CHARACTER CERTIFICATES
in the
GENERAL LAND OFFICE
OF TEXAS

Edited by
Gifford White

From the files of the
General Land Office
Austin, Texas

CLEARFIELD

Reprinted for
Clearfield Company, Inc. by
Genealogical Publishing Co., Inc.
Baltimore, Maryland
1993, 1996, 1998, 2001

CONTENTS

Empresario Grants.

1 Felisola's Grant.
2 Burnet's   "
3 Vehlin's   "
4 Zavalla's   "
5 Austin's Colony.
6 Robertson's Grant.
7 S. F. Austin's "
8 Milam's   "
9 DeWitt   "
10 DeLeon's   "
11 Bexar District
12 McMullin & McGloire's Grant.
13 Power's   "
14 John Cameron's   "

Pecan Pt.

Red   R.

14

S. Little R.

Robins R.

DEPARTMENT

Tanaha

Texas   Nacogdoches

San Augustine

Gain's
Ferry

Sabine R.

2

Ft. Teran

Viesca

6

Bobbin's
Crossing

NACOGDOCHES

Bevil

3

Colorado

7

Tenoxticlan

CONTRABAND TRAIL

Alabama C.S.

4

Guadalupe River

8

Bastro

Washington

Coles Settlem't

LAID OUT IN 1829

Jacinto

Liberty

San Felipe

Lynchburg

Gonzales

San
Antonio

DEPARTMENT

Harrisburg

Powels

Anahuac

San Antonio
(Battle of Rosalis 1813

La Grange

N. Washington

OF

BRAZOS

Richmond

Columbus

5

Galveston

DEPARTMENT

9

11

Brazoria

OF   BEXAR

Victoria

Texana

San   Antonio

Goliad

10

Refugio

Copano

12

Lipanlitlan

TAMAULIPAS

Laredo

Pedro Creek

San Antonio
&
Environs
Old Mill

Powder House

Mier

Rio Grande

Town Stormed
by Texans
Dec'r 9th, 1835

Redoubt

Alamo Mar. 6th, 1836

Alamo
1813

LA BAHIA ROAD

TEXAS

In 1834

Scale

Miles 10 20 30 40 50   100

Matamoras

Grass Fight 1835

Conception Oct. 1835

A PICTORIAL HISTORY OF TEXAS
Rev. Homer S. Thrall, St. Louis, 1879

FOREWORD

A goal of the Texas General Land Office is to make the land records maintained and preserved in the Archives and Records Division more accessible to the public. Gifford White, who has produced several books based on these records, provides a service for both the Land Office and genealogists with his Character Certificates in the General Land Office of Texas.

The government of Mexico, in allowing the settlement of Texas by people other than its own residents, wanted to ensure that the new Anglo-American settlers were of high character. It did not want the province to become a haven for the criminal element or for the non-productive. Therefore the authorities, through the colonization laws, directed that, among other requirements, the immigrants prove their good character either by providing credentials from their homeland or having two witnesses to vouch for them.The character certificate was the result.

Information pulled from these files should be welcomed by genealogists and historians. Place of origin, marital status, occupation, and family size can help to fill in the missing pieces for those doing family histories. The finding of other items, such as the letter to Stephen F. Austin reporting on Texas political affairs , should interest historians.

Researchers owe Gifford White a big "thank you."

Michael Q. Hooks

Texas General Land Office

ACKNOWLEDGEMENTS

I am especially indebted to Dr. Michael Q. Hooks, Director and Archivist, Archives & Records Division, General Land Office of Texas, for allowing me free access to the records of the Spanish Collection in which this historically important material is found. The staff of the Archives & Records Division has, as always, given unfailing assistance during the long hours that this transcription required. Mr. Galen Greaser, Spanish Translator, supplied critical aid in working over difficult spots. Genealogists who benefit from these abstracts will owe them their sincere thanks.

Gifford White
Austin 1985

PREFACE

The Character Certificate File in the General Land Office of Texas is a product of the events that formed the Texas land system and its records. The history of public land in Texas is complex and to understand it, Ref. 1 (Ericson) or Ref. 2 (Taylor) or other sources should be consulted. No short summary can be made, but a few critical dates can be cited as a reminder of the time of important changes.

1821 Before this date, Texas was a part of Colonial Mexico under Spain. After this date, Mexico was an independent nation, and Texas was a part of the State of Coahuila and Texas.

1824 Stephen F. Austin, as the first contractor (Empresario) to bring settlers into Texas under the new colonization laws of Mexico, gave out Titles to "The Old 300" in the Austin Colony. The movement of American settlers to Texas was under way.

1834 Before this date, there was no effective system to give Title to lands in any of eastern Texas. Many had been on chosen land for 10 years or more.

13 Nov 1835. The provisional government of the revolutionary forces in Texas closed the Mexican land offices in November and all Titles issued after 13 November 1835 were later declared not valid. This ended the Mexican land system in Texas, and the issue of lands would not be resumed until January 1838 under the Republic of Texas.

2 March 1836. Texas declared its independence of Mexico and was a Republic until statehood in the U.S.A. was agreed upon in late 1845. The date of 2 March 1836 became an important "cut-off" in later determination of the amount of land a settler would receive from the Republic of Texas.

All records of the granting of public land in Texas are contained in the Archives & Records Division of the General Land Office of Texas in Austin.

The Character Certificate File

As described more fully in References 1 and 2, an immigrant into Texas under one of the colonization acts of Mexico between say 1825 and 1835 had to meet specific requirements before becoming eligible to receive land. He was required to apply to the officials of the Municipality or to the Commissioner where he proposed to settle and to prove his good character by bringing credentials from his place of origin, or by two creditable witnesses. He had further to swear to support the laws and Constitution, and to adhere to the established Church as a condition to receiving a certificate of admittance. The oath to obey the laws of Mexico was formally sworn.

The laws also required the statement of place of origin, marital status, occupation, and the size of the family in the petition for admission. The petition for admission was at times separate from the certificate of admission as will be seen in some of the documents from the Austin Colony. These records are important sources of genealogical information.

Many of the entrance records have already been published. For example, those of the Austin Colony appear in <u>Austin's Register of Families</u> (Ref. 3). Those of the DeWitt Colony are incorporated with the bound land records and have been published in Ref. 4.

Those issued in Nacogdoches may also appear in duplicate in the Nacogdoches Archives, Texas State Archives, Austin.

The Character Certificate file contains all of the loose papers relating to this admission process as gathered up when the local land office records were assembled into the General Land Office. A brief description of the different documents is warranted.

Some of the documents dated before 1834 are related to applications for admission into Austin's Colony, as will be seen by comparison with the entries in <u>Austin's Register</u> (Ref. 3). Some seem to be the original made out by the applicant to meet the requirements of the Colonization Law, and personally signed by him. They were later copied into the Register. A few Certificates of Reception are found, which should have been originally issued to the settler. These were signed by Austin or Williams. A few Mexican passports issued in New Orleans survive. Miscellaneous notes will also be in the file.

A major part of the file consists of Character Certificates dated 1834-35 and given out in the Department of Nacogdoches, which included all of east Texas. Special legislation appointed Commissioners for the area at this time, and started a sudden flurry of applications. See Ref. 1 or Ref. 2 for a further explanation. Those actually given out in Nacogdoches are in Spanish and copies will be found in the Nacogdoches Archives. Other Certificates as for example those from San Augustine and Liberty are in English. Filed with some of these is the Order of Survey made out after the settler had been accepted into one of the Empresario grants. See the Map for the several areas granted to the Empresarios. The surveyor often made interesting notes on the Certificate when it was returned with the Field Notes to be incorporated into the Title. Many of the Character Certificates were issued too late to complete the Title before the unexpected closing of the land offices in November 1835.

Some historically important letters and other records have also been gathered into this file, without actually being related to the process of settling immigrants. For example see No. 1476, a letter from J.A. Navarro to S.F. Austin on political affairs in Texas. A rare baptismal certificate by Father Michael Muldoon appears in No. 1736. Some are difficult to classify and may be correctly called bits of paper.

Unfinished Titles

The records relating to land were gathered from the various local land offices after the end of the Texas Revolution in 1836, into the General Land Office. The Titles incomplete or dated after 13 November 1835 were collected under the name of each Commissioner and finally bound into several permanent volumes in the Spanish Collection. The Petition in each Title repeats the personal information that appeared in the Character Certificate (after allowing for changes caused by lapse of time). Some show differences that could not be reconciled although a special effort was made to detect discrepancies. See Page 202 for a more complete explanation. Abstracts begin on Page 203.

Using the Abstracts of the Character Certificates

The file in the General Land Office called by this name has been alphabetically arranged and a personal name appears on a file folder. Each folder has been given a number. Both name and number may be helpful in asking for copies of the full document. If a paper had more than one name on it, as in a list, the last name may have been chosen for the file name. See the Personal Names Index for all internal names.

If a file has more than one document, this will be made clear in the abstracts.

Names as they appear on the file tab may not agree with that in the record and may have been taken from other records in the Archives. Some honest differences in writing and reading may appear.

Many of these records are in Spanish as is usually noted by [S]. The translation given here may suffer from faded records and legibility problems. If the information is important, a photostat of the original is mandatory.

In the Personal Name Index, the principal name on the file does not reappear, but all internal names were copied out. Repeated names of Alcaldes, Commissioners, Surveyors and other officials were not Indexed because their presence on a document usually did not bear on the genealogical information contained in it.

To Search for A Name

1. Look in the Character Certificate abstracts which are already alphabetically ordered.
2. Look next in the Personal Names Index for further occurences.

REFERENCES

1. Ericson, Carolyn Reeves. Nacogdoches--Gateway to Texas. Ft. Worth: Arrow/Curtis Pub., 1974.

2. Taylor, Virginia H. The Spanish Archives of the General Land Office of Texas. Austin: The Lone Star Press, 1955.

3. Williams, Villamae. Stephen F. Austin's Register of the Families. St. Louis: Ingmire Publications, 1984.

4. Rather, Ethel Zivley. "De Witt's Colony". Quart. of the Texas State Historical Assoc., Vol. VIII (1904), pp. 95-191.

5. Miller, Thomas Lloyd. The Public Lands of Texas 1519-1970. Norman: Univ. of Oklahoma Press, 1972.

ABBREVIATIONS

Alc.	Alcalde
[ ]	Insertion by the Editor
[?]	Doubtful reading
[E]	Document in English
[S]	Document in Spanish
( )	Used only as they appear in the original
Elision	... Material omitted
X	Mark by a person who did not write his signature
[Sig]	Appears to be signed by the person named
[Note]	Denotes an added notation on the document
[Unf]	Unfinished Title as noted by a clerk at some later date
Teste	Witness
Man of good...	or a similar expression stands for a formal and extended statement of good character and readiness to sign the oath of loyalty to the Mexican government.

El Ciudadano *Radford Berry*, alcalde
Constitucional de esta villa y su municipalidad
Certifico en cuanto puedo, debo
y el derecho me permita de manera que haga
fe que el Estrangero *Thomas J. Rusk*
es un hombre de muy buena moralidad
Costumbres é industrioso, amante a la constitución
tucion y leyes del pais y de la religión
Cristiana, de estado Casado con familia
todo lo expresado arriba ha sido probado
por un testigo y a pedimento de la parte
le doy la presente en esta villa de
Nacogdoches a 23 de Mayo de 1835

                 Radford Berry

CHARACTER CERTIFICATES

1. **ACOSTA, JOSE MARIANO [S]**
Nacogdoches   19 July 1835
Citizen Jose Mariano Acosta is a man
of good character, married with family ...has not obtained land...
                    Radford Berry

1a. **[E]**
Nacogdoches   10 Sept 1835
Sir: You are hereby authorized to
survey the sitio and labor of land
which Mr. Jose Maria Acosta will
designate to you ...
                    Geo M. Smyth Comr

2. **ACOSTA, MANUEL [S]**
Nacogdoches   3 August 1835
Citizen Manuel Acosta is a man of
good character, born in this municipality, single without family, has
not obtained land...
Jn Egne Michamps Alcalde Interim

3. **ADAMS, JOHN [S]**
Nacogdoches   17 Sept 1835
Foreigner John Adams is a man of
very good character, married with
family...   Radford Berry
[Rev] Acceptd in Burnet   A.Henrie

4. **ADAMS, JOHN W. [S]**
Nacogdoches   24 March 1835
Foreigner J.W. Adams is a man of
good character, married with family.
                    Radford Berry
4a. **[E]**
Nacogdoches   May 21st 1835
To: G.A. Nixon Esq
Please deliver to Chas S. Taylor...
          John W. Adams by Chas S. Taylor

5. **ADAMS, LEWIS H. [E]**
San Augustine   10 Oct 1835
I certify that Lewis H. Adams is a
native of the state of Georgia that
he is a man of family consisting of
a wife ... emigrated to Texas in the
year 1833.   A. Hotchkiss P. Judge
5a. **[E]**
San Augustine   9 Oct 1835
I, Lewis H. Adams appoint Richard
Haley my attorney in the petition to
Geo W. Smyth Comr for one league and
1 labor of land.
          [Signed] Lewis H. Adams

6. **ADAMS, THOMAS [E]**
[Field notes] Survey for 1 league
and 1 labor for Thomas Adams, Nueces
above Frio

7. **ALANCIO, MARIA CONCEPCION [S]**
Nacogdoches   4 April 1835
Certify that citizen Maria Consec-
ion Alancio is a resident of the Municipality, born in this country,
widow with a family, has not obtained land...   Radford Berry

8. **ALDRICH, COLLIN [S]**
Nacogdoches   28 November 1834
Certify that Collin Aldrich is a man
of good character, married with a
family...   Vital Flores
[Note in English] Wife & 3 children.
Adjoining Cummings Survey on the
Mustang Ravine. Vehlein.   Robinson
8a. **[E]**
Mustang Prairie   March 14, 1835
Geo A. Nixon Esq. Dear Sir:
Please send my land title by Mr.
Cummings provided my field notes
have been recd ...   Collin Aldrich

9. **ALEXANDER, AMOS [E]**
Austin [de San F.]   March 31, 1832
To: Mr. S.F. Austin Empresario
I am desirous of being admitted as a
colonist in your contract of July
1828. I am married and my family
consists of a wife and 4 children
who are now residing in Bradford
County, Pennsylvania. My name is
Amos Alexander 46 years of age
my wife Hannah 41 years
2 male, 2 female children
                    Amos Alexander

10. **ALEXANDER, HANNAH [E]**
San Augustine   April 5, 1835
I certify that Hannah Alexander is a
native of Georgia of the USA...is a
woman of family consisting of three
persons.   A. Hotchkiss P. Judge

11. **ALFORD, JAMES [E]**
San Augustine   August 20, 1835
Certify James Alford native of Georgia of the USA...is a man of family
consisting of three persons. Alford
emigrated to this country in 1832.
                    Saml Thompson Alcd

1

12. ALLEN, ETHAN [E]
Viesca   Dec 14, 1834
We certify that Ethan Allan is a na-
tive of the State of New York, a
millright by trade and a man of fam-
ily consisting of three persons.
Samuel Lindley   Wm Rankin
I certify the above applicant merit-
ing to become a citizen.
                      James J. Foster
Commissioner   Precinct of Viesca

13. ALLBRIGHT, ALEXANDER F. [E]
San Augustine   Sept 1, 1835
Certify Alexander F. Allbright a native of Georgia a man of family of
three persons...emigrated 1831...
                  Samuel Thompson Alcd

14. ALLEN, A.C. [S]
Nacogdoches   11 Oct 1834
Certify citizen of the Villa, A.C.
Allen,   married and with family,
man of good...   Luis Procela

15. ALLEN, ELISHA [E]
Department of Nacogdoches
Jurisdiction of Liberty 20 Dec 1834
I, Commissioner for the precinct of
Cow   Bayou do hereby certify that
Elisha Allen, native of the State of
Louisiana, is a young man of good
morals and industrious habits...
                      Geo A. Pattillo
[Note] Single man = W.line John Cole

16. ALLEN, GEORGE   [E]
Department of Nacogdoches
Precinct of Cow Bayou Dec 20th 1834
George Allen, a native of the State
of   Louisiana is a man of a family
consisting of himself and wife...
                  Geo A. Pattillo Comr

17. ALLEN, JOHN [E]
Jurisdiction of Liberty Nov 25,1834
I certify that John Allen is a native of   the State of Tennessee, is
a man of family consisting of
four, man of good...
          Wm Hardin, Primary Judge
[Note] Widower 4 ch on the Sabine R
adjoining Ballews N line. F. Hardin
17a. [Field notes of survey]

18. ALLEN, JOHN K. [E]
Recd of G.A. Nixon Commissioner
Twenty-five titles granted to the
following   persons.   Jacob Roth
Thos J. Hagerty   Wm Clark
Stephen Eaton Babtiste Andre Vacocu
[Name not legible] Willis B. Wattson
Hugh Morgan   James Latheam
John Childers   Birtan Odum
Thos McDonald   Walter Little
Lewis Latheam   Domingo Ybarbo
James Johnson   Maria Ja Rios
Andrew J. Yates   Cosimo Garcia
Cazanova M.N.S.de Elisha M. Collins
Hugh Means   Wm Means
Jesse McGee   Jose Garcia
Nacogdoches Feby 13th 1836
                      Jno K. Allen

19. ALLEN, NATHANIEL [E]
Department of Nacogdoches
District of Bevil   April 3d 1835
I certify that Nathaniel Allen is a
native of the State of Georgia in
the US of the North, hath a family
consisting of two persons, good ...
              Wm Williams, Alcalde
19a. [Field notes with no date]

20. ALLEN, NATHANIEL N.G. [S]
Nacogdoches   Sept 22, 1834
Foreigner Nathaniel N.G. Allen is a
man of very good morals ...
          Luis Procela Alcalde Interim
[Note] his wife and 4 children
                  Burnet = Wm Brookfield

21. ALLEN, WILLIAM S. [S]
Nacogdoches   25 May 1835
Foreigner William S. Allen is a man
of very good morals and habits, mar-
ried with a family...
Juan Eugo Michamps, Interim Alcalde

22. ALLISON, ELIHU (ELISHA) C. [S]
Nacogdoches   2 June 1835
Foreigner Elihu C. Allison is a man
of very good...married with family..
      Jn E. Michamps Alcalde Interim

23. ALLISON, JAMES [S]
Nacogdoches   30 May 1835
Foreigner James Allison is a man of
very good...married, with family...
Jn Egn Michamps   Alcalde Interim

2

24. ALLISON, WILLIAM F. [S]
Nacogdoches   11 May 1835
Foreigner William F. Allison is a
man of good...married with family...
                    Radford Berry
24a. [E] [Receipt]
William F. Allison by Arthur Henrie
    William F. Allison $22
Received of J.A. Nixon Commissioner
William F. Allison's Title for him
October 28th, 1835   Arthur Henrie

25. ALPHIN, RANSOM [E]
Naches District   May 2d 1835
This is to certify that I have been
acquainted with Ransom Allphin for a
con siderable time...a man of family...a farmer by occupation.
                    Wm Whiteley
Commissioner for the Naches District

26. ALLPHIN, SHELTON [E]
Naches District   May 2, 1835
I have been acquainted with Shelton
Allphin for some considerable time.
He is a man of family...farmer by
occupation.
Commissioner of the Naches District
                    Wm   Whiteley

27.   ALTIG,   EDMUND   [S]
Nacogdoches   18 June 1835
Foreigner Edmond Altig...married
with family, man of good...
Jn Egn Michamps Alcalde Interim

28. AMORY, NATHANIEL [E]
Received of Nathaniel Amory eight
dollars   which is in full for my
fees   on his title   and   plat.
Oct 31st 1835   Arthur Henrie

29. ANDERSON, BAILEY JR. [E]
San Augustine   August 18, 1835
I do certify that Bailey Anderson
Jun is a native of the State of
South Carolina,   that he is a man
of family consisting of a   wife and
ten children...emigrated to Texas
in the year 1821.
            A. Hotchkiss, P. Judge

30. ANDERSON, BAILEY SR [E]
San Augustine   August 18, 1835
Certify that Bailey Anderson Snr is
a native of the State of Virginia
and that he is a man of family consisting of five children. Emigrated
in 1822...   A. Hotchkiss, P. Judge

31. ANDERSON, BENJAMIN [E]
San Augustine   May 18, 1835
Certify Benjamin Anderson is a native of the State of South Carolina
man of family of a wife and twenty
one children...
            A. Hotchkiss, P. Judge

32. ANDERSON, ELI J.   [S]
Nacogdoches   27 April 1835
Certify foreigner Eli J. Anderson is
a man of good...married with family
                    Radford Berry

33. ANDERSON, HOLLAND [E]
San Augustine   August 18, 1835
Certify Holland Anderson is a native
of Kentucky...man of family consisting of wife and two children...emi-
grated to Texas in the year 1830.
            A. Hotchkiss P. Judge

34. ANDERSON, JONATHAN [E]
San Augustine   Aug 17, 1835
Certify Jonathan Anderson is a native of the State of Kentucky that
he is a man of family consisting of
a wife and six children...emigrated
to Texas in the year 1819.
            A. Hotchkiss, P. Judge
34a.
San Augustine   Oct 5, 1835
Personally appeared before me...Jon-
athan Anderson...he has & has had
for some time an old improvement on
the north side of Tenaha Crick on
the trace leading from the settlement of the Sabine and that someone
without his knowledge or consent has
surveyed it in the name of BN as
appears on the marks of the trees.
        [Signed] Jonathan Anderson
Sworn before me A.Hotchkiss P.Judge

George W. Smyth Esq.
    Dear Sir: At top you have Mr.
J. Anderson affidavit in regard to a
piece of land on Tenaha Creek. I wish
you to examine into the matter when
                                    3

such Survey may be returned as he
do protest against it.
                        John English

35. ANDERSON, (OLIVER) HAZZARD [E]
San Augustine   August 18, 1835
Hazzard Anderson is a native of the
State of Indiana that he is a man
of family consisting of a wife and
child...emigrated to   Texas in the
year 1821.
         A. Hotchkiss, Primary Judge

36. ANDERSON, URIAH   [E]
Jurisdiction of Liberty 26 March1835
Uriah Anderson, a native of the
State of Tennessee, is an unmar-
ried man...
                    Wm Hardin Judge
36a.
Jorge Antonio Nixon Comr
Sir: Please to give the bearer my
title   and he will settle with you
for   the   expenses incurred &c
                  Uriah X Anderson
Test: James Robinson

37. ANDERSON, WILLIAM B.   [E]
San Augustine   14 March 1835
Mr. Wm B. Anderson, a native of
Maryland,   of the United States of
the North is a man of family consisting of two persons...he emigrated in the year 1834.
             R.C. McDaniel, C.P.O.
37a.
Nacogdoches   Augt 12, 1835
Mr. Surveyor: You are hereby required to   survey in Zavalas Grant
the sitio of land   which Mr. Wm B.
Anderson will designate...
              Jorge Anto Nixon

38. ANDING, DANIEL   [E]
San Augustine   Sept 1st 1835
Daniel Anding is a native of the
State of Mississippi, that he is a
single man, im- migrated to Texas
in the month of February 1834.
A. Hotchkiss, P. Judge

39. ANDING, GEORGE   [E]
San Augustine   May 19, 1835
George Anding a native of South Carolina,   a man of family of a wife &
one child...
           A. Hotchkiss, P. Judge
4

40. ANDREWS, RICHARD   [E]
San Felipe de Austin   June 29, 1830
To S.F.   Austin   Empresario
I have emigrated to the Colony...my
name is Richard Andrews, age 30
years. Single, occupation farmer &
stock raiser. Removed from Georgia.
Arrived in this Country in 1827.
              Richd Andrews

41. ANGLIN, ELISHA
Tenoxtitlan   22 May 1834
To Empresarios Austin & Williams
I have emigrated to Texas, I am
married my wifes name Catherine and
6 children. My age 37 my wifes age
21.   Elisha Anglin

42. ANTHONY, DANIEL W.   [E]
To Mr. S.F. Austin Empresario
I have emigrated to this Country...
Daniel W. Anthony, 25 years of age.
Unmarried. Austin Oct 10, 1832
              D.W. Anthony

43. ANTHONY, FREDERICK   [E]
San Augustine   29 August 1835
Frederick Anthony is a citizen of
this Country...a native of Tennessee
emigrated to this Country in the
year 1830.
        Saml Thompson   Alcd

44. ANTHONY, JACOB   [E]
San Augustine   August 20, 1835
I certify from the statement of two
respected persons that Jacob Anthony
is a native of Tennessee is a man of
family consisting of three persons..
emigrated to this Country in 1831.
        Saml Thompson   Alcd

45. ANTHONY, RHODDY   [E]
San Augustine   Aug 20 1835
Rhoddy Anthony a native of Tennessee
is a man of family consisting of
eight persons, emigrated to this
Country in 1831.
        Saml Thompson   Alcd

46. APPLEGATE, JOHN   [E]
San Augustine   August 18, 1835
John Applegate is a man of family
consisting of a wife and two children, emigrated to Texas in the year
1829.
           A. Hotchkiss, P. Judge

47. ARMSTRONG, JACOB   [E]
Jurisdiction of Liberty 24 Feb 1835
Jacob Armstrong is a native of the
State of Kentucky, a single man...
                    Wm Hardin Judge

48. ARROCHA, JOSE ANDRES [S]
Nacogdoches   8 Sept 1835
Certify Citizen Jose Andres Arrocha
single without family, resident of
this municipality since 1820...has
not received land...
                    Radford Berry

49. ARROCHA, JOSE MA.   [S]
Nacogdoches   15 Aug 1835
Certify Jose Ma Arrocha...a resident
of this Municipality since 1827...
married with family...has not received land...   Radford Berry

50. ARTHUR, JOHN   [S]
Nacogdoches   11 June 1835
Foreigner John Arthur...single
without family...man of good...
Jn Egn Michamps   Interim Alcalde

51. ASHABRANNER, HENRY   [E]
San Augustine   August 17, 1835
Henry Ashabraner a native of North
Carolina a man of family consisting
of three persons...emigrated to this
country in 1830...
                    Saml Thompson Alcd

52. ASHLEY, AARON   [E]
San Augustine   15 June 1835
Aaron Ashley a native of Virginia of
the United States of the North is a
man of family consisting of five
persons, that he emigrated to Texas
in the year 1834...
                    R.C. McDaniel C.P.O.

53. ASHWORTH, AARON   [E]
Jurisdiction of Liberty 25 Apr 1835
Aaron Ashworth, a native of the
State of South Carolina, a man of
family...   Claiborne West Judge

54. ASHWORTH, ABNER   [E]
Jurisdiction of Liberty 12 Jan 1835
I, John Stewart, Commissioner of the
Precinct of Cow Bayou...Abner Ash-
worth a native of the State of Loui-

siana, a man of family consisting of
his wife and five children...
                    John Stewart
[Note] On his improvement in Duncans
woods lower end = Jno A. Veatch

55. ASHWORTH, WILLIAM   [E]
Jurisdiction of Liberty Nov 24,1834
Wm Ashworth a native of South
Carolina is man of family consisting
of six...   Wm Hardin
[Note added] On the Sabine adjoining
Jno Allen = Jno A. Veatch

56. ATKINSON, JESSE B.   [E]
To Empresario Austin and Williams
                    May 6th 1834
I have emigrated to Texas, I am mar-
ried wifes name is Margaret and have
one child.
My age thirty six, my wifes eighteen
                    Jesse B. Atkinson

57. AUGINBAUGH, JESSE AUGUSTINE [S]
Nacogdoches   8 July 1835
Certify Jesse Augustine Aughinbaugh,
married with family...man of good...
Jn Egn Michamps Alcalde Interim

58. AUGUSTINE, HENRY W.   [E]
San Augustine   Feby 19, 1835
H.W. Augustine is a native of the
State of South Carolina in the Unit-
ed States of the North, that he is a
man of family consisting of a wife
and two children...
      A. Hotchkiss   Primary Judge
58b. [Receipt]
Henry W. Augustine
Recd the above title for the owner
                    Arthur Henrie
58a.
To Mr. S.F. Austin Empresario
I am desirous to be admitted...
Henry W. Augustine 24 years of age
Cynthia his wife   19 years of age
Moved from Alabama and arrived in
this Colony in Nov 1831.
                    W.W. Augustin [sic]

59. AVENT, DURHAM   [S]
Nacogdoches   23 May 1835
I certify that foreigner Durham
Avent...married...man of good...
                    Radford Berry

5

59a. Nacogdoches   9 October 1835
I certify that foreigner Derrum
Avent...married with family and res-
ident of this   Department since
Jany 1834...   Radford Berry
59b.   [E]
Nacogdoches   24 Oct 1835
William Brookfield Sir:
You are hereby authorized to survey
the sitio & labor of land what Mr.
Durham Avent will designate.
                  Geo W. Smyth Comr

60. AWALT, HENRY   [S]
Nacogdoches   23 January 1835
I certify that foreigner Henry Awalt
from   the United States of the
North, age 28 years, married with
family, occupation   farmer & cattle
raiser...   Radford Berry

61. AYRES, DAVID   [E]
Austin [de San F.] February 5, 1833
To Mr. S.F. Austin, Empresario
I have emigrated to the country with
a   view to settle my self in it ...
Family wife & 6 children
From New York   David Ayers

62. AYRES, (LEWIS) LUIS   [E]
Survey of one league for Luis Ayres.
Situated on the West Bank of the Rio
Frio   [Field notes, undated]

63. BAILEY, GAINES   [E]
Town of Austin   6 July 1830
To Mr. S.F. Austin, Empresario
I wish to be included in your con-
ract...I   have resided in the coun-
try for more than   eight years...
Gains Bailey 25 years old
             [Signed] Gaines Bailey

64. BAILEY, HENRIQUE   [S]
Nacogdoches   7 Oct 1834
I certify that foreigner Henrique
Bailey   is a man of very good...
married with family...
        Luis Procela 1st Regidor

65. BAILEY, HOWARD   [S]
Nacogdoches   17 Aug 1835
I certify foreigner Howard Bailey is

a man of very good...single without
family, resident of this municipality since the year 1832.
              Radford Berry

66. BAIRD, CHARLES   [E]
[Reverse notation]: Application
Chas Baird   )
Frances E. Baird   ) Wife & son
Richd W. Baird   )
Black servants:
  Scott   One league fronting
  Berry   on the Brasis commen-
  John   cing at the centre of
  Godfrey   Wica Village and ex-
  Flora   tending up and down
  Tenor   the River
  Malinda
  Moriah
  Celia
  Amanda

66a. [A slip of paper with nothing
      further on it]
Chas Baird
Frances E. Baird (wife)
Richd William Baird (son)
Isaac Betsel) White servants
Tho Lewis   )
Black servants;
  Scott   Tenor
  Berry   Malinda
  John   Moriah
  Godfrey   Amanda
  Flora   Celia

67. BAIRD, DAVID   [E]
Nacogdoches   Aug 13, 1835
Mr. Surveyor: You are hereby required to survey in Zavalas Grant
the sitio of land which Mr. David
Baird will designate to...
            Jorge Anto Nixon
67a.   [E]
San Augustine   27 June 1835
I certify that Mr. David Baird,
native of the US of the North is a
man of family of 4 persons, emigrated to Texas in the Spring of
1835.   R.C. McDaniel C.P.O.

68. BAIRD, JOSEPH   [E]
Nacogdoches   May 23, 1835
Mr. Surveyor. Sir:
You are authorized to survey in the
D.G. Burnet Grant the quarter sitio
of land which Mr. Joseph Baird [the
name crossed out] will designate.
                    Jorge Anto Nixon
[Added note] West of Trinity
[Rev] Changed by consent to Vehlein
Sept 28, 1835   Order of Survey for
Mr. Joseph Baird

69. BAKER, LARKIN   [S]
Nacogdoches   10 June 1835
Certify that foreigner Larkin Baker
is a man of good...married with
family...
        Jn Egn Michamps Alcalde Interim

70. BAKER, MOSELEY   [E]
Jurisdiction of Liberty Oct 2, 1834
I do certify that Moseley Baker, a
native of Virginia, is a man of family consisting of his wife and one
child...   Wm Hardin Primary Judge

71. BALLANOVA, MARIA   [S]
Nacogdoches   7 Sept 1835
Citizen Maria Ballanova is a woman
of very good character, inhabitant
of this municipality and born here,
widow with a family has not received land...   Radford Berry

72. BALLEW, RICHARD   [E]
Jurisdiction of Liberty Nov 24, 1834
Richard Ballew is a native of the
State of Tennessee, is a man of
family consisting of six...
                    Wm Hardin Judge
[Note] Wife & 5 children. Z. On the
Sabine at the place he has improved.

73. BANKSTON, S.P.   [E]
San Augustine   3 April 1835
S.P. Bankston is a native of the
United States of the North is a man
of family consisting of two per-
sons...that he emigrated to Texas in
1834...   R.C. McDaniel
73a.
Nacogdoches   Aug 7, 1835
Mr. Surveyor
You are required to survey in Zava-
las Grant the sitio of land which

Mr. S.P.Bankston will designate...
                    Jorge Anto Nixon
[Note]: On the West Bank of the
Neches

74. BARCLAY, ANDERSON   [E]
District of Bevil Octr the 6th 1834
Anderson Barclay is a native of
Tennessee in the US of the North,
hath a family consisting of four
persons...   John Bevil Alcalde
[Note]: Place where he now lives
74a.
[Field Notes] Anderson Barclay sitio
on the waters of Wolf which runs
into the Naches...
                    George W. Smyth Surveyor

75. BARCO, CALVIN   [E]
San Augustine   May 26, 1835
Calvin Barco is a native of the
State of South Carolina, that he is
a man of family consisting of a wife
and no children...
                    A. Hotchkiss Primary Judge

76. BARRELA (BARELLA), ANASTACIO
Nacogdoches   [S]   4 April 1835
Citizen Anastacio Barrela is a resident of the municipality, born in
this country, married with family,
has not received land
                    Radford Berry

77. BARNETT, GEORGE M.   [E]
To Empresarios Austin and Williams
I have emigrated to Texas...I am
married my wifes name Eliza & have 3
children, my age 40, my wife age 32
Tenoxtitlan   23 May 1834
                    Geo M. Barnett

78. BARNETT, ISAAC   [S]
Nacogdoches   1 June 1835
Certify foreigner Isaac Barnett...
married with family...man of good...
        Jn Egne Michamps Alcalde Interim
[Reverse] Accepted in Burnet
                    A. Henrie

79. BARNHILL, WILLIAM   [S]
[Printed form in Spanish]
Tenoxtitlan   3 June 1834
To Stephen F. Austin & Samuel M.
Williams I certify that Wm Barnhill
is one of the colonists...is married

and his family consists of ten persons.   Spencer H. Jack, Agent
79a. [Printed form in English]
To Empresarios Austin and Williams
I have emigrated to Texas...I am
married   my wifes name is Cintha
I have eight children.
4 male 4 female My age seventy five
[wife] sixty three
Tenoxtitlan   June 3, 1834
        [Signed]   Wm Barnhill
[Added note]: from Tennessee

80. BARNHILL, WILLIAM   [S]
Nacogdoches   9 Oct 1834
Certify foreigner William Bainehill
married with family...man of good
                        Luis Procela
80a.
Nacogdoches   22 Sept 1835
I certify foreigner William Barnhill...married with family and resident of the   Department since 1833
man of good...
                        Radford Berry

81. BARNS, TAYLOR S.   [S]
Nacogdoches   23 April 1835
I certify foreigner Taylor S. Barns
single, man of good... Radford Berry

82. BARR, ALANSON   [E]
San Augustine   August 17, 1835
Alanson Barr is a native of the
State of Vermont...that he is a man
of family consisting of a wife and
five children...emigrated to Texas
in 1821.   A. Hotchkiss P.Judge

83. BARR, ELANSIN   [E]
Municipality of San Augustine
To: Mr. Geo W. Smyth Commissioner
    The petition of Elans Barr of
[San Aug] would respectfully represent that he emigrated to the
country in the year A.D.   1821 and
settled and improved land with   the
faith that the government would make
him a Title...drove your petitioner
from his home and his improvements
and set the same up to publick sale
and displaced your petitioner by
Strong Arm and your petitioner further showeth that one John Merchant
is now in possession...this is to

inform you that it is an old claim..
protest...that you make your petitioner a Title as Commissioner.
August the 19th 1835   Elansen Barr

84. BARR, ISAAC   [S]
Nacogdoches   5 Oct 1835
Certify that Isaac   Barr...single
without a family, inhabitant of this
Department since 1832...man of good
                        Radford Berry

85. BARR, ROBERT   [E]
To Mr. S.F. Austin Empresario
I have emigrated to this country and
am desirous to be admitted as a
Colonist to your Coast Colony.
Robert Barr, 30 years of age,
single, from the State of Ohio.
Austin   5 Dec 1832   R. Barr

86. BAREA (BARRERRA) MARIA DAMACIA
Nacogdoches   [S]   9 Sept 1835
Citizen of Mexico, gives Power of
Attorney to Jose Ramires to repre-
sent her in obtaining land...an old
settler, and cannot personally do
this because she has been ill...
                Ma Damacia Barea
Witnesses
Antonio ---   Julio Sazarin

87. BARRON, THOMAS   [E]
Austins Colony   April 1831
This certifies that we the undersigned have known Thomas Barron two
years on the Red River and one year
in this Colony in eighteen hundred
and twenty two. We never have hear
any thing alledged to the said Thomas Barron dishonest or disrespect-
full but always believing him to be
an honest industrious good citizen.
                Walter Sutherland
                William Cooper
                Abner Kuykendall

88. BARTEE, WILLIAM   [S]
Nacogdoches   20 Sep 1834
Certify that foreigner William Bartee is a man of character...married
with family...
            Luis Procela Alc Interim

8

89. BASQUEZ, JUAN FRANCISCO [S]
Nacogdoches   Sept 14, 1835
Certify that Citizen Juan Francisco
Basques...married with family, resi-
dent in this State many years and
has not received land...
                       Radford Berry
89a.   [E]
Nacogdoches   Sept 18th 1835
Sir: You are authorized to Survey
the   sitio & labor of land which
Juan Francisco Basques will desig-
nate...   Geo W. Smyth Comr

90. BATEMAN, A.D.   [S]
Nacogdoches   4 June 1835
Certify that foreigner A.D. Bateman
is a man of good...married with
famly...
Jn Egn Michamps Alcalde Interim
[Rev] Accepted in Zavala. A.Henrie

91. BATES, SAMUEL JR.   [E]
San Augustine   17 July 1835
I certify that Mr. Samuel Bates Jr.
is a   native of Indiania of the
United States of the North; is a man
of family consisting of six persons, that he emigrated to Texas
in June 1835. R.C. McDaniel C.P.O.
91a.
Nacogdoches   Augt 9th 1835
Mr. Surveyor: You are hereby required to survey in Zavalas Grant
the sitio of land   which Mr. Saml
Bates will designate.
                 Jorge Anto Nixon Comr

92. BAUME, JOSE DE LA   [S]
Austin   21 December 1832
To Empresarios Austin & Williams
I am European by birth, married in
Nacogdoches, wish to be admitted
with my family to the Colony...wish
a league...my name is Jose de la
Baume born in Montpelier and origin-
ally of the Canton of B---, enclave
in the Canton of Auvignon in France.
Married in Nacogdoches and have five
children, three boys and two girls,
of age hundred and one years. The
name of my spouse is Maria Louisa
Couturier native of New Orleans,
of age fifty years.
Austin   21 December 1832
[Signed]   Jose de la Baume
Certificate granted 21 Dec 1832
                       Austin

93. BAUME, PEDRO SANCIRIO DE LA [S]
To Empresarios Austin & Williams
I am Mexican by birth...wish to be
admit-ted as Colonist to receive
the quantity of land conceded to
Mexican colonials who have no family. My name is Pedro de la Baume,
native of Nacogdoches, single and
of age 25 years.   21 Dec 1832
         Pedro Sanciro de la Baume
[Note] Certificate granted in Bejar
21   December 1832   Austin

94. BEALE, BENJAMIN   [E]
To Mr.S.F. Austin
I have emigrated to this Country...
my name is Benjamin Beale, 26 years
of age, single from New York and
arrived 2 March 1832.
Austin 31 March 1832
          [Sig]   Benj Beale

95. BEASLEY, BERRY   [S]
Nacogdoches   29 Septy 1835
Certify that foreigner Berry Beas-
ley... married with family...man of
good...   Radford Berry
[Rev] Accepted in Vehlein. A.Henrie

96. BEASLEY, WILLIAM [S]
Nacogdoches   29 Sept 1835
Certify that foreigner William Beas-
ley is married with family...man of
good...   Radford Berry
[Rev] Accepted in Vehlein. A.Henrie

97. BEATY, JOHN   [S]
Nacogdoches   8 Dec 1834
Certify that foreigner John Beaty
married with family...man of good...
                       Vital Flores
[Note] John Beaty wife and five
children Bank Hurricane Bayou west
to the river survey of Strode.

98. BEAUCHAMP, JEROBOAM R.   [E]
San Augustine   Aug 18, 1835
I certify that Jeroboam R. Beacham
is a native of Kentucky of the USA,
a single man, emigrated to Texas in
the year 1831.
          Nathan Davis Commissioner

9

99. BEAUCHAMP, JOHN [E]
San Augustine   22 Sept 1834
Certify that John Beauchamp a native
of   Delaware is a man of family of
six persons
        Benjamin Lindsey Alcalde

100. BEBE, MARIA   [S]
Nacogdoches   22 Sept 1835
I certify that Maria Bebe is a woman
of   very good character...resident
of this municipality, born here and
citizen with all rights...widow with
family of 3 children, has not obtained land   Radford Berry

101. BEBE, SANTIAGO   [S]
Nacogdoches   4 Aug 1835
I certify that citizen Santiago Bebe
is an old citizen of this municipality, widower with family...has
not obtained land... Radford Berry
101a.   [E]
Nacogdoches   Aug 4, 1835
Sir: You are hereby authorized to
survey   the sitio & labor of land
which Mr. Santiago Bebe will
designate..   Geo W. Smyth Comr
[Reverse] The within order has been
executed.   Wm Brookfield Surveyor

102. BECK, JESSE   [E]
Austin   4 April 1832
To S.F. Austin Empresario
I am desirous of being admitted...
I am married, my family is not in
the Country but will be here in the
Spring. My name is Jesse Beck 45
years of age.
Milly my wife 45 years of age
4 male, 5 female children
                        Jesse Beck

103. BECKER, J.   [E]
Mr. J.L. Ewing   Sir: You are to
survey the third of a sitio which
Mr. J. Becker will designate ...
                    Geo W. Smyth Comr

104. BECKHAM, ALEXANDER W.   [S]
Nacogdoches   8 June 1835
Certify foreigner Alexander W.Beck-
ham...married with family...man of
good...
Jn Egn Michamps Alcalde Interim
[Rev] Accepted in Zavala. A.Henrie

105. BEERS, DAVID   [S]
Nacogdoches   19 March 1835
Certify foreigner David Beers...man
of good...married with family...
                       Radford Berry
105a.   [E]
Nacogdoches   October 5, 1835
Received of Jorge Anto Nixon, Mr.
David Beers title.   J.H. Cummins

106. BELL, GEORGE A.   [E]
Town of Austin   May 25, 1830
To Mr. S.F. Austin Empresario
I have emigrated to this Colony...
George A. Bell 47 years of age un-
married. Moved from Louisiana and
arrived in this colony in 1828.
                   [Sig] Geo A. Bell

107. BELL, JOHN D.   [S]
Nacogdoches   25 April 1835
Certify foreigner John D. Bell...man
of good...married with family...
                       Radford Berry

108. BELT, SAMUEL T.   [E]
Nacogdoches   Octr 14th 1834
Mr. Jno A. Veatch, Surveyor Sir:
You are to survey in Lorenzo Zavalas
Grant a sitio which Mr. Saml T. Belt
will designate...
          Jorge Anto Nixon Comr
[Note] The place where he lives
[Rev] I return to the Commissioner
George A. Nixon the Order of Sur-
vey, as I have declined taking a
title from him as a Colonist...
[No date]   S.T. Belt

109. BENARD, GENEREUX   [S]
Nacogdoches   11 Dec 1834
Mr. Genereux Benard is a man of
good...   Vital Flores

110. BENHAM, WILLIAM D.   [E]
[Field Notes] Survey of one league
for William D. Benham on the left
bank of the Rio Frio..

111. BENNETT, JAMES   [E]
San Augustine   17 September 1835
I certify that James Bennett a native of Virginia in the US of N.A.
emigrated to his country in the year
1830, family consisting of four
persons...   Saml Thompson Alc

10

111a. [E]
Sabine District   15 September 1835
Sir: Please to deliver to James
Bennett my Order of Survey. He will
pay your fee. I am a citizen of Sa-
bine District. Maj. Bennett has my
Certificate of Citizenship alle-
gience &c.   Wm Bennett
Teste: William F. Sparks

112. BENNETT, THEODORE   [E]
Brazoria   31 December 1831
To Empresario S.F. Austin:
I have emigrated to this Colony...
My name is Theodore Bennett, single,
20 years of age, removed from New
York. [Signed]   Theodore Bennet

113. BENNETT, WILLIAM R.   [S]
Passport   [By Mexican Consul]
New Orleans   9 June 1832
Passport to Mr. William R. Bennett,
native of New York, to Brazoria...
personal business...
              [Sig] Wm R. Bennett

114. BENNETT, ZIMRI   [E]
San Augustine   Oct 4, 1834
I certify Zimri Bennett...native of
Connecticut, man of family of six
persons... Benjamin Lindsey Alcalde
[Note] Wife & four children = Burnet
       Head of Angelina

115. BENNINGHOA, FR.   [E]
To his excellenty the governor,
Austin at   Sn Felipe de Austin by
Mr. Betty. My residence at present
is at Harrisburg   After having left
Germany my native country to live in
the US of NA, I was, when sojourn-
ing in New York...written by Burnet
[relative to] Province of Texas...
[Then follows 8 detailed questions]
1 January 1833   Fr. Benninghoa
[Note says Austin replied on
 29 Jany 1833]

116. BERMEA, ANDRES   [E]
Received of Comr G.A. Nixon the
title of Mr. Andres Bermea.
August 3, 1835   Jn Bt Cazenave

117. BERMEA (VERMELLA),PEDRO [S]
Nacogdoches   6 April 1835
Certify Pedro Vermella is a citizen

of this Municipality for many years,
widower   without   family...has not
received land...   Radford Berry

118. BERRY, MILLY   [S]
Nacogdoches   Sept 12, 1835
Citizen Milly Berry is a woman of
good...widow with family, resident
in this Department since year 1830.
                      Radford Berry

118a. [E]
Nacogdoches   Sept 12, 1835
Sir: You are hereby authorized to
survey the sitio & labor which Mrs.
Milly Berry will designate...
                   Geo W. Smyth Comr

119. BETTNER, CHARLES A.   [E]
To Empresario S.F. Austin
Dec 31, 1831 I have emigrated to
this Colony...My name is Charles A.
Bettner, aged 30 years, single. Re-
moved from New York. Chas A. Bettner

120. BEVIL, ALFRED   [E]
San Augustine   December 20, 1834
I certify Alfred Bevil, a native of
Georgia of the US of A is a single
man...   E. Rains Alcalde Interim

121. BEVIL, JEHU   [S]
Nacogdoches   31 Oct 1834
I certify that Foreigner Jehu Be-
vil...single...a man of good...
                      Vital Flores
[Note] The place where he lives. Z.

122. BEVIL, JOHN   [E]
San Augustine   24 September 1834
I certify that John Bevil is a native of North Carolina of the US...
a man of family...of nine persons
             Benjamin Lindsey Alcalde
122a.
[Field Notes] John Bevil's sitio on
the north bank of Sandy Creek in
Zavala's Gr

123. BIGNER, FREDERICK   [E]
Department of Nacogdoches
Jurisdiction of Liberty   9 Jan 1835
I John Stewart Commissioner for the
Precinct of Cow Bayou, do hereby
certify that Frederick Bigner a na-
tive of the State of Louisiana, a
single man...of good morals...
                      John Stewart

11

124. BINNS, HENRY   [E]
San Augustine   9 June 1835
I certify that Mr. Henry Binns, a
native   of the US of the North is
a man of family   consisting of
seven persons, that he emigrated to
Texas in the fall of 1834...
                R.C. McDaniel C.P.O.
124a.   [E]
Nacogdoches   Aug 20th [1835]
Mr. Surveyor. Sir:
You are hereby required to survey in
Zavalas Grant the sitio which Mr.
Henry Binns will designate...
                Jorge Anto Nixon Comr

125. BIRDSELL, WARREN   [S]
Nacogdoches   18 Sept 1834
I certify that foreigner Warren
Birdsill   is a man of good...mar-
ried with family... Luis Procela

126. BITTICK, JONATHAN   [E]
San Augustine   Aug 18, 1835
I certify that Jonathan Bittick a
native of Tennessee of the US of A,
a man of family consisting of seven
persons, and a man   of good...
emigrated to this country in b830.
                Nathan Davis Commissioner

127. BLACKMAN, BENNETT   [E]
[Field notes, no date] Bennett
Blackman   Survey 20,249,353 sq vs
south side of Taylor Bayou...
        Reported by Burton Surveyor
127a.   [E]
Department of Nacogdoches
Jurisdiction of Liberty 28 Decr 1834
I William Hardin Judge...certify
that Bennett Blackman a native of the
State of [blank] is a man of family
consisting of his wife and [blank]
children...a man of good...
                Wm Hardin

128. BLACKMAN, BURRELL   [E]
I James B. Woods Alcalde for the
Jurisdiction of Liberty certify Burrell Blackman is a native of Mississippi is a man of family consisting
of himself & his wife, is a man of
good...
27 day of Dec 1834   J.B. Woods

[Note] Wife = Cypress Creek below
the little fenced in Alabama Village
        F. Hardin = Vehlein = No. 127
128a.
Liberty   March 10th 1835
George A. Nixon Esqr.
Dear Sir: You will please deliver my
tite to my league to Mr. Jos Bryan
Teste: Wm Hardin Burrell X Blackman

129. BLACKMAN, JOAB JOHN   [E]
I James B. Woods Alcalde for the
Jurisdiction of Liberty do certify
that Joab John Blackman is a man of
family consisting of himself, his
wife, and one child & a man of
industrious...
27 December 1834   J.B. Woods
[Note] Joab = adjoining James
Blunts west line.
        F. Hardin = Vehlein No. 130
129a.
George A. Nixon. Dear Sir:
You will please to deliver my title
papers to my league to Mr. Jos
Bryan.
                Joab John X Blackman
Teste: Wm Hardin March 10, 1835

130. BLAIR, JOHN   [E]
San Augustine   Nov 30th 1834
I certify that John Blair, native of
Tennessee is a man of family consisting of three persons and a man
of good...
        James W. Bullock Alcalde pro tem
[Note] Wife and one child - Zavala
20 miles west from Santa Ana
on the road to Trinity - D. Brown
130a.
[Field Notes] John Blair's sitio
near Wolf Point, about 20 miles west
of Santa Ana in prairie...
                D. Brown Surveyor
130b.
San Augustine   October 4, 1837
Sir: Be so good as to let my son
have the copy of John Blair's land
title which paid you for when at my
place also Mr.James Rowe's and he
has put by him for it.
                A. Huston
[To] Geo A. Nixon Esqr. Nacogdoches

131. BLAKE, BENNET   [S]
Nacogdoches   25 August 1835
I certify foreigner Bennett Blake is
a man of good...widower with family
                    Radford Berry
[Rev] Accepted in Vehlein. A.Henrie

132. BLANCHARD, PLINY   [S]
Nacogdoches   27 May 1835
I certify that foreigner Pliny Blanchard is a man of good...married
with family... Jn Egne Michamps
                    Alcalde Interim

133. BLANCHET, PIERRE   [S]
[Passport. Consul of Mexico in N.
Orleans] Give passport to Mr.Pierre
Blanchet citizen of this state to go
by the American   Sloop La Hetta,
Captain Lewis, to go to Empresario
S. Felipe Austin by way of Matagorda
New Orleans   5 June 1831
        [Sig] Pierre Blanchet

134. BLAND, JOHN   [E]
Department of Nacogdoches
Jurisdiction of Liberty 14 Feb 1835
I John Stewart, Commissioner for the
Precinct of Cow Bayou, certify that
John   Bland a native of the State
of Louisiana, a man of family con-
sisting of his wife and two
children...   John Stewart

135. BLEDSOE, GEORGE L.   [S]
Nacogdoches   13 Nov 1834
George L. Bledsoe is a man of good
married with family...Vital Flores
[Note] My wife & one son.
                    Wm Robinson
135a.   [E]
Nacogdoches   Nov 13, 1834
Mr. Wm Robinson, Surveyor Sir:
You are required to survey in Joseph
Vehleins Grant the sitio of land
which Mr. Geo L. Bledsoe will
designate.

136. BLOODGOOD, WILLIAM   [E]
Department of Nacogdoches
Jurisdiction of Liberty June 30,1835
I Wm Hardin one of the Judges...
certify   that Wm Bloodgood, a na-
tive of the US of NA and state of
New Jersey is a man of family
consisting of a wife and three

children and emigrated to this country in the year eighteen hundred
twenty four.   Wm Hardin

137. BLOSSOM, HIRAM   [E]
San Augustine   7 Oct 1835
Know that I Hiram Blossom have this
day appointed Franklin Fuller my
attorney...to petition George M.
Smyth Comr for one league and labor
of land. Hiram Blossom
[Wit] Thos H. Garner   W.J. Talbert
A. Harelson   A.B. Davis
W.L. Scott
137a.   [E]
Precinct of Tennahaw   21 Sept 1835
I certify that Hiram Blossom a native of Vermont of the US of A, a
man of family consisting two persons, a man of good... immigrated to
the country in the year 1829
           Nathan Davis Commissioner

138. BLOSSOM, MINOR   [E]
San Augustine   1 Sept 1835
I certify that Minor Blossom a native of New York, single man...
emigrated to this country in 1830.
           E. Thompson Alcalde

139. BLOUNT, JAMES H.   [E]
Department of Nacogdoches
District of Bevil   April 5, 1835
I certify that James H. Blount is a
native of the State of North Carolina in the US of the North, is a single man of good...
           Wm Williams Alcalde

140. BLUNT, BASHEBA   [S]
Nacogdoches   6 June 1835
I certify that foreigner Basheba
Blunt is a woman of very good...
widow with family...
G. Pollitt Alcalde Interim
[Note] Accepted in Vehlein,
where she lives.   A. Henrio

141. BLUNT, JAMES   [E]
Department of Nacogcoches
Jurisdiction of Liberty 26 Dec 1834
James Blunt a native of North Caro-
lina is man of family consisting of
his wife and two children...
           J.B. Woods
[Note] Big Sandy= at the crossing of
an Indian trace. Vehlein.
                    F. Hardin
                         13

141a.
George A. Nixon Esqr. Dear Sir:
You will please to deliver to Mr.
Joseph Bryan my title to my league.
[Signed]   James Blunt
Test: March 10th 1835
    Wm Hardin Liberty

142. BLUNT, JOHN S.   [S]
Nacogdoches   17 July 1835
Certify that John S. Blunt is a man
of very good...married with family
                    Radford Berry

143. BLUNT, STEPHEN W.   [S]
Nacogdoches   18 Sept 1835
Certify that Stephen W. Blunt is a
man of very good...single without
family...   Radford Berry

144. BLUNT, WILLIAM S.   [S]
Nacogdoches   12 Aug 1835
Certify that William S. Blunt is a
man of   very good...married with
wife and child
    Jn Egne Michamps Alcalde Interim
[Rev] Accepted in Zavala. A. Henrie

145. BLYTHE, CHAMPAIN   [S]
Nacogdoches   17 Sept 1835
Certify that Champain Blythe is a
man of good...married with family...
                    Radford Berry

146. BODEN, JUAN LORENZO   [S]
Nacogdoches   5 May 1835
Certify that Juan Lorenzo Boden is a
resident of this municipality for
many years,   married with family...wants land...   Radford Berry

147. BODEN, JUAN NICOLAS [S]
Nacogdoches   5 May 1835
Certify that citizen Juan Nicolas
Boden is a resident of this muni-
cipality for many years, married
with family...   Radford Berry

148. BODEN, MARIA TERESA   [S]
Nacogdoches   15 June 1835
Certify that citizen Maria Teresa
Bodin   is resident of this municipality and born here, a woman of
very good...widow with family... has
not obtained land...
    Jn Egne Michamps Alcalde Interim

149. BODEN, MARIA MADALENA   [S]
Nacogdoches   15 Aug 1835
Certify that Ma Madalena Boden is a
woman of very good...resident of
this municipality, single with family...has not obtained land...
                    Radford Berry
149a.
Nacogdoches   Aug 15, 1835
Mr. J. Smith. Sir: You are hereby
authorised to survey the sitio &
labor of land which Ma Madalena
Boden will designate...
                    Geo W. Smyth Comr

150. BURDINE, JOHN   [E]
San Augustine   Sept 27, 1834
I certify that John Burdine is a
native of No Carolina of the US of
A, is a man of a family consisting
of six persons...
            Benjamin Lindsey Alcalde

151. BONTANE, JOSE ANTO   [E]
Nacogdoches   14 July 1835
I received from the Land office by
Major Nixon Commissioner of this
Department the land title for Mr.
Jose Anto Bontane
                    Joseph H---

152. BOON, SIMON   [E]
San Augustine   5 January 1835
I certify that Simon Boon, a native
of Indiana of the US of the North is
a man of family consisting of five
persons, that he emigrated to Texas
in the year 1833...
                R.C. McDaniel C.P.O.
152a.
Nacogdoches   Oct 4, 1835
Mr. Surveyor. Sir:
You are hereby required to survey in
D.G. Burnett's Grant the sitio of
land which Mr. Simon Boon will
designate...
                Jorge Anto Nixon Comr

153. BOREN, JOSEPH   [E]
To Empresarios Austin and Wiliams
I have emigrated to Texas...
I am unmarried my age is 24 years
Tenoxtitlan 26 May 1834
                    Joseph Boren

14

154. BOREN, MICUL   [E]
To Empresarios Austin and Williams
I have emigrated to Texas...
I am married my wifes name Elizabeth
and her three children. My age 27
my wifes age 23 years.
Tenoxtitlan   27 May 1834
                   Micul Boren

155. BOREN, NANCY   [E]
To Empresarios Austin and Williams
I have emigrated to Texas...
I am a widow, my age 64 years
Tenoxtitlan   27 May 1834
                   Nancy Boren

156. BORSOLEY, MARIA JOSEFA   [S]
Nacogdoches   4 April 1835
Certify that Maria Josefa Barsoley,
an old resident of this municipality, and widow with family...has
not obtained land...
                   Radford Berry

157. BOSTICK, JAMES H.   [E]
To Mr. S.F. Austin Empresario
I have emigrated to this Colony...
James H. Bostic unmarried
Moved from Tennessee and arrived in
March 22, 1830.
[Signed]   J.H.   Bostick
Town of Austin   20 May 1830

158. BOULTER, JAMES   [S]
Nacogdoches   4 May 1835
Certify that foreigner James Bolter
is a man of very good...married with
family...   Radford Berry
158a.
[Receipt on a slip of paper]
Recd Levi Btikes title this 20th of
June 1835   James Boulter

159. BOURLAND, GABRIEL L.   [S]
Nacogdoches   1 Jan 1835
Certify that foreigner Gabriel L.
Bourland is a man of good...mar-
ried with family...
Jn Egne Michamps Alcalde Interim
[On reverse] Accepted in Zavalas. A.He
159a.
[Field notes] Sitio west of the
Sabine also on Houson Bayou. 6 la-
bors arable
[No date]   David Brown Surveyor

160. BOURLAND, OLIVER P.   [S]
Nacogdoches   1 June 1835
Certify that foreigner Oliver P.
Bourland is a very good...single
without family...
Jn Egne Michamps Alcalde Interim
[Reverse] Accepted in Z. A. Henrie
160a.
[Field Notes] Quarter sitio, west
boundary of Green Cooks Survey...1
labor arable
[No date]   Pennington Surveyor

161. BOREN, RHODA   [E]
Tenoxtitlan   30 March 1834
To The Empresarios
          Austin and Williams
I have emigrated to Texas...I am a
widow and two children, my age 28
years.   Rhoda Boren

162. BOWEN, ELI A.   [S]
Nacogdoches   16 May 1835
Certify that foreigner Eli A. Bowen
is a man of very good...married with
family...wants land... Radford Berry

163. BOWERS, JOHN   [E]
[Field notes, no date, no signature]
Left bank Attascoso Crk...one league

164. BOWIE, JOHN   [E]
San Augustine   May 19, 1835
I do certify that John Bowie is a
native of the State of Louisiana,
that he is a single man...
     A. Hotchkiss   Primary Judge

165. BOWIE, STEPHEN   [E]
Town of Austin   19 Feby 1831
To Mr. S.F. Austin Empresario
I have emigrated to this Colony...
Stephen Bowie 31 years of age unmar-
ried. Occupation farmer, moved from
Louisiana and arrived in this Colony
26 Nov 1830.   Stephen Bowie

166a. BOWKER, ELIAS   [E]
San Augustine   February 10th 1835
I certify that Elias Bowker, a na-
tive of Massachusetts of the US of
A, is a single man and of good...
          James S. Hanks Alcalde
166. [Field notes, no date].
NE corner of William Cook Survey 6
labors arable

15

166b. G.A. Nixon Dear Sir:
Please let Thos B. Huling have my
land title.   E. Bowker
Zavalla   Oct 2, 1835

167. BOWLIN, JAMES   [E]
San Augustine   Aug 18, 1835
I certify that James Bowlin is a
native of Tennessee a man of family of a wife and child, emigrated
to Texas in 1826...
                 A. Hotchkiss P. Judge

168. BOWLIN, JEREMIAH   [E]
San Augustine   August 18, 1835
I certify that Jeremiah Bowlin is a
native of Virginia a man of family
of a wife and two children...emi-
grated to Texas in the year 1826.
                 A. Hotchkiss P. Judge

169. BOWLIN, MARY ANN   [E]
San Augustine   31 August 1835
I, Mary Ann Bowlin appoint Wm G.
Logan & John K. Allen attorneys to
petition for a sitio and labor of
land which I am entiled to...being
an old settler of the Country.
                 Mary Ann X Bowlin
 Attest to mark: Ann Gray
Wit: Henry B. Clark, Nathan Davis
169a.
San Augustine   31 August 1835
I certify on this day personally appeared before me Mary Ann Bowlin...
took the oath.
        William Davis Commissioner
169b.   [E]
San Augustine   August 31, 1835
I certify that Mary Ann Bowlin a native of Tennessee of the US of A and
emigrated to the country in April
1826 and is the head of a family
consisting of two in number...
        Nathan Davis Commissioner

170. BOWLIN, SOLOMON   [S]
Nacogdoches   1 November 1834
Solomon Bowlin, a man of very
good...married with family...
                 Vital Flores
[Note] Solomon Bowlin wife and four
children. Adjoining McNealy's Survey
Burnet Grant.   Brookfield

170a.
Major Geo Anto Nixon   Dear Sir:
You will please to let Mr. Thorn
have my title & oblige. Yours
        Sol Bolin   per H.H. Edwards

171. BOX, JAMES   [E]
Naches   February 19, 1835
This is to certify that I have been
acquainted with James Box for some
time...farmer by profession, he has
a family...   Wm Whiteley
        Comr for the Naches District

172. BOX, JOHN   [S]
Nacogdoches   28 Nov 1834
Certify foreigner John Box is a man
of very good...married with fam-
ily...   Vitlal Flores
[Rev] Accepted in Vehlein. A.Henrie

173. BOX, JOHN A.   [E]
Naches   February 19, 1835
This is to certify that I have been
acquainted with John A. Box for some
time, a man of family, a farmer by
profession...   Wm Whiteley
        Comr for the Naches District
173a.
Nacogdoches   16 December 1835
Received of Comr G.A. Nixon, John A.
Box and title for one league & labor
                 R.W. Box

174. BOX, JOHN M.   [S]
Nacogdoches   1 June 1835
Certify foreigner John M. Box is a
man of very good...married with
family...
        Jn Egne Michamps Alcalde
[Rev] Accepted in Burnet. A. Henrie

175. BOX, NELSON   [S]
Nacogdoches   1 June 1835
Certify that foreigner Nelson Box is
a man of very good...single without
family...
        Jn Egne Michamps Alcalde Interim
[Rev] Accepted in Burnet 1/4 sitio
                 A. Henrie

176. BOX, ROLEN W.   [E]
Naches   February 19, 1835
I have been acquainted with Rolen W.

16

Box for some time...a farmer...A man
of family   Wm Whiteley
     Comr for the Naches Precinct

177. BOX, SAMUEL   [E]
Naches   February 19, 1835
I have been acquainted with Samuel
Box for some time...he is a man of
family, a farmer by·profession.
               Wm Whiteley
     Comr for the Naches Precinct

178. BOX, STEPHEN   [S]
Nacogdoches   28 November 1834
Certify foreigner Stephen Box is a
man of very good...married with
family...   Vital Flores

179. BOX, STEPHEN JR.   [E]
Naches   August 14, 1835
I have been acquainted with Stephen
Box Junr for some time...has no
family, farmer by profession.
               William Whiteley
Commissioner for the Naches Precinct
[Rev] Accepted in Vehlein. A.Henrie
179b.
Nacogdoches   August 15, 1836 [?]
Maj. Nixon: Will oblige his friend
by letting Bearer have my title.
               Stephen Box Junr

180. BOX, STILLWELL   [E]
Naches   January 25, 1835
I have been acquainted with Stillwell Box for some time...he is a man
of family... a farmer by occupation.
               Wm Whiteley Comr
[Rev] Accepted where his improvement
is.   A. Henrie

181. BOX, WILLIAM S.   [E]
Naches   December 14, 1835
I have been acquainted with William
S. Box for some time...a man of a
family, farmer by profession.
               Wm Whiteley
     Comr for the Naches Precinct
[Reverse] Accepted in Burnet
                    Authur Henrie
181a.   [E]
Naches   December 12, 1835
This day came before me William

Whiteley Commissioner for the Naches
Precinct, John S. McCoy...says that
he carried the chain for Wm McDaniel
Surveyor to survey a league of land
for William S. Box on the east side
of the Naches River and that he
crost the league in different direc-
tions and saw no improvements on the
land whatever...   Wm Whiteley
     Comr for the Naches Precinct
181b.
Naches   December 14, 1835
[Essentially the same statement as
above was made by John Beaty]

182.. BOYCE, JEPTHA   [E]
Austin [de San F.]   30 October 1832
To Mr. S.F. Austin Empresario
I have emigrated to this Country...
Jepsey Boyce 32 years of age
Unmarried   [Sig]   Jeptha Boice

183. BOYD, JOHN   [S]
Nacogdoches   16 May 1835
Certify foreigner John Boyd is a man
of very good...married with family.
                    Radford Berry

184. BRADLEY, ELEANOR   [S]
Nacogdoches   5 August 1835
Certify foreigner Helena Bradley is
a woman of very good...widow with
family, resident of this munici-
lpality since the year 1831...
                    Radford Berry
184a.   [E]
Nacogdoches   August 1835
Mr. Brookfield Sir:
Survey the sitio & labor which Mrs.
Eleanor Bradley will designate...
               Geo W. Smyth Comr
184b.
Nacogdoches   Sept 7, 1835
Mr. Wm Brookfield, Surveyor Sir:
You are required to survey in Bur-
nets Grant the sitio of land Mrs.
Eleanor Bradley will designate...
          Jorge Anto Nixon Comr

185. BRADLEY, FRANCES [FANNY]   [S]
Nacogdoches   7 Octr 1835
Certify citizen Frances Bradley a

woman of very good...widow with family... Radford Berry [Reverse] Accepted. A. Hotchkiss attorney for Joseph Vehlein

186. BRADLEY, JOHN [E]
San Augustine August 22, 1835
I certify that John Bradley a native of Georgia of the US of A is a single man and a man of good...emigrated to the Country in 1831...
Saml Thompson Alcalde

187. BRADLEY, JOHN M. [E]
San Augustine August 17, 1835
Certify that John M. Bradley is a native of the State of North Carolina that he is a man of family consisting of four children...that he came into Texas and settled in 1832 in February.
A. Hotchkiss P. Judge
187a.
San Augustine August 1835
Mr. S.O. Pennington Sir:
You are hereby authorized to survey the sitio & labor which Mr. John M. Bradley will designate...
Geo W. Smyth Comr

188. BRADLEY, MARK M. [E]
San Augustine 21 August 1835
I certify that Mr. Mark M. Bradley a native of Indiana ...is a man of family of four persons, that he emigrated to Texas in 1834...
R.C. McDaniel C.P.O.
188a.
Nacogdoches
Mr. Surveyor: You are requested to survey in Zavala's Grant the sitio which Mr. Mark M. Bradley will designate...
[No date] Jorge Anto Nion Comr

189. BRADSHAW, JAMES [S]
Nacogdoches 25 May 1835
I certify foreigner James Bradshaw is a man of very good...married with family Jn Egne Michamps
Alcalde Interim
189a.
Nacogdoches 9 Sept 1837
Received of Majr Geo Anty Nixon Title issued out of Joseph Vehlein's Colony. James Bradshaw

190. BRENNAN, MRS. M. Passport
New Orleans 8 June 1832
Passport to Da M. Brenan native of this State to go in the American Schooner named Brasoria, her Captain Rowland, passage to Brazoria with her two children on personal business. [Consul Martinez]

191. BRENNAN, MARY
Survey of one league for Maria Brennan. [Rev] 1 League Nueces

192. BRENAN, THOMAS H. [E]
Austin [de San Felipe] Aug 25, 1832 To Mr. S.F. Austin Empresario
I have emigrated to this Country... My name is Thomas H. Brenan 22 years of age. Unmarried, arrived in this Colony in March 1832.
Thomas H. Brenan

193. BREWER, GREEN B. (GRANBURY)
Nacogdoches [S] 20 Sept 1834
Certify Green B.Brewer a man of good...married with family...
Luis Procela Alc
[Note] Wife and five children
193a.
Nacogdoches 9 Oct 1835
I certify that foreigner Greenbury Brewer is a man of very good...married with family and resident of this municipality since the year January 1834... Radford Berry

194. BREWER, HENRY [S]
Nacogdoches 20 Sept 1834
Certify that foreigner Henry Biwel is a man of very good...married man with wife, wants land...
Luis Procela Alcd
[Note] Wife and five children
Henry Brewer true name

195. BREWER, HENRY M. [S]
Nacogdoches 20 Sept 1834
Certify foreigner Henry M. Brewer is a man of very good...wants land
[Note] Single man Luis Procela Alcd
Henry M. Brewer true name

196. BREWER, WILLIAM [S]
Nacogdoches 7 Aug 1835
Certify that foreigner William Brew-

18

er is a man of very good...married with family, resident of this municipality since the year 1831...
Radford Berry

196a.
Nacogdoches   Aug 7, 1835
Sir: You are hereby authorized to survey the third sitio which Mr. William Brewer will designate...
Geo W. Smyth Comr

197. BREWER, WILLIAM G.   [S]
Nacogdoches   23 May 1835
Certify foreigner William G. Brewer is a man of very good...married with family...   Radford Berry

198. BREWER, WILLIAM T.   [S]
Nacogdoches   9 Oct 1835
Certify foreigner William T. Brewer a man of very good...married with family and resident of this Department since the year   1834 March...
Radford Berry

199. BREWER, WILLIAM T.   [S]
Nacogdoches   20 Sept 1834
Certify that foreigner William T. Bower is a man of very good...
Luis Procela Alc
[Note] His wife and two children
Wm T. Brewer true name
[Rev] The name of the person mentioned on the face of the Certificate is unintelligible.

200. BRIDGES, ELIZABETH [E]
San Augustine   Jany 24, 1835
Certify that Elizabeth Bridges a native of Georgia...a woman of family of four persons...
James S. Hanks Alcalde

201. BRIDGES, JAMES   [E]
San Augustine   Sept 22, 1834
I certify that Mr. James Bridges, certified to by two respectable citizens, a native of Louisiana, a man of family of three persons...
Benjamin Lindsey Alcalde

202. BRIDGES, JAMES   [E]
San Augustine   Sept 26, 1834
I certify that James Bridges a native of No Carolina of the USA is a man of family consisting of eight persons...
Benjamin Lindsey Alcalde

203. BRIDGES, ROSS M.   [E]
San Augustine   22 Sept 1834
Certify that Ross M. Bridges from the evidence of two respectable persons is a native of Georgia of the US of the North and a man of family consisting of three persons...
Benjamin Lindsey Alcalde

204. BRIDGES, THOMAS   [E]
Matagorda   1 December 1833
To Col. S.F. Austin Empresario
San Felipe, Texas
I take the liberty to inform you that I am now in Texas with your colony. It is my desire to become a colonist...I have a family consisting of a wife and one child. I expect my family in the country in a short time.   Thomas Bridges
204a.
Austin [de San Felipe] June 24, 1835
I Francis W. Johnson, Judge of the first instance, hereby certify that Thomas Bridges has taken the oath.
F.W. Johnson

205. BRIMBERRY, SAMUEL   [S]
Nacogdoches   8 August 1835
Certify foreigner Samuel Brimberry married with family, resident of this Municipality since 1833...
Radford Berry

206. BRITTON, WHITNEY   [S]
Nacogdoches   6 October 1835
Certify foreigner Whitney Britton a man of good...married with family...
G. Pollitt Alcalde Interim
[Rev] Accepted. Hotchkiss Agent for
Joseph Vehlein

207. BROOKFIELD, WILLIAM C.   [S]
Nacogdoches   8 August 1835
Certify that foreigner Wm Charles Brookfield is a man of very good... single without family, resident of this Municipality since the year 1830...   Radford Berry
207a.
Nacogdoches   August 8, 1835
Sir: You are hereby authorised to survey the third sitio of land which Mr. Wm C. Brookfield will designate.
Geo W. Smyth Comr

19

[Rev]   The within order has been
executed.   Wm Bradfield Surveyor

208. BROOKS, GEORGE W. [E]
San Augustine   9 March 1835
I certify that George W. Brooks a
native of South Carolina of the US
of the North is a man of family consisting of nine persons, that he
emigrated to the country in 1834...
                 R.C. McDaniel C.P.O.
208a.
Nacogdoches   Augt 7, 1835
Mr. Surveyor: You are required to
survey in Zavala's Grant the sitio
of land which which Mr.Geo W. Brooks
will designate...
         Jorge Anto Nixon Comr
[Note] On the west bank of R Neches

209. BROOKS, GILBERT [E]
Department of Nacogdoches
Jurisdiction of Liberty 24 Apl 1835
I William Hardin Judge of the first
instance...certify Gilbert Brooks a
native of the State of Connecticut
is a man of family consisting of
himself and wife...   Wm Hardin

210. BROWN, DAVID [E]
San Augustine   24 Sept 1834
I certify that David Brown is a na-
tive of Virginia that he is a man of
family consisting of two persons...
              John Bevil Alcalde
210a.
Received of George Antonio Nixon
Comr, three titles (vz) John M.
Neely, R.D. Wood, and Lefroi Gedrup.
This July 30th 1835   David Brown
210b.
John Coughran   Daniel Phares
John McGinnes   John Gates
James Scott   Nimrod Sulser
Wright Coley   David Huffman
Thomas Wilson   Enoch Frazier
James Mitchell   Patrick Mullin
James English   Levi Mann
Michael Shreves   W.B. Graham
Also Susanna Frances Fitch
Received the above Titles
October 12th 1835   David Brown

210c. [Field notes]
West bank of the river Naches...
David Brown's sitio and labor...
[No date]   J.A. Veatch Surveyor

210d.
              Sept 25th 1837
I have received orders of Survey for
the following persons and executed
their surveys for the same on which
they have had their titles executed
by George A. Nixon Commissioner previous to the closing of the land office by the Consultation at San Felipe de Austin in one thousand eight
hundred and thirty five which orders
of survey I promised to send to the
Commissioner Generals Office if not
lost or misplaced.
John Coughran   John McGinnis
John Gates   James Scott
Nimrod Selser   Wright Coley
David Huffman   John Haley
James Mitchell   Patrick Mullin
[Four more names heavily struck]
                     David   Brown

211. BROWN, HIRAM [E]
San Augustine   Sept 25th 1834
I certify that Hiram Brown is a native of the State of New York in the
US of the N, that he hath a family
consisting of three persons...
              John Bevil Alcalde
211a. [Field notes]
Hiram Brown Survey...west bank of
the marsh of the River Naches...
              Geo W. Smyth Surveyor

212. BROWN, JAMES M. [E]
San Augustine   Oct 10, 1835
I certify that James M. Brown is a
native of No Ca[rolina] of the USA
is a man of family consisting of two
persons...   Saml Thompson Alcd
212a.
San Augustine   Oct 10, 1835
I hereby authorise Samuel Stivers to
petition George W. Smyth Comr in my
name for one league and labor of
land...   James M. Brown
Teste: E.O. Legrand
              Saml Thompson Alcd

20

213a. BROWN, LUCRETIA [E]
San Augustine   Sept 22, 1834
I certify that Lucretia Brown a
native of Kenida [sic] is a widow
woman of a family consisting of
four persons...
          Benjamin Lindsey Alcalde
213.
Nacogdoches   16 Dec 1835
Before me Juan Eugenio Michamps Alcalde ad interim of the aforesaid
municipality personally appeared
Thomas Cartwright...who says that
he [line missing] order of survey issued from Commissioner George
Anto Nixon in Zavala's Colony and
in favor of Lucretia Brown numbered
No. 81 and dated the 24th Sept 1834.
                    Thomas Cartwright
213b.
San Augustine   2 June 1837
George A. Nixon Esq Sir:
Please to let Mr. Benjamin Thomas
have my land title out of the
office by his paying the fees due
on the same.
          [Signed] Leucretia Brown

214. BROWN, REUBEN   [E]
Naches   March 18, 1835
Certify that I have been acquainted
with Reuben Brown for some consid--
erable time say one year or more.
He is a man of good moral character
a man of family. He is a farmer by
occupation...
               Wm Whiteley Comr
          for the Naches Precinct

215. BROWN, SAMUEL P.   [E]
To Mr. S.F. Austin Empresario
I have emigrated to this Colony...
Samuel P. Brown 35 years old married
Susan 27 years old my wife
3 male and 1 female [children].
Arrived in April.
May 22, 1830   Saml P. Brown

216. BROWN, SQUIRE   [E]
San Augustine   24 Sept 1835
Certify that Squire Brown is a native of the State of New York of
the US of the North, is a single
man...
          John Bevil Alcalde

217. BROWN, STEPHEN JR. [E]
San Augustine   Oct 10, 1835
Certify Stephen Brown junr a man of
family of four persons and a native
of No Ca[rolina]...emigrated in 1831
               Saml Thompson Alcd
217a. [E]
San Augustine   Oct 10, 1835
I hereby authorise Samuel Stevers to
petition George W. Smyth Comr in my
name for one league and labor of
land.
Test   [Signed] Stephen Brown Jun
Test: E.O. Legrand
               Saml Thompson Alcd

218. BROWN, WILSON C.   [S]
Nacogdoches   17 Aug 1835
Certify foreigner Wilson C. Brown is
a man of very good...married with
family, resident of this Municipality since the year 1829...
               Radford Berry

219. BROWNRIGG, GEORGE B.   [E]
Nacogdoches   Apl 13, 1835
Mr. S.C. Hiroms, Surveyor
Sir: You are hereby required to
survey in Joseph Vehlein's Grant the
sitio of landwhich Mr. Geo B. Brown-
rigg designates...
               Jorge Anto Nixon Comr
[Reverse]
I return the within order and dont
wish to become a Collenest.
August 5th 1835   G.B. Brownrigg

220. BRUCE [BREECE], THOMAS H. [E]
San Augustine   Nov 12, 1834
I certify that Thos H. Breece is a
native of Pennsylvania of the USA
and a man of family consisting of
three persons...
          John Bodine Secent Regidore
               third Alcalde in turn
[Note] 1st Survey above Ashworth's
Ferry Zavala wife and one child
220b.
[Field notes] Breeces sitio on East
Bank of the Naches River
               J.A. Veatch Surveyor

221. BRYANT, JOHN   [E]
San Augustine   Sept 1st, 1835
I certify that John Bryant a na-

tive of Georgia...is a single man
emigrated to the Country in 1831.
Saml Thompson Alcd

222. BRYAN, JOHN W.   [S]
Nacogdoches   25 May 1835
Certify foreigner John W. Bryan a
man of good...single without family.
                     Radford Berry
222a.
San Augustine   Sep 25th 1837
To George A. Nixon   Sir:
Please deliver to Mr. C. Dart my
title   which was advertised in your
office.
     [Signed]   John Bryan

223. BUCHETTI, JEAN FRANCISCO [S]
Bejar   13 Dec 1832
To Empresario Stephen F. Austin &
Samuel M. Williams
I am European by birth, married to a
Mexican woman in the City of Bejar.
I want to be admitted with the Colo-
nists...My name is Juan Francisco
Buchetti native of the Canton of
Falais in Switzerland, 48 years old.
My wife, Da Getrudis de LaBaume y
Buchetti, native of Nacogdoches, 18
years old.   Juan Francisco Buchetti
          G. de la Baume Buchetti
[Note] Certificate opened
Decr 21, 1832 in Bexar S.F. Austin
[Reverse] Petition for land of Dr.
Esteban Austin y Samuele Williams

224. BUCKEL, JOHN D.   [S]
Nacogdoches   10 Oct 1834
Certify that foreigner John D.
Buckes is a man of very good...mar-
ried with family... Luis Procela

225. BUCKLY, TERRY [TYRE] [E]
San Augustine   August 18, 1835
I certify that Terry Buckly is a
native of   the State of Mississippi
that he is a sin- gle man. Emigrated to Texas in the year 1822.
     A. Hotchkiss Primary Judge

226. BUFORD, THOMAS Y.   [S]
Nacogdoches   2 June 1835
Certify that foreigner Thomas Y.
Buford is   a man of very good...
single without family
 Jn Egne Michamps Alcalde Interim
[Rev] Accepted in Burnet. A. Henrie
22

227. BULLOCK, ALLEN C.   [S]
Nacogdoches   6 March 1835
Certify that foreigner Allen C.
Bullock is a man of very good...mar-
ried with family.
     Radford Berry   Alcd

228. BULLOCK, DAVID   [S]
Nacogdoches   11 August 1835
Certify that foreigner David Bullock
is a man of very good...widower with
family...resident of this Municipality since the year 1833...
                     Radford Berry

229. BULLOCK, DAVID   [E]
                     8 December 1834
This may certify that David Bullock
whos a natif of the you nited States
of the North has a family consisting
of five persons and is a good sete-
son and a man of good morrels...
John   Bodine   secont   Regedore
Third Alcalde in turn   [Note]
David Bullock, Zavala, Wife and
three children adjoining G. Thompson
Survey, below on the Naches.
                     J.A. Veatch

230. BULLOCK, JAMES W.   [E]
San Augustine   Sept 24th 1834
I certify that James W. Bullock a
native of North Carolina is a man of
family consisting of nine and a man
of very good...
          Benjamin Lindsey Alcalde
230a. [Field notes] West side Neches
River near a place known by the name
of Spindle Top...
          David Brown   Surveyor
231. BULLOCK, WILLIAM C.   [E]
San Augustine   May 18th 1835
I do certify that William C. Bullock
is a native of the State of Georgia
that he is a man of family consisting of a wife and four children.
     A. Hotchkiss Primary Judge

232. BUNKER, ISAAC [E]
San Augustine .   Nov 12th 1834
I certify that Isaac Bunker is a
native of Ohio of the US of A, is a
man of family consisting of thirteen
persons...
     John Bodine   secont Regedore
     the third Alcalde in turn

[Note] Wife and nine children. Zavala about 5 miles from A. Savery's
Survey   J.A. Veatch

233. BURDITT, WILLIAM B. [E]
San Augustine   May 25, 1835
I do hereby certify that William C.
Burditt is a native of the State of
Tennessee   that he is a man of fam-
ily consisting of a   wife and one
child... A. Hotchkiss, Primary Judge
[Rev] Accepted in Vehlein. A.Henrie
233a.
Nacogdoches   Oct 11, 1834
Mr. Wm Robinson, Surveyor
Sir: You are required to survey in
Vehlein's Grant the sitio of land
which Mr. Wm Whitaker [the name
was XXd out and the   following
written above it in a different
hand] Wm B. Burditt will designate.
              Jorge Anto Nixon Comr
[Note] On the league selected by Mr.
Edinburgh in Robinson's Settlement
[Reverse]
August 15, 1835 I return the within
order and renounce all   claim to it
and don't wish to be consider   a
Collonist.   Wm Whitaker
Order of Survey for W.B. Burditt

234. BURGES, JOHN [S]
Nacogdoches   27 April 1835
I certify that foreigner John Burges
is a man of very good...married with
family...   Radford Berry

235. BURK (BIRKE), ANN
[Field notes, no date, no signature]
Survey for Ann Birke of one league
and one   labor, being League No.4,
on the East Bank   of the Eastern
Fork of the Aransas

236. BURKE, BENJAMIN [E]
San Augustine   23d Sept 1834
I certify that Benjamin Burke is a
native of the US of the North he is
a man with   family consisting of
seven persons...   John Bevil Alc
236a.
San Augustine   23 Sept 1834
Mr. G.W. Smyth, Surveyor
Sir: You are required to survey in
Zavala's Grant the sitio of land

which Mr.Benjn Burke will designate.
              Jorge Anto Nixon Comr
236b.
Bevils Settlement   March 8, 1835
George A. Nixon Commissioner
Sir: You will please to deliver my
title to Wyatt Hanks. Benjamin Burke
[Reverse]   Sir: Please send by S.H.
              Everett   W. Hanks
236c. [Field notes]
East bank of the Neches River...
sitio of land...

237. BURKE, JOHN C.   [E]
San Augustine   29 Aug 1835
I certify that John C. Burk a native
of South Carolina of the US of A is
a man of family consisting of seven
in number...emigrated to this Country in 1820...
              Nathan Davis Commissioner
237a.
San Augustine   29 Aug 1835
I do certify that John C. Burk has
taken the oath of allegiance...
              Nathan Davis Commissioner
237b.
San Augustine   29 Aug 1835
I John C. Burk...appoint Edward O.
Legrand my attorney...to petition
George W. Smyth Comr for one league
and labor...being an old settler in
the Country. [Signed]   John C. Burk
Attest   John Harding
         H.L. Wiggins
         John Haley
         John Choat
         Jesse Amason

238. BURLESON, EDWARD
Town of Austin   June 18, 1830
To Mr. S.F. Austin Empresario
I have emigrated to this Colony...
Edwd Burleson 33 years old married
Sarah my wife   35 years old
3 male and one female children
Moved from Tennessee and arrived in
the Colony in 1st May 1830.
         [Signed]   Edward Burlesson
[Note] Wants his land on the West
side of the Colorado or on the East
side in the neighborhood of Varner's
Prairie.

239. BURLESON, JACOB
To Mr. S.F. Austin Empresario
I am desirous of becoming a Colonist
in your Contract of 1827...
Jacob Burleson 24 years of age
Elisabeth my wife 20 yrs
One male child
Passport 28 March
[No further signatures or dates]

240. BURLESON, HOPSON   [S]
Nacogdoches   6 June 1835
Certify...foreigner Hopson Burleson
is a man of very good...married with
family...   George Pollitt
                     Alcalde Interim
[Rev] Accepted Burnet   A. Henrie

241. BURLESON, JONATHAN   [E]
Selection of land in the Little Col-
ony. Jonathan Burleson has located
No. 12 South   of the St. Antonio
Road and West of the   Colorado.
Martin Ramsey has selected League
No. 28   S. of the St. Antonio Road
& West of Colorado.
[Also a plat on the same page]
Leagues Nos 1 & 2, --- have been se-
lected by Mr. Bisell --- be held in
reserve until   the 1st of October
1835.   Sims & Shackelford D.S.S.
[--- means word missing]

242. BURLESON, JOHN   [E]
Austin [de San Felipe] June 2, 1832
To Mr. S.F. Austin Empresario
I have emigrated to this Country...
John Burleson   27 years of age
Rebecca my wife 22   do
One male child
Moved from Tennessee and arrived in
this Colony in April
          [Signed]   John Burleson
[Note] Issued Certificate

243. BURLESON, JONATHAN by
      JAMES BURLESON
            April the 20, 1835
Mr. Borden. Sir:
You will find in my letter that I
have selected two leagues of land
one for Jonathan Burleson No. 12 the
other for Martin   Ramsby No. 28.
You will please enter them for me

and oblige your friend with out fail
and please drop me a few lines by
the barer conserning the matter and
I will be down to see you quick as I
can. Jonathan is mared and is inti-
tled to three quarters and his Brother will   take the other quarter
with him. [Signed] James Burlinson

244. BURLESON, JOSEPH   [E]
San Augustine   June 1, 1835
I do certify Joseph Burleson is a
native of the State of Tennessee
that he is a man of family consisting of a wife and six children...
        A. Hotchkiss Primary Judge
[Reverse] Accepted in Zavala
                     Arthur Henrie
244a.
San Augustine   August 17, 1835
I certify that Joseph Burleson a native of Tennessee of the US of A is
a man of family consisting of eight
persons...man of good...emigrated to
the Country in 1833.
          Saml Thompson Alcd
244b.
[Slip of paper with various items]
Sir:
Borden I wish you to enter League
No. 15 to the heirs of David Warren,
the survey and return is in the
office maid by Sims.
             Yours respectfully
Edward Burleson   James Rogers &
                     James Burleson

J. Burleson Junr has selected League
N. situated in Plumb Creek and shape
thus [four sided plot sketched]

Joseph Burlson Senior has selected
League No. 13 below the Road and
laying on Austin Boundary line on
Walnut Creek.   Application, James
Rogers, Jas Burleson
Attended to
244c.
Nacogdoches   June 2, 1835
Mr. Surveyor. Sir:
You are hereby required to survey in
Lorenzo de Zavala's Grant the sitio
of land which Mr. Joseph Burleson
will designate.
          Jorge Anto Nixon Comr
This order returned

[Reverse]   George Anto Nixon, Sir:
I hereby relinquish the right of the
order to any person you may wish to
give it, as I have taken land under
Mr. Smith. Yours &c Joseph Burleson

245. BURLINGTON, JOHN   [S]
Nacogdoches   29 May 1835
Certify...foreigner John Burlington
is a man of very good...single with-
out family. Jn Egne Michamps
          Alcalde Interim
[Reverse] Accepted   Arthur Henrie

246. BURNET, CRAWFORD   [E]
Town of Austin [de S.F.] 28 May 1830
I have emigrated to this Colony...
Crawford Burnett 24 years of age
married
Anne my wife   22 years of age
One male, one female children
Moved from Luisiana and arrived in
December 1829.   Crafforde Burnett

247. BURNET, CRAWFORD   [S]
Nacogdoches   19 June 1835
Certify...Crowford Burnett is a man
of very good...married with family.
   Geo Pollitt   Alcalde Interim
[Reverse] Burnet's Colony

248. BURNET, JOSEPH   [E]
San Augustine   May 24, 1835
Certify that Joseph Burnet native of
South   Carolina is a single man of
good...   A. Hotchkiss Primary Judge

249. BURNETT, WILLIAM   [E]
Town of Austin [de S.F.] 29 Apr 1830
To Mr. S.F. Austin Empresario
I have emigrated to this Colony...
William Burnett 28 years old married
Nancy my wife   28 years old
Two male, three female children
Occupation farmer, moved from Luisi-
ana and arrived in March 1830.
                 William Burnett

250. BURNETT, WILLIAM   [E]
San Augustine   17 Sept 1835
Certify that William Burnett a native of Virgiania of the US of A
emigrated to this Country in the
year 1830, that he is a man of family consisting of three persons.Took
the oath of allegiance...
          Saml Thompson Alcd

251. BURNHAM, STEPHEN   [S]
Nacogdoches   5 Sept 1835
Certify foreigner Stephen Burnham is
a man of very good...single without
family, resident of this Municipali=
ty since the year 1821...
                 Radford Berry
251a.
Nacogdoches   Sept 4, 1835
You are authorized to survey the
sitio of land which Mr. Stephen
Burnham will designate...
                 Geo W. Smythe Comr
[Reverse]
Executed the within Sept 5, 1835
          by James Bradshaw Surveyor

252. BURREL, A.A.   [E]
San Augustine   20 July 1835
Certify that A.A. Burrel, a native
of the US of the North is a man of
family consisting of seven persons,
that he emigrated to Texas in the
year 1834.   R.C. McDaniel C.P.O.
252b.
Nacogdoches   18 Aug 1835
Mr. Surveyor   Sir:
You are hereby authorized to survey
in Zavala's Grant the sitio of land
which Mr.A.A. Burrel will designate.
               Jorge Anto Nixon Comr

253. BURREL, DAVID   [E]
Department of Nacogdoches
Jurisdiction of Liberty 28 Jan 1835
Certify that David Burrell is a native of the State of Louisiana, is a
man of family consisting of himself
and wife...   Wm Hardin

254. BURRUS, SAMUEL   [S]
Nacogdoches   6 June 1835
Certify foreigner Samuel Buress is a

man of very good...single without
family... Geo Pollitt
[Reverse]. Accepted in Vehlein's
near where he lives. 1/4 sitio.
Arthur Henrie

255. BURROUGHS, JAMES [S]
Nacogdoches 26 May 1835
Certify foreigner James Burrows is a
man of very good...married with
family... Jn Egne Michamps
Provisional Alcalde

256. BURRUS, THOMAS [S]
Nacogdoches 15 Nov 1834
Thomas Burrus is a man of very
good...who has lived in this De-
partment for ten years is a widower
with family... Vital Flores
[Note] Two child.
256b.
Fort Teran March 1835
Mr. Jorge Anto Nixon, Land Commis-
sioner in Nacogdoches. Sir:
Please to deliver my Title to Mr.
M.B. Menard. He will in the same
time satisfy you for your charges.
[Signed] Thomas Burrus

257. BURTON, ISAAC W. [S]
Nacogdoches 7 Sept 1835
Certify foreigner Isaac W. Burton is
a man of very good...married with
family resident of this Municipality
since the year 1831... Radford Berry
257a.
Recd of George Anto Nixon the Title
of Stephen Jackson & Bennet Blackman
both for Zavala's Colony.
Sept 12, 1835 I.W. Burton
257b.
Nacogdoches 2 June 1835
Certify foreigner Joses W. Burton is
a man of very good...married with
family...
Jn Egne Michamps
Provisional Alcalde

258. BURTON, WILLIAM B. [S]
Certify foreigner William B. Burton
is a man of very good...married
with family...
Geo Pollitt Provisional Alcalde

[Rev] Accepted in Zavala. A. Henrie
258a.
Recd of J.A. Nixon Commissioner
Wm B. Burton's Title.
Oct 22, 1835 Arthur Henrie

259. BURTS, DENNIS B. [S]
Nacogdoches 7 Nov 1834
Certify foreigner Dennis B. Burts is
a man of very good...married with
family... Vital Flores
[Note] Wife. On the 3 Cabin Bayou
adjoining Mr. Hry Martin's Survey,
Wm Robinson
259a.
Nacogdoches Nov 7, 1834
Mr. Wm Robinson, Surveyor. Sir:
You are hereby required to survey in
David G. Burnet's Grant, the sitio
of land which Mr. Dennis B. Burts
will designate.
Jorge Anto Nixon Comr
Adjoining Hry Martin's Survey
on 3 Cabin Bayou

260. BUSBY, WILLIAM [S]
Nacogdoches 15 April 1835
Certify foreigner William Busby is a
man of very good...married with
family... Radford Berry

261. BUSH, JOHN [S]
Nacogdoches 24 Oct 1835
Certify foreigner John Bush is a man
of very good...single resident of
this Department since the year 1831.
Radford Berry
[Reverse] John Bush No. 594
261a.
Nacogdoches Oct 28, 1835
Sir: You are authorized to survey
the third sitio of land which Mr.
John Bush will designate...
Geo W. Smyth Comr
[Reverse] John Bush No. 594

262. BUSH, JOHN [S]
Nacogdoches 7 May 1835
Certify foreigner John Bush is a man
of very good...single without family
Radford Berry

263. BUSTIC, BENJ. [E]
San Augustine 18 Aug 1835
Certify that Benjamin Bustic is a citizen of this Municipality is a native of Virginia of North A is a man of family consisting of four persons...that he emigrated to this Country in about 1821.
Nathan David Commissioner

264. BUTLER, AHIRA [E]
San Augustine August 17, 1835
Certify Ahira Butler is a single man that he is a native of Tennessee that he emigrated to Texas in the year 1828. A. Hotchkiss P. Judge

265. BUTLER, GEORGE [E]
San Augustine 27 Sept 1834
I certify that George Butler a native of Georgia of the USA is a man of family consisting of five persons... Benjamin Lindsey Alcalde

266. BUTLER, JOSEPH [E]
San Augustine Sept 23, 1834
I certify that Joseph Butler a native of Georgia of the US of the N is a man of family consisting of nine persons...
Benjamin Lindsey Alcalde

267. BUTTLER, WILLIAM F.C. [S]
Nacogdoches 9 December 1835
Certify foreigner Wm F.C. Buttler is a man of very good...married with family... Jn Egne Michamps
Provisional Alcalde

268. BYERLEY, ADAM [E]
Nacogdoches December 18, 1834
Adam Byerley is a native of the State of S.Carolina in the US of the N, is a single man...
John Bevil Alcalde
268a.
Department of Nacogdoches
District of Bevil August 28, 1835
Adam Byerley is a native of the State of South Carolina in the US of the N, emigrated to this Country in the year one thousand eight hundred and thirty three...
is a single man...
Wm Williams Alcalde

269. BYERLEY, MARTIN [E]
Department of Nacogdoches
District of Bevil August 25, 1835
Martin Byerley is a native of the State of South Carolina of the US of the N, hath a family consisting of three persons...Wm Williams Alcalde

270. BYERLEY, WILLIAM [E]
Department of Nacogdoches
District of Bevil August 25, 1835
William Byerley is a native of the State of South Carolina of the US of the N, is a single man...
Wm Williams Alcalde

271. BYRNS, MATTHEW
[Field notes] Survey of one third of a league for Matthew Byrns being part of League No. 8. Situated on the right bank of the Rio Frio.

272. William Barret Travis Agent for S.D. BYROM
Tenoxtitlan 29 April 1834
To the Empresarios Austin and Williams I have emigrated to Texas... I am married my wife name [blank] and have [blank]
John S.D. Byrom
by Wm Barret Travis Agent

273. CADDEL, ANDREW [E]
San Augustine April 3d 1834
Andrew Caddel is a native of North Carolina in the US of A is a man of family consisting of eight persons.
A. Hotchkiss Pry Judge
273a.
[Field notes] Set post for beginning corner of Andrew Caddel's sitio on the NE bank of the Angelina... 4 labors arable

274. CADENA, JUANA BERGAR DE [S]
Nacogdoches 30 July 1835
Citizen Juana Bergar de Cadena born in this State, woman of very good...widow with a family...has not obtained land. Radford Berry
274a.
Nacogdoches August 4, 1835
Sir: You are authorized to survey

the sitio & labor of land which
Juana Bergar Cadena will designate.
Geo W. Smyth Comr

275. CADENA, MARIA JOSEFA   [S]
Nacogdoches   3 Aug 1835
Certify that citizen Maria Josefa
Cadena a woman of very good...wi-
dow with family, resident of this
Municipality since the year 1829...
Jn Egne Michamps
Alcalde Provisional

276. CAFFEY, HOOPER   [E]
To Mr. S.F. Austin Empresario
I have emigrated to this Colony...
My name is Hooper Coffey
40 years of age
My wifes name Mary 37 years
I have 5 children of which 3 are
male and 2 female. Moved from the
State of Alabama. H. Caffey [Coffey]

277. CAGE, B.F.   [S]
Nacogdoches   11 Aug 1835
Certify that foreigner B.F. Cage is
a man of very good...single without family,   resident of this state
since the year 1832...
Radford Berry

278. CAIN, JAMES C.   [E]
San Augustine   [no date. 1835?]
I certify that James C. Cain a native of Louisiana of the USA is a
single man...emigrated to this country in 1832...   Saml Thompson Alcd
278a.
San Augustine   Sept 1, 1835
Sir: You are authorized to survey
the third sitio Mr. James C. Cain
will designate... Geo W. Smyth Comr

279. CALDERON, ANTONIO   [S]
Nacogdoches   17 July 1835
Certify Antonio Calderon is a man of
very good...single without family...
Radford Berry

280. CALDERON, GUADALUPE   [S]
Nacogdoches   9 Sept 1835
Certify that citizen Guadalupe Cal-
deron is a woman of very good...
widow with family, resident of this
Municipality since the year 1833...
has not obtained land...
Radford Berry

281. CALDWELL, JAMES P.   [E]
Austin [de San F.]   10th May 1831
To Mr. S.F. Austin Empresario
I have emigrated to this Colony...
James P. Caldwell 36 years of age
widower. A native of Kentucky.
Jas P. Caldwell

282. CALDWELL, WILLIAM   [E]
Nacogdoches   24 Oct 1835
Citizen William Caldwell declares
that some time in the month of July
last past or thereabouts, he obtained an order of survey from Commissioner George Anto Nixon for one
league of land in Joseph Vehlein's
Colony, and that a few days after-
ward he lost said order and further
supposed that said was stolen...
[wants duplicate]
[Sig] William Caldwell
G. Pollitt Alcalde Interim
282b.
San Augustine   June 9, 1835
I certify William Caldwell a native
of N.Carolina of the USA is a man of
family consisting of nine persons.
A. Hotchkiss P. Judge
[Rev] Accepted in Zavala. A. Henrie

283. CAMPBELL, WILLIAM   [S]
Nacogcohes   17 June 1835
Certify foreigner William Campbell
is a man of good...married with
family...
Jn Egne Michamps Alcalde Interim

284. CAMUNEZ, JUANA   [S]
Nacogdoches   Ausust 4, 1835
Sir: You are hereby authorized to
survey...sitio & labor which Mrs.
Juana Camunez will designate...
Geo W. Smyth Comr

[Reverse]   Juana Camunez

285. CANFIELD, ALANSON W.   [E]
District of Sabine   May 20th 1835
This is to certify that Alanson W.
Canfield, a native of Connecticut,
USA, is now a citizen of the Dis-
trict aforesaid, has a family

consisting of three persons.
B.Holt Commissioner
[To] Major George A. Nixon,
Nacogdoches

286. CANFIELD, BUCKMAN [E]
Austin [de San F.]   March 26, 1833
To Mr. S.F. Austin Empresario
I have emigrated to this Country...
My name is Buckman Canfield 33 years
of age, Harriet my wife 23 years of
age. One male child. Moved from the
State of New York and arrived
6th Feby.
[Signed]   Buckman Canfield

287. CANFIELD, HENRY   [S]
Nacogdoches   4 June 1835
Certify foreigner Henry Canfield is
a man of very good...married with
family...
Jn Egne Michamps
Provisional Alcalde

288. CANNON, FRANCIS B.   [E]
Naches   January 18, 1835
I have been acquainted with Mr.
Francis B. Cannon for some time and
he is a man of family, of good...
Wm Whiteley Comr

289. CANNON, MARTIN   [E]
Department of Nacogdoches
Jurisdiction oi Liberty 31 May 1835
I certify that Martin Cannon, a na-
tive of Ireland, is a married man,
man of good... Wm Hardin P. Judge
[Rev] Accepted in Vehlein's Grant
A. Henrie
Wants his quarter near John Welshes,
which is No. 5 surveyed by Genl
Russel

290. CANTU, MARIA DE   [S]
Nacogdoches   6 April 1835
Certify citizen Maria de Cantu is a
resident of this Municipality since
many years and of very good...wi-
dow with family...has not obtained
land...   Radford Berry

291. CAPLE, ELIJAH
Austin [de San F.]   24 Novr 1831
To S.F. Austin Empresario
I have emigrated to this Country...
Elijah Caple 28 years of age

2 female children
Farmer moved from Arkansas and ar-
rived in this Colony March 1831.
[Signed]   Elijah Caple

292. CARLETON, WILLIAM   [E]
Mr. Carleton by his agent Geo
Sutherland applies for land.
England. Family wife & one child
Dec 15, 1834   John Sutherland
[Rev] Wm Carleton application

293. CARLISLE, ROBERT   [E]
Navadad   Decr 19th 1835
Mr. Borden. Dear Sir:
Last May when the land office was
open you will find my name recorded
in your Book applying for land. I
had made choice of a quarter which
was said to be forfeited by Aldridge
on West Crankeway believing that to
be the situation of land and being
willing to comply with the Regula-
tions of the Land Law...
Robt Carlisle

294. CARMONA, MANUEL   [S]
Nacogdoches   9 Sept 1835
Certify citizen Manuel Carmona is a
man of very good...resident of this
Department since the year 1822,
married with family, has not obtained land...   Radford Berry

295. CARMONA, MARIA DE LOS ANGELES
Nacogdoches   [S]   1 July 1835
Certify citizen Ma de los Angeles
Carmona is a woman of very good...
resident of the Municipality and
born here, woman with a family...has
not obtained land...
Jn Egne Michamps
Provisional Alcalde

295a.
Nacogdoches   August 25, 1835
Sir: You are authorized to survey
the sitio Mrs. Ma de los Angelos
Carmona willvdesignate...
Geo W. Smyth Comr

296. CARMONA, MARIA GERTRUDEZ   [S]
Nacogdoches   9 September 1835
Certify citizen Maria Gertrudiz Carmona, a woman of very good...widow
with family, resident of this Municipality since the year 1820...

29

has not obtained land...
Radford Berry

297. CARNER, PATRICK   [S]
Nacogdoches   27 April 1835
Certify foreigner Patrick Carner is
a man of very good...single...
Radford Berry

298. CARO, JOSE AGATON   [S]
Naogdoches   4 May 1835
Certify citizen Jose Agaton Caro is
a resident of this Municipality and
born here, a man of very good...
single...has not obtained land...
Radford Berry

299. CARO, JOSE ANTONIO   [S]
Nacogdoches   5 May 1835
Certify that citizen Jose Antonio
Caro, a resident of this Municipality, born here, a man of very good...
married with family. has not obtained land... Radford Berry

300. CARO, JOSE SEBASTIAN   [S]
Nacogdoches   23 July 1835
Certify Jose Sebastian Caro is a
resident   of this Municipality and
born here, man of very good...single
without family...has not obtained
land...   Radford Berry
300a.
Nacogdoches   Sept 28, 1835
Sir: You are authorized to survey a
sitio of land which Mr. Jose Sebastian Caro will designate...
Chas S. Taylor Comr

301. CARO, PEDRO JOSE   [S]
Nacogdoches   4 April 1835
Certify citizen Pedro Jose Caro is a
resident of this Municipality, born
in the country, married with family
has not obtained land...
Radford Berry

302. CARO, AGATON   [E]
San Augustine   Sept 1st 1835
I certify that Agraton Carr is a
native citizen, is a man of family
consisting of   six persons, and a
man of good... Saml Thompson Alcd

303. CARR, ANDERSON B.   [S]
Nacogdoches   2 May 1835
Certify that foreigner Anderson B.
30

Carr is a man of very good...
married with family
Radford Berry
303a.
Nacogdoches   May 2, 1835
Mr. Surveyor   Sir:
You are hereby required to survey in
Joseph Vehlein's Grant the sitio
which Mr. Anderson B. Carr will
designate.   Jorge Anto Nixon Comr
[Note] On West Bank of Trinity

304. CARR [CARO], ANASTACIO   [E]
San Augustine   Sept 1, 1835
I certify that Anastacio Carr is a
native citizen, is a single man...
Saml Thompson Alcd

305. CARR, WILLIAM   [E]
Department of Nacogdoches
Jurisdiction of Liberty 28 Dec 1834
Certify that William Carr is a na-
tive of the State of Louisiana, is a
man of family consisting of his wife
and eight children.
Wm Hardin P. Judge

306. CARRODINE, ISAAC   [E]
San Augustine   August 21, 1835
Certify that Isaac Carrodine is a
native of the State of Mississippi,
a man of family consisting of a wife
and one child...that he emigrated to
Texas in the year 1827...
A. Hotchkiss

307. CARRODINE, ROBERT   [E]
San Augustine   August 31, 1835
I Robert Carradene...appoint A.
Houston my attorney to   petition
George W. Smyth Comr for one third
of a league to which I am entitled
as an old settler...
Robert X Carodin
Certified by A. Hotchkiss, P. Judge
307a.
San Augustine   Aug 31, 1835
Certify that Robert P. Carodine is a
native of Mississippi that he is a
single man...emigrated to Texas in
the year 1827.
A. Hotchkiss P. Judge
He has taken the oath of allegiance

308. CARROL, ELIZABETH   [E]
San Augustine   6 Sept 1835
I certify that Elizabeth Carrol is a

native of South Carolina...woman of family consisting of two persons... Emigrated to Texas in the year 1824.
Nathan Davis Commissioner
308a.
San Augustine   12 September 1835
I Elizabeth Carrol appoint Wm Jones my agent to obtain for me an order of survey from Mr. Geo W. Smyth Comr.   Elizabeth X Carrol
Witness: John English

309. CARROLL, JOHN   [S]
Nacogdoches   8 November 1834
Certify foreigner John Carroll is a man of very good...single...
Vital Flores
309a.
[Field notes] Survey one league of land for John Carroll. Beginning on the bank of the river...Lake Santa Margarita...
[Reverse] Nueces
309b.
Maj. Nixon, Commissioner   Sir:
Please to deliver my deed to Martain Murchison when it is ready.
Decr 28th 1834   John Carroll

310. CARROLL, MARY   [E]
[Field notes] Survey of one league of land for Mary Carroll.   Situated at the   head of the Eastern Branch of Aransas Creek...League No. 6.

311. CARROLL, MOSES A.   [E]
Liberty   Octr 1st 1834
I certify that Moses A. Carroll a native   of Louisiana is a man of family consisting of himself and wife...   Wm Hardin P. Judge
311a.
Turtle Bayou   Sept 19th 1835
Majr G.A. Nixon, Comr   Sir:
You will please deliver to Mr. Wm M. Logan my land title...
Moses X Carroll
Witness: F. Hardin

312. CARROLL, PATRICK   [E]
[Field notes] Survey of one league and   one labor of land for Patrick Carroll, known as League No. 7,

situated on the head waters of the Aransas   Creek...
312a.
Nacogdoches   April 27, 1835
Mr. H. Hiroms, Surveyor
Sir: You are hereby required to survey in Jos Vehlein's Grant the quarter sitio which Mr. Patrick Carroll will designate...
Jorge Anto Nixon Comr
[Note] In a vacant place on Menard Creek

313. CARROLL, PHILLIP   [S]
Nacogdoches   9 September 1835
Certify foreigner Philip Carrol is a man of very good...married with a family...   Radford Berry
[Reverse] Accepted in Vehlein's
Arthur Henrie

314. CARSON, JOHN   [E]
San Augustine   May 19, 1835
I do hereby certify that John Carson is a native of the State of Georgia, that he is a man of family consist- ing of eight children...
A. Hotchkiss   Primary Judge

315. CARTER, GEORGE   [E]
Sabine   District [no date; 1834?]
I do certify that George Carter a native of North Carolina has a fami- ly...emigrated to Texas in the year 1824.   B. Holt Commissioner

316. CARTWRIGHT, JOHN
San Augustine   Oct 29, 1835
I John Cartwright of the Municipali- ty of San Augustine appoint W.M. Ragland my agent to apply to George W. Smyth Comr at Nacogdoches for a league and labor... John Cartwright
Witnesses: Jefferson Wilson
M. Cartwright
A. Hotchkiss
316a.
San Augustine   Oct 29, 1835
I do hereby certify that John Cart- wright is a native of the State of North Carolina that he is a man of family consisting of wife and seven children...emigrated to Texas in the year 1825.   A. Hotchkiss P. Judge

317. CARTWRIGHT, JOHN   [E]
Town of Austin [de S.F.] 3 May 1828
To Mr. S.F. Austin Empresario
I have visited your Colony for the
purpose of procuring a settlement in
it for my family that are now re-
siding in the District of Aises in
the Republic. I wish to move to
your Colony...
John Cartwright 43 years old
Mary my wife   42 years old
Five male, two female children.
Eleven dependents.   Occupation
farmer. Moved from Mississippi.
Jno Cartwright

318. CARTWRIGHT, M.   [E]
George A. Nixon, Esqr. Dec 3rd 1835
Mr. Dennis Hegerty will call on you
for Titles for the following persons
who have undertaken to clear out of
the land office, A.W. Canfield and
others which he has a list of
names & oblige   M. Cartwright
[Reverse]
Received on account of the written
order the following titles.
Isaac Greeson   Henry Canfield
Widow Russell   Matthew Cartwright
Isaac Powel
Decr 3d 1835   Dennis Hegerty

319. CARTWRIGHT, MATTHEW   [S]
Nacogdoches   7 May 1835
Certify foreigner Mathew Cartwright
is a man of good...single without
family...   Radford Berry

[Field notes] Commence at the
Northwest corner of Speers Survey
for the beginning corner of Mathew
Cartwright...quarter sitio on the
East Bank of the Atoyaque...2 labors
arable   John Harvey Surveyor

320. CARTWRIGHT, ROBERT G.   [E]
District of Sabine   April 7th 1835
This will certify that Robert G.
Cartwright of this place has resided
in the District of Ayish Bayou since
March 1826, a young man of moral
habits...   B. Holt Commissioner

321. CARTWRIGHT, THOMAS   [E]
San Augustine   Sept 26, 1834
I certify that Thomas Cartwright a
native of Georgia of the US of A is
a man of family consisting of seven
persons... Benjamin Lindley Alcalde
321a.
Nacogdoches   Sept 26, 1834
Mr. Surveyor. Sir:
You are required to survey in Joseph
Vehlein's Grant the sitio of land
which Mr. Thomas Cartwright will
designate...   Jorge Anto Nixon
[Note] NW of Menard's Survey

322. CARUTHERS, JOHN   [S]
Nacogdoches   14 Oct 1834
Certify foreigner John Caruthers is
a man of very good... Luis Procela

[Note] John Caruthers wife and four
children, between the head waters of
the San Jacinto and Trinity Rivers

323. CAZNEAU, W.L.   [E]
To Mr. S.F. Austin Empresario
I have emigrated to this Country...
My name is Wm L. Cazneau 22 years of
age. From Boston and arrived in the
Colony June 1831.   W.L. Cazneau

324. CASTANEDA, FRANCESCA   [E]
Nacogdoches   April 4th 1835
I do hereby certify that Franca Castaneda was married to a solger in
the 12th Battalion by the name of
Toribio Marufo and that her husband
died in the ospital in this town---
and that she has two orfan children.
P.E. Bean

325. CASTANEDA, PEDRO   [S]
Nacogdoches   26 May 1835
Certify citizen Pedro Castaneda is a
resident of this Municipality, man
of very good...married with family.
Has not obtained land...
Jn Egne Michamps Alcalde Interim

326. CASTILLO, MANUEL ITURRI   [S]
To Empresarios Esteban F. Austin &
Samuel M. Williams
I am married to a Mexican in the

city of Bexar, fifteen years of residence in the same. I am a farmer and rancher, with seven persons in my family. I am Manuel Iturri Castillo of 42 years. My wife D̲a̲ Maria Josefa Rodriguez of 29 years and daughter of 16 years. Also two small female children and one small male child which I have raised as if they were my own children. Another little girl put in my charge and 3 young servants.
Bexar   20 Dec 1832
          Manuel Iturri Castillo
[Note] Gave a certificate 23 Dec 1832 in Bexar.   [signed] Austin

327. CASTLEBERRY, AARON   [E]
San Augustine   May 23, 1835
I certify that Aaron Castleberry is a native of Georgia of the US of A is a man of family consisting of twelve persons...
          John Chumley 2d Regdr
          Alcalde in turn

328. CASTLEBERRY, WILLIAM   [E]
San Augustine   May 23, 1835
I certify that William Castleberry is a native of Georgia of the US of A is a man of family consisting of seven persons...   John Chumley
          2d Regdr Alcalde in turn
[Reverse] Accepted. Arthur Henrie

329. CASTRO, FRANCISCO   [S]
Nacogdoches   7 May 1835
Certify citizen Francisco Castro, a resident of this Municipality for many years is a man of good...married...has not obtained land...
          Radford Berry
[Note] Two children

330. CASTRO, MARIA GUADALUPE DE
Nacogdoches   [S]   6 April 1835
Certify citizen Maria Guadalupe de Castro is a resident of this Municipality for many years, is a woman of very good... widow with family...has not obtained land
          Radford Berry

331. CASANAVE, JUAN BAPTISTE   [S]
Nacogdoches   28 May 1835
Certify foreigner Juan Baptiste Casanave is a man of very good...wi-

dower with family...
     Jn Egne Michamps Alcalde Interim
331a. [Field notes] Waters of Big Alabama Creek about 6 or 7 miles south of A. Bartlett and about 12 miles west of the bluff on the Naches known as Bacon Bluff and on the west side of a branch of Village Creek...   Burton Surveyor

332. CERVANTES, JOSE   [E]
San Augustine   Sept 22, 1835
I certify that Jose Cervantes a naive citizen is a man of family consisting of eight persons...
          Saml Thompson Alcd
332a.
San Augustine   23rd Sept 1835
I Jose Cervantes...appoint William Inglish my attorney to petition George W. Smyth Comr for one league and labor to which I am entitled...
          Jose X Cervantes
Wit: A.E.C. Johnson
     C. Thompson
     Saml Thompson Alcd

333. CERVANTES, JOSE MARIA   [S]
Nacogdoches   22 August 1835
Certify citizen Jose Maria Servantes de Bejar is a man of very good... resident of this Municipality since the year 1820...single without family...has not obtained land...
          Radford Berry

334. CERVANTES, PEDRO   [S]
Nacogdoches   25 August 1835
Certify citizen Pedro Servantes native of the Hacienda Palmira is a man of very good...resident of this Municipality since the year 1834... single without family...has not obtained land...   Radford Berry

335. CHAFFIN, JOHN   [E]
Tenoxtitlan   29 April 1834
To Empresarios Austin and Williams I have emigrated to Texas...
I am single.   John Chaffin

336. CHAFFIN, THOMAS   [S]
Nacogdoches   3 June 1835
I certify foreigner Thomas Chaffin is a man of very good...married with family...   Jn Egne Michamps
          Alcalde Interim

337. CHAMBERS, JESSE H. [S]
Nacogdoches 22 April 1835
Certify foreigner Jesse H. Chambers
is a man of very good...single
without family. Radford Berry

338. CHAPA, IGNACIO [S]
Nacogdoches 6 April 1835
Certify citizen Ignacio Chapa is a
resident in this Municipality since
many years, married with family...
has not obtained land...
Radford Berry

339. CHAPLIN, CHICHESTER [E]
San Augustine 22 Sept 1834
I certify that Chichester Chaplin
from the evidence of two persons is
a native of Ireland a man of family
consisting of five persons...
Benjamin Lindsey Alcalde
339a.
[The record below is 3 pieces of
paper of unproven relationship]
I do certify that Col Martin Palmer
is a Gentleman of honor and property
and is under a good character, in
our Parish and State
[These may not be Texas names]
Peter Leatherman   George Grounds
Charles Rodes   John Grounds
Jonathan Knox   Jesse Grounds
Thomas Price   Conrad Grounds
Farqueson Haile   John Lamb
Wm Driskill   Obadiah Driskill
John Leewright   Danl S.D. Moore

By A.B. Roman
Governor of the State of Louisiana
I certify that Chichester Chaplin...
was at the signing of this, is now
Parish Judge of the Parish of
Claiborne...
New Orleans   23 March 1831
George A.Waggoner   A.W. Roman
Secretary of State
339c.
[Field Notes] Chichester Chaplin on
the west bank of Ayish Bayou...8
labors arable land.
T.S. McFarland Surveyor

340. CHAPPELL, H.J. [E]
San Augustine August 20, 1835
Certify that H.T. Chappele is a na-
tive of the State of Virginia, that

he is a man of family consisting of
a wife...emigrated to Texas in the
yr 1833. A. Hotchkiss P. Judge

341. CHAPPELL, SARAH [E]
San Augustine August 20, 1835
Certify that Sarah Chappell a native
of Tennessee a widow woman with a
family of two persons emigrated to
this Country in 1828.
Saml Thompson Alcd

342. CHASE, WILLIAM [S]
[Printed Certif. of Admission]
Villa de Austin 23 Decem 1829
Certify that Mr. William Chase is
one of the Colonists; came to this
Colony in Nov 1823; married, family
of 4 persons Esteban F. Austin

343. CHAVANA, ANTONIO
Nacogdoches Sep 15, 1834
Order of Survey for Antonio Chavana
Mr. Wm Brookfield, Surveyor
Sir: You are hereby authorized to
survey in Vehlein's Grant the sitio
Mr. Antonio Chavana will designate
Jorge Nixon Comr
[Reverse] The within order has been
executed by me. William Brookfield

344. CHAVANA, JOSE RAMON [E]
Nacogdoches Sep 15th 1834
Mr. Wm Brookfield, Surveyor
Sir: You are hereby required to
survey in Vehlein's Grant the sitio
of land which Mr.Jose' Ramon Chavana
will designate... Jorge Anto Nixon
344a.
Recd of Jorge Anto Nixon Comr
The title of Jose' Ramon Chavana
Nacogdoches Sep 29, 1835
Jose Antonio Sepulveda

345. CHAVANA, SANTIAGO [S]
Nacogdoches 25 August 1835
Certify citizen Santiago Chavan is a
man of good...resident of this Municipality and born here...single
without family...has not obtained
land... Radford Berry

346. CHEAIRS, JOHN [S]
Nacogdoches 25 May 1835
Certify foreigner John Cheairs is a
man of good...married with family... Radford Berry

347. CHEAIRS, JOHN F. [S]
Nacogdoches 25 May 1835
Certify foreigner John F. Cheairs is
man of good...single without family... Radford Berry

348. CHEAIRS, SAMUEL [S]
Nacogdoches 25 May 1835
Certify Samuel Cheairs is a man of
good...single... Radford Berry

349. CHEAIRS, WILLIAM [S]
Nacogdoches 25 May 1835
Certify forigner William Cheairs is
a man of good...single without
family... Radford Berry

350. CHEATHAM, JAMES L. [S]
Nacogdoches 3d June 1835
Certify foreigner James L. Cheatham
is a man of good...single without
family... Jn Egne Michamps

351. CHERMNEY, ARMSTEAD [E]
San Augustine 22 Sept 1834
I certify that Armsted Chermney is a
native of Arkansas...is a man of
family consisting of four persons
and that he is a man of good...
Benjamin Lindsey Alcalde

352. CHERRY, AARON [E]
Nacogdoches Apl [torn]
Mr. F. Harding, Surveyor
Sir: You are required to survey in
Veh- lein's Grant the sitio which
Aaron Cherry will designate...
Jorge Anto Nixon Comr
[Note] Near Menard on the East Bank
of the Trinity (adjn Blanchd) at
his own improvement
[Reverse]
Returned and I dont want to reserve
land as a Collenest Aaron X Cherry

353. CHERRY, DAVID [E]
San Augustine September 1st 1835
I certify that David Cherry a native

of South Carolina is a man of family
of six persons...emigrated in 1830.
Saml Thompson Alcd

354. CHERRY, JOHN [E]
Department of Nacogdoches
Jurisdiction of Liberty Dec 18, 1834
I James B. Woods Alcalde...certify
that John Cherry a native of the
State of Ohio is a man of family
consisting of himself his wife and
three children and that he is a man
of good... J.B. Woods

355. CHERRY, JOHN V. [E]
San Augustine September 1st 1835
I certify John V. Cherry a native of
No Carolina is a man of family of
three persons and a man of good...
emigrated 1833 Saml Thompson Alcd

356. CHERRY, SMITH R. [E]
San Augustine September 1st 1835
Smith R. Cherry native of No Caroli-
na...single man, emigrated in 1830
Saml Thompson Alcd

357. CHESSER, DANIEL [E]
Dept of Nacogdoches
District of Bevil Oct 10th 1834
Daniel Chessher is a native of the
State of Georgia is a single man...
John Bevil Alcalde
[Note]
At place where his father lives
357a.
Maj Henrie Dear Sir:
In the Book of Notes which I first
put in your possession you will find
one in the name of David Dawson.
This is the place petitioned for by
Daniel Chesshe in Order No. 164.
You will therefore have the goodness
to examine & make out the note of
said Survey of one fourth sitio. Mr.
Chesher is a single man, and there-
fore entitled to no more although
the order is by mistake given for
one sitio. Feb 8, 1835
Geo W. Smyth
357b.
[Field Notes] No. 164. Daniel
Chessser quarter sitio on the north
bank of Sandy Creek...
Geo W. Smyth Surveyor

358. CHESSHER, DANIEL [E]
Dept of Nacogdoches
District of Bevil   August 29th 1835
I certify that Daniel Chessher is a
native of the State of Georgia and
emigrated   to this Country in the
year 1829, hath a   family consisting of three persons...
           Wm Williams Alcalde

359. CHESSHER, JAMES   [E]
Dept of Nacogdoches
District of Bevil   Octr 10th 1834
I certify James Chessher is a native
of the State of Georgia hath a fam-
ily consisting of six persons...
           John Bevil Alcalde
[Note] Wife and 5 children. Zavala
Mouth of Wrights Creek J.A.V.

360. CHESSHER, JAMES   [E]
Dept of Nacogdoches
District of Bevil   August 29th 1835
I certify that James Chessher is a
native of the State of Georgia and
emigrated to the Country in 1824,
hath a family consisting of eight
persons...   Wm Williams Alcalde

361. CHILDERS, JOHN   [E]
District of Sabine   6th June 1835
This will certify that John Childers
a   native of Tennessee, now a citizen of the   District aforesaid, has
a family consisting of two persons.
           B. Holt Commissioner

362. CHENNITH, E.D.   [E]
San Augustine   Sept 1, 1835
I certify that E.D. Chenneth a native citizen is a single man and man
of good...   Saml Thompson Alcd

363. CHIRINO, BAUTISTE   [S]
Nacogdoches   29 Aug 1835
Certify citizen Bautiste Chirino is
a man of good...resident of this
Municipality for many years, married with family, has   not obtained
land...   Radford Berry

364. CHIRINO, MANUEL   [S]
Nacogdoches   27 April 1835
Certify citizen Manuel Chirino resi-

dent of this Municipality and born
here...man of very good...married
with family...has not obtained land
           Radford Berry
364a.
[Field Notes] West corner of David
Burrell Survey in prairie in the
fork of Taylors Bayou...Manuel
Chirino sitio...   Burton Surveyor

365. CHIRINO, MARIA CANDIDA   [S]
Nacogdoches   8 April 1835
Certify citizen Maria Candida Chi-
rino is a resident of this Munici-
pality for many years, widow with a
family...has not obtained land...
           Radford Berry
365a.
[Field Notes] Maria Candidade
Chirino Survey on the margin of the
Alleseaso...   by Brown Surveyor

366. CHISUM, JOHN   [S]
Nacogdoches   16 Sept 1834
Certify foreigner John Chisum is a
man of good...proved by four witnesses... Luis Procela Alcalde Interim
366a.
Nacogdoches   August [torn]
Mr. William Brookfield   Sir:
You are to survey the third sitio
which Mr. John Chisum will designate...   Geo W. Smyth Comr
[Rev] This order has been executed
by me   Wm Brookfield   Surveyor

367. CHISUM, WILLIAM P.   [S]
Nacogdoches   14 August 1835
Certify foreigner Wm P. Chisum is a
man of good...single without family,
resi-dent of this Municipality since
1833... wants land... Radford Berry

368. CHOATE, DAVID   [E]
Department of Nacogdoches
Jurisdiction of Liberty 6 Jan 1835
I John Stewart Commissioner of the
Precinct of Cow Bayou do hereby
certify that David Choate Junr is a
native of Louisiana and a single man
of good...   John Stewart
     Comr of Precinct of Cow Bayou
[Reverse] David Choat, Edward Choat

369. CHOATE, DAVID   [S]
Nacogdoches   27 October 1834
Certify foreigner David Choate is a
man of very good...married with
family...   Vital Flores
369a.
Mr. Geo A. Nixon   Sir:
Please deliver my Title to Mr. J.C.
Martin   August 7th 1835
     [Signed] David Choate

370. CHOATE, JOHN   [E]
San Augustine   May 23d 1835
I certify that John Choat a native
of Tennessee and man of family consisting of three persons...
          Nathan Davis Comr

371. CHOATE, MOSES L.   [S]
Nacogdoches   9 October 1834
Certify resident of this Villa Moses
L. Choate is a man of very good...
married at Nuestra Santa Madre
Church in this Villa.
          Luis Procela

372. CHOATE, REDMOND   [S]
Nacogdoches   4 May 1835
Certify foreigner Redmond Choate is
a man of very good...married with
family...   Radford Berry

373. CHOATE, THOMAS   [S]
Nacogdoches   18 May 1835
Certify foreigner Thomas Choate is a
man of very good...married with
family...   Redford Berry

374. CHRIST, ISAAC   [S]
Nacogdoches   22 November 1834
Certify that Isaac Christ is a man
of very good...married with family
          Vital Flores
374a. Order of Survey
Nacogdoches   Nov 22, 1834
Mr. William Brookfield, Surveyor
Sir: You are to survey in Vehlein's
Grant the sitio which Mr. Isaac
Crist will designate...
          Jorge Anto Nixon Comr
[Note]
Above Judge Hardin's half league on
Vehlein's Grant, Trinity River

375. CHRIST, JEREMIAH   [S]
Nacogdoches   22 Sept 1834
Certify that Jeremiah Christ is a
man of very good...married with
family...   Vital Flores

376. CRIST, JOHN   [S]
Nacogdoches   29 January 1835
Certify foreigner John Crist is a
man of very good...married with
family...   Radford Berry

377. CRIST, STEPHEN   [S]
Nacogdoches   22 Feb 1835
Certify foreigner Stephen Crist is a
man of very good...married with
family...   Radford Berry
[Note] Wife & 6 children. Burnet

378. CHRISTIAN, THOMAS   [E]
Austin [de San F.]   April 26, 1832
To Mr. S.F. Austin Empresario
I am desirous of becoming a Colon-
ist...My name is Thomas Christian 32
years of age, married,
moved from Illinois.
Mary my wife 32 years
One male 4 female children
          [Signed] Thomas Christian
Passport dated 2d April

379. CLAPP, ELISHA   [S]
Nacogdoches   14 October 1834
Certify foreigner Elisha Klape is a
man of very good...married with
family...   Luis Procela
[Note] Elisha Clapp. D.B. Burnet
Grant Wife and four children.
1-1/2 miles from Mustang Prairie of
the road

380. CLARK, BARTON   [S]
Nacogdoches   2 April 1835
Certify foreigner Barton Clark is a
man of very good...married with
family...   Radford Berry

381. CLARK, ELIJAH   [E]
San Augustine   Nov 12, 1834
I certify that Elijah Clark is a na-
tive of Mississippi, is a single man
of good...
     John Bodine secont Regedore
          third Alcalde in turn
[Note]
Housen Bayou, Zavala. McFarland

381a.
Nacogdoches   Oct 12, 1835
Sir: You are authorized to survey
for   Elijah Clark...19,750,000 sq
varas...   Geo W. Smyth Comr
381b.
Major Nixon Sir: Please to send by
the   bearer Mr. Robert Smith my
land Title...
29 August 1835   Elijah Clark

382. CLARK, ELIJAH   [E]
San Augustine   18 September 1835
I certify Elijah Clark a native of
Mississippi emigrated to this coun-
try in 1824, man of family consist-
ing of two persons...
                  Saml Thompson, Alcd
382a.
[Field Notes]   Corner of James
Clark's survey for Elijah Clark's
quarter sitio... John A. Veatch

383. CLARK, JAMES   [E]
San Augustine   Nov 12, 1834
I certify James Clark is a native of
Mississippi, is a single man of
good... John Bodine secont Regedore
         third Alcalde in turn
[Note] Housen Bayou adjoining John
Clark Survey, Zavala. Thos McFarland
383a. [Field Notes]

386. CLARK, JAMES   [S]
Nacogdoches   11 Dec 1835
Certify foreigner James Clark is a
man of very good...married with family, resident of this Department
since 1819...   Radford Berry

387. CLARK, JAMES   [E]
To Mr. S.F. Austin Empresario
I have emigrated to this Colony...
James Clark 40 years old
Susan S my wife 34 years of age
4 male, 5 female children
Moved from Kentucky where his family
now resides. Arrived 1 Nov 1831.
              [Signed] Jas Clark

388. CLARK, JOHN   [E]
San Augustine   September 24th 1834
I certify John Clark a native of the
State   of Mississippi, man of fami-
ly consisting of two persons...
             Benjamin Lindsey Alcalde

389. CLARK, JOHN   [S]
Passport by Mexican Vice-Consul, New
York To John Clark native of Ireland
Citizen of the same, age 28 years,
farmer.   Pass to Galveston
8 March 1831 James Treat,Vice-Consul
[Reverse, several endorsements with
very poor legibility]
Presented in this Military Command
Anahuac, April 23d 1831
              John Davis Bradburn

Nacogdoches   18 July 1831
Presented: Manuel de los Santos Coy

389a. [Field Notes] [No proof that
this belongs to the above JohnClark]
Corner of James Clark sitio...
John Clark sitio... Veatch Surveyor

390. CLARK, M.B.   [S]
Nacogdoches   11 Sept 1835
Certify foreigner M.B. Clarck is a
man of very good...single without
family...   Radford Berry

391. CLARK, WILLIAM   [S]
Nacogdoches   23 April 1835
Certify foreigner William Clark is
a man of very good...married with
family...   Radford Berry

392. CLARK, WILLIAM   [S]
Nacogdoches   30 October 1835
Certify foreigner William Clark is a
man of very good...widower with family, resident of this Department
since March 1834   Radford Berry

393. CLARK, WILLIAM   [E]
San Augustine   October 10, 1835
Certify that Wm Clark is a native of
the State of Connecticut, that he
is a man of family consisting of one
child, emigrated to Texas in the
year 1831 as said by Mr.Haley...
          A. Hotchkiss Primary Judge
393a.
San Augustine   9 October 1835
I William Clark appoint Richard
Haley my attorney to petition for
one league and labor... Wm X Clark
Wit. A. Hotchkiss Oct 10, 1835

394. CLARK, WILLIAM   [E]
San Augustine   September 24th 1834
Wm Clark is a native of South Caro-
lina...a man of family consisting of
eight persons...
            Benjamin Lindsey Alcalde
394a.
[Field notes] William Clark Survey
John Clark's North [torn]
            John A. Veatch Surveyor

395. CLARK, WILLIAM F.   [E]
District of Sabine   June 9th 1835
William F. Clark now a citizen of
the District has a family consisting
of four persons...
            B. Holt Commissioner
[Reverse]
Accepted in Zavalas. A. Henrie

396. CLARKE, ANTHONY R.   [S]
[Printed Certificate of Reception]
Villa de Austin 23 December 1829
No. 77   Certify that Anthony R.
Clarke is one of the Colonists...
Arrived Novr 1824; single...
            Estevan F. Austin

397. CLARKSON, JAMES   [S]
Nacogdoches   18 May 1835
Certify foreigner James Clarkson is
a man of very good...married with a
family...   Radford Berry

398. CLEGHORN, JOHN W.   [E]
San Augustine   Feb 2, 1835
John W. Cleghorn is a man of family
consisting of a wife and two children, native of Georgia...man of
good... A. Hotchkiss Primary Judge

399. CLEVELAND, DANIEL   [S]
Nacogdoches   19 June 1835
Certify foreigner Daniel Cleaveland
is a man of very good...single with-
family   Jn Egne Michamps
[Reverse]
Accepted in Vehlein, A.Henrie

400. CLEVER, ISAAC   [S]
Nacogdoches   15 September 1835
Certify foreigner Isaac Clover is a
man of   very good...married with
family, resident   of this District
since 1823...   Radford Berry

401. CLEVER, ROBERT   [E]
San Augustine   August 17, 1835
Certify Robert Clever is a native of
Virginia, that he is a single man...
emigrated to Texas in 1833.
            A. Hotchkiss P. Judge
401a.
San Augustine   [E] August 17th 1835
You are ordered to survey the third
sitio which Mr. Robert Clever will
designate...   Geo W. Smyth Comr

402. CLIFFT, JESSE   [E]
To Mr. S.F. Austin Empresario
I have emigrated to this Colony...
Jesse Clifft 31 years old married
Mary my wife 16 years old
Occupation Farmer & Blacksmith
Moved from Luisiana and arrived in
this Colony Feby 1830.
            [Sig]   Jesse Clifft

403. COALE, JAMES   [E]
Department of Nacogdoches
Jurisdiction of Liberty 9 Jany 1835
I   John Stewart Commissioner for the
Precinct of Cow.Bayou, certify James
Coale is a native of Louisiana, a
man of family consisting of his wife
and ten children, a man of good...
            John Stewart
[Note] On Long King's Cr = F. Hardin
    Vehlein

404. COBBS, JAMES   [S]
Nacogdoches   10 October 1834
Certify foreigner Santiago [James]
Cobbs is a man of very good...
single...   Vital Flores
[Note]   James Cobbs, single, the
place by Mathew Sims near the ---
            Brookfield

405. COCHRAN, HENRY [E]
Department of Nacogdoches
District of Bevil   April 11th 1835
Henry Cochran a native of Indiana is
a single man of good...
            Wm Williams Alcalde
405a.
District of Ayish   4 Feby 1833
Personally appeared Henry Cochran
who took the oath to support the
Constitution...and proves permanent-
ly locating himself between the
first and fifteenth of March 1833.
            William McFarland Alcalde
39

406. COCHRAN, JAMES [E]
Town of Austin   July 14, 1833
To Mr. S.F. Austin Empresario
I have moved to this Colony...
James Cochran 30 years of age.
Occupation farmer, moved from Ala-
bama. Arrived in the Colony in
July 1829. [Signed] James Cochran

407. COITEUX, FRANCIS [E]
State of Missouri, Perry Co.
Decr 20, 1830 We the undersigned
are acquainted with Francis Coiteux, a resident of the County, a
man of good...we know him to have
been born and raised under the
Spanish Gov. in upper Louisiana...
M. Wilkinson
[4 Missouri signers]
407a.
State of Missouri Perry Co.
13 Jan 1831 I Frederick C. Hase
Clerk of the Co. Ct. certify [the
above names]

408. COLBURN, JOHN [E]
Austin [de San F.]   Jany 6, 1831
Mr. S.F. Austin Empresario
I have emigrated to the Colony...
John Colburn 36 years of age
Pamelia my wife 33 years of age
1 female child
Family in the State of New York,
arrived in Novr 1831
[Sig] John Colburn
Passport 10 Octbr

409. COLE, JOHN [S]
Nacogdoches   2 May 1835
Certify foreigner John Cole is a man
of very good...married with family...
Radford Berry

410. COLEMAN, B.M. [E]
Tenoxtitlan   8 Feby 1834
To Empresarios Austin & Williams
I have emigrated to Texas...
I am a married man my wifes name is
Elizabeth, I have three sons & two
daughters. My age 36, my wifes 30.
[Sig] B.M. Coleman

411. COLEMAN, NICHOLAS [E]
San Augustine   19 July 1835
I certify Mr. Nicholas Coleman a na-
40

tive of the US is a man of family
consisting of three persons, that he
emigrated to Texas in June 1835...
R.C. McDaniel C.P.O.
411a.
Nacogdoches   Aug 15, 1835
Mr.Surveyor   Sir:
You are to survey in Zavala's Grant
the sitio which Mr. Nicholas Coleman
Jorge Anto Nixon Comr

412. COLEY, WRIGHT [E]
Precinct of Sabine October 9, 1834
Wright Coley a native of North Carolina a man of no family...good citizen... Elbert Hines Commissioner

413. COLLARD, ELIJAH [E]
San Jacinto   Novr 10th 1834
We certify that we have been ac-
quainted with Mr. Elijah Collard...
good citizen...
Joseph Lindly
Samuel Lindley
John Sadler
This is to certify that I know all
of the above... James J. Foster
Commissioner for the precinct of
Viesca
[Note] Wife & 5 children at his
improvement on San Jacinto, Vehlein.
Wm Rankin

414. COLLARD, FREDERICK [S]
Nacogdoches   2 Dec 1834
Certify foreigner Frederick H. Col-
lard a man of very good...married
with family... Vital Flores
[Note] Opposite the town of Zavala
Side of the Angelina
Wife & 7 children = Jno A. Veatch

415. COLLARD, JOBE S. [E]
Jorge Anto Nixon,Comr at Nacogdoches
Sir: I have taken an order of survey for a certain sitio...and I find
the selection to be an old claim. I
therefore made an other selection
and had it surveyed...May 18th 1835
Job S. Collard
415a.
Naches District   May 8th 1835
I have been acquainted with Jobe S.
Collard...man of good...man of family, a farmer... Wm Whiteley Commissioner for the Naches District

416. COLLARD, LEMUEL M.
San Jacinto   August 21st 1835
Mr. George Antonio Nixon,
Commissioner
Sir: You will please send my Land
Title by Hiram Little by his paying
fees.   Lemuel M. Collard
[Also on the same sheet]
San Jacinto   21 August 1835
Mr. George A. Nixon, Commissioner
Sir: You will oblige me by sending
my Land Title by Mr. Little by his
paying the fees.   Samuel Lindley
416a.
San Jacinto   Novr 10, 1834
We certify that we have been ac-
quainted with Lemuel M. Collard for
a considerable time...
                  Joseph Lindley
                  William Ware
I certify I am personally acquainted
with all the above.   11 Novr 1834
     John B. Foster Comr Pct Viesca
[Note] Wife & 5 children
At a place surveyed on the Sn Jacto
for Cameron. Wm Robinson =
Vehlein

417. COLLINS, E.M.   [E]
District of Sabine   June 8, 1835
E.M. Collins a native of Tennessee
now a citizen of the District aforesaid, has a family consisting of
four persons, a currier & tanner to
trade...   B. Holt Commissioner
[Rev] Accepted Zavala A. Henrie

418. COLLINS, GEORGE T.W.   [E]
San Augustine   Sept 23d 1834
George T.W. Collins a native of Lou-
isiana is a single man of good...
          Benjamin Lindsey Alcalde

419. COLVILL, THOMAS   [S]
Nacogdoches   2 May 1835
Certify foreigner Thomas Colvill is
a man of very good...married...
                  Radford Berry

420. COLVIN, JOHN   [S]
Nacogdoches   4 January 1835
Certify foreigner John Colvin is a
man of very good...single without
family...   Radford Berry
[Note] 1/4 at a spot 8 miles to the
NE of Mr. Cummings= Hiroms= Vehlein

421. COLWELL, WILEY   [S]
Nacogdoches   25 September 1835
Certify foreigner Wiley Colwell is
a man of very good...married with
family...   Radford Berry
[Reverse] Accepted in Vehlein.
                  Arthur Henrie

422. COLWELL, WILLIAM   [S]
Nacogdoches   25 September 1835
Certify foreigner William Colwell is
a man of very good...single without
family...   Radford Berry
[Reverse] Accepted in Vehlein
                  Arthur Henrie

423. CONE, HENRY H.   [S]
Nacogdoches   2 May 1835
Certify foreigner Henry H. Cone is
a man of very good...married...
                  Radford Berry

424. CONN, JAMES   [E]
San Augustine   22 Sept 1834
James Conn a native of the US...man
with family consisting of five
persons...   John Bevil Alcalde
424a.
Geo A. Nixon   Sir:
You will please send me my Title by
Dr. S.H. Everett
March 22d 1835   James Conn

425. CONN, ROBERT   [E]
Department of Nacogdoches
District of Bevil   Octr 15th 1834
Robert Conn is a native of S. Caro-
lina...single man of good...
               John Bevil Alcalde
[Note]
The place where his father lives
425a. [Field notes]
Begin at John Bevils Survey for
Robert Conns quarter sitio...

426. CONNAWAY, ISAAC   [S]
Nacogdoches   16 April 1835
Certify foreigner Isaac Conaway is
a man of very good...married with
family...   Radford Berry
426a.
G.A. Nixon:
Let T.B. Huling have my Title
Sept 30th 1835   Isaac Connaway

427. CONNELLY, ELIJAH M.   [E]
Town of Austin   13 May 1830
I have emigrated to this Colony...
Elijah M. Connly 34 years of age,
single. Mariner from Luisiana ar-
rived Apl 1830. Elijah M. Connelly

428. CONNELLY, JAMES   [E]
San Augustine   August 19, 1835
James Connalley is a native of the
State of N York...single emigrated
to Texas in the year 1832...
         A. Hotchkiss P. Judge

429. CONWAY, JOHN
[Field notes] 1/3 Lea Atascosa
Survey of 1/3 league for John Conway... part of League No. 3...left
bank of the   Attascosa Creek...

430. COOK, DAVID   [E]
This is to certify that I have been
acquainted with David Cook for some
time   January 31, 1835
        Wm Whiteley Commissioner
        for the Naches Precinct

431. COOK, GREENBERRY [E]
Precinct of Sabine Feb 23, 1835
Greenberry Cook is a native of Mississippi is a man of family
consisting of two persons...
         B. Holt Commissioner

432. COOK, HENRY C.   [S]
Nacogdoches   18 May 1935
Certify foreigner Henry C. Cook is
a man of very good...married...
         Radford Berry

433. COOK, JAMES   [S]
Nacogdoches   8 Dec 1834
Certify foreigner James Cook is a
man of good...married...
         Vital Flores
[Note] Wife. Near the Neches above
Williams Ferry adjoining Gibbs Sur-
vey. Burnet   J. Strode

434. COOK, JOSEPH T.   [S]
Nacogdoches   15 Dec 1834
Certify foreigner Jose T. Cook is a
man of very good...married with
family...   Vital Flores
[Note] Joseph T. Cook. Wife & 11
ch. N of L. Gibbs about 7 or 8
miles = Burnet
42

435. COOK, WILLIAM A.   [S]
Nacogdoches   12 November 1834
Certify foreigner William A. Cook is
a man of very good...married with
family...   Vital Flores
[Note] Wife & 4 children
Vehleins 5 mi West of Caruthers.
         Robinson

436. COOTE, WILLIAM M.   [E]
Department of Nacogdoches
District of Bevil January 21, 1835
William Coote is a native of Ire-
land in Europe, has a family con-
sisting of four persons...
         Wm Williams Alcalde
436a.
[Field notes] West bank of the
Ayish Bayou for the beginning of
William Cootes sitio...
         D. Brown Surveyor

437. COPE, THOMAS   [E]
Town of Austin   31 May 1830
I have emigrated to this Colony...
Thomas Cope 28 years of age, unmar-
ried. Occupation farmer, moved from
Luisiana and arrived in the Colony
in July 1829. [Signed]   Thos Cope
437a.
Department of Nacogdoches
Jurisdiction of Liberty 19 Dec 1834
Certify Thomas Cope is a native of
Maryland, is single unmarried...
         James B. Woods Alcalde
[Note] Single man. Vehlein =
F. Hardin Between Wm Hardin and ---
Survey on the West Bank of Trinity
River

438. COPELAND, JAMES   [E]
Town of Austin   29 May 1830
I have emigrated to this Colony...
James Copeland 28 years of age un-
married. Farmer. Moved from Georgia
and arrived in Aug 1827.
         [Sig]   James Copeland

439. COPELAND, JOHN   [S]
Nacogdoches   3 April 1835
Certify foreigner John T. Copeland
is a man of good...married with
family...   Radford Berry

440. COPELAND, MARK   [S]
Nacogdoches   18 April 1835
Certify foreigner Mark Copeland is a

man of good...married with family...
                    Radford Berry

441. CORDER, WILLIAM A.   [S]
Nacogdoches   12 Oct 1835
Certify foreigner William A. Corder
is a man of good...married with
family...
                    Radford Berry
[Rev] Accepted. A. Hotchkiss Attor-
ney for Joseph Vehlein. The above
may be changed to Burnets if the
Commissioner should think proper.
A. Hotchkiss At for D.G. Burnet

442. CORDOVA, DAMIAN [S]
Nacogdoches   16 July 1835
Certify citizen Damian Cordova is a
man of very good...widower with
family, one   daughter...
                    Radford Berry
442a.
Nacogdoches   26 August 1835
Sir: You are to survey the sitio
and labor which Mr. Damian Cordova
will designate.   Geo W. Smyth Comr

443. CORDOVA, FRANCISCO   [S]
Nacogdoches   8 May 1835
Certify citizen Francisco Cordova is
a resident of this Municipality and
born here, married...has not
obtained land...   Radford Berry
443a.
Nacogdoches   2 Sept 1835
Certify citizen Francisco Cordova is
a man of good...resident of this
Municipality, born here...married
with family...has not obtained
land...   Radford Berry
443b.
Nacogdoches   May 8, 1835
Mr. Surveyor   Sir: You are to
survey in David G. Burnets Grant the
sitio which   Mr. Franco Cordova
will designate
                Jose Anto Nixon Comr
[Rev] I am authorized to return
this Order of Survey.
25 Sept   F. Thorn

444. CORDOVA, TELESFORO   [S]
Nacogdoches   11 May 1835
Certify citizen Telesforo Cordova a
resident of this Municipality and
born here...single, has not
obtained land...   Radford Berry

445. CORNWALL, WILLIAM   [E]
Precinct of Tennahaw 1 Sept 1835
William Cornwall native of Caintuckey...family consisting of three persons, emigrated to the Country in
1829.   Nathan Davis Commissioner
445a.
San Augustine   Sept 1, 1835
Sir: You are to survey the sitio &
labor which Mr. Wm Cornwall will
designate...   Geo W. Smyth Comr

446. CORTES, MARIA DE LA
              CRUZ RODRIGUEZ Y
Nacogdoches   10 June 1835
Certify citizen Maria de la Cruz
Rodriguez y Cortes is a woman of
very good...widow with family...
                    Radford Berry

447. CORTINAS, MIGUEL   [S]
Nacogdoches   29 May 1835
Certify citizen Miguel Cortinas is a
resident of this Municipality for
many years, man of good...married
with family...has not obtained
land...   Jn Egne Michamps
                    Alcalde Interim
[Reverse] Accepted in Burnet
                    Arthur Henrie

448. CORZINE, SHELBY
Tuskaloosa, Alabama   20 Novr 1834
Mr. Shelby Corzine the bearer...in-
tending to visit the province of
Texas and probably to remove there
with his family. I have been ac-
quainted...
[Governor of Alabama]   John Gayle
[Reverse]
Livingston   Jany 13th 1835
[another similar testimonial]
                    Saml Chapman
448a. [Field notes]
Commence at North East corner of
Pevetoes Survey for beginning of
Shelby Corzine...
                    Veatch Surveyor

449. COSTLEY, NICHOLAS   [S]
Nacogdoches   23 May 1835
Certify foreigner Nicholas Costley
is a man of good...married with
family...   Radford Berry

450. COSTLEY, MICHAEL   [S]
Nacogdoches   28 Oct 1835
Certify foreigner Michael Costly is
a man of good...married with family,
resident of   this Department since
1832...   Radford Berry

451. COTTLE, LEONARD   [E]
Austin [de San F.]   Feb 4th 1830
To Mr. S.F. Austin Empresario
I have emigrated to this Colony...
My name is Leonard W. Cottle, I am
21 years of age. I removed from
Missouri and arrived in the Colony
in February 1828
        [Signed]   Leonard Cottle

452. COTTON, JOHN   [S]
Nacogdoches   7 October 1835
Certify foreigner John Cotton is a
man of good...married with family
and resident of this Department
since the year 1821...
                      Radford Berry
452a
October 13th 1835
Mr. William Brookfield   Sir:
You are to survey the sitio & labor
which   Mr. John Cotton will
designate...   Geo W. Smyth

453. COTTON, JOHN J.E.   [E]
San Augustine   August 20, 1835
Certify John J.E Cotton is a native
of Tennessee that he is a man of
family consisting of a wife and
four children...emigrated to Texas
in 1833.   A. Hotchkiss P. Judge

454. COUGHRAN, JOHN   [E]
San Augustine   Sept 23, 1834
John Caughran is a native of Ken-
tucky, is a single man of good...
            Benjamin Lindsey Alcalde
454a.
Nacogdoches   5 August 1835
Certify foreigner John Caughhorn is
a man of good...single without fam-
ily, resident of this Municipality
for four years...   Radford Berry
454b.
Nacogdoches   August 1835
Mr. Roark   Sir:
You are to survey the third sitio

which John Coughran will designate.
            Geo W. Smyth Comr

455. COWAN, JOHN B.   [E]
Austin [de San F.]   October 1, 1832
Mr. S.F. Austin Empresario
I have emigratd to this Colony...
John B. Cowan 39 years of age, mar-
ried. Sarah my wife 33 years of age
3 male, 2 female children
Moved from the State of Alabama
                      John B. Cowan

456. COX, JAMES   [E]
Austin [de San F.]   April 26, 1832
To Mr. S.F. Austin Empresario
I am desirous of becoming a Colonist
My name is James Cox 33 years of
age, married. Moved from Kentucky
where his family resides.
My wifes name Anne
2 female children   James Cox
Passport dated 2d April

457. COX, JOHN   [E]
Austin [de San F.]   April 26, 1832
To Mr. S.F. Austin Empresario
I have come to this Country desirous
of settling in your Contract...
John Cox 29 years of age
Mary my wife 26
1 male 3 female children
Moved from Kentucky where his family
resides.   John Cox

458. COX, LEWIS   [E]
San Jacinto   November 16th 1834
We certify that we are acquainted
with the bearer of this
Mr. Lewis Cox...   Joseph Lindly
                    Elijah Collard
I certify that the above ...
        James J. Foster Commissioner
        for the Precinct of Viesca
[Note] Wife & 4 ch. At his im-
provements adjoining Wm McDonald's
Survey, North
            Vehlein. Wm Robinson

459. COX, WILLIAMSON N.   [E]
San Augustine   2 February 1835
Williamson N. Cox is a native of
Tennessee is a man of family con-

sisting of six persons, emigrated to Texas in January 1834.

R.C. McDaniel C.P.O.

459a.
Nacogdoches   Agt 6th 1835
Mr. Surveyor   Sir:
You are to survey in Zavala's Grant the sitio which Mr. Williamson N. Cox will designate.

Jorge Anto Nixon Land Comr
[Note]
On the West side of River Neches

460. COY, IGNACIO DE LOS SANTOS
Nacogdoches   [S]   15 May 1835
Certify citizen Ignacio de los Santos Coy a resident of this Municipality, born here, man of good... married with family...has not obtained land...   Radford Berry

461. COY, MARIA JESUSA
              DE LOS SANTOS   [S]
I am a widow with children of my late husband Ignacio, six children power of attorney to Pedro Estocoman...because I am sick and unable to appear...has not received land...
      Maria de los Santos X Coy
      Saml Thompson Alcalde

462. CRABB, HILLARY M.   [E]
Georgia, Harris Co.   29 Decem
We the undersigned do hereby certify that Mr. Hillary M. Crabb... [good character]   [9 Georgia signatures]
[Note] Mr. Hillary M. Crabb also a certificate of E. Hamilton, Governor of Georgia
462a.
February 13th 1835
Mr. G.A. Nixon   Sir: Please send my Title by barer by his paying the office fees   Hilary M. Crabb

463. CRAIG, ROBERT   [E]
District of Tennehaw   1 July 1835
I certify Robert Craig is a native of Kentucky, a man of family consisting of seven persons...emigrated to the Country in the year 1834...
      Nathan Davis Commissioner

464. CRAIN, JOEL B.   [E]
San Augustine   May 24, 1835
Joel B. Crain is a native of Tennes-

see...single man...
      A. Hotchkiss Primary Judge
[Reverse] Accepted in Burnet 1/4
sitio.   A. Henrie

465. CRAIN, WILLIAM J.   [E]
San Augustine   August 1835
William J. Crain is a native of Tennessee a man of family consisting of a wife and three children, emigrated to Texas in the year 1831.
      A. Hotchkiss Primary Judge

466. CRANE, JOHN   [E]
San Jacinto   Novr 16, 1834
We certify that we are acquainted with the bearer Mr. John Crane...
      John Lindley
      Elijah Collard
I certify [to the above names]
      James J. Foster Commissioner
      for the Precinct of Viesca
[Note] Wife & 7 ch. on Cumming's Trace near Jesse Parker's Survey.
Vehlein   Wm Robinson

467. CREAGER, WILLIAM   [S]
Nacogdoches   ´14 December 1835
Certify foreigner William Creager is a man of very good...married with family, resident of this Department since 1822...   Radford Berry

468. CRENSHAW, CORNELIUS   [E]
San Augustine   Sept 1st 1835
Cournelious Crenshaw is a native of South Carolina, a married man of family consisting of seven persons emigrated to this Country in 1831.
      Saml Thompson Alcd

470. CRENSHAW, DANIEL   [E]
San Augustine   September 1st 1835
Daniel Crenshaw a native of Georgia...man of family consisting of three persons, emigrated to this Country in 1831.
      Samuel Thompson Alcd

471. CRIPPIN, JOHN   [E]
San Augustine   Sept 27, 1834
John Crippin a native of New York... man of family consisting of four persons... Benjamin Lindsey Alcalde

472. CRISSMAN, S.   [E]
San Augustine   May 18th 1835
S. Crisman a native of the United
States is a man of family consist-
ing of six persons...
                R.C. McDaniel C.P.O.
472a.
Nacogdoches   August 10, 1835
Mr. Surveyor   Sir:
You are to survey in Zavala's Grant
the sitio which Mr. S. Crissman will
designate   Jorge Anto Nixon Comr

473. CRISWELL, ANN D.   [E]
Liberty   Octr 12th 1834
Mrs. Ann Creswell a native of Mis-
souri is a woman of family consist-
ing of three...
              Wm Hardin Primary Judge
                 Jurisdiction of Liberty
473a.
Trinity   March 17th 1835
Mr. Jorge Anto Nixon Land Commis-
sioner in Nacogdoches   Sir:
Please deliver my Title to Mr. M.B.
Menard   Ann D. Criswell

474. CRONKRITE [CONKRITE], JOHN
Wayne [N.Y.]   [S]   Novr 3, 1830
We do certify John Cronkrite and
Albert   Selsbe of Wayne County of
Steuben, State of New York, are of
good moral character [3 New York
signers. Certification of the
County Clerk]

475. CRONKRITE, DR. LYMAN   [E]
Marysville, Union County, Ohio
November 24, 1830
I have been acquainted with Dr.
Lyman   Cronkrite for several years
past... [Certification by Union
County Clerk]

476. CROW, JOHN   [E]
San Augustine   Sept 1, 1835
John Crow a native citizen is a man
of family consisting of five persons
                Saml Thompson Alcd
476a.
San Augustine   1 Sept 1835
I, John Crow, do appoint James Eng-
lis my   attorney to petition Geo W.
Smyth for a league & labor to which
I am entitled...   John X Crow
Wit: Saml Thompson Alcd

477. CROW, LEVI M.   [E]
San Augustine   Oct 30th 1834
Levi M. Crow a native of Tennessee
and a single man...
James W. Bullock Cindico
              and Alcalde pro tem
[Note] Soltero [single]
Adjoining on the north east side of
Ayes Bayou, Zavala   G. McFarland
477a.
Mr. George A. Nixon   Dear Sir:
Please send me my Title by the bear-
er Mr. W.F. Allison
November 20, 1835   Levi M. Crow
Teste: John Wrightsell
       Elihu C. Allison

478. CRUSE [CRUISE], SQUIRE   [E]
San Augustine   23 September 1834
Squire Cruse is a native of the U.S.
a man of family consisting of three
persons...   John Bevil Alcalde
478a. [Field notes] Begin at corner
Anderson Barclay's Survey for Squire
Cruise Survey...waters Wolf Creek
running into the Neches...
478b.
Nacogdoches   Oct 8, 1835
Rec of the Comr Maj Geo Antonio
Nixon the titles of possession of
Squire Cruise & Briton Hall.
              Geo W. Smyth

479. CULLEN, JONATHAN S.   [S]
Nacogdoches   26 May 1835
Certify foreigner Jonathan S. Cullen
is a man of very good...single with-
out family...
Jn Egne Michamps Alcalde Interim

480. CUMMINGS, JOHN H.   [S]
Nacogdoches   20 Sept 1834
Certify foreigner John N. Cummings
is a man of good...proved by three
witnesses...   Luis Procela Alcalde
480a.
Nacogdoches   30 June 1834
Received of Citizen Antonio Menchaca
from the papers left in his possession...a concession of one league...
granted in 1827 of which I am to be
put in possession by the Alcalde of
this town...   John H. Cummings

481. CUMMINS, MESHACK   [E]
Presink of Sabine   8 December 1834
Meshack Cummings a native of South
Carolina a man of family consisting
of six persons... Elbert Hines Comr
[Note] Meshack Cummings
Wife and four children. The place
where he   lives adjoining Nelson's
Survey on Bear Creek.
Zavala.   J.A. Veatch
481a. [Field notes]
Commence at S. Nelsons southwest
corner   for M. Cummings Survey...
Veatch
481b.
To George Nixon Land Comr
Dear Sir: Please to send by
Robert Smith my Title
August 29, 1835   Meshack Cummins

482. CUNNINGHAM, ANDREW P.   [S]
Nacogdoches   18 Nov 1834
Certify foreigner Andrew P. Cunningham is a man of good...married with
family...   Vital Flores
[Note] Wife & 2 ch
2 Survey above the mouth of Hurricane Bayou N side.   Burnets
Wm Robinson

483. CUNNINGHAM, DAVID   [S]
Nacogdoches   4 December 1834
Certify foreigner David Cunningham
is a man of good...married with
family...   Vital Flores
483a. [Field notes]
Commence northwest corner William
Zigler's   Survey for David A.
Cunninhgam quarter sitio...
John A. Veatch   Surveyor
483b.
Nacogdoches   Oct 23, 183-
Recd of Majr J.A. Nixon, Mr. Stephen
J. Stanley Title for said Stanley
David A. Cunningham

484. CURRY, JAMES A.   [E]
San Augustine   Sept 27, 1834
James A. Curry is a native of Georgia, hath a family consisting of
nine persons. John Bevil Alcalde
484a. [Field notes]
Beginning corner James A. Curry
sitio on the north east boundary
of James McKeny Survey...
J.A. Veatch Surveyor

485. CURRY, WILLY   [S]
Nacogdoches   16 May 1835
Certify foreigner Willy Curry a man
of good...married with a family...
Radford Berry

486. CURTNEY, JEREMIAH   [S]
Nacogdoches   25 May 1835
Certify Foreigner Jeremiah Curtney
is a man of good...married with
family...   Jn Egne Michamps
Alcalde Interim

487. CUSHING , THEOPHILUS
[Field notes]   Set post on west
bank of the Naches for corner of
Theophilus Cushing sitio...

488. CUTTS, DAVID   [E]
San Augustine   May 17, 1835
David Cutts native of the U.S. a man
of family consisting of six persons,
that he emigrated to Texas in 1834.
R.C. McDaniel C.P.O.
488a.
Nacogdoches   11 August 1835
Mr. Surveyor   Sir:
You are to survey in Zavala's Grant
the sitio which Mr. David Cutts will
designate.Jorge Anto Nixon Land Comr

489. DALE, CHARLES   [E]
Matagorda   December 1, 1833
To Col. S.F. Austin Empresario
I take the liberty of informing you
that I am now in Texas within your
Colony. It is my desire to become a
colonist...I have a family within
the Country resident at this town,
consisting of a wife & one child...
Charles Dale

490. DALTON, WILLIAM R.   [E]
Jurisdiction of Liberty Dec 27,1834
Certify Wm R. Dalton a native of
Louisiana is a man of family con-
sisting of himself his wife & four
children & a man of...   J.B. Woods

491. DOUGHERTY, JOHN [S]
Nacogdoche   5 August 1835
Certify foreigner John Daugherty is
a man of good...married with family,

47

resident of this Municipality since
1831...   Radford Berry

492. DAUGHERTY, PATRICK   [S]
Nacogdoches   14 August 1835
Certify Citizen Patrick Daugherty is
a man of good...resident of this
Municipality since 1833...married
with family...has not obtained land
                   Radford Berry
492a.
Nacogdoches   August 11, 1835
Mr. William Brookfield   Sir:
You are to survey the sitio & labor
which   Mr. Patrick Daugherty will
designate...   Geo W. Smyth Comr

493. DAVIDSON, URIAH   [E]
San Augustine   29 Feby 1835
Certify Uriah Davidson a native of
Alabama is a man of family consist-
ing of 4 persons, that he emigrated
to Texas in   April 1834, man of
good...   R.C. McDaniel C.P.O.
493a.
Nacogdoches   Aug 8, 1835
Mr. Surveyor   Sir:
You are to survey in Zavala's Grant
the sitio which Mr. Uriah Davidson
will designate...
        Jorge Anto Nixon Land Comr
[Note]
On the west side of River Neches

494. DAVIS, ALFRED B.   [E]
Precinct of Tennahaw   -- Sep 1835
Certify that Alfred B. Davis a native of   South Carolina, man of
family consistsing of three persons
and man of good...immigrated to
this Country in 1828.
         Nathan Davis Commissioner

495. DAVIS, ALFRED B.   [S]
Nacogdoches   29 May 1835
Certify foreigner Alfred B. Davis is
a man of very good...single without
family...   Jn Egne Michamps
                 Alcalde Interim
[Reverse]
Accepted. 1/4 sitio   Arthur Henrie

496. DAVIS, CADWALDER   [E]
District of Sabine   April 20th 1835
Certify that Mr. Cad Davis of this
District, a native of Virginia,

emigrated to this place in Novembver
last with his family consisting of
nine persons...good citizen...farmer
              B. Holt Commissioner
       of the Precinct of Sabine
496a.
[Field notes] Beginning Cadwalder
Davis survey...waters of Sabine...
496b.
Maj. Nixon   May 12, 1835
Sir: Send my land title by Mr.
Robert Smith...   Cad W. Davis

497. DAVIS, EDWARD   [S]
Nacogdoches   28 January 1835
Certify foreigner Edward Davis is a
man of good...single...
Jn Egne Michamps Alcalde Interim

498. DAVIS, ELIAS K.   [E]
San Augustine   May 8, 1835
Certify Elias K. Davis is a citizen,
that he is a native of Kentucky, man
of family consisting of a wife and
four children...good citizen...
         A. Hotchkiss Primary Judge
498a.
San Augustine   May 8, 1835
[Oath of Allegiance which he signed]
                     Elias K. Davis
I certify that Elias K. Davis is
unable to travel from this to Nacog-
doches...low state of health.
   John Bodine   Alcalde pro tem
498b.
Nacogdoches   1 June 1835
Mr. Surveyor   Sir:
You are to survey in Jose' Vehlein's
Grant the sitio which Mr. Elias K.
Davis will designate...
        Jorge Anto Nixon Land Comr

499. DAVIS, HARRISON   [E]
San Augustine   10 Dec 1834
Certify Harrison Davis is a native
of Illinois, is a man of family
consisting of two persons...good
citizen...   E. Rains Alcalde

500. DAVIS, JAMES R.   [E]
San Augustine 25 September 1834
Certify James R. Davis a native of
Georgia is a single man...very
good... Benjamin Lindsey Alcalde

501. DAVIS, JOHN [S]
Nacogdoches   5 January 1835
Certify Citizen Juan Davis is a
good...married...
           Jn Egne Michamps Alcalde Int
[Note]
Ajoining the sitio of Jas Dewit.
Wife & child.   Hiroms   Vehlein
501a.
Nacogdoches   6th January 1835
Maj Nixon   Dear Sir
You will deliver to John H. Cummins
our deeds for our land
                John X Davis
                John X Colvin

502. DAVIS, MRS. NANCY   [E]
San Augustine   September 25th 1834
Certify Mrs. Nancy Davis is a native
of Georgia, a widow woman of family
consisting of four persons and a
woman of good...
            Benjamin Lindsey Alcalde
502a.
[Field notes] Beginning corner Nancy
Davis sitio...East bank of the
Naches...   A. Veatch Surveyor

503. DAVIS, NATHAN SR.   [E]
San Augustine   August 18th 1835
Certify Nathan Davis is a native of
South Carolina, man of family consisting of a wife and six children.
man of good... Emigrated to Texas
in 1822.   A. Hotchkiss Pry Judge

504. DAVIS, SAMUEL   [E]
San Augustine   August 18, 1835
Certify Samuel Davis is a native of
North Carolina, man of family con-
sisting of a wife and one child...
emigrated to Texas in 1833.
           A. Hotchkiss P. Judge

505. DAVIS, SAMUEL   [E]
San Augustine   September 25th 1834
Certify Samuel Davis a native of
Georgia is a single man of good...
           Benjamin Lindsey Alcalde
505a. [Field notes]
Beginning of Samuel Davis quarter
sitio,   edge of the marsh of the
east side of the   Neches...

506. DAVIS, TIMOTHY   [E]
Town of Austin   21st June 1830
To Mr. S.F. Austin Empresario
I have emigrated to this Colony...
Timothy Davis 50 years old moved
from North Carolina and arrived in
this Colony in Octr 1829.
      [Signed]   Timothy Davis
[Note] Wants his land on the forks
of the Creek above Wilbargers
called Big Creek

507. DAVIS, WILLIAM   [S]
Nacogdoches   12 January 1835
Certify foreigner William Davis is a
man of good...married with family...
           Jn Egne Michamps
[Note] Wife and 4 children = on the
San Pedro Creek at his improvements.
Burnet
507a.   Mr. Arthur Henry   Sir:
October 14, 1835   Please to send
by Mr. Leonard Williams my Deed
                William Davis

508. DAVIS, WILLIAM   [E]
San Augustine   25 Sept 1834
Certify William Davis a native of
Georgia a single man of good...
           Benjamin Lindsey Alcalde
508a. [Field notes]
Commence West corner of Samuel Davis
for corner of William Davis quarter
sitio...

509. DAVIS, WILLIAM M.   [S]
Nacogdoches   29 December 1834
Certify foreigner William M. Devis
is a man of good...married with
family...   Vital Flores
[Note] Wm M. Davis Zavala.
Wife and five children. At a cane
head West bank of Neches.
                Wm McFarland
509a. [Field notes] Set post for
William M. Davis sitio between the
Naches & Trinity about 15 miles
south west from David Choates Survey
                Wm McFarland

510. DAY, F.H.K.   [S]
Nacogdoches   10 August 1835
Certify foreigner F.H.K. Day is a
man of good...single without family,
resident of the Municipality since
March 1834...   Radford Berry

511. DAY, SUSAN [E]
San Augustine   1st Sept 1835
Certify Susan Day a native citizen
is a widow woman of family consisting of six persons...
          Saml Thompson Alcd

512. DAYLY, REDMOND [E]
Sabine District   Sept 16th 1835
Redmond Dayly has a family and has
resided in the District of Ayish
since 1829...
          B. Holt Commissioner
512a.
District of Sabine   16 Sept 1835
I, Redman Dayly of the District of
Ayish   Bayou empower W.H. Landrum
to act for me   in procuring...an
order of survey of land according
to my headright as an old settler
and a citizen having a family...
          Redmond X Dayly
Witness R.A. Burny
          Jas Hughes
[Oath of Allegiance]   Personally
appeared Redmun Dayly and took
the necessary oath...
          B. Holt Commissioner

513. DEAN, JOHN M. [E]
San Augustine   June 22nd 1835
John M. Dean a native of the US is a
man of family consisting of seven
persons, that he emigrated to Texas
in 1833, that he is a moral...
          R.C. McDaniel C.P.O.
513a.
Nacogdoches   Aug 10, 1835
Mr. Surveyor   Sir:
You are to survey in Zavala's Grant
the sitio which Mr. Jno M. Dean will
designate
          Jorge Anto Nixon Land Comr

514. DEAN, SOFIA [S]
Nacogdoches   3 December 1834
Certify Sofia Dean is a woman of
very good...widow... Vital Flores
[Note] Widow, 2 children   Zavalla
Between Pine Island Bayou and the
Neches   D. Brown
514a.[Field notes]   Beginning of
Sophia Dean's sitio about 15 miles
west of Santa Anna...
          D. Brown Surveyor

50

515. DEARK, DELILY [E]
San Augustine   May 23, 1835
Certify Delily Deark a native of
Tennessee is a woman of family con-
sisting of two persons and a woman
of good... Nathan Davis Commissioner
[Reverse] Accepted. Arthur Henrie

516. DEBARD, ELIJAH J. [S]
Nacogdoches   3 October 1834
Certify foreigner Elijah J. Debard
is a man of good...Vicente Cordova

517. DEEN, CALLOWAY [E]
San Augustine   Jan 1, 1835
Certify Calloway Deen is a native of
Tennessee, that he is single...man
of good...
          A. Hotchkiss Primary Judge
[Reverse] Acceptd in Zavala. 1/4
sitio   A. Henrie

518. DEFEE, WILLIAM [E]
District of Sabine   2 Sept 1835
Certify William Defee a native of
South Carolina is a man of good...
has a family consisting of 9 persons...emigratd in 1830
          B. Holt Commissioner
518a.
Precinct of Sabine   Nov 15th 1835
Certify William Defee a native of
South Carolina is a man of family
consisting of nine persons and a man
of good...
          Elbert Hines Commissionr
[Note] Wife & 7 children. At his
improvement fronting on the River
Sabine & Colony line & running back
for complement.   Zavala   Brown
518b.
Mr. Hogkist and Mr. Nixon Commissioners   Please to send me a title
for my league on the Sabine
              William Defee
David Huffman   January the 1, 1835
518c. [Field notes]   Set post west
bank of the Sabine River

519. DELEANY, CHARLES [E]
District of Bevil   April 26, 1835
Charles Deleany a native of Mississippi hath family consisting of four
persons...   Wm Williams Alcalde

520. DELGADO, MIGUEL, PEDRO, JUAN,
NEPOMUCENO [S]
Survey of four leagues for Miguel,
Pedro, Juan and Nepomuceno Delgado
jointly

521. DENISON, SAMUEL [E]
Matagorda November 20th 1833
To Col. S.F. Austin Empresario
I...am in Texas.I intend to become a
Colonist under you...I have a family
of a wife & one child who I expect
in the Country in a short time. I
wish to settle Sam D. Denison

522. DENMAN, JAMES [E]
Department of Nacogdoches
District of Bevil August 26, 1835
I certify that James Denman is a na-
tive of Louisiana, a single man of
good... Wm Williams Alcalde
[Rev] James Denman. Emigrated 1831

523. DENMAN, OBEDIAH [E]
Department of Nacogdoches
District of Bevil October 9th 1834
I certify Obediah Denmon is a native
of Louisiana, a single man of
good... John Bevil Alcalde

524. DENMAN, OBEDIAH
Department of Nacogdoches
District of Bevil August 26, 1835
Obediah Denman is a native of Louis-
iana, single man of good...
Wm Williams Alcalde
[Reverse] Emigrated in 1831
524a.
District of Bevil August 26, 1835
Sir: You are to survey the sitio
which Mr. Obediah Denman will
designate... Geo W. Smyth Comr

525. DENSON, THOMAS C. [E]
Naches September 7, [torn]
I have been acquainted with Thomas
C. Denson for some time...man of
family and a farmer...
Wm Whiteley Comr
[Rev] Accepted in Vehlein.
Arthur Henrie

526. DENTON, WILLIAM [E]
Department of Nacogdoches
Jurisdiction of Liberty 25 Apr 1835
William Denton is a native of Ten-
nessee, a man of family, is a man of
good... Claiborne Wright Judge
526a. September 23d 1835
Mr. Commissioner: Please let Wm
Smedlie have my title on his paying
fees William X Denton
Witness William Mussat

527. DEVORE, JESSE [E]
Department of Nacogdoches
Jurisdiction of Liberty 17 Apr 1835
Jesse Devore a native of Pennsylva-
nia is a man of family of his wife
and four children...man of good...
Wm Hardin Judge

528. DEVORE, TIMOTHY [E]
San Augustine 22 Sept 1834
Timothy Devore a native of the US,
man of family of three persons, a
man of good...
Benjamin Lindsey Alcalde

529. DEWITT, JAMES [S]
Nacogdoches 3 October 1834
Certify foreigner Santiago Duiet a
man of good... Vicente Cordova
529a.
Nacogdoches Oct 3d 1834
Mr. Wm Robinson, Surveyor Sir:
You are to survey in Vehlein's Grant
the sitio which Mr. James Dewitt
will designate...
Jorge Anto Nixon Land Comr
[Note] Title made to Adams[?]
[Reverse] By request of owner &c.
The within order has been executed
by me. Feb 17th 1835
Wm Brookfield Surveyor

Major Henrie will please get my fee
on this survey $40.00 before Plating
and also all other which I may send
in, which are not endorsed "Paid".
Wm Brookfield

530. DIAS, AUGUSTIN [S]
Nacogdoches 2 Sept 1835
Certify citizen Augustin Dias is a
man of good...resident of this Municipality since 1815...single without
family and has not obtained land...
Radford Berry

531. DIAS, FRANCISCO [S]
Nacogdoches 25 August 1835
Certify citizen Francisco Dias is a

51

man of very good...resident of this
Municipality and born here...single
without family and has not obtained
land...   Radford Berry

532. DIAS, MARIA ESCOLASTICA [S]
Tenoxtitlan   2 April 1834
To Empresarios Austin and Williams
I have come to Texas with the inten-
tion of settling here and wish to be
admitted...I am a widow, have one
daughter, my age 22
Because I do not know how to write
          M̲a Escolastica Dias
          [by] Spence H. Jack

533. DIAS, MARIA GERTRUDIS [S]
Nacogdoches   29 June 1835
Certify citizen M̲a Gertrudez Dias is
a resident of this Municipality for
many years, woman of very good...
widow with family...wants land...
has not obtained   land...
Jn Egne Michamps Alcalde Interim

534. DIAZ, MARIA SALOME [S]
Nacogdoches   2 April 1835
Certify citizen Maria Salome Diaz is
a resident of this Municipality for
many   years, a widow with family
has not obtained land   Radford Berry

535. DIAS, MARIA VICENTE [S]
Nacogdoches   Oct 22nd 1835
Sir: You are to survey the sitio &
labor which M̲a Vicente Dias will
designate...   Geo W. Smyth Comr

536. DICKERSON, JOHN
Nacogdoches   December 2d 1834
Mr. Jno A. Veatch, Surveyor Sir:
You are to survey in Vehlein's Grant
the sitio which Mr. Jno Dickerson
will designate...
          Jorge Anto Nixon Land Comr
[Note] At his improvement about 15
miles W. of Fort Teran
I return the within order and dont
wish to take land as a Collenest.
Sept 14, 1835   John Dickerson

537. DICKERSON, SAMUEL [E]
San Augustine   Oct 10, 1835
I certify that Samuel Dickerson is a
native of Kentucky, is a man of family consisting of three persons and
52

a man of very good...emigrated to
the Country in 1831
          Samuel Thompson Alcd
537a.
San Augustine   10 Oct 1835
I hereby authorize Samuel Stevers to
petition Geo W. Smyth in my name for
one league & labor...
          Samuel Dickerson
Witness E. Legrand
          Saml Thompson Alcd

538. DICKSENSON, WALTER [S]
Nacogdoches   13 Oct 1835
Certify foreigner Walter Dickenson
is a man of good...single without
family...resident of this Department
since 1833...   Radford Berry

539. DIEGO, MARIA DEL CARMEN [S]
Nacogdoches   6 Aril 1835
Certify citizen Maria del Carmen
Diego is a resident of this Munici-
pality and born here, widow with
family...has not obtained land...
          Radford Berry

540. DIKES, JOSIAH [S]
Nacogdoches   18 June 1835
Certify foreigner Josiah Dikes is a
man of good...married with family...
Jn Egne Michamps Alcalde Interim
[Rev] Acceptd Zavala. A. Henrie

541. DIKES, LEVY B. [S]
Nacogdoches   6 May 1835
Certify foreigner Levy B. Dikes is a
man of good...married with family...
          Radford Berry

542. DIKES, WESLEY [S]
Nacogdoches   18 June 1835
Certify foreigner Wesley Dikes is a
man of good...married with family
Jn Egne Michamps Alcalde Interim
[Reverse] Accepted in Zavala's.
          A.Henrie

543. DILLARD, JOHN B. [E]
San Augustine   August 10th 1835
Certify John B. Dillard is a native
of North Carolina, man of family
consisting of the wife and seven
children, emigrated to Texas in the
year 1830.

          A. Hotchkiss Primary Judge

543a.
San Augustine   August 18th 1835
Sir: You are to survey the sitio &
labor which Mr. John B. Dillard
will designate   Geo W. Smyth Comr
[Note]
Where he lives & on Plumb Creek

544. DILLARD, THOMAS
Austin   May 24, 1832
I have emigrated to this Country...
My name Thomas Dillard 34 years of
age. Occupation Physician. Unmar-
ried. Moved from Alabama and arrived
Novr 1830   Thomas Dillard

545. DIMORY, ALLEN   [S]
Nacogdoches   11 Feb 1835
Certify foreigner Allen Dimory is a
man of   good...married with family...   Radford Berry

546. DINSMORE, JOHN   [E]
Town of Austin   July 14, 1830
To Mr. S.F. Austin Empresario
I have emigrated to the Colony...
John Dinsmore 40 years of age. Occu-
pation farmer. Moved from New Hamp-
shire and arrived this Colony in
July 1829.   John Dinsmore

547. DONOHOE, DANIEL   [E]
Department of Nacogdoches
District of Bevil   March 21st 1835
I certify Daniel Donohoe is a native
of   South Carolina, hath a family
consisting   of nine persons...man
of good...   Wm Williams Alcalde

548. DONOHO, DANIEL   [E]
Department of Nacogdoches
Jurisdiction of Liberty 28 May 1835
Daniel Donoho, a native of South
Carolina is a man of family...his
wife and four children...
                 Wm Hardin Judge

549. DONOHO, LEWIS   [E]
Department of Nacogdoches
District of Liberty June 3d 1835
Lewis Donoho is a native of Louisi-
ana, hath a family of four persons.
                 Wm Williams Alcalde
[Rev] Accepted in Zavala, the grant
he is now a living in.   Henrie

549a.
Bevils Settlement   June 3, 1835
Major Henrie: Respectful Sir:
The gentleman handing you this is
Mr. Donaho, a son-in-law to Col.
Lewis, has resided in Texas several
years, has a wife and 2 children. He
wishes an order on the waters of the
Sabine. He holds a good...
                 W. McFarland

550. DONOHO, LEWIS   [E]
Department of Nacogdoches
District of Bevil October 2d 1835
Certify Lewis Donoho is a native of
Mississippi and emigrated to this
Country in 1831, hath a family con-
sisting of four persons, is a man of
good...   Wm Williams Alcalde

551. DONOHO, MOSES   [E]
Department of Nacogdoches
Jurisdiction of Liberty 28 May 1835
Certify that Moses Donoho, a native
of South Carolina is a man of family
consisting of his wife and six chil-
dren...man of good.. Wm Hardin Judge
[Reverse]
Accepted in Zavala. A. Henrie

552. DONAHO, WILLIAM   [E]
Department of Nacogdoches
Jurisdiction of Liberty 28 May 1835
Certify William Donaho a native of
South Carolina is a man of family
consisting of his wife and eight
children...man of good
                 Wm Hardin Judge
[Reverse]
Accepted in Zavala. A. Henrie

553. DONOHOE, WILLIS   [E]
Department of Nacogdoches
District of Bevil   March 21, 1835
Certify Willis Donahoe ia a native
of Mississippi, single man of
good...   Wm Williams Alcalde

554. DONAHO, WILLIS   [E]
Department of Nacogdoches
District of Bevil   Septr 28 1835
I certify Willis Donaho is a native
of Mississippi, emigrated to this
Country January 1831, hath a family
consisting of two persons, is a
good man...   Wm Williams Alcalde

53

554a.
District of Bevil   Sept 29th 1835
Sir: You are to survey the sitio &
labor which Mr. Willis Donaho will
                Geo W. Smyth Comr

555. DONAHO, WILLIS   [S]
Nacogdoches   4 June 1835
Certify foreigner Willis Donahoe is
a man of good...married with family
  Jn Egne Michamps Alcalde Interim
[Reverse]
Accepted in Zavala. A. Henrie

556. DONAVAN, AMOS   [S]
Nacogdoches   16 Feb 1835
Certify foreigner Amos Donavan is a
man of good...married with family...
                    Redford Berry

557. DOOLIN, JOHN   [E]
Nacogdoches Dept December 4th 1834
Certify John Doolin a native of Ireland in Europe, hath a family of two
persons, man of good...
                  John Bevil Alcalde

558. DORR, JOHN M.   [S]
Nacogdoches   24 June 1835
Certify foreigner Juan M. Dor is a
man of   good...married with family,
resident of the State of Tamaulipas
since 1822 and of this Department
since 1830...   Radford Berry

Nacogdoches   Sept 3, 1835
Mr. Benjamin Tennell   Sir:
You are to survey the sitio & labor
which   Mr. John M. Dorr will desig
nate...   Geo W. Smyth Comr

559. DOR, JOHN M.   [S]
Nacogdoches   29 May 1835
Certify John M. Dor is a man of
good...single without family...land
  Jn Egne Michamps Alcalde Interim

560. DORSETT, JOHN   [E]
San Augustine   22 Sept 1834
John Dorset, a native of Georgia, a
man of family of eleven persons, a
man of good...
            Benjamin Lindsey Alcalde
[Note]
Wife & 9 children on the W. side of
Horatio Hanks Sabine Bay

54

561. DOWNS, JOHN F.   [E]
District of Tenehaw Sept 3d 1835
Certify John F. Downs a native of
Louisiana, a man of family consist-
ing of three persons...man of good
emigrated to the Country in 1832.
        Nathan Davis Commissioner
[Reverse] Accepted.   A. Henrie

562. DOYLE, FESTUS
[Field notes] Survey of one league
and one labor for Festus Doyle,
League No. 4, East bank of the
Attascoso...

563. DOYLE, MATTHEW   [S]
Nacogdoches   13 August 1835
Certify foreigner Matthew Doyle is a
man of good...married with family,
resident of this Municipality since
1831...   Redford Berry

564. DRAKE, JAMES   [E]
Dept. of Nacogdoches Decr 10, 1834
James Drake is a native of New Jer-
sey, hath a family consisting of
three persons. John Bevil Alcalde
[Note]
Wife & 1 ch. On the Neches 2 miles
above Charles or Tevis Bluff at the
place he has improved.   Zavala's
564a.
[Field notes] Beginning corner of
Jas Drake Survey on west bank of the
Naches...   Burton Surveyor
565. DRAKE, MARY   [E]
Department of Nacogdoches
Town of Liberty   26 Sept 1835
Certify that Mary Drake a native of
Louis-iana is a widow woman with
family consisting of herself and six
children, has been for some time
resident in this Jurisdiction woman
of good...   Edwd Tanner
[Reverse] Accepted in Vehleins
                   Arthur Henrie
565a.
Town of Liberty   25 Sept 1835
Personally appeared Mary Drake, widow...a long resident...entitled to
a league of land as a Colonist, that
owing to infirmities of old age...
unable to travel to Nacogdoches to
present [took the oath]
                Mary X Drake
Wit: Robert Pelham, J.W. Moreland
     Burrel Ea---, J. Devour,
     Edwd Tanner

566. DRODDY, JOHN [E]
Department of Nacogdoches
District of Bevil   March 27, 1835
Certify John Droddy native of Virginia hath a family of six persons good...   Wm Williams Alcalde

567. DRY, DANIEL [E]
San Augustine   September 23d 1835
Certify Daniel Dry is a native of Germany is a man of family consisting of four per-   sons and a man of good...emigrated to this Country 1830...   Saml Thompson Alcd

San Augustine   23 Sept 1835
I Daniel Dry...appoint William Inglish my attorney to petition George W. Smyth Comr for one league and labor...   Daniel Dry
Witnesses
A.E. Johnson, Saml Thompson Alcd

Ncogdoches   October 9th 1835
Sir: You are to survey the sitio & labor which Mr. Daniel Dry will designate...   Geo W. Smyth Comr

568. DRY, JOHN   [E]
San Augustine   23 Sept 1835
John Dry a native of Germany is a man of   family consisting of five persons   and a   man of good...emgrated to the Country in 1830.
                Saml Thompson Alcd

San Augustine   22d Sept 1835
I, John Dry appoint William Inglish my attorney to petition George W. Smyth for one league & labor...
                John Dry
Witnesses
A.E. Johnson, Saml Thompson, Alcd

Nacogdoches   Oct 9, 1835
Sir: You are to survey the sitio & labor which Mr. John Dry will designate...   Geo W. Smyth Comr

569. DRY, JOHN F.   [E]
San Augustine   Sept 23d 1835
Certify John F. Dry a native of Germany is a man of family consisting of three per-   sons and a man of good...emigrated to the Country in 1830...   Saml Thompson Alcd

San Augustine   22d Sept 1835
I John F. Dry appoint William Inglish my attorney to petition George W. Smyth Comr for one league and labor...   John F. Dry
Witnesses
A.E.C. Johnson, Saml Thompson Alcd

Nacogdoches   October 9th 1835
Sir: You are to survey the sitio & labor which Mr. John F. Dry will designate...   Geo W. Smyth Comr

570. DRY, PAUL   [E]
San Augustine   Sept 23d 1835
Certify Paul Dry a native of Germany is a man of family consisting of two persons, is a man of good...emigrated to the Country in 1830.
                Saml Thompson Alcd

San Augustine   Sept 22d 1835
I Paul Dry appoint William Inglish my attorney to petition George W. Smyth Comr for one league & labor.
                Paul X Dry
Witnesses:
    A.E.C. Johnson, Saml Thompson

Nacogdoches   October 9, 1835
Sir: You are to survey the sitio & labor which Mr. Paul Dry will designate...   George W. Smyth Comr

571. DUGGANS, THOMAS HINDS   [E]
Dept. of Nacogdoches
Jurisdiction of Liberty 10 Sept 1835
Certify Thomas Hinds Duggan is a native of Mississippi, a man of family consisting of his wife and one child man of good...
                Wm Hardin Primary Judge
[Rev] Accepted on Vehlein A. Henrie

572. DUNCAN, ELISHA   [E]
San Augustine   19 May 1835
Elisha Duncan a native of the US is a man of family of three persons, that he emigrated to the Country in May 1835...   R.C. McDaniel C.P.O.

Nacogdoches   August 8, 1835
Mr. Surveyor Sir: You are to survey in Zavala's Grant the sitio which Mr. Elisha Duncan will designate...
                Jorge Anto Nixon Land Comr
[Note] On west side of the Neches

573. DUNCAN, GEORGE H.   [S]
Nacogdoches   10 November 1834
Certify foreigner Geo H. Duncan is a
man of good...married with family...
wants land   Vital Flores
[Note] Reuben McKenzie.
       Wife, 5 children on Grahams
       west by --- Duncans

Nacogdoches   22 October 1835
Certify Geo H. Duncan is a man of
good...married with family, resident
in the State since December 1833...
                   Radford Berry

Nacogdoches   Oct 23rd 1835
Sir: You are to survey the sitio &
labor which Mr. Geo H. Duncan will
designate...   Geo W. Smyth Comr

574. DUNCAN, JACOB   [S]
Nacogdoches   7 May 1835
Certify foreigner Jacob Duncan is a
man of good...single without family.
                   Radford Berry

575. DUNCAN, JAMES   [E]
Matagorda   March 2d 1833
To Mr. S.F. Austin Empresario,
San Felipe
I am now in your Colony with my
family consisting of myself, wife &
three children. I wish to be a settler...My children are all daughters. My own age is 44 years   my
wife 40, my daughters Eliza 21, Ann
17, Sophia 12 years...I appoint as
my agent   J.R. Lewis Esqr.
                   James Duncan

576. DUNCAN, JAMES H.   [S]
Nacogdoches   21 September 1835
Certify foreigner James H. Duncan is
a man of good...married with family
                   Radford Berry
[Reverse]
Accepted Vehleins   Arthur Henrie

577. DUNCAN, MEREDITH   [E]
Dept. of Nacogdoches
Municipality of Liberty July 8, 1835
Certify that I am acquaintedf with
Meredith Duncan, a native of South
Carolina,   a man of family...man of
good...   Jno A. Williams

56

I am acquainted with Meredith Duncan and hold him in the same esti-
mation...July 8, 1835   Wm Duncan

Liberty   July 10, 1835
Maj. A. Nixon Sir: You will send
my title by Mr. D.L. Kokernot
                   Meredith Duncan

578. DUNCAN, SARAH ANN   [S]
Nacogdoches   30 May 1835
Certify foreigner Sarah Ann Duncan
is a woman of good...widow with
family...
     Jn Egne Michamps Alcalde Interim
[Rev] Accepted. Arthur Henrie
       In Vehleins near McClain

579. DUTY, THOMAS
[Field notes] Survey of one third
of a league for Thomas Duty, left
margin of the Enmedio Creek

580. DWELL, LEWIS   [S]
Nacogdoches   13 May 1835
Certify foreigner Lewis Dwell is a
man of good...married with family
                   Radford Berry

581. DWYER, SIMON
[Field notes] Survey of one league
and one labor for Simon Dwyer being
League No. 5 head waters of the
western fork of Aransas Creek...

582. DYKES. GEORGE P.   [E]
Georgia   [Passport]
By His Excellency Jared Irvin Gov.
Know ye, George P. Dykes having been
recommended to me...Baldwin County,
I give him and his family my per-
mission to travel through the Chero-
kee Nation...
Milledgeville   31 March 1808
582a.
We the undersigned citizens of Tus-
cumbia and Franklin County in Alaba-
ma have long been acquainted with
George P. Dykes and his four sons...
Tuscumbia   Decr 17th 1830
[Signatures of 19 Alabama friends]

583. DIKES, LOVICK P.   [S]
Nacogdoches   Sept 15, 1835
Certify foreigner Lovick P. Dikes is
a man of good...married with family

resident of this State since 1831...
                              Radford Berry
583a.
Nacogdoches   Sept 15th l835
Sir: You are to survey the sitio &
labor which Mr. Lovick P. Dikes
will designate
                         Geo W. Smyth Comr

584. DYSON, JAMES   [E]
Dept of Nacogdoches   12 Jan 1835
Jurisdiction of Liberty
I, John Stewart Commissioner for the
precinct of Cow Bayou, certify James
Dyson a native of Louisiana, man of
family consisting of his wife and
three children   John Stewart
584a.
[Field notes] Commenced at NE
corner of William Dyson Survey...
sitio on Cow Bayou
          John M. Henrie, Surveyor

585. DYSON, JESSE   [S]
Nacogdoches   31 January 1835
Certify foreigner Jesse Dyson is a
man of good...married with family...
     Jn Egne Michamps Alcalde Interim
[Note] Wife & 1 child
At improvements, Bear Island on the
E side of Cow Bayou. Zavala.

586. DYSON, WILLIAM   [S]
Nacogdoches   6 January 1835
Certify foreigner William Dyson is a
man of good...married with family...
                              Radford Berry
[Note] Wife & 1 child. On the
Neches at the place has improved
adjoining Col. Davis. Zavala. Veatch
586a.
[Field notes] East side Cow Bayou
for William Dyson Survey.
                         John A. Veatch

587. EADON, CHARITY   [S]
Nacogdoches   1 Aug 1835
Certify Foreigner Charity Eadon is a
woman of good...widow with family
                              Radford Berry

588. EARL, MATTHEW   [E]
District of Sabine August 20th 1835
Certify Matthew Earl a native of

Louisiana has resided in the District aforesaid since 1824, has a
family consisting of five persons...
              B. Holt Commissioner
588a.
District of Sabine   25th August 1835
I, Matthew Earl appoint my son William Earl to act for me before the
Comr...order of survey for my headright...old settler.
                    Matthew X Earl
Witnesses: Wm Johnston
     Sampson D. McGee   B. Holt, Comr

589. EARLE, ROBERT   [S]
Nacogdoches   1 Sept 1835
Certify foreigner of the State of
Missouri Robert Earl is a man of
good...married with family, resident
of the Municipality since 1830...
                              Radford Berry
[Note] Two in family
[Reverse]
Nacogdoches   1 Sept 1835
[Certification that oath of allegi-
ence taken]   Radford Berry

590. EARL, WILLIAM   [E]
District of Sabine August 20, 1835
Certify William Earl, a native of
Louisiana, has resided in the dis-
trict ever since the year 1824...
                         B. Holt Comr

591. EARL, MARY   [S]
Nacogdoches   7 September 1835
Certify citizen Mary Earl is a woman
of good...widow with family, resident of this Department since 1823.
                              Radford Berry

592. EASLEY, DANIEL   [E]
San Augustine   Sept 27, 1834
Certify Daniel Easley a native of
Georgia hath a family consisting of
nine persons. is of good...
                    John Bevil Alcalde
592a.
[Field Notes] Corner of Samuel
Easley sitio on South side of Pine
Island Bayou.   Veatch Surveyor
592b.
Comr George Anto Nixon
Sept 22d 1835 Dear Sir: Please to
deliver my title to A. Horton.
                         Daniel Easley

593. EATON, STEPHEN   [S]
Nacogdoches   27 May 1835
Certify Foreigner Stephen Eaton is a
man of good...married with family...
    Jn Egne Michamps Alcalde Interim

594. EDDINGS, ABRAM   [E]
Town of Austin   May 20, 1830
To Mr. S.F. Austin Empresario
I have emigrated to this Colony...
Abram Eddings 22 years old unmar-
ried, moved from Alabama and arrived
in this Colony in March 1830.
              [Sig] Abram Eddins

595. EDDINGS, THEOPHILUS   [E]
To Mr. S.F. Austin Empresario
I have emigrated to this Colony...
Theophilus Eddings 56 years old,
married Nancy my wife 40 years old
Four male and three female child-
ren. Moved from Alabama and arrived
in this Colony 1st April 1830.
        [Sig] Theophilus Edd[torn]

596. EDINBURG, CRISTOBAL   [S]
Nacogdoches   8 September 1834
Certify foreigner Cristobal Eden-
burgh is a man of good...married...
      Luis Procela Alcalde Interim

597. EDENS, JOHN   [S]
Nacogdoches   30 January 1835
Certify foreigner John Edens is a
man of good...married with family...
              Radford Berry Alcd
[Note] Wife & 3 children on the
Elkhart above the fork on the N.
bank

598. EDWARDS, DANIEL F.   [E]
San Augustine   1 June 1835
Certify Daniel F. Edwards, a native
of the US is a man of family consisting of three persons, that he emigrated to the Country in 1834...
              R.C. McDaniel C.P.O.
598a.
Nacogdoches   August 9, 1835
Mr.Surveyor Sir: You are to survey
in Zavala's Grant the sitio which
Mr. Danl F. Edwards will designate
    Jorge Anto Nixon Land Comr

599. EDWARDS, HADEN H.   [S]
Nacogdoches   26 October 1835
Certify foreigner Haden Edwards is a
man of good...single without fami-
ly, resident of the Department since
1825...   Radford Berry
599a.
Nacogdoches   Oct 26, 1835
Sir: You are to survey the third
sitio which Mr. Haden H. Edwards
will designate Geo W. Smyth Comr
599b.
Nacogdoches   3 July 1835
Received of Maj. Geo Anto Nixon. Mr.
Geo Mays & Mr. --- titles for one
league each   H.H. Edwards
599c.
Nacogdoches   11 April 1837
Received of Major Geo Ant Nixon.
Seven land titles as follows:
Jacob Duncan for 1/4
Jose N.Manchaca 1/4
Larkin Robertson 1
Warrick Ferguson 1
Thos Jackson 1   Maria Trinidad
Francisco Peres 1
For which I have paid him the cash
in hand   F. Thorn   H.H. Edwards

600. ELDER, JAMES   [E]
San Augustine   31 Aug 1835
Certify James Elder a native of
Pennsylvania, single man of good...
emigrated in 1831.Saml Thompson Alcd

601. ELDRIDGE, SAMUEL   [E]
San Augustine   Oct 10, 1835
Samuel Eldridge is a native of Tennessee that he is a man of family
consisting of a wife ...good citizen
emigrated to Texas in 1833.
A. Hotchkiss P. Judge
601a.
San Augustine   9 Oct 1835
I, Samuel Aldridge appoint Richard
Haley my attorney to petition for
one league & labor...
              Samuel X Eldridge
602. ELLERY, JOSEPH   [E]
San Augustine   7 March 1835
Joseph Ellery a native of New York,
a man of family consisting of four
persons, emigrated to Texas in Sept
1834...   R.C. McDaniel C.P.O.

58

602a.
Nacogdoches   August 7th 1835
Mr. Surveyor Sir: You are to survey
in Zavala's Grant the sitio which
Mr. James   Ellery will designate
          Jorge Anto Nixon Land Comr
[Note]
On the west side of the River Naches

603. ELLIOTT, F.P.   [E]
San Augustine   4 May 1835
F.P. Elliott a native of the US is a
man of family consisting of three
persons, emigrated to Texas in
1834... good...   R.C. McDaniel
C.P.O.
[Reverse] Accepted   A. Henrie
603a.
Nacogdoches   Augt 19, 1835
Mr. Surveyor Sir: You are to survey
in   Zavala's Grant the sitio which
Mr. F.P.   Elliott will designate...
          Jorge Anto Nixon Land Comr
[Note]
On the west side of the Neches

604. ELLIOTT, NICHOLAS   [E]
San Augustine   7 April 1835
Nicholas Elliott a native of the US,
man   of family consisting of four
persons, emigrated to Texas in 1825
                 R.C. McDaniel C.P.O.
604a.
Nacogdoches   9 Aug 1835
Mr. Surveyor Sir: You are to survey
in   Zavala's Grant the sitio which
Mr. Nichls Elliott will deignate
          Jorge Anto Nixon Land Comr

605. ELLIOTT, PETER S.   [S]
Nacogdoches   18 May 1835
Certify foreigner Peter S. Elliott
is a man of good...married ...
                 Radford Berry

606. ELLIOTT, WILLIAM   [S]
Nacogdoches   18 Sept 1834
Certify resident William Elliott is
a man   of good... Vicente Cordova
606a.
Major George Anto Nixon   Sir:
You will please deliver over to Mr.
Haden Edwards my land title when
completed...
18 Feby 1835   Wm Elliott

607. ELLIS, ALFRED   [E]
San Augustine   20 April 1835
Alfred Ellis, native of Missouri,
man of family consisting of six per-
sons, emigrated to Texas April 1835
                 R.C. McDaniel C.P.O.
607a.
Nacogdoches   Aug 7th 1835
Mr. Surveyor Sir: You are to survey
in Zavala's Grant the sitio which
Mr. Alfred Ellis will designate...
          Jorge Anto Nixon Land Comr

608. ELLIS, BENJAMIN F.   [S]
Nacogdoches   2 May 1835
Certify foreigner Benjamin F. Ellis
is a man of good...single without
family...   Radford Berry

609. ELLIS, GEORGE   [E]
Dept of Nacogdoches
Jurisdiction of Liberty May 10, 1835
George Ellis a native of Scotland,
is at present a resident of this
jurisdiction, man of family consisting of himself & wife, is a
carpenter...   Wm Duncan Judge

610. ELLIS, JOSEPH L.   [S]
Nacogdoches   2 May 1835
Certify foreigner Joseph L. Ellis is
a man of good...single...
                 Radford Berry
610a.
Nacogdoches   July 17, 1835
M.S. Womack   H.H. Cone
J.L. Ellis   B.F. Ellis
M.L. Patton   R.S. Patton
Capt. S.C. Hiroms will please pay
for the titles of the above written
names...Maj. G.A. Nixon will please
deliver to S.C. Hiroms.
                 Jos Ellis

611. EMANUEL, ALBERT   [S]
Nacogdoches   23 March 1835
Certify foreigner Albert Emanuel is
a man of good...married with family
                 Radford Berry

612. ENETT, LEWIS
Town of Austin   17 June 1830
I have emigrated to this Colony...
Lewis Enat   27 years old married.
Occupation farmer

Mary my wife 15 years old.
Moved from Mississippi and arrived
in this Colony June 1830.
                [Signed] Lewis Enett

613. ENGLIDOW, CREED S. [S]
Nacogdoches   16 May 1835
Certify foreigner Creed S. Englidow
is a man of good...married with
family...   Radford Berry

614. ENGLEDOW, JOHN [S]
Nacogdoches   25 May 1835
Certify foreigner John Englidow is a
man of good...married with family...
Jn Egne Michamps Alcalde Interim

615. ENGLISH, ARCHIBALD [E]
Precinct of Tennahaw   16 Aug 1835
Archable English is a native of
Tennessee man of one person only,
man of good...   Nathan Davis Comr

616. ENGLISH, ELIZABETH [E]
Precinct of Tenahaw   25 May 1835
Elizabeth English is a native of
Tennessee, is a woman of family
containing two persons and a woman
of good...   Nathan Davis Comr

617. ENGLISH, GEORGE [E]
San Augustine   Sept 22, 1834
George English a native of Tennessee single man of good...
          Benjamin Lindsey Alcalde
617a.
[Field notes] Set post east boundary of Martin White's survey for
the beginning of George English
sitio...   D. Brown Surveyor
617b.
Mr. Nixon Commissioner Sir:
Pleae deliver to Benjamin Lindsey my
Title of one quarter of a league on
Bare Creek
30 July 1835   George English

618. ENGLISH, JAMES [E]
San Augustine   May 28, 1835
James English a native of Tennessee,
single man of good...
          A. Hotchkiss P. Judge
[Reverse] Accepted A. Henrie

60

619. ENGLISH, JAMES [E]
San Augustine   August 18, 1835
James English a native of North
Carolina, man of family consisting
of a wife and seven children...
emigrated to Texas in 1827.
          A. Hotchkiss P. Judge

620. ENGLISH, JAMES [E]
San Augustine   August 17, 1835
James English a native of Tennessee,
a single man of good...emigrated to
Texas in 1829.
          A. Hotchkiss Primary Judge

621. ENGLISH, JAMES [E]
San Augustine   27 Sept 1834
James English a native of Tennessee
single man of good...
          Benjamin Lindsey Alcalde

622. ENGLISH, JOHN [E]
San Augustine   August 18, 1835
John English is a native of Tennessee, man of family consisting of a
wife and five children...emigrated
to Texas in 1825.
          A. Hotchkiss P. Judge

623. ENGLISH, JOHN
San Augustine   May 24, 1835
John English is a native of South
Carolina, man of family consisting
of a wife and five children, emi-
grated to Texas in 1825.
     Nathan Davis Commissioner
San Augustine   May 24, 1835
I certify that Nathan Davis Commis-
sioner of the Precinct of Tanahaw,
Municipality of San Augustine...
          A. Hotchkiss P. Judge

624. ENGLISH, JONAS [E]
San Augustine   August 17, 1835
Jonas English is a native of Tennessee, man of a family consisting of a
wife...emigrated to Texas in 1824.
          A. Hotchkiss P. Judge

625. ENGLISH, JOSEPH [E]
San Augustine   August 18, 1835
Joseph English is a native of Tennessee, man of family consisting of
a wife and two children...emigrated
to Texas in 1823.
          A. Hotchkiss P. Judge

626. ENGLISH, JOSHUA [E]
San Augustine   August 18, 1835
Joshua English is a native of Ten-
nessee, man of family consisting of
a wife and no child...emigrated to
Texas in 1826.
                    A. Hotchkiss P. Judge

627. ENGLISH, RICHARD B.   [E]
San Augustine   Sept 1st 1835
Richard B. English is a native of
Tennessee, single man of good...
emigrated to this Country in 1827.
                    Saml Thompson Alcd

628. ENGLISH, STEPHEN   [E]
San Augustine   August 17th 1835
Stephen English a native of Tennessee is a man of family consisting
of four persons emigrated to Texas
in 1825.   Saml Thompson Alcd

629. ENGLISH, THOMAS   [E]
San Augustine   17 Aug 1835
Thomas English is a native of Tennessee, man of family consisting of
a wife and eight children...emi-
grated to Texas in 1825.
                    A. Hotchkiss P. Judge

630. ENGLISH, WILLIAM   [E]
San Augustine   24 Sept 1834
William Inglish a native of Tennessee, man of family consisting of
nine persons...
                    Benjamin Lindsey Alcalde

631. ENGLISH, WILLIAM   [E]
San Augustine   Oct 18, 1835
To George W. Smyth   Sir:
A few days since, I purchased from
J.B. Humble his land right...He
has since as I am informed, applied
for his order of survey. This is to
give you notice that I   protest
against any act of his...
                    [Signed]   Wm Inglish

632. ENGLISH, WILLIAM   [E]
Republic of Texas, Shelby County
Geo A. Nixon Comr.
Seeing in the Nacogdoches papers
that a title in the name of William English decd. Having bought
said land...as Administrators. We
request that you send said title by
James English. He will pay you the

fees on same.   Jonathan Anderson
Sept 20th 1837 George Engilsh Admrs

633. ENOCH, JEREMIAH   [E]
District of Tenehaw August 10,1835
Jeremiah Enoch a native of South
Carolina is a man of family consist-
ing of five persons...emigrated to
this Country in 1833.
                    Nathan Davis Comr

634. EQUIS, TRINIDAD   [S]
Nacogdoches   8 April 1835
Certify citizen Trinidad Equis resident of this Municipality and born
here, widow with family...has not
obtained land...   Radford Berry

635. EVANS (ERVIN), ROBERT   [E]
Precinct of Tanahaw   17 Aug 1835
Robert Ervan a native of South Carolina, man of family consisting of
seven persons, man of good...
                    Nathan Davis Comr

636. ESCOBEDA, BARTOLO   [S]
Nacogdoches   20 April 1835
Certify citizen Bartolo Escobeda is
a resident of this Municipality for
many years, married with family...
has not obtained land...
                    Radford Berry
636a.
Recd of Majr Nixon   Commissioner
Bartolo Escobedo title Sept 28,1835
                    P. X Roblow
Witness: Arthur Henrie

637. ESTRADA, MARIA GERTRUDIS   [S]
Nacogdoches   30 July 1835
Certify citizen Maria Gertrudis Estrada is a resident of this Municipality and born here, woman of
good...widow with family...has not
obtained land...   Radford Berry
637a.
Nacogdoches   Aug 3d 1835
Sir: You are to survey the sitio &
labor which Mrs. Ma Gertrudis Estrada will designate...
                    Geo W. Smyth Comr

638. EUBANK, ELIAS M.   [S]
Nacogdoches   28 May 1835
Certify foreigner Elias M. Eubank is
a man of good..married with family
Jn Egne Michamps Alcalde Interim

61

639. EVANS, DR. HOLDEN [E]
This is to certify that we have
known Dr. Holden Evans for the last
year...   Signed 2nd Decr 1834
in Ayish Bayou, Texas
[this is a copy; signers unlisted]
[Evans] has reported himself to
Jacob Garret Alcalde and taken the
oath.....   Jacob Garret Alcalde
[Witness]   John Cartwright

640. EVANS, JESSE J.   [E]
The State of Alabama, Perry County
Whereas Jesse J.Evans of the State
and County aforesaid makes known...
intends removing to the province of
Texas...certify that we know Jesse
Evans...   17th day of July 1830
[about 16 Alabama signers]

641. EVERITT, RICHARD
[Field notes] Survey one league and
one labor for Richard Everitt in the
forks of Nueces and Rio Frio...

642. EVERITT, STEPHEN H.   [E]
San Augustine   22 Sept 1834
S.H. Everitt is a native of the US,
single but a house keeper with
servants, good...   John Bevil
[Rev] S.H. Everitt can have his
survey made without interfering with
any other survey.   John Bevil
San Augustine Sept 22, 1834
642a.
[Field note] Beginning corner of
Stephen H. Everitt sitio on Thickety
Fork Cow Creek...
            Geo W. Smyth Surveyor

643. EWING, EDLEY   [E]
San Augustine   August 17, 1835
Edley Ewing is a native of Tennessee
a man of family consisting of a wife
and four children...emigrated to
Texas in 1833...
            A. Hotchkiss Primary Judge

644. EWING, EDLEY   [E]
San Augustine   25 Sept 1834
Edley Ewing is a native of Tennessee
a man of family consisting of three
persons...man of good...
            Benjamin Lindsley Alcalde
[Note] Edly Ewing, wife and three
chidren. Near Mr.Townsend. Burnet.

645. EWING, JAMES L.   [S]
Nacogdoches   10 June 1835
Certify foreigner James L. Ewing is
a man of good...married with family
    Jn Egne Michamps Alcalde Interim
[Reverse]
Accepted Burnet's Arthur Henrie

646. EWING, WILSON   [S]
Nacogdoches   14 August 1835
Certify foreigner Wilson Ewing a man
of good...married with family, resident of this Municipality since 1832
                     Radford Berry
646a.
Nacogdoches   Aug 14, 1835
Mr. William Brookfield   Sir:
You are to survey the sitio & labor
which Mr. Wilson Ewing will
designate...   Geo W. Smyth Comr

647. EWING, WILSON   [E]
San Augustine   June 1, 1835
Wilson Ewing is a native of Tennes-
see a man of family consisting of a
wife and eight children...
            A. Hotchkiss Primary Judge
[Reverse]
Accepted in Burnet   A. Henrie

648. FADDEN, JOHN
[Field notes] Survey of one third
league John Fadden, on left bank of
Rio Frio...

649. FADDEN, PATRICK
[Field notes] Survey of one league
and labor for Patrick Fadden on left
bank of the River Nueces...

650. FADDIS, JAMES   [E]
San Augustine   5 Oct 1835
I James Faddis appoint Henry Teal my
attorney to petition for one league
and labor... [Signed] James Faddis
Witnesses   E.O. Legrand
Samuel Stivers   George English
James English   Thos H. Garner

651. FALCON, JOSE   [S]
Nacogdoches   27 April 1835
Certify citizen Jose Falcon is a
resident of this Municipality for
many years, man of good...married
with family...   Radford Berry

62

651a. [Field notes] On waters of
Great Alabama, 7 miles from A. Bart-
lett & 12 miles from Town Bluff on
Naches...sitio   Burton Surveyor

652. FALCON, JOSEFA PEREZ   [S]
Nacogdoches   6 April 1835
Certify citizen Josefa Perez Falcon,
resident of this Municipality for
many years, a woman of good...widow
with family...has not obtained
land...   Radford Berry

653. FALCON, JUAN   [S]
Nacogdoches   21 April 1835
Certify citizen Juan Falcon is resident of this Municipality and born
here, man of good...married with
family...has not obobtained land...
                   Radford Berry

654. FANTHORPE, HENRY   [E]
Austin [de San F.]   June 11, 1832
Mr. S.F. Austin Empresario
I have emigrated to this Colony...
My name is Henry Fanthorpe, a native
of England, 47 years of age and a
widower without any children in this
Country, but have one child in Eng-
land. I arrived in   Novr 1831.
        [Signed] Henry Fanthorp
Coast Colony

655. FARIS, SAMUEL   [E]
Nacogdoches
District of Bevil September 28, 1835
Samuel Faris is a native of Kentucky
emigrated to this Country February
1834, hath a family consisting of
four persons... Wm Williams Alcalde

656. FARMER, HOUTT   [E]
San Augustine   October 12, 1835
Houtt Farmer is a native of Tennessee a man of family consisting of
three persons,emigrated to the Country in 1829...   Saml Thompson Alcd
656a.
San Augustine   Oct 12, 1835
I authorize Samuel Stivers to petition for one league and labor...
                   Houtt Farmer

657. FASSITE, GEORGE A.   [E]
San Augustine   June 8, 1835
George A. Fassete is a native of

Massachusetts is a single man of
good...   A. Hotchkiss P. Judge

658. FAULK, JOHN
Dept of Nacogdoches
Jurisdiction of Liberty 17 Apr 1835
John Faulk a native of Louisiana, a
man of family of wife and six child-
ren...   Wm Hardin

659. FAULK, JOHN R.
Dept of Nacogdoches
Jurisdiction of Liberty 22 Feb 1835
John R. Faulk a native of Virginia,
a man of family of wife and six
children...   Wm Hardin
x
660. FELDER, CHARLES A.   [E]
San Augustine   11 May 1835
Charles A. Felder a native of Maryland man of family consisting of six
persons, emigrated to Texas in January 1835...   R.C. McDaniel C.P.O.
660a.
Nacogdoches   Aug 8, 1835
Mr. Surveyor Sir: You are to survey in Zavala's Grant the sitio
which Mr. Chs A. Felder will designate...
[Note]
On the west side of River Neches

661. FERGUSON, ALSTON   [S]
Nacogdoches   9 October 1835
Certify foreigner Alston Feguson, a
man of good...married with family...   Luis Procela

662. FERGUSON, JOHN   [S]
Nacogdoches   26 May 1835
Certify foreigner John Forguson is a
man of good...married with family...
Jn Egne Michamps Alcalde Interim

663. FERGUSON, JOHN   [S]
Nacogdoches   9 October 1834
Certify foreigner John Ferguson is
a man of good...married with family
                   Luis Procela
663a.
[Field notes] West bank Naches for
beginning of John Ferguson sitio...
              William Brookfield

664. FERGUSON, JOSEPH   [S]
Nacogdoches   9 October 1834
Certify foreigner Joseph Fergusond
a man of good...married with
family...   Luis Procela

665. FERGUSON, WARRICK   [S]
Nacogdoches   29 May 1835
Certify Warrick Ferguson is a man of
good, married to a woman of the
country [Mexico]
    Jn Egne Michamps Alcalde Interim
[Rev] Accepted. Arthur Henrie. In
Burnet. Married a Mexican
1-1/4 league

666. FIELD, ISAIAH   [S]
Nacogdoches   11 December 1834
Certify foreigner Isaiah Field is a
man of good...married with family...
                     Vital Flores
[Note] Isaiah Fields, wife and three
children. East side of Trinity,
Vehlein. The place where he lives.

666a. [Faded "Receipt for Title"]

667. FIELDS, THOMAS   [S]
Nacogdoches   10 June 1835
Certify Thomas Fields man of good...
single without family...
    Jn Egne Michamps Alcalde Interim

668. FISH,JOSEPH   [E]
San Augustine   Octr 5, 1835
Joseph Fish a native of Georgia a
man of family of four persons, man
of good...emigrated to the Country
in 1829.   Saml Thompson Alcd
668a.
San Augustine   8 Oct 1835
I, Joseph Fish appoint James C.
Caine my attorney to petition for
one league and one labor to which
I am entitled...
Witnesses [Signed]   Joseph Fish
    E.O. Legrand
    Morris May   E.W. Cullen

669. FISHBACK, ISAAC H.   [S]
Nacogdoches   11 Dec 1835
Certify foreigner Isaac H. Fishback
is a man of good...married with
family, resident of this Municipality since 1827... Radford Berry

64

670. FISHER, GEORGE   [S]
Villa de Austin   May 15, 1830
Sr Empresario:
I wish to acquire land in this Colony...My family is Elizabeth my wife,
and three sons, one daughter, and
seven dependents.   Jorge Fisher

671. FISHER, JOHN   [E]
San Augustine   17 June 1835
John Fisher is a native of Kentucky,
with family of four persons, emigrated to Texas in June 1835, man of
good...   R.C. McDaniel C.P.O.
671a.
Nacogdoches   Aug 6, 1835
Mr. Surveyor Sir: You are to survey in Zavala's Grant the sitio
which Mr. Jno Fisher will designate
          Jorge Anto Nixon Land Comr
[Note]
On the west side of River Neches

672. FISHER, SAMUEL R.   [E]
San Augustine   17 June 1835
Saml R. Fisher native of Kentucky,
man of family of five persons, emi-
grated to Texas in June 1835...
          R.C. McDaniel C.P.O.
672a.
Aug 6, 1835.   Mr. Surveyor Sir:
You are to survey in Zavala's Grant
the sitio which Saml R. Fisher will
designate
          Jorge Anto Nixon Land Comr
[Note]
On the west side of the Neches

673. FITCH, JABEZ   [S]
Nacogdoches   8 June 1835
Certify foreigner Jabez Fitch is a
man of good...single without family
    Jn Egne Michamps Alcalde Interim
[Rev] Accepted in Burnet.
1/4 sitio.   A. Henrie

674. FITZGERALD, EDWARD   [S]
Nacogdoches   2 June 1835
Certify foreigner Edward Fitzgerald
is a man of good...single without
family...
    Jn Egne Michamps Alcalde Interim

675. FITZGIBBINS, WILLIAM   [E]
Mr. S.F. Austin Empresario
I have emigrated to this Colony...
William Fitzgibbins 46 years married

Nancy my wife 50 years old.
One female child. Occupation farmer.
Moved from Luisiana and arrived this
Colony 1822
Town of Austin   4 May 1830
   [Signed]   William Fitzgibbins

676. FLACK, ELISHA   [E]
To S.F. Austin Empresario
I have emigrated to this Colony...
Elisha Flack 31 years old. Occupa-
tion farmer. Moved from Kentucky and
arrived Feby 1830.
Town of Austin   1 June 1830
   [Signed]   Elisha Flack
[Note] Wants land below Henry Jones

677. FLOREZ, ANTONIO   [E]
Nacogdoches   Sept 22, 1834
Mr. Wm Brookfield Surveyor Sir:
You are to survey in Vehlein's Grant
the sitio which Mr. Anto Florez will
designate
        Jorge Anto Nixon Land Comr
[Reverse] Executed. Wm Brookfield

678. FLOREZ, FELIX   [S]
Nacogdoches   13 July 1835
Certify citizen Felix Florez is a
man of goòd...married with family,
resident of this Municipality for
many years...   Radford Berry
Nacogdoches   Aug 3, 1835
Sir: You are to survey the sitio
which Mr. Felix Flores will designate...   Geo W. Smyth Comr

679. FLORES, JUAN   [S]
Nacogdoches   6 April 1835
Certify citizen Juan Flores is a
resident   of this Municipality and
born here, married with family...
has not obtained land
        Radford Berry

680. FLORES, MARIA TENOLIA   [S]
Nacogdoches   19 July 1835
Certify citizen Maria Tinolea Flores
is a woman of good...widow with
family...has not obtained land...
        Radford Berry
680a.
Nacogdoches   Sept 11, 1835
Sir: You are to survey the sitio &
labor which Mrs. Maria Tenolea
Flores will designate...
        Geo W. Smyth Comr

681. FLORES, PATRICIO DE   [S]
Nacogdoches   Sept 8, 1835
Sir: You are to survey the sitio &
labor which Mr. Patricio de Flores
will designate...Geo W. Smyth Comr

682. FOOTE, ROBERT   [S]
Nacogdoches   16 May 1835
Certify foreigner Robert Foote is a
man of good...single without family
        Radford Berry

683. FOOTE, ROBERT H.   [E]
San Augustine   Sept 1, 1835
Robert H. Foot a native of South
Carolina single man of good...emi-
grated in 1830.
        Saml Thompson Alcd
683a.
I Robert H. Foote appoint George W.
Jones my attorney to take an order
of survey...   R.W. Foote
Witnesses: A.E.C. Johnson
Redding A. Jordan   J.D. Henry
I certify the foregoing Power of
Attorney   Saml Thompson Alcd
Mr. G.W. Smith   Sir:
I have previously taken the oath...
        R.H. Foote

684. FORBES, GEORGE   [S]
Nacogdoches   30 May 1835
Certify foreigner George Forbes is a
man of good...married with family...
   Jn Egne Michamps Alcalde Interim
[Reverse] Accepted. A. Henrie

685. FORBES, JOHN   [S]
Nacogdoches   28 April 1835
Certify foreigner John Forbes is a
man of good...married with family...
        Radford Berry

Nacogdoches   Nov 26, 1835
Received of Jorge Antonio Nixon Esq
Comr The following individual deeds:
John Adams   David Wilson
John Wade   John Waugh
William B. Reed   J. Quinilty
        [By] John Forbes

686. FORD, D.S.   [E]
Town of Austin   19 June 1830
To Mr. S.F. Austin Empresario
I have emigrated to this Colony...
Drury S. Ford, 26 years old, unmar-
ried Moved from Pennsylvania and
arrived in   this Colony Feby 1830.
      [Signed]   D.S. Ford

687. FORD, JAMES   [S]
Nacogdoches   24 September 1835
Certify foreigner James Ford a man
of good married with family and resident of this Department since
1829...   Radford Berry

688. FORSYTH, JAMES   [E]
San Augustine   August 15, 1835
James Forsythe is a native of Kentucky, man of family of a wife and
three children, emigrated to Texas
in June 1821; his wife is a
Mexican. A.Hotchkiss Primary Judge

689. FORSYTHE, JOHN   [E]
San Augustine   August 19, 1835
John Forsyth is a native of Kentucky, man of family of a wife and
three children...emigrated to Texas
in 1822.
        A. Hotchkiss Primary Judge

690. FOSTER, JAMES   [E]
Town of Austin   17th June 1830
To Mr. S.F. Austin Empresario
I have emigrated to this Colony...
James Foster 26 years old unmarried.
Occupation farmer. Moved from
Luisiana and arrived in this Colony
June 1830.   James Foster

691. FOSTER, JOHN   [E]
To Mr. S.F. Austin Empresario
I have emigrated to this Colony...
John Foster 26 years of age, unmar-
ried. Moved from Carolina and ar-
rived in this Colony in Feby 1830
[No date]   John Foster

692. FOWLER, JAMES F.   [E]
District of Tennehaw 11 August 1835
James F. Fowler a native of Tennessee man of family of three persons
emigrated to the Country in 1834.
        Nathan Davis Comr

693. FRANCIS, SEBASTIAN   [E]
Precinct of Tennahaw Sep 7, 1835
Sebastian Francis a native of South
Carolina, man of family two persons
emigratd to the Country in 1830.
        Nathan Davis Comr
693a. Nacogdoches   Oct 10th 1835
Sir: You are to survey the sitio &
labor which Mr. Sebastian Francis
will designate   Geo W. Smyth Comr

694. FRAZER, HARMON   [S]
Nacogdoches   7 April 1835
Certify foreigner Harmon Frazer is a
man of good...married with family...
        Radford Berry
694a. Nacogdoches   Apl 7, 1835
Mr. Surveyor Sir: You are to survey
the sitio which Mr. Harman Frazer
will designate...
    Jorge Anto Nixon Land Comr
[Note] On the Naches

695. FRAZER, SUSAN   [E]
Department of Nacogdoches
Jurisdiction of Liberty 12 Jan 1835
Susan Frazer native of Louisiana,
woman of family of one child.
        John Stewart
695a.
[Field Notes] On the marsh of the
Naches for the beginning corner of
Susan Frazer Survey...
        John M. Henrie Surveyor

695A. FREELAND, CHOYL   [E]
San Augustine   Sept 1, 1835
Choyl Freeland a native of Louisiana
man of family of three persons...
emigrated to this Country in 1827.
        Saml Nathan Alcd

696. FREELAND, ISAAC   [E]
San Augustine   Sept 17, 1835
Isaac Freeland is a native of Ken-
tucky, man of family of two persons,
emigrated to this Country in 1830.
        W. McFarland Primary Judge
696a. San Augustine   17 Sept 1835
I, Isaac Freeland appoint William
Inglish my attorney; to petition for
one league & labor...
        Isaac X Freeland
Witnesses
W. McFarland, Primary Judge
E.O. Legrand   J.S. Lacey

697. FREEMAN, BENJAMIN   [E]
Dept of Nacogdoches
Jurisdiction of Liberty 26 May 1835
Benjamin Freeman a native of Vermont
is unmarried man of good...Wm Hardin
[Rev] Accepted Vehlein A. Henrie

698. FRENCH, JOHN J.   [E]
Dept of Nacogdoches
Jurisdiction of Liberty 28 Decr 1834
John J. French native of Connecti-
cut, man of family his wife and four
children...   Wm Hardin
698a.
[Field Notes] Commence at William
Carr SE corner for John J. French
sitio...

699. FRIAR, DANIEL B.   [E]
Austin [de San F.] 30 October 1832
To Mr. S.F. Austin Empresario
I have emigrated to this Country...
Daniel B. Friar 31 years of age,
married Anne my wife 22 years of age
2 male 1 female children
                    [Sig] D.B. Friar

700. FRIER, ENECK   [E]
San Augustine   May 18, 1835
Eneck Frier is a man of family wife
and fore children, man of good...
native of Cain Tuckey.
     John Bodine Alcalde pro tem

700A. FRISBY, WILLIAM   [S]
Nacogdoches   27 May 1835
Certify foreigner William Frisby is
a man of good...married with family
Jn Egne Michamps Alcalde Interim

701. FROST, WILLIAM   [E]
Neches   May 9th 1835
I have been acquainted with William
Frost a considerable time. He is a
man of a family and been in the
Country for one year or more,
farmer...   William Whiteley
Commissioner for Neches Precinct

702. FULCHER, ELIZABETH   [E]
San Augustine   Sept 26, 1834
Mrs. Elizabeth Fulcher is a native
of Kentucky, is a widow woman of
family of three persons...
          Benjamin Lindsey Alcalde

703. FULCHER, FRANCIS   [S]
Nacogdoches   7 April 1835
Certify foreigner Francis Fulcher is
a man of good...married with family...   Radford Berry

704. FULCHER, JOSHUA   [S]
Nacogdoches   5 September 1835
Certify foreigner Joshua Fulcher is
a man of good...married with family
resident of this Municipality and
born here...   Radford Berry
704a.
Nacogdoches   Sept 5, 1835
Sir: You are to survey the sitio
and labor which Mr. Joshua Fulcher
will designate...Geo W. Smyth Comr

704A. FULCHER, JOSHUA   [S]
Nacogdoches   16 Sept 1834
Certify resident Joshua Fulcher is a
man of good...married at Nuestra
Santa Madre Yglesia [Church] in this
villa...
     Luis Procela Alcalde Interim

704B. FULCHER, JOSHUA
Nacogdoches   Sept 18, 1834
Mr. Wm Robinson Surveyor Sir:
You are to survey the sitio in David
G. Burnetts Grant which Mr. Joshua
Fulcher will designate...
          Jorge Anto Nixon Comr
[Note] 2 miles north of Ranes Creek
[Reverse] This order returned by --

705. FULLENWIDER, PETER H.   [E]
To the Empresarios Austin and
Williams
I have emigrated to Texas...
I am married my wifes name Balinda,
my age 37, my wifes 21.
Tenoxtitlan   21 April 1834
     [Signed] Peter H. Fullinwider

705A. FULLER, BENJAMIN   [E]
San Augustine   May 23, 1835
Benjamin Fuller a native of South
Carolina man of family of five per-
sons...   John Chumley 2d Regidor
          Alcalde in turn
[Reverse] Accepted. Arthur Henrie
[See next column]

705Aa.Nacogdoches   May 28, 1835
Mr. Surveyor Sir: You are to survey
the sitio which Mr. Benjamin Fuller
will designate...
            Jorge Anto Nixon Comr
[Note] On the waters of Neches

705B. FULLER, DANIEL   [E]
San Augustine   May 23, 1835
Daniel Fuller a native of South
Carolina is a man of family of six
persons...   John Chumley 2d Reg
            Alcalde in turn
[Reverse] Accepted. Arthur Henrie

705Ba.San Augustine   27 Sept 1835
Daniel Fuller a native of South
Carolina emigrated to this Country
in 1830, man of family of six
persons...   Saml Thompson Alcd
Daniel Fuller has already taken the
oath of allegiance.

705Bb.San Augustine Sept 28th 1835
Mr. Commissioner:
Mr. Thomas M. Smullin is authorized
by me to receive from you in my name
an order of survey for a league &
labor..   Daniel Fuller
Witness: George English
705Bc.
I, Thomas M. Smullin have appointed
Samuel Stevers my attorney to sign
for me...the names of the settler
mentioned in said certificate.
Thomas M. Smullin
[Reverse] Daniel Fuller

705C. FULLER, EZEKIEL M.
Nacogdoches   22 Sept 1835
Certify foreigner Z.M. Fuller is a
man of good...married with family
and resident of this Department
since 1829...   Radford Berry

Nacogdoches   Sept 22, 1835
Sir: You are to survey the sitio &
labor which Ezekiel Fuller will
designate...   Geo M. Smyth Comr
[Reverse] The within order has been
executed by me. Wm Brookfield

705D. FULLER, FRANKLIN   [S]
Nacogdoches   12 September 1835
Certify foreigner Franklin Fuller is
a man of good...married with family
and resident of this Department
since 1831...   Radford Berry

Nacogdoches   Sept 12, 1835
Sir: You are to survey the sitio &
labor which Mr. Franklin Fuller will
designate   Geo M. Smyth Comr
[Rev] This order has been executed.
                    Wm Brookfield

705E. FULLERTON, HENRY   [E]
To the Empresarios Austin and
Williams
I have emigrated to Texas...
I am married, my wifes name Sarah
and have 9 children. My age 50 my
wifes 45 years
Tenoxtitlan   22 May 1834
                    Henry Fullerton

706. GAGNE, JEAN BAPTISTE   [S]
Nacogdoches   7 May 1835
Certify foreigner Jean Baptiste
Gagne man of good...married...
                    Radford Berry

707. GAINES, RADING   [S]
Nacogdoches   16 May 1835
Certify foreigner Rading Gaines is a
man of good...married with family...
                    Radford Berry

708. GAINES, THOMPSON C.   [S]
Nacogdoches   1 June 1835
Certify foreigner Thomson C. Gaines
is a man of good...married with
family...
   Jn Egne Michamps Alcalde Interim
[Rev] Accepted in Zavala. A. Henrie
708a. [Field notes] Beginning corner
of Thompson C. Gaine sitio near head
waters of Pine Island Bayou...

709. GALBRAITH, GEORGE
[Faded Certificate of Recommendation which is not readable]

709a. --- Creek   2 March 1831
I beg leave to introduce to you the
bearer George Galbraith. He came

into our neighborhood...I employed
him and find him to be very
industrious... [not legible]

710. GALLION, JOHN C.   [E]
San Augustine   Sept 27, 1834
John C. Gallion is a native of Ken-
tucky hath a family of six persons.
                John Bevil Alcalde
710a. [Field notes]   Begining
corner of John Gallion sitio on
Sandy Creek, waters of Sabine
River...   Veatch Surveyor

711. GALOWAY, PETER   [E]
San Augustine   Sept 22, 1834
Peter Galoway from the evidence of
two   respectable persons is a native of South Carolina, man of
family of three persons
            Benjamin Lindsey Alcalde
711a. [Field notes]   Beginning
corner of Peter Galloways sitio on
the north bank of the Angelina...
                Brown Surveyor

712. GAMBO, JOSE   [S]
Nacogdoches   29 Aug 1835
Certify citizen Jose Gambo is a man
of good...resident of this Municipality since 1812, married with
family of 4 persons...has not obtained land...   Radford Berry

713. GANDY, DANIEL R.
The State of Alabama, Perry County
Whereas Daniel R. Gandy of the State
and County aforesaid intends going
immediately to the Province of Texas
[to] obtain land   October 18th 1830
                Joseph Martin J.P.
[11 Alabama signers]

714. GARCIA, GREGORIO   [S]
Nacogdoches   4 April 1835
Gregorio Garcia is resident of the
Municipality, born in the Country,
married with family...has not
obtained land...   Radford Berry
Certify that mentioned Garcia is not
a deserter or a soldier.   Berry
714a. [Field Notes]   Head waters of
Pine Island Bayou for beginning of
Gregorio Garcia sitio...   D. Brown

715. GARCIA, JOSE   [S]
Nacogdoches   25 May 1835
Jose Garcia born on Mexican soil but
a citizen of the US of the North...
man of good...married with family...
    Jn Egne Michamps Alcalde Interim

716. GARCIA, MARCOS   [S]
Nacogdoches   14 August 1835
Certify citizen Marcos Garcia is a
man of good...resident of this Municipality since 1827...single without
family...has not obtained land...
                Radford Berry
716a.
Nacogdoches   August 15, 1835
Mr. J. Snively   Sir: You are to
survey the sitio Mr. Marcos Garcia
will designate   Geo W. Smyth Comr

717. GARCIA, SANTOS   [S]
Nacogdoches   28 August 1835
Certify citizen Santos Garcia is a
man of good...resident of this Muni-
cipailty since 1814, single without
family...has not obtained land...
                Radford Berry

718. GARLING, MRS. CHRISTINA
Nacogdoches   May 29, 1835
Mr. Surveyor Sir: You are to survey
in Zavala's Grant the quarter sitio
which Mrs. Christina Garling will
designate... Jorge Anto Nixon Comr

719. GARNER, ARTHUR   [S]
Nacogdoches   2 Feb 1835
Certify foreigner Arthur Garner is a
man of good...married with family...
    Jn Egne Michamps Alcalde Interim
[Faded note] Wife & 7 ch. W side
Trinity at his improvement adjoining
Mathew Hubert

720. GARNER, BRADLEY   [E]
Dept of Nacogdoches
Jurisdiction of Liberty 15 Apr 1835
Bradley Garner a native of Virginia,
a man of family...   Claiborne West

721. GARNER, DAVID   [S]
Nacogdoches   2 May 1835
Certify foreigner David Garner is a
man of good...married with family...
                Radford Berry

721a. Nacogdoches   August 10th 1835
Received of J.A. Nixon, Comr,
Stephen Jetts Title   David Garner

722. GARNER. EDWARD & JAMES
[Field notes] Survey of one league
and one labor for James Garner being
Survey   No. 6...Rio Frio.
[Field notes] Survey of one third
league part of Survey No. 8 for
Edward Garner...   East bank of
Attascoso Creek.

723. GARNER, JAMES A.   [S]
Nacogdoches   29 September 1835
Certify foreigner James A. Garner is
a man of good...single without
family...   Radford Berry
[Rev] Accepted in Vehlein. A.Henrie

724. GARNER, JAMES J.   [S]
Nacogdoches   2 February 1835
Certify James J. Garner is a man of
good, married with family...
     Jn Egne Michamps Alcalde Interim
[Note] Wife = west side of Trinity,
below the long King's trace at his
improvement.

725. GARNER, THOMAS H.   [E]
San Augustine   3 April 1835
Thomas H.Garner is a native of North
Carolina, a man of family of seven
persons   R.C. McDaniel Sindico
Which I certify   May 18, 1835
          A. Hotchkiss P. Judge

726. GARNETT, JAMES N.   [E]
District of Tennehaw   9 August 1835
James N. Garnett of South Carolina,
man of family of six persons...man
of good...emigrated to the Country
in 1834. Nathan Davis Commissioner

727. GARRETT, ALSE   [S]
Nacogdoches   7 September 1834
Certify foreigner Alse Garrett is a
man of good...married man...
     Luis Procela Alcalde Interim
[Note] Alse Garrett and wife

728. GARRTT, CLEBORN   [E]
San Augustine   Sept 26, 1834
Clebourn Garrett a native of Tennes-
see, single man of good...
          Benjamin Lindsey Alcalde

728a. Nacogdoches   21st Oct 1834
Mr. Samuel C. Hiroms Surveyor Sir:
You are to survey in Joseph Veh-
lein's Grant the sitio which C.
Garrett will designate...
     Jorge Anto Nixon Comr
[Note] No. 20 adjoining M.B.
     Menard's Survey, 4th sitio

729. GARRETT, ELI   [E]
San Augustine   March 30, 1835
Eli Gerrett native of New York a
single man...
     John Bodine Alcalde pro tem

730. GARRETT, JACOB   [E]
San Augustine   Sept 27, 1834
Jacob Garrett a native of Tennessee,
man of family of two persons...
          Benjamin Lindsey Alcalde

731. GARRETT, MILTON   [S]
Nacogdoches   13 May 1835
Certify foreigner Milton Garrett is
a man of good, single...
          Radford Berry

732. GARRETT, THOMAS B.   [E]
San Augustine   May 29, 1835
Thomas B. Garrett a native of Ten-
nessee man of family of a wife and
seven children...
     A. Hotchkiss Primary Judge
[Reverse] Accepted   Arthur Henrie

733. GARZA, JOAQUIN DE LA
[Field notes] Survey of Number One
in Class number two, made for Goagin
de la Garza...north side of the
Attascoso...

734. GARZA, JUAN DE LA
[Field notes] Survey of one league
and one labor for Juan de la Garza
Number 1, Class third, on Nueces
River...

735. GARZA, LUCIANO   [S]
Tenoxtitlan   18 March 1834
To Empresarios Austin and Williams
I have emigrated to Texas...
I am married, my wife is named Maria
Antonia. My age is 39, my wife 33.
          Luciano X Garza
Witness: F.W. Johnson

736. GATES, BARTHOLOMEW [S]
Nacogdoches   11 May 1835
Certify foreigner Bartholomew Gates
is a man of good...married with
family...   Radford Berry
736a. San Augustine August 18, 1835
B. Gates is a native of Georgia, man
of family, emigrated to Texas in
1831.   A. Hotchkiss P. Judge
736b.
Nacogdoches   11 May 1835
Mr. Surveyor: You are to survey in
David G. Burnett's Grant the sitio
which Mr. Bartholomew Gates will
designate... Jorge Anto Nixon Comr
[Note] On the waters of the Angelina
[Reverse] Returned by Col. F. Thorn

737. GATES, CHARLES   [E]
San Augustine   August 18, 1835
Charles Gates is a native of Kentucky, man of family of a wife and four
children...emigrated to Texas in
1831.   A. Hotchkiss P. Judge

738. GATES, GREENBERRY   [E]
San Augustine   August 20, 1835
G. Gates is a native of Kentucky, a
single man...emigrated to Texas in
1831.   A. Hotchkiss P. Judge

739. GATES, JOHN   [S]
Nacogdoches   9 October 1835
Certify foreigner John Gates is a
man of good...married with family
and resident of this Department
since 1829...
         G. Pollitt Alcalde Interim

740. GATES, JOHN   [E]
San Augustine   May 26, 1835
John Gates of the U.S. is a man of
family of seven persons and man of
good... John Chumley Alcalde in turn

741. GATES, JOHN   [E]
District of Nacogdoches
Jurisdiction of Liberty 10 Sep 1835
John Gates a native of Tennesee is a
man of family of his wife and one
child, man of good...   Wm Hardin
[Rev] Accepted in Vehlein. A.Henrie

742. GATES, WILLIAM   [S]
Nacogdoches   11 May 1835
Certify foreigner William Gates is a
man of good...married with family...
                 Radford Berry

743. GATES, WILLIAM G.   [S]
Nacogdoches   9 October 1835
Certify foreigner Wm W. Gates is a
man of good...married with family,
resident of this Department since
1831.   Radford Berry
[Rev] Wm G. Gates [note discrepancy]

744. GEDRUY, LEFROI   [E]
Nacogdoches   Decr 4th 1834
Certify Lefroi Gedruy is a native
of Louisiana, man of family of two
persons...   John Bevil Alcalde
[Note] Wife only. Adjoining G.W.
Tevis's survey on the Neches.
Zavala. D. Brown
[Reverse] L. Gedery
744a.
[Field notes] Upper end of Davises
Prairie, west of an improvement for
the beginning corner of Lefroi
Gedrup...   D. Brown

745. GEE, EASON   [S]
Nacogdoches   25 May 1835
Certify Eason Gee is a man of
good...married with family...
    Jn Egne Michamps Alcalde Interim

746. GEORGE, HESEKIAH   [S]
Nacogdoches   8 August 1835
Certify foreigner Hezekiah George is
a man of good...single without family...resident of this Municipality
since 1828...   Radford Berry

747. GEORGE, JOHN B.C.B.   [S]
Nacogdoches   6 May 1835
Certify foreigner John B.C.B. George
is a man of good...married with
family...   Radford Berry

748. GEORGE, STEPHEN   [S]
Nacogdoches   23 May 1835
Certify foreigner Stephen George is
a man of good...single without
family...   Radford Berry

749. GEORGE, WILLIAM [S]
Nacogdoches 5 Sept 1835
Certify foreigner William George is
a man of good...married with family,
resident of this Municipality since
1832... Radford Berry

750. GERISH, JAMES JR. [E]
San Augustine 22 Sept 1834
James Gerish is a native of England, is a man of family of a wife
and 3 children...
Benjamin Lindsey Alcalde
750a.
[Field Notes] Commencing at the SW
corner of David Shoats Survey for
corner of James Gerish Junr sitio
750b.
To the Commissioner or Empresario
Gentlemen: You will please send me
by Mr. Thos Wilson my Title for my
league of land which is situated on
the Neches River and surveyed by
D. Brown. J. Gerish Jur

751. GERISH, JAMES SR. [E]
San Augustine Sept 23d 1834
James Gerish Senr is a native of
England, is a man of family of two
persons and man of good...
Benjamin Lindsey Alcalde

[Field notes] Set post west line
Hustons Survey, about 10 miles
west of Santa Anna corner James
Gerish sitio... D. Brown

752. GIBBS, ZACHEUS [S]
Nacogdoches 1 December 1834
Certify foreigner Zacheus Gilbes is
a man of good...married with family
Vital Flores
[Note] Zacheus Gibbs. One child.
Burnett on the Aynai trace 5 miles
west of Bowles Plantation.
Strode Surveyor

753. GIBSON, ABSALOM [S]
Nacogdoches 24 November 1834
Certify foreigner Absalom Gibson is
a man of good...married with family
Vital Flores
[Note] Absalom Gibson. Wife & 3
children on an improvement he has
purchased of Wm Barbee = Brookfield

753a. Maj. A. Nixon Commissioner
Sir: Please to deliver my deed to
Mr. John J. Simpson.
Decr 28th 1834 Absalom Gibson

754. GIBSON, JAMES L. [E]
San Augustine May 27th 1835
James L. Gibson a native of Kentucky
and a man of family two children...
Nathan Davis Commissioner
[Reverse] Accepted. Arthur Henrie

755. GIBSON, JESSE [S]
Nacogdoches 29 May 1835
Certify Jesse Gibson is a man of
good... married with family...
Jn Egne Michamps Alcalde Interim
755a.
Nacogdoches May 29, 1835
Mr. Surveyor Sir: You will survey
in Burnett's Grant the sitio which
Mr. Jesse Gibson will designate...
Jorge Anto Nixon Comr
[Note] Between Neches & Trinity

756. GIBSON, URIAH [E]
Dept of Nacogdoches
Jurisdiction of Liberty 16 Feb 1835
I John Stewart Commissioner for the
Precinct of Cow Bayou...Uriah Gibson
a native of Louisiana, a man of
family of himself and wife...
John Stewart

757. GILBERT, DANIEL [S]
Nacogdoches -- July 1835
Certify foreigner Daniel J. Gilbert
is a man of good...single without
family... Radford Berry
[Rev] Accepted in Vehlein. A.Henrie

758. GILBERT, JOHN [E]
San Augustine January 22d 1835
John Gilbert a native of South Carolina is a married man of family of
nine persons...
James S. Hanks Alcalde
758a.
[Field Notes] Commencing NW corner
of James Clark Survey for beginning
of John Gilbert's sitio... John A.
Veatch Surveyor

759. GILLCHRIST, CHARLES   [E]
Dept of Nacogdoches
District of Bevil   Octr 10th 1834
Charles Gilchrist a native of Loui-
siana, family of four persons...
            John Bevil Alcalde
[Note] Wife and four children
Zavala on the south side of Wm Jor-
dan's land.   D. Brown
759a.
Mr. Geo Anto Nixon Comr   Sir:
You will please deliver to Geo W.
Smyth my title   Oct 3d 1835
        Charles X Gillchrist

760. GILLCHRIST (KILLCREASE), JOHN
Nacogdoches [S] 13 January 1835
Certify foreigner John Killcrease is
a man of good...married with family
            Radford Berry Alc
[Note] Gilchrist = wife & 7 children. At his improvement on the N.
side of Pine   Island Bayou, adjoining Menard. Zavala   Geo W. Smyth

761. GILLILAND, ELY   [S]
Nacogdoches   18 November 1834
Certify Mr. Ely Gilleland is a man
of good...married with family and
for six years has lived in the
Country...   Vital Flores
[Note] Wife, 7 ch. Vehlein
On a branch of the Angelina about 4
miles above Robt Bridges NW

762. GILLILAND, E.W.   [E]
San Augustine   May 18, 1835
E.W. Gilliland is a native of North
Carolina, a man of family of two
persons...   A. Hotchkiss P. Judge

763. GLASS, GEORGE   [E]
San Augustine   Sept 22d 1835
George Glass native of the Country,
a man of family of five persons...
            Saml Thompson Alcd
763a. San Augustine   23d Sept 1835
I, George Glass appoint William
Inglish my attorney to petition
for a league and labor of land...
            George Glass
Witnesses C. Thompson
            A.E.C. Johnson

763b. Nacogdoches Oct 9th 1835
Sir: You are to survey the league &
labor which Mr. George Glass will
designate... Geo W. Smyth Comr

764. GLASS, PETER   [E]
San Augustine   23d Sept 1835
Peter Glass is a native citizen, man
of family of three persons...
            Saml Thompson Alcd
764a. San Augustine   22d Sept 1835
I, Peter Glass appoint William Ing-
lish my attorney to petition for one
league & one labor...Peter X Glass
Witnesses
A.E.C. Johnson
C. Thompson   Saml Thompson Alcd

764b. Nacogdoches October 9th 1835
Sir: You are to survey the sitio &
labor which Mr. Peter Glass will
designate.   Geo W. Smyth Comr

765. GLENN, JAMES L.   [E]
District of Tennehaw 1st July 1835
James L. Glenn a native of Tennessee, a man of family of two persons...emigrated in 1835.
            Nathan Davis Commissioner

766. GLENN, SALLY   [E]
Dept of Nacogdoches
District of Bevil   Oct 10th 1834
Sally Glenn a native of Kentucky,
widow with a family of four persons
            John Bevil Alcalde
[Note] Widow with three children
The place she has improved.
            Zavala GWS

767. GLENN, SAMUEL   [E]
District of Tennehaw 1st July 1835
Samuel Glenn a native of Tennessee,
man of family of three perons...
emigrated in the Spring of 1835.
            Nathan Davis Comr
[Note] Accepted. Henrie

768. GLENN, SARAH
[Field notes] Zavala 49. Corner
Sarah Glenn's sitio, waters Walnut
Creek... [See SALLY GLENN above]

769. GOLIGHTLY, T.J.   [S]
Nacogdoches   25 August 1835
Certify foreigner T.J. Golightly is
a man of good...single without fam-

ily, resident of this Municipality
since July 1835...   Radford Berry
Accepted in Vehlein. 1/4 sitio.
                    A. Henrie

770. GOLLIHER, MATTHEW   [S]
Nacogdoches   11 May 1835
Certify foreigner Mathew Gollaihar
is a man of good...married with
family...   Radford Berry

770a.Mr. G.A. Nixon
Dear Sir: Please send me my title
by the barer Mr. George May...
July 2, 1835   Mathew X Golliher
Witnesses
Jno ---   Benjamin G. Reed

771. GOMEZ, JESUS   [S]
Nacogdoches   30 August 1835
Certify citizen Jesus Gomez is a
man of good...resident of this Municipality since 1812...married with
family...has not obtaimed land...
                  Radford Berry
771a. Nacogdoches   Sept 25, 1835
Mr. J. Snively Sir: You are to
survey the sitio & labor which
Mr. Jesus Gomez will designate...
            Geo W. Smyth Comr

772. GONZALES, DOMINGO   [E]
San Augustine   August 19, 1835
Domingo Gonzales is a native Mexican, a man of family of a wife and
one child... A. Hotchkiss P. Judge

773. GONZALES, MARIA SINFOROSA [S]
Nacogdoches   29 April 1835
Certify citizen Maria Sinforosa Gonzales is a woman of good...resident
of this Municipality for many years,
widow with family...has not obtained
land...   Radford Berry

773a. Nacogdoches   May 13th 1835
Major Nixon: Please deliver my
title to   R. Smith.
            Maria X Sinforosa Gonzales
Witness   J.G. Parker

774. GONZALES, ROMANO   [S]
Nacogdoches   8 April 1835
Romano Gonzales, soldier...married
in the city of Durango with Maria
Cuellar on 2 August 1832...because
of war...lost his left arm.
74

Because I am destitute...my wife
is a long way off...petition that he
be given one league of land...
8 April 1835   Jose Pineda
[Radford Berry certifies petitioner
entitled to land]
Nacogdoches   May 13, 1835
Major Nixon: Please deliver my
title to Robt Smith.
            Roman X Gonzales
Witnesses
L. Mortimer Thorn   John Morriss

775. GONZALES, TRINIDAD   [S]
Nacogdoches   4 Septembr 1835
Citizen Trinidad Gonzales is a woman
of good...resident of this Municipality, born here, a widow with
family...has not obtained land
                  Radford Berry

776. GOOD, EDWARD   [E]
Dept of Nacogdoches
District of Bevil October 8th 1834
Edward Good is a native of Virginia,
hath a family of eight persons...
            John Bevil Alcalde
776a. [Field notes] Beginning cor-
ner of Edward Good sitio...John
Bevils Survey on Sandy Creek...

777. GOOD, JAMES D.   [E]
Dept of Nacogdoches
District of Bevil October 8th 1834
James D. Good is a native of Missou-
ri, single...   John Bevil, Alcalde

778. GOODMAN, JOHN
To Mr. S.F. Austin Empresario
I have emigrated to this Colony...
John Goodman 48 years
Rebecca my wife 42 years
6 [8?] Male, 2 female children
Moved from Tennessee and arrived in
this Colony.   John Goodman
778a.
State of Tennessee, Madison County
To the inhabitants of Austin Grant
of Texas. Greetings:
Whereas our neighbor Mr. John Good-
man has signified to us his inten-
tion of emigrating to your Country
We recommend... 5th February 1831
[About 35 signatures in Tennessee]

779. GOODRICH, B.B.
War Department   Jany 20, 1834
Sir: ...your letter of 19th inst the
recommendation of B.B. Goodrich for
appointment of Enrolling Agent
amongst the Cherokees of Alabama
shall be placed on file...
779a.
Municipality of Austin Octr 8th 1834
Having been acquainted with Doctr
B.B. Goodrich both in the State of
Alabama and in this Country...man of
fair reputation
          Jesse Grimes, Prim Judge
          Municipality of Austin
779b.
San Jacinto   May 25th 1835
Col Nixon   Sir:
During my absence in the U.S., Mr.
Blanchet has promised to attend to
my land matters. He will present my
field notes for a title...
          B.B. Goodrich

780. GOODRICH, ANDREW W.   [E]
San Augustine   August 18th 1835
Andrew W. Goodrich a native of Tennessee, a man of family of three
persons...emigrated to Texas in
1830.   Nathan Davis Comr

781. GOODWIN, HENRY   [E]
San Augustine   [no date]
Henry Goodwin a native of Georgia
is a man of family of three
persons...   Nathan Davis Comr
[Reverse] Accepted. A. Henrie

782. GOODWIN, ROBERT   [E]
San Augustine   May 23d 1835
Robert Goodwin a native of Tennessee
is a man of family of eight persons
          Nathan Davis Comr
[Reverse] Accepted. A. Henrie

783. GOODWIN, SHEARLY   [E]
San Augustine   May 23d 1835
Shearly Goodwin is a native of Geor-
gia a man of family of five persons
          Nathan Davis Comr
[Reverse] Accepted. Arthur Henrie

784. GORDON, HORACE   [E]
Brasoria   March 11th 1830
To Samuel M. Williams   Sir:
I have known Mr. Horace Gordon some
time, his conduct...justly merits a
grant.   John Austin
784a.
Mouth of the Brazos 10th March 1830
To Samuel M. Williams   Dear Sir:
The bearer Horace Gordon is a young
man that I have been personally
acquainted with for nine months...
His mother is a widow with four
children.   Asa Mitchell

785. GORDON, SAMUEL   [E]
To Mr. S.F. Austin Empresario
I have emigrated to this Colony...
I am a single man aged 23, a farmer
by occupation. Removed from Kentucky
and arrived in this Colony 5th
August 1829.   Samuel Gordon
785a.
Brazoria   May --, 1830
This is to certify that ---[faded]
Mr. S.Gordon that I find him to be a
very good and industrious young man.
          Shubael Marsh

786. GOSS, THOMAS   [S]
Nacogdoches   25 April 1835
Certify foreigner Thomas Goss is a
man of good...married with family...
          Radford Berry

787. GOSSETT, ELIJAH   [S]
Nacogdoches   28 November 1834
Certify foreigner Elija Gosett is a
man of good...married with family...
          Vital Flores

788. GOSSETT, JAMES L.   [S]
Nacogdoches   28 November 1834
Certify foreigner James L. Gossett
is a man of good...married with
family...   Vital Flores

789. GOUGH, HENRY   [S]
Nacogdoches   23 September 1835
Certify Henry Gough is a man of
good...married with family...
          Radford Berry
[Rev] Accepted in Vehlein. A.Henrie

790. GRAGG, JOHN [S]
Nacogdoches 11 December 1835
Certify foreigner John Gragg is a
man of good...married with family
and resident of this Department
since 1820... Radford Berry

791. GRAGG, MOSES [S]
Nacogdoches 27 May 1835
Certify foreigner Moses Gragg is a
man of good...married with family...
Jn Egne Michamps Alcalde Interim

792. GRAYHAM, ELIZABETH [E]
San Augustine [no date]
Elizabeth Grayham is a native of
Kentucky a widow woman of family of
seven persons, emigrated to this
Country 1 January 1833.
Nathan Davis Commissioner

792a. I certify that Elizabeth Gray-
ham has taken the oath...this 29th
Aug 1835 Nathan Davis Commissioner
792b.
I, Elizabeth Grayham appoint Edward
O. Legrand my attorney to petition
for one league and one labor...
Elizabeth X Grayham
Wignesses| Peter C. Ragsdale
Joseph Jewett Charles Haley
Jesse Amason

793. GRAHAMS, JOHN [S]
To the Empresarios Austin and
Williams
I have emigrated to Texas...
I am unmarried, my age 56 years
Tenoxtitlan 27 May 1834
John Grahams

794. GRAHAM, JOHN H. [S]
Nacogdoches 8 June 1835
Certify foreigner John H. Graham is
a man of good...married with family
Jn Egne Michamps Alcalde Interim
[Rev] Accepted in Zavala. A.Henrie

795. GRAHAM, SAMUEL L. [S]
Nacogdoches 8 June 1835
Certify Samuel L. Graham is a man of
good...single without family...
Jn Egne Michamps Alcalde Interim
[Rev] Accepted in Zavala. 1/4 sitio.
A. Henrie

796. GRAHAM, WALTER B. [S]
Nacogdoches 9 June 1835
Certify Walter B. Graham is a man of
good...single without family...
Jn Egne Michamps Alcalde Interim
[Reverse] Accepted in Z. 1/4 sitio
A. Henrie

797. GRANGE, MARCELANT [E]
Department of Nacogdoches
[Dist of Bevil?] Dec 10th 1834
Certify Marcelant Grange is a native
of Louisiana...hath a family of two
persons John
Bevil Alcalde [Reverse] Accepted in
Zavala. A. Henrie

798. GRANT, JAMES [S]
Nacogdoches 25 May
1835 Certify foreigner James
Grant is a man of good...single...
Jn Egne Michamps Alcalde Interim

799. GRAVES, PHILLIP [E]
San Augustine August 19,
1835 Phillip Graves is a native
of Tennessee, single man, emigrated
to Texas in 1824...
A. Hotchkiss P. Judge

800. GRAY, ALLEN G. [S]
Nacogdoches August 11, 1835
Mr. Surveyor Sir: You are to survey
in Zavala's Grant the sitio which
Mr. Allen G. Gray will designate...
Jorge Anto Nixon Comr

801. GRAY, PLEASANT [E]
San Jacinto March 16, 1834
We certify that we are acquainted
with the bearer of this, Mr. Pleasant Gray and recommend him as an
honest and industrious man and a
good citizen.
Joseph Lindley Elijah Collard

I certify that I am personally ac-
quainted with the men that have
recommended... 16th Nov, 1834
James J. Foster Commissioner
for the Precinct of Viesca
[Note] Wife and 3 ch. Adjoining
Birdsell's Survey to the South =
Vehlein Wm Robinson

76

802. GRAY, THOMAS   [E]
Town of Austin   5th June 1830
To Mr. S.F. Austin Empresario
I have emigrated to this Colony...
Thomas Gay 25 years old unmarried.
Moved from Georgia and arrived in
this Colony in   May 1830.
                  Thomas Gary
[Reverse] Thos Gay, Thos Gray

803. GREAVES, ALEX   [E]
San Felipe de Austin 25 July 1832
To Mr. S.F. Austin Empresario
I have emigrated to this Country...
I am single, 49 years of age, by
birth an Englishman.
                  Alexr Greaves

804. GREEN, BENJAMIN M.   [E]
Dept of Nacogdoches
Jurisdiction of Liberty 28 Mar 1835
Benjamin M. Green is a native of
Louisiana man of family of wife and
one child...   Wm Hardin

805. GREEN, FRANCIS L.   [E]
San Augustine   May 26th 1835
Francis L. Green is a native of Ala-
bama, man of family of two persons
     A. Hotchkiss Primary Judge
[Reverse] Accepted. A. Henrie

806. GREENLOW, A.   [S]
Nacogdoches   25 September 1835
Certify foreigner A. Greenlow is a
man of good...single without
family...   Radford Berry
[Reverse] Accepted in Vehlein.
1/4 sitio   Arthur Henrie

807. GREENWAY, JEHU H.   [E]
San Augustine   Aug 18th 1835
Jehue H. Greenway is a native of
Tennessee, emigrated to Texas in
1831, is a single man...
          Nathan Davis Commissioner

808. GREENWOOD, GARRISON   [E]
Municipality of Austin Jany 2, 1835
I certify Garrison Greenwood is a
native of the U.S., a man of family
of ten persons. Jesse Grimes Judge
                  Dept of Brasos
[Note] Wife & 8 ch. Robinson
     North fork of Elkhart

808a. Nacogdoches   Feb 27th 1835
Major Nixon Comr:
Be so good as to let Mr. M. Murchi-
son have my land papers for a sitio
north fork of Elkhart in Burnett's
Grant.   Garrison Greenwood

809. GREENWOOD, JOHN T.   [E]
District of Tennehaw 10 Aug 1835
John T. Greenwood is a native of
Kentucky a man of family of eight
persons...emigrated to the Country
1833   Nathan Davis Commissioner
[Reverse] Accepted. A. Henrie

810. GREESON, ISAAC   [E]
San Augustine   May 17, 1835
Isaac Grason is a native of Georgia,
man of family of a wife & three[?]
children. A. Hotchkiss Prmy Judge

811. GREGORY, JOHN   [S]
Nacogdoches   31 October 1835
Certify foreigner John Gregory is a
man of good...married with family...
     G. Pollitt Alcalde Interim

811a.   November 28th 1835
Received of the Comr J.A. Nixon,
John Gregory title...
                  Arthur Henrie

812. GRESHEN, JAMES   [E]
[Type script copy of Vol. 22-191]
San Augustine   Sept 23d 1834
John Greshen is a native of England,
man of family of two persons...
          Benjamin Lindsey Alcalde
Z39. Field Notes of Greshen's
     league   D. Brown
[Note says "Originals are missing"]

813. GRIFFIN, JACKSON H.   [E]
Dist of Nacogdoches
Jurisdiction of Liberty 18 Apr 1835
Jackson H. Griffin is a native of
Mississippi, a man of family of
himself and wife   Wm Hardin Judge

814. GRIGSBY, ELBERT   [S]
Nacogdoches   7 October 1835
Certify foreigner Elbert Grigsby is
a man of good...single without fami-

ly, resident of this Department
since 1831...   Radford Berry

815. GRIGSBY, JOHN   [S]
Nacogdoches   14 November 1835
Certify John Grigsby is a man of
good...married with family...
                    Vital Flores
[Note] Wife & 8 ch. Vehlein.
      Big Sandy.   Hiroms

816. GRIGSBY, JOSEPH   [E]
Dept of Nacogdoches
District of Bevil   Octr 10th 1834
Joseph Grigsby is a native of Virginia, family of six persons...
                    John Bevil Alc
[Note] Wife and four children.
Zavala. On the Neches near the
mouth, the place he has improved.
                    Geo W. Smyth
816a. [Field Notes]   Marsh near
the Neches River, on west side,
for Joseph Grigsby's sitio...

817. GRIGSBY, NATHANIEL   []
San Augustine   23d Sept 1834
Certify Nathaniel Grigsby is a native of the U.S., a single man...
                    John Bevil Alc
817a. [Field Notes]   North bank
of Sandy Creek...quarter sitio
for Nathaniel Grigsby...

818. GRILLET, CLERI   [S]
Nacogdoches   20 October 1835
Certify foreigner Clairy [over-writ-
ten "Cleri"] Grillet is a man of
good...married with family, resident
in this Department since 1825.
                    Radford Berry

819. GRIMES, GEORGE   [S]
[photocopy of Cert. of Reception]
Villa de Austin   1 January 1830
Certify that George Grimes is one of
the Colonists who came --- 1827;
married with family of eleven
persons... [Note] Received his land.
                    Stephen F.Austin

820. GROSS, CHRISTIAN   [E]
San Augustine   August 20th 1835
Christian Gross is a native of No
Carolina man of family of three
persons...emigrated to this Country
in 1828.   Saml Thompson Alc
78

821. GROSS, MRS. ELIZABETH   [E]
San Augustine   May 19, 1835
Mrs. Elizabeth Gross is a native of
South Carolina, widow lady of family
of six children.
                    A. Hotchkiss Prmy Judge

822. GROSS, LARKIN   [E]
San Augustine   Sept 23d 1834
Larkin Gross is a native of Kentucky, man of family of two persons.
                    Benjamin Lindsey Alcalde
822a. [Field Notes]   At SE corner
of Benjamin Lindsey's Survey for
beginning of Larkin Gross sitio...
                    Brown Surveyor

823. GROUNDS, GEORGE   [E]
San Augustine   August 20th 1835
George Grounds native of Missouri,
man of family of five persons...
emigrated in 1828
                    Saml Thompson Alcd

824. GRUBBS, THOMAS   [S]
Nacogdoches   30 September 1835
Certify foreigner Thomas Grubbs a
man of good...married with family...
                    Radford Berry
[Rev] Accepted in Vehlein. A.Henrie

825. GUTHRIE, WILLIAM   [E]
Dept of Nacogdoches
District of Bevil   Octr 12th 1834
William Guthrie is a native of Vir-
ginia, hath a family of five
persons...   John Bevil Alcalde
[Note] Wife and 3 children.
        Place where he lives.
                    Zavala. G.W.S.
825a.
Nacogdoches   Oct 31st 1834
Mr. Geo W. Smyth   Surveyor Sir:
You are to survey in Zavala's Grant
the sitio which Mr. William Guthrie
will designate...
                    Jorge Anto Nixon Comr
[Reverse] I have declined taking
land as a Colonist. Oct 4th 1835
                    William Guthrie

826. GUTIERREZ, ISABELLA   [S]
Nacogdoches   10 September 1835
Certify citizen Isabella Gutierez is
a woman of good...widow with family,
resident of this Municipality since
1831...has not obtained land...
                    Radford Berry

827. HAGERTY, THOMAS J.   [E]
San Augustine   May 19, 1835
Thomas J. Hagerty is a native of
Georgia, a man of family of a wife
and two children.
       A. Hotchkiss Primary Judge

828. HAIL, JONAS J. [E]
San Augustine   22 Sept 1834
Jonas J. Hale from two witnesses is
a native of North Carolina, man of
family of four persons.
       Benjamin Lindsey Alcalde
[Note] Jonas J. Hale wife and three
children. Adjoining Townsons.Burnet
928a.
San Augustine   August 17, 1835
Jonas Haile is a native of North
Carolina a man of family of a wife
and four children...emigrated to
Texas in 1834.
       A. Hotchkiss P. Judge

829. HALBERT, NATHAN   [S]
Nacogdoches   2d May 1835
Certify foreigner Nathan Halberd is
a man of good...married with family
       Radford Berry

830. HALE, GEORGE C.   [E]
Austin [de San F.] 29th Novr 1831
To Mr. S.F. Austin Empresario
I have emigrated to this Colony...
George C. Hale 30 years of age.
Unmarried. Moved from New York and
arrived in this Colony Novr 1831.
       George C. Hale

831. HALEY, ALLEN   [E]
San Augustine   August 18, 1835
Allen Haley is a single man, native
of Tennessee...emigrated to Texas in
1822. A. Hotchkiss Primary Judge

832. HALEY, ALLEN   [E]
San Augustine   August 18, 1835
Allen Haley is a single man, a na-
tive of Tennessee, emigrated to
Texas in 1821.
       A. Hotchkiss Prmy Judge

833. HALEY, CHARLES   [E]
San Augustine   Oct 10, 1835
Charles Haley is a native of Louisiana, single...emigrated to Texas in
1821. A. Hotchkiss Primary Judge

833a. San Augustine   9 Oct 1835
I, Charles Haley appoint Richard
Haley my attorney to petition for
one third of a league...
       [Sig] Charles Haley

834A. HALEY, JOHN   [E]
San Augustine   22 Sept 1835
John Haley from evidence of two
persons is a man of family of eight
persons...
       Benjamin Lindsey Alcalde

834A. HALEY, JOHN   [E]
San Augustine   August 10, 1835
John Haley is a native of North
Carolina a man of family of a wife
and ten children, emigrated to Texas
in 1822.   A. Hotchkiss P. Judge

835. HALEY, MARK   [E]
San Augustine   August 19, 1835
Mark Haley a native of Allabama is a
man of family of a wife and one
child...emigrated to Texas in 1825.
       A. Hotchkiss P. Judge

836. HALEY, MARY ANN   [E]
San Augustine   August 19th 1835
Mary Ann Haley a native of Georgia
is a woman of family of four persons...emigrated to the Country in
1828.   Saml Thompson Alcd

837. HALEY, MICHAEL
[Field Notes]. Survey one league &
labor for Michael Haley, right bank
of Rio Frio

838. HALEY, R.B.   [E]
San Augustine   August 29, 1835
R.B. Haley is a native of Tennessee,
man of family of two persons...
emigrated to this Country in 1822.
       Nathan Davis Commissioner
Certify that R.B. Haley has taken
the oath of allegiance.
22 August 1835.
838a.
San Augustine   22 August 1835
I, R.B. Haley appoint Edwin O. Legrand my attorney to petition for 1
league and 1 labor...   R.B. Haley
Wit| John Haley   James T. Howard
   Charles Haley Mark Haley
   R. Haley

839. HALEY, RICHARD   [E]
San Augustine   August 17, 1835
Richard Haley is a native of North
Carolina, man of family of a wife
and eight children...emigrated to
Texas in 1822.
            A. Hotchkiss P. Judge
839a.
San Augustine   August 20, 1835
George W. Smith Comr
Being informed that James McAdams
has obtain from you an order of
Survey for one league and labor,
that said McAdams has it in cont-
emplation to make an encroachment
on my land...I have had my land
surveyed.   Richard Haley

840. HALEY, THOMAS   [E]
San Augustine   August 18, 1835
Thomas Haley is a single man, native
of Allabama, emigrated to Texas in
1822.   A. Hotchkiss P. Judge
840a.
San Augustine   August 18th 1835
Mr. Sydn O. Pennington   Sir:
You are to survey the third sitio
which Mr. Thomas Haley will designate...   Geo W. Smyth Comr

842. HALL, BRITAIN   [E]
Dept of Nacogdoches
District of Bevil   Oct 10th 1834
Britain Hall is a native of Georgia...hath a family of eight
persons...   John Bevil Alcalde
842a. [Field Notes]   Commencing
NW corner of Turners Survey beginning corner of Britain Hall's
Survey on the west of Thickety Fork
of Cow Creek

843. HALL, BURGESS G.   [E]
Dept of Nacogdoches
District of Bevil   Sept 15, 1835
Burgess G. Hall is an old settler of
this district and emigrated from
North Carolina in 1828, do possess
good...   B. Holt Comr

843a. Dist. of Sabine   15 Sept 1835
I, Burgess G. Hall appoint Benjamin
Lindsey my agent to procure an order
of survey   Burgess G. Hall
Wit: W.H. Landrum, James Hughes,
            B. Holt Comr

844. HALL, ELI W.   [E]
District of Tenehaw   Aug 10th 1835
Eli W. Hall is a native of New York,
a man of family of eight persons...
emigratd to the Country in 1833.
            Nathan Davis Commissioner

845. HALL, HAYWOOD H.   [S]
Nacogdoches   4 May 1835
Certify foreigner H.H. Hall is a man
of good... single without family...
            Radford Berry
845a.
Nacogdoches   May 4, 1835
Sir: You are to survey in David G.
Burnett's Grant the sitio which
Haywood H. Hall will designate...
            Jorge Anto Nixon Comr
[Note] Quarter sitio
845b.
Nacogdoches   Oct 10, 1835
Sir: You are to survey the third
sitio which H.H. Hall will
designate... Geo W. Smyth Comr

846. HALL, HARVEY   [E]
San Augustine   29 Aug 1835
Harvey Hall is a citizen of this
Country, a native of Tennessee...
emigrated to this Country in 1829.
            Saml Thompson Alcd

847. HALL, JAMES   [S]
Nacogdoches   14 Novr 1834
Certify James Hall is a man of
good...proved by two witnesses...
            Vital Flores
[Note] Wife & 1 child   20 below
Sabine on W. side of the Neches
above the Survey of Little & Elliott

848. HALL, JAMES JR.   [E]
San Felipe de Austin July 3, 1830
To S.F. Austin Empresario
I have removed to this Colony...
My name James Hall Jr. aged 55 years
My wife Wineferd aged 54 years.
One servant. Removed from Illinois.
Two male children.
Arrived in this Colony 3d June last.
            James Hall Jr.

849. HALLMARK, GEORGE W.   [E]
Neches   August 14th 1835
I have been acquainted with George
W. Hallmark...farmer by occupation.
    William Whiteley Commissioner
    for the Neches Precinct

850. HAM, CAIAPHAS K.   [E]
To Mr. S.F. Austin   [no date]
I have emigrated to this Colony...
My name is Caiaphas K. Ham, 28 years
of age. Unmarried, arrived in the
Colony in Feby 1830 Caiaphas K. Ham

851. HAMBLETON, NATHANIEL   [E]
San Augustine   Sept 1st 1835
Nathaniel Hambleton is a native of
Tennessee, a single man of good...
emigrated to this Colony in 1831.
            Saml Thompson Alcd

852. HAMILTON, FRANCIS   [E]
San Augustine   Sept 29, 1835
Francis Hamelton a native of Missou-
ri, family of twelve persons...emi-
grated to the Country in 1827.
            Nathan Davis Comr
852a.
San Augustine   7 October 1835
I authorize Franklin Fuller to peti-
tion for one league and labor...
    [Sig] Francis Hamelton
Wit: E.O. Legrand   James Mason
     J.B. Davis   D. Moses [?]
     W.L. Scott

853. HAMILTON, HANCE C.   [S]
Nacogdoches   11 June 1835
Certify foreigner Hance C. Hamilton
is a man of good...married with
family...
    Jn Egne Michamps Alcalde Interim
[Reverse] Accepted in Burnet.
            Arthur Henrie

854. HAMILTON, JAMES   [S]
Nacogdoches   25 May 1835
Certify foreigner James Hamilton a
man of good...married with family.
            Radford Berry

855. HAMMOND, JOHN J.   [E]
San Augustine   26 Sept 1834
John J. Hammond from evidence of two
persons is a native of Kentucky,

man of family of five persons.
            Benjamin Lindsey Alc
[Note] The above named party has
only been sworn
856. HAMMER, ROSALIE   [E]
San Felipe de Austin 6 July 1830
To the Empresario S.F. Austin:
I have removed to this Country...
My name is Rosalie Hammer 24 years.
Acting for myself, my husband having
abandoned me in Louisiana.
One male child, one servant.
Removed from Louisiana. Arrived in
this Colony April last.
        [Sig] Rosalie Hammer

859. HAMPTON, ALEXANDER   [E]
San Augustine   May 20th 1835
Alexander Hampton a native of the
U.S., a man of family of four persons...emigrated to Texas in 1834.
            R.C. McDaniel C.P.O.
957a.
Nacogdoches   Aug 20, 1835
Mr. Surveyor   Sir: You are to
survey in Zavala's Grant the sitio
which Mr. Alexr Hampton will
designate... Jorge Anto Nixon Comr

860. HAMPTON, LAWRIE G.   [S]
Nacogdoches   13 November 1834
Certify Lawrie G. Hampton has lived
in the Country about seven years or
more...married, has five children.
            Vital Flores
[Note] Wife & 5 children on the
waters of Big Sandy
            Hiroms - Vehlein

861. HAMPTON, WILLIAM   [E]
Neches Precinct   April 27th 1835
I have been acquainted with Wm Hamp-
ton for three years...man of family
and a farmer by occupation.
        Wm Whiteley Commissioner
        for the Naches Precinct
861a.
Nacogdoches   Apl 28, 1835
Mr. Jeremiah Strode   Surveyor
Sir: You are to survey in Burnett's
Grant the sitio which Mr. William
Hampton will designate...
        Jorge Anto Nixon Comr

862. HANKS, BURREL L. [E]
Austin [de San F.]   15 March 1833
To S.F. Austin Empresario
I have emigrated to this Country...
Burdell Hanks 28 years
Sarah Anne R. 18 years of age
Moved from Tennessee   B.L. Hanks
[Reverse] Burrel L. Hanks

863. HANKS, ELIJAH F.   [S]
Nacogdoches   28 May 1835
Certify foreigner Elijah F. Hanks is
a man of good...married with family
Jn Egne Michamps Alcalde Interim

864. HANKS, ISABELLA   [E]
San Augustine   Sept 27, 1834
Isabella Hanks is a native of Virginia, hath a family of two persons,
is a lady of good...John Bevil Alcd

865. HANKS, JAMES S. [E]
San Augustine   Sept 23, 1835
James S. Hanks is a native of Ken-
tucky, man of family of three per-
sons...   Benjamin Lindsley Alcalde
[Note]
Sworn and admitted. J.A. Nixon

866. HANKS, SAMUEL G.   [E]
Department of Nacogdoches
District of Bevil   Oct 5th 1835
Samuel G. Hanks is a native of In-
diana and emigrated to this Country
in 1827, hath no family...
            Wm Williams Alcalde

867. HANKS, WESLEY W.   [S]
Nacogdoches   28 May 1835
Certify foreigner Wesley W. Hanks is
a man of good...single without
family...
    Jn Egne Michamps Alcalde Interim

868. HANKS, WYATT   [E]
San Augustine   23d Sept 1834
Wyatt Hanks is a native of the U.S.,
a man of family of nine persons...
            John Bevil Alc
868a.
[Field Notes] East bank of the
Neches River for beginning corner of
Wyatt Hanks sitio...

869. HANLEY, JAMES   [S]
Nacogdoches   12 Aug 1835
Certify foreigner James Hanley is a
man of good...married with family...
            Radford Berry
[Rev] Accepted in Vehlein. A.Henrie

870. HARDIN, AUGUSTIN B.   [E]
Dept of Nacogdoches
Jurisdiction of Liberty 19 Dec 1834
Augustin B. Hardin a native of Geor-
gia a man of family of his wife and
two children   B. Woods
[Note] Wife & 2 ch. Vehlein. Half a
league on the Trinity NE below
Whitlock and Orr

871. HARDIN, MILTON A.   [E]
Dept of Nacogdoches
Jurisdiction of Liberty Dec 19, 1834
Milton A. Hardin a native of Georgia
is a single unmarried man...
            J.B. Woods
[Note] Single man. Vehlein. On mid-
dle branch of Long King's Creek
adjoining on the west Blanchet
            Saml C. Hiroms

872. HARDIN, WILLIAM   [E]
Dept of Nacogdoches
Jurisdiction of Liberty Dec 19, 1834
William Hardin, a native of Georgia
is a man of family of his wife and
two children   J.B. Woods
872a.
Nacogdoches   Sept 18, 1835
Received of the Commissioner George
Anto Nixon four titles, to wit,
John Stewart   Francis McMillon
George Allen   Joseph Morgan
            [by] Wm Hardin

873. HARDIN, WILLIAM B.   [E]
Dept of Nacogdoches
Jurisdiction of Liberty 19 Dec 1834
William B. Hardin a native of Ten-
nessee a man of family of himself
and wife and three children...
            J.B. Woods

874. HARDING, WILLIAM J.   [S]
Nacogdoches   1 October 1835
Certify foreigner William J. Harding
is a man of good...single without
family and resident of this Department since 1831... Radford Berry

875. HARDISON, JAMES   [S]
Nacogdoches   October 10th 1835
Sir: You are to survey the sitio &
labor which Mr. James Hardison will
designate...   Geo W. Smyth Comr

876. HARDISON, JOHN   [E]
Precinct of Tannahaw Oct 7, 1835
John Hardison a native of Caintuckey
is a man of family of too persons...
emigrated to the Country in 1830...
                    Nathan Davis Comr
[Reverse] James Hardison

877. HARDWICK, NATHAN   [E]
San Augustine   Oct 5th 1835
Nathan Hardwick a native of Georgia
is a man of family of seven persons
emigrated to this Country in 1830,
and has taken the oath of
allegiance.   Saml Thompson Alcd
877a.
San Augustine   6th October 1835
I, Nathan Hardwick appoint James C.
Cain to petition for one league &
labor.   [Sig] Nathan Hardwick
Witnesses: E.O. Legrand
        Morris Mays E.W. Cullene

878. HARKINS, WILLIAM   [E]
District of Tenehaw Aug 12th 1835
William Harkins is a native of Virginia a man of family of seven persons...emigrated to the Country
1830, has taken the oath of
allegiance.   Nathan Davis Comr

879. HARLAN, ISAIAH   [S]
Nacogdoches   14 November 1834
Certify Mr. Isaiah Harlan is a man
of good...married with family...
                    Vital Flores
[Note] Wife & 9 ch. Vehlein.
Hiroms Big Sandy or Bear Creek

880. HARMON, E.D.   [E]
Mina   Feb 20th 1835
Col Samuel M. Williams   Dear Sir:
I located a league of land Feb 2nd
1835 in Col. Austin's lower Colony
plan made for me byCapt. Bartlett
Sims, which plat I forward for your
inspection by Mr. Mathew Duty...I
shall leave here for San Felipe...
                    E.D. Harmon

880a. [Plat of surveys on Sandy
Creek, Seader Creek, Walnut Creek]

881. HARMON, JOHN   [E]
San Augustine   June 13, 1835
John Harmon a native of Tennessee a
man of family of wife...
                    A. Hotchkiss
[Note] Mr. Harmon has been in Texas
        since 1826.
881a.
Cow Bayou   Aug 8th, 1835
Mr. Nixon   Dear Sir:
Please send me the title to my land
by David Garner or bearer.
            [Sig] John Harmon

882. HARMON, JOHN   [E]
Dept of Nacogdoches
Jurisiction of Liberty 27 Nov 1834
John Harmon a native of Louisiana is
a man of family of his wife and
five children.   Wm Hardin
[Note] John Harmon.Wife and five
children. The place where he lives
on the Sabine. First bluff below Big
Cow Creek. Zavala   F. Hardin
882a.
[Field Notes] SE corner of Anthony
Harrises Survey for the beginning
corner of John Harmons Survey...
                    Hardin Surveyor

883. HARNESS, WILLIAM   [S]
Nacogdoches   14 August 1835
Certify foreigner William Harness is
a man of good...single without family...resident of this State since
1833.   Radford Berry

844. HARPER, BENJAMIN J.   [E]
Dept of Nacogdoches
Jurisdiction of Liberty 19 Decr 1834
I, James B. Woods Alcalde...Benjamin
J. Harper is a native of Virginia,
is a man of family of himself and
wife.   J.B. Woods
[Note] Wife. On the Long King's
Creek head waters N. of Blanchet's
Survey. Vehlein   Franklin Hardin

885. HARPER, HENRY   [E]
San Augustine   Oct 7, 1835
Henry Harper is a native of Vir-
ginia, a man of family of eight

persons...emigrated in 1826 and has taken the oath of allegiance
                    Nathan Davis Comr
885a.
San Augustine   7th Oct 1835
I authorize Franklin Fuller to petition George W. Smyth Comr for one league & labor...[Sig] Henry Harper
Witnesses
E.O. Legrand   W.L. Scott
James Mason   A.B. Davis
Edmund ---

886. HARREL, HENRY   [E]
To Mr. S.F. Austin Empresario
I am desirous of becoming a Colonist...Henry Harrel 26 years of age, unmarried. Moved from Georgia and arrived in this Colony in Novemr 1831.
[no date]   [Sig] Henry Harrel

887. HARRELL, JOSIAH   [E]
Austin [de San F.]   4 Octr 1832
To Mr. S.F. Austin Empresario
I have emigrated to this Country...
My name is Josiah Harrell and 27 years of age. Married.
Elisa is my wife.
2 Male and 1 female children.
                    Josiah T. Harrell

888. HARRIS, ANTHONY   [E]
Dept of Nacogdoches
Jurisdiction of Liberty 10 Feb 1835
I, John Stewart Comr for Cow Bayou certify Anthony Harris is a native of Louisiana, a single man...
                    John Stewart

889. HARRIS, EDWARD C.   [E]
San Augustine   May 18, 1835
Certify Edward C. Harris is a native of North Carolina, that he is a man of family of a wife and seven children...   A. Hotchkiss

890. HARRIS, ISAAC   [E]
To S.F. Austin Empresario
I have emigratd to this Colony...
Isaac Harris 25 years
Martha my wife 23 years
One boy. Moved from Louisiana.
Jany 12, 1832 Isaac X Harris

891. HARRIS, JAMES   [E]
San Augustine   Oct 5, 1835
James Harris a native of Alabama is a man of family of two persons... emigrated in 1830 and has taken the oath of allegiance.
                    Nathan Davis Comr
891a. San Augustine   7th Oct 1835
I hereby authorize Franklin Fuller to petition for 1 league and labor
                [Sig] James Harris
Witnesses: E.O. Legrand
        James Gibson   James Mason
A.B. Davis   Daniel Blount [?]

892. HARRIS, JOHN   [S]
Nacogdoches   29 May 1835
Certify foreigner John Harris is a man of good...single without family
            Egne Michamps Alcalde Interim

893. HARRISON, ALMOND   [E]
San Augustine   Sept 1st, 1835
Almond Harrison a native of New York, single man...emigrated to the Country in 1830...
                    Saml Thompson Alcd

894. HARRISON, JONAS   [E]
San Augustine   August 17th 1835
Jonas Harrison a native of New Jersey, man of family of and wife seven children...emigrated January 1821...
                    A. Hotchkiss Prmy Judge

895. HARRISON, F.J.[T.J.]   [E]
San Augustine   14th August 1835
F.J. Harrison a native of Mississippi man of a family of three persons emigrated to Texas in 1834...
                    R.C. McDaniel C.P.O.
895a.
Nacogdoches   Aug 7, 1835
Mr. Surveyor Sir: You are to survey in Zavala's Grant the sitio which Mr. T.J. Harrison will designate...   Jorge Anto Nixon Comr
[Note] On the Neches on the west side of said river.

896. HART, GUSTAVUS   [S]
Nacogdoches   28 May 1835
Certify foreigner Gustavus Hart is a

man of good...single without family
Jn Egne Michamps Alcalde Interim

897. HART, JOHN
[Field Notes] Survey one league for
John Hart beginning on bank of
River Nueces...

898. HARVEY, BLASSINGAME W. [E]
San Augustine   23d Sept 1834
Blassingame W. Harvey a native of
South Carolina man of a family of
six persons   Benjamin Lindsey Alcd
898a.
[Field Notes] NE side of Rio Ange-
lina for   beginning of B.W. Harvey
Survey...

899. HASKELL, CHARLES C. [S]
Nacogdoches   16 May 1835
Certify Charles S. Hiskall is a man
of good...single... Radford Berry
899a.
Nacogdoches   8 Aug 1835
Certify foreigner Charles C. Hies-
kill is a man of good...single without family, resident of this Munici-
vpality since 1822... Radford Berry

900. HATCH, HARLEN [E]
To Mr. S.F. Austin Empresario
I am desirous of locating myself and
family in the Colony...
Harlen Hatch aged 23
Mary my wife aged 19
One female child.
February 10, 1830 [Sig] Harlen Hatch

901. HAUGHEY, BRIDGET
[Type script, "Original missing"]
[Field Notes] Survey of one league
and labor for Bridget Haughey, No.
7, on E bank of Attascoso Creek...

902. HAUGHTELING, JAMES [S]
Nacogdoches   25 September 1835
Certify foreigner James Haughteling
is a man of good...single without
family...resident of this Dept since
March 1834... Radford Berry
902a. Nacogdoches   Sept 25th 1835
Sir: You are to survey the third
sitio which Mr. James Haughteling
will designate   Geo W. Smyth Comr

903. HAWLEY, JOEL EDWIN [S]
Nacogdoches   1 June 1835
Certify foreigner Joel Edwin Hawley
is a man of good...married with
family...
Jn Egne Michamps Alcalde Interim
[Rev] Accepted Zavala. A.Henrie
903a.
[Field Notes] Commence at NE corner
of Gregorio Garcia's Survey for beginning of J. Edwin Hawley sitio on
head waters of Pine Island Bayou...

903A. HAYES, STEVEN
[Typescript "Originals Missing"]
[Field Notes] Steven Hayes one
league and labor right bank of
Attascoso Creek...

904. HAZEL, SETH [E]
San Augustine   Sept 7, 1835
Seth Hazel a native of South Carolina a man of family of five persons
has taken the oath...emigrated to
this Country in 1830.
          Nathn Davis Comr   904a.
Nacogdoches   Sept 8th 1835
Sir: You are to survey the sitio &
labor which Mr. Seth Hazel will
designate...   Geo W. Smyth Comr

905. HEALTH, WILLIAM [S]
Nacogdoches   6 April 1835
Certify foreigner William Health is
a man of good...single without
family...   Radford Berry

906. HENDERSON, HUGH [S]
Nacogdoches   3 August 1835
Certify foreigner Hugh Henderson is
a man of good...single without family...resident of this Municipality
since 1832...
Jn Egne Michamps Alcalde Interim

907. HENDERSON, PETER M. [E]
San Augustine   6 January 1835
Mr. Peter M. Henderson a native of
the U.S., man of family of seven
persons... eimgrated in 1834.
          R.C. McDaniel C.P.O.
907a.
Nacogdoches   Aug 9, 1835
Mr. Surveyor Sir: You are to survey
in Zavala's Grant the sitio which
P.M. Henderson will designate...
          Jorge Anto Nixon Comr

908. HENDRICK, EDWIN [E]
San Augustine   August 18, 1835
Edwin Hendrick is a native of Kentucky, man of family of a wife and
three children came to Texas in
1824...   A. Hotchkiss Prmy Judge

909. HENDRICK, HENRY [E]
San Augustine   August 17th 1835
Henry Hendrick a native of Virgin-
ia... a single man...emigrated
June 1824.   Saml Thompson Alcd

910. HENDRICK, OBEDIAH [E]
San Augustine   December 8th 1834
Obediah Hendrick a native of Kentuc-
ky...single man.   John Bodine
secont Regidor Third Alcalde in turn
[Note] Single. 1/4 sitio. The place
where his father lives Ayes Bayou.
                    G.McFarland
910a.
Nacogdoches   Dec 10th 1834
Mr. Thos McFarland, Surveyor Sir:
You are to survey in Zavala's Grant
the fourth sitio which Mr. Obediah
Hendrick will designate...
                    Jorge Anto Nixon Comr

911. HENDRICK, OBEDIAH [E]
San Augustine   Sept 1st 1835
Obediah Hendrick a native of Kentucky...single man...emigrated 1826.
                    Saml Thompson Alcd
911a.
Nacogdoches   Sept 11, 1835
Sir: You are to survey the third
sitio which Mr. Obediah Hendrick
will designate Geo W. Smyth Comr

912. HENNESSY, THOMAS [E]
[Field notes] Survey of one third
of a sitio for Thomas Henesy on the
E bank of the Attascsco adjoining
Edward O'Boyle's Survey...

913. HENRIE, ARTHUR [E]
John Steenson   John Howard
John Lucas   Stephen Jones
James Thomas   Carter J. McKinza
Recd my fees on the above surveys
from   David Brown. Arthur Henrie
Received the within titles.
December 2, 1835   David Brown

914. HENRIE, JOHN M.
[Field Notes] Set post in the Swamp
of Cow Bayou for beginning corner of
John M.Henrie's quarter sitio...

915. HENRIQUE, MARIA GERTRUDIS [S]
Nacogdoches   29 April 1835
Certify Citizen Maria Gertrudis Henrique is a widow with family, resident of this Municipality for many
years...has not obtained land...
                    Radford Berry
915a.
Nacogdoches   May 13, 1835
Major Nixon will please deliver my
title to Robt Smith.
      Maria Gertrudis X Henrique
Wit: Jesse Chamber, Anto Calderon

916. HENRY, HARVEY M. [E]
San Augustine   10 March 1835
Harvey M. Henry a native of the
U.S., man of family of three[?]
persons, that he emigrated to Texas
in 1834.   R.C. McDaniel C.P.O.
916a.
Nacogdoches   Apr 13, 1835
Mr. Surveyor   Sir: You are to
survey in Vehlein's Grant the sitio
which Mr. Harvey M. Henry will
designate... Jorge Anto Nixon Comr

917. HENRY, ISAAC D. [E]
San Augustine   6 September 1835
Isaac D. Henry a native of Robertson
County, Tennessee, emigrated to this
Country 1833 a single man...
                    Saml Thompson
917a.
San Augustine   6th September 1835
I, Isaac D. Henry appoint Burrel
Thompson my attorney to petition
for one league and one labor...
                    I.D. Henry
Witnesses D. McDonald
           H.H. Lockridge
I certify Isaac D. Henry took the
oath...   6 September 1835
                    Saml Thompson Alcd

918. HENRY, PATRICK [E]
[Field Notes] Survey one third for
Patrick Henry on left bank of Rio
Frio...
919. HENRY, THOMAS [E]
[Field Notes] Survey one league and

one labor for Thomas Henry in two tracts, one tract on the right margin of the Rio Frio, one Attascoso.

920. HENRY, WALTER   [E]
[Field Notes] Survey one third league for Walter Henry on right bank of Attascoso

921. HENSLEY, WILLIAM R.   [E]
Austin [de San F.]   6 Jany 1832
To Mr. S.F. Austin Empresario
I have emigrated to this Colony...
Wm Hensley 31 years of age
Mary my wife 22 years of age
3 Male 1 female children. Moved from Indiana and arrived in this Colony in 1831.
        [Sig] Wm R. Hensley

922. HERFORD, CHARLES   [E]
San Augustine   April 3d 1835
I know Charles Herford a native of North Carolina is a man of family of seven persons...
        A. Hotchkiss Prmy Judge

923. HERNANDES, DOLORES   [S]
Nacogdoches   9 September 1835
Certify Citizen Dolores Hernandez is a man of very good...resident of this Municipality since 1830, married with family...has not obtained land...   Radford Berry

924. HERNIAN, GUILLERMO J.   [S]
Nacogdoches   9 November 1834
Certify foreigner Guillermo J. Hernian is a man of good...married with family...   Vital Flores

925. HERRERA, MANUEL   [S]
Nacogdoches   6 April 1835
Certify Citizen Manuel Herrera is a resident of this Municipality for many years, married with family... has not obtained land...
        Radford Berry

926. HERRERA, MARIA GERTRUDIZ   [S]
Nacogdoches   8 May 1935
Certify Citizen Maria Gertrudis Herrera a woman of very good...resident of this Municipality for many years, widow with family...has not obtained land...   Radford Berry

927. HERRERA, MIGULEL DE   [S]
Nacogdoches   30 May 1835
Certify Citizen Miguel de Herrera is a man of good...resident of this Municipality for many years, married with family...has not obtained land.
   Jn Egne Michamps Alcalde Interim
[Rev] Accepted in Zavala. A. Henrie

928. HERRERA, YGNACIO   [E]
[Field Notes] Survey Number two in Class 2 made for Ignacio Herrera... on the north side of Attascoso Creek in McMullen's Colony about thirty miles from Bexar...
928a.
[Field Notes] Survey Number three in Class 2 for Ignacio Herrera on the north side of Attascoco Creek...

929. HERRIN, MOSES   [S]
Nacogdoches   26 May 1835
Certify foreigner Moses Herrin is a man of good...married with family...
   Jn Egne Michamps Alcalde Interim
929a. Recd of Majr Nixon, Moses Herrin Title for him (Herrin).
Arthur Henrie   Decr 10th 1835

930. HIDEN, NATHANIEL   [E]
San Augustine   March 3, 1835
Nathaniel Hiden a native of Tennessee, man of family of three persons
        James S. Hanks Alcalde
[Note] Wife & 1 child

931. HIGGIN (HAGAN) JUAN   [S]
Nacogdoches   9 January 1835
Certify foreigner Juan Higgin is a man of good...married with family...
        Radford Berry
[Note] At the place where he lives Hagan = wife 3 ch = E of Thos Townsend, on both sides of the river =
        Strode

932. HILL, FRANCIS   [E]
San Augustine   Sept 22d 1834
Francis Hill a native of No Carolina a single man...
        Benjamin Whiteley Alcalde

933. HILL, JACOB   [E]
San Augustine   26 January 1835
Jacob Hill a native of the U.S. a

man of family of three persons,
emigrated to Texas in 1834.
                R.C. McDaniel C.P.O.
933a.
Nacogdoches   Aug 20, 1835
Mr. Surveyor Sir: You are to survey in Zavala's Grant the sitio
which Jacob Hill will designate...
        Jorge A Nixon Comr

934. HILL, COL. WILLIAM K.   [E]
Jurisdiction of Liberty 28 Mar 1835
Col. Wm K. Hill a native of Virginia
a man of family of his wife and five
children   Wm Hardin
[Reverse] I affirm the within from
personal...long acquaintance with
Col. Hill.   James Houston

935. HILLHOUSE, JOHN   [E]
San Augustine   Sept 22, 1835
John Hillhouse a native citizen is a
man of family of nine persons...
            Saml Thompson Alcd

935a.San Augustine   22 Sept 1835
I, John Hillhouse appoint William
Inglish my attorney to petition for
one league and labor...
        [Sig]   John Hillhouse
Witnesses
A.E.C. Johnson
Saml Thomnpson Alcd

935b. Nacogdoches   October 19, 1835
Sir: You are to survey the sitio &
labor which Mr. John Hillhouse will
designate...   Geo W. Smyth Comr

936. HINES, ALLEN   [E]
District of Sabine   17 June 1835
Allen Hines has a family of three
persons and has resided in this bis-
trict eleven years...
        B. Holt Commissioner
936a.
Nacogdoches   Sept 10, 1835
Sir: You are to survey the sitio &
labor which Mr. Allen Hines will
designate...   Geo W. Smyth Comr

937. HINES, ELBERT   [E]
San Augustine   Sept 23d 1834
Elbert Hines a native of Georgia is
a man   of family of seven persons
        Benjamin Lindsey Alcalde
88

937a.
District of Sabine 25 Aug 1835
Elbert Hines a native of Georgia has
resided in the District of Sabine
the last ten years for which time I
have been intimate acquainted with
him...family of six persons...
            B. Holt Comr

938. HINES, WILLIAM   [E]
San Augustine   Sept 23d 1834
William Hines is a native of Geor-
gia, man of family of seven persons
        Benjamin Lindsey Alcalde

938a. San Augustine   Sept 1st 1835
William Hines a native of Georgia a
man of family of seven persons...
emigrated to this Country in 1823.
            Saml Thompson Alcd

938A. HISKALL, CHARLES
[Typescript of Vol. 62-194]
[This is the same as Charles C.
Haskell, under No. 899. Editor]

939. HIXON, JOHN B.   [E]
Precinct of Tannahaw Oct 12, 1835
John B. Hixon a native of Virginia
is a married man of family of
four[?] persons, immigrating to the
Country in 1828.
        Nathan Davis Commissioner

940. HOLDY (HOBDY), JOSES   [E]
San Augsutine   Feby 22d 1835
I, Joses Hobdy do nominate Mr. Cartwright my attorney for a survey of
land upon which I now live laying &
being in Zavalas Collony...
        [Sig]   Joses Holedy [Hobdy?]
940a.
State of Tennessee, Davidson County
Know ye that Joses Holedy a citizen
of this County...being about to
emigrate and settle in Texas...
21 November A.D. 1825   R. Weakley
940b.
[Field Notes] East side of the
Ayish Bayou for the beginning of
Joses Hobdy sitio
            David Brown Surveyor

941. HOBSON, HENRY H.   [S]
Nacogdoches   19 Sept 1835
Certify foreigner Henry H. Hobson is

a man of good...married with family
resident of this Department since
1822...   Radford Berry

942. HODGES, JOSEPH   [E]
San Augustine   Sept 26, 1834
Joseph Hodges from the evidence of
two persons is a native of Virgin-
ia...man of family of two persons
            Benjamin Lindsey Alcalde
[Note] The party above named has
       been duly sworn.

943. HODGES, NEWELL C.   [E]
San Augustine   Sept 26, 1834
Newel C. Hodges a native of Tennes-
see, a man of family of three per-
sons... Benjamin Lindsey Alcalde
[Note] The above named party has
       been duly sworn.

944. HOFFMAN, DAVID   [E]
San Austine   24 Sept 1834
David Huffman a native of South
Carolina is a man of family of ten
persons...
            Benjamin Lindsey Alcalde
944a.
October the 2 day of 1835
Mr. George W. Smith Dear Sir:
I can .inform you that Mr. Defees has
been legally made and has been in-
truded on by a Mr. Mason and Smullen
and they perhaps may apply for a
title before I can come up. You will
be so good as to stop the proceeding
until I see you which will be in a
short time. Mr. Brown surveyed Def-
fees   land and returned it to you
which you will find by examination.
Your compliance will confer a favour
on your friend. D. Huffman & Defee

945. HOFFMAN, DAVID   [S]
Nacogdoches   13 Oct 1835
Certify foreigner David Hufman is a
man of good...married with family
and resident of this Department
since 1829...   Radford Berry
945a.
Nacogdoches   October 13th 1835
Sir: You are to survey the sitio &
labor which Mr. David Hoffman will
designate...   Geo W. Smyth Comr

946. HOFFMAN, DAVID A.   [S]
Nacogdoches   27 May 1835
Certify foreigner David A. Hoffman
is a man of good...married with
family...
   Jn Egne Michamps Alcalde Interim

947. HOGAN, SEBASTIAN   [S]
Nacogdoches   29 May 1835
Certify foreigner Sebastian Hogan is
a man of good...single without
family...
   Jn Egen Michamps Alcalde Interim

948. HOGGAT, JAMES   [E]
Dept of Nacogdoches
District of Bevil   Sept 28, 1835
James Hoggatt is a native of Missis-
sippi, hath a family of .three
persons... Wm Williams Alcalde
[Reverse] Accepted in Zavala's in
place of Samuel Phares. A. Henrie

949. HOIT [HAIT], SAMUEL   [E]
Town of Austin   18 June 1830
To Mr. S.F. Austin Empresario
I have emigrated to this Colony...
Samuel Hoit 46 years old. Widower.
Occupation Farmer. Moved from Mis-
sissippi and arrived in this Colony
in May 1830. 4 dependants.
                     Thomas Hait

950. HOLLAND, PHILLIP   [E]
San Augustine   18 May 1835
Mr. Philip Holland a native of N.
Carolina, man of family of three
persons, emigrated to Texas in Decr
1834...   R.C. McDaniel C.P.O.
950a. Nacogdoches   12 Aug 1835
Mr. Surveyor Sir: You are to survey in Zavala's Grants the sitio
which Mr. P. Holland will
designate... Jorge Anto Nixon Comr

951. HOLLEY, MARY A.   [E]
To Empresario S.F. Austin
I have emigrated to the Colony as
one of the Colonists which you are
authorised to settle, and I request
that you will admit me...
November 20, 1831
   [Signed]   Mary A. Holley

952. HOLLOWAY, CALEB   [E]
San Augustine   August 17, 1835
Caleb Holloway a native of Mississippi, a single man...emigrated to
this Country in 1821...
              Saml Thompson Alcd

953. HOLLOWAY, DANIEL   [E]
San Augustine   August 18th 1835
Daniel Holloway a native of South
Carolina, single man...emigrated to
this Country in 1821...
              Saml Thompson Alcd

954. HOLLOWAY, LEWIS   [S]
Nacogdoches   13 August 1835
Certify foreigner Luis Holiway is a
man of good...married with family,
resident of this Department since
1821...   Radford Berry

955. HOLLOWAY, SIMPSON   [E]
San Augustine   August 17, 1835
Simpson Holloway a native of South
Carolina is a man of family of three
persons, emigrated to this Country
in 1821...   Saml Thompson Alcd

956. HOLMAN, ISAAC   [S]
Nacogdoches   10 February 1835
Certify foreigner Isaac Holman is a
man of good...married with family...
              Radford Berry

957. HOLMAN, ISAAC   [S]
Nacogdoches   28 May 1835
Certify foreigner Isaac Holman is a
man of good...married with family...
Jn Egne Michamps Alcalde Interim
[Reverse] Accepted.   A. Henrie

958. HOLMAN, JOHN W.   [S]
Nacogdoches   27 May 1835
Certify foreigner John W. Holman a
man of good...single without family
Jn Egne Michamps Alcalde Interim
[Reverse] I give my consent that the
Bearer J.W. Holman shall have one
1/4 league of land in Zavala's Grant
May 27th 1835   Lorenzo de Zavala
        by his Attorney Arthur Henrie
958a.
Andrew D. Batemen   Nathaniel Hiden
Wm. T. Shannon   Hiram Hughes

Jas L. Ewing   Jefferson Wilson
J.W. Johnson   Isaac Holmes
Recd the above Titles   Decr 8th 1835
John H. Holman

958b.   Republic of Texas,
County of Nacogdoches
Personally appeared...John W.Johnson
he has lost the following land
titles which were in his possession:
   One league to Andrew D. Batemen
   One league to Wm P. Shannon
   One fourth to Hiram Hughes
All in Zavala's Grant. Also a league
for James L. Ewing and one fourth
for himself in Vehlein's Grant.
   John W. Johnson
7th April 1837.   Wm Hart, J.P.

959. HOLMAN, RUFUS   [E]
District of Tennehaw   10 August 1835
Rufus Holman is a native of Tennes-
see, a man of family of four per-
sons, man of good...emigrated to the
Country in 1834. Nathan Davis Comr
[Reverse] Accepted. A. Henrie

961. HOMES (HOLMES), ANTHONY
[Field Notes] Anthony Homeses quar-
ter sitio on the west bank of Adams
Bayou...   J.M. Henrie Surveyor

962. HOMES, SAMUEL   [E]
Precinct of Tannahaw   Sept 17, 1835
Samuel Homes a native of Caintuckey
a man of family of too persons...
emigrated to the Country in 1829.
   Nathan Davis Commissioner

963. HOMES (HOLMES), STEPHEN
To Geo W. Smyth, Comr
Nacogdoches   December 17th 1835
I...have been in occupancy of a
tract of land on the Sabine near the
Trescianas or Three Prairies...for
about five years...considerable
improvements. It is an old settled
place...about the year 1818, and
about the last of October or first
of Sept last a Mr. Nathan Smith came
with his Surveyor, Mr. Pennington
and ran a league of land ...and paid
no regard to me...Therefore I do
most solemnly protest...
   Stephen Holmes

964. HOLMES, THOMAS C.   [E]
District of Bevil   Oct 8th 1834
Thomas C. Holmes is a native of N.
Carolina, hath a family of three
persons, is a man of good...
              John Bevil Alcalde

965. HOLT, BENJAMIN   [E]
San Augustine   August 18, 1835
Benjamin Holt is a native of Mississippi a man of family of a wife and
six children, emigrated to Texas in
1825.   A. Hotchkiss P. Judge
965a.
San Augustine   24 Sept 1834
Benjamin Holt a native of Mississi-
pi, a man of family of eight persons
              Benjamin Lindsey Alcalde

966. HOLT, THOMAS C.   [S]
Nacogdoches   6 June 1835
Certify foreigner Thomas C. Holt is
a man of good...married with family
         G. Pollitt Alcalde Interim

967. HOLTHAM, JOHN G.   [E]
Town of Austin   5 June 1830
To S.F. Austin Empresario
I have emigrated to this Colony...
John G. Holtham 29 years of age,
unmarried moved from Louisiana in
November 1829   John G. Holtham

968. HOOKIT, EDWARD   [S]
Nacogdoches   25 May 1835
Certify foreigner Edward Hookit is a
man of good...married with family...
   Jn Egne Michamps Alcalde Interim
[Reverse]   Edward W. Kohet

969. HOOVER, HENRY   [E]
San Augustine   5 Oct 1835
I, Henry Hoover appoint Henry Teal
my attorney to petition for 1 league
& 1 labor   Henry X Hoover
Witnwsses
E.O. Legrand   George English
Saml ---   Thos H. Garner
James English

970. HOOVER, JOHN S.   [E]
District of Tenehaw   Aug 10th 1835
John S. Hoover a native of N. Caro-
lina, a family of four persons...

emigrated in 1832.
              Nathan Davis Comr
[Reverse] Accepted. Henrie

971. HOPKINS, JAMES E.   [S]
Nacogdoches   11 Decr 1835
Certify James E. Hopkins a man of
good...married with family...resi-
dent of this Department since 1824
              Radford Berry

972. HORNE, CHARLES   [E]
San Augustine   22 June 1835
Charles S. Horne a native of Kentucky, a man of family of two persons,
emigrated to Texas in June 1835.
              R.C. McDaniel C.P.O.
972a.
Nacogdoches   Aug 13, 1835
Mr. Surveyor Sir: You are to survey in Zavala's Grant the sitio
which Mr. Chs S. Horne will
designate... Jorge Anto Nixon Comr

973. HORNSBY, REUBEN   [E]
Town of Austin   5 June 1830
To Mr. S.F. Austin Empresario
I have emigrated to the Colony...
Reuben Hornsby 37 years old married
Sarah my wife 35   do
5 Male 1 female children. Occupation
farmer, moved from Mississippi and
arrived in this Colony 15 Feb 1830.
              [Sig] Reuben Hornsby
[Note] Wants land on the Colorado
adjoining James Gilliland above

974. HORET (HORST), BALTAZARA [E]
Nacogdoches   9 Decr 1834
Certify Senor Baltazar Horst is a
man of good...married with family...
              Vital Flores
[Note] Baltazar Horet. Wife and one
child. The place where he lives
adjoining Cummings Survey near the
Trinity. Vehlein   Saml C. Hirom

975. HORTON, ALEXANDER   [E]
San Augustine September 24th 1834
Alexander Horton a native of North
Carolina is a single man of good...
              Benjamin Lindsey Alcalde

975a. [Field Notes] NE corner of
John Blairs Survey near Wolf Point
for beginning corner of A. Horton's
Quarter sitio...

976. HORTON, MRS. SUSAN [E]
San Augustine   27 Sept 1834
Mrs. Susan Horton a native of No
Carolina is a widow woman of a
family of eight persons...
            Benjamin Lindsey Alcalde
976a.
[Field Notes] Commence at NW corner
of Sophia Deans Survey about 17
miles W of Santa Anna for beginning
corner of Susan Horton's sitio...
            David Brown Surveyor

977. HOTCHKISS, AUGUSTINE   [E]
Mr. S.F. Austin Empresario
I have emigrated to this Colony...
My name is Augustus Hotchkiss
Age thirty years. Married
My wife Ann. Two male children, one
servant. I removed from Cincinnati,
State of Ohio. [Sig] Aug Hotchkiss
977a.
San Augustin   Sept 22, 1834
Augustin Hotchkiss a native of
Chishen in the U.S., a man of family
of wife and three children.
            Benjamin Lindsey Alcalde
977b.
[Field Notes] Corner of Augustus
Hotch-   kiss sitio...west bank of
Ayish Bayou...Zavala's Grant No. 4

978. HOULIHAN, JOHN
[Field Notes] Survey of one league
and one labor for John Houlihan situated on E bank of the Attascoso...

979. HOULSHOUSEN, CLAIBOURNE [E]
Department of Nacogdoches
Jurisdiction of Liberty 29 Dec 1834
Claibourne C. Houlshousen a native
of Alabama is an unmarried man...
            Wm Hardin Judge

980. HOUNDSHELL, JOSEPH   [SZ
Nacogdoches   30 Oct 1835
Certify foreigner Joseph Houndshell
is a man of good...married with
family and resident of this Department since 1832... Radford Berry

981. HOUSE, GEORGE   [E]
To Mr. S.F. Austin Empresario
I have emigrated to this Colony...
George House 45 years of age, mar-
ried Sally my wife 35 years of age
3 Male 2 female children.
Moved from Luisiana and arrived in
this Colony in Decr 1830.
Jany 10, 1832
            [Sig] George House

982. HOUSTON, SAMUEL PAUL   [S]
Nacogdoches   21 April 1835
Certify foreigner Samuel Pablo Houston is a man of good...single without family...   Radford Berry

983. HOWARD, HARTWELL   [E]
San Augustine   August 20, 1835
Hartwell Howard a native of Virginia
is a man of family of five persons
emigratedto this Country in 1823.
            Saml Thompson Alcd

984. HOWARD, JAMES   [E]
Tanahaw District   Oct 8, 1835
I James Howard authorize Richard
Haley to apply for an order of
survey...   [not signed]

James Howard a native of Kentucky is
a mared man [with family] of three
persons, taken the oath...emigrated
to this Country in 1833.
            Nathan Davis Comr

985. HOWARD, JAMES L.   [E]
San Augustine   May 27th 1835
James L. Howard is a native of Mississippi, emigrated to Texas in
1829...   Nathan Davis Comr

986. HOWARD, JOHN   [E]
San Augustine   April 3d 1835
Certify John Howard a native of
South Carolina is a man of family of
ten persons.
            A. Hotchkiss Primary Judge

987. HOWE, JOSEPH   [E]
San Augustine   Sept 1st 1835
Joseph Howe a native of Ohio a
single man, emigrated to this Country in 1827.   Saml Thompson Alcd

988. HOXEY, ASA   [E]
Austin [de San F.]   April 20, 1832
I have emigrated to this Colony...
Asa Hoxey 30 years of age.
Unmarried. Moved from Alabama.
                [Sig] Asa Hoxey
Passport 2 April 1832

Tenoxtitlan   8 Feby 1833
To Empresarios Austin & Williams
I have emigrated to Texas...
I am a married man. My wifes name
Elizabeth. I have a family consist-
ing of 28 persons. [Sig] Asa Hoxey

[No N.] HOYE, CATHARINE
[Type script "Orig Missing"]
[Field Notes]| One third of a league
for Catharine Hoye. On the left bank
of Attascoso adjoining John
Houlighan Survey...

989. HUBBEL, JOHN   [E]
San Augustine   August 19, 1835
John Hubbel a native of Missouri a
man of family of a wife ...came into
Texas while an infant, and his first
wife a Mexican.
                A. Hotchkiss P. Judge

990. HUBERT, MATTHEW   [E]
To Mr. S.F. Austin Empresario
I have emigrated to this Colony...
Mathew Hubert 34 years old married.
Frances my wife 32.
2 Female children. Moved from Ala-
bama and arrived 20 Jan 1830
May 27, 1830   M. Hubert
990a.
Municipality of Austin Nov 30, 1832
Matthew Hubert a native of Missis-
sippi, a man of family of six per-
sons. Jesse Grimes Primary Judge
[Note] of the Mun. of Austin
W side of the Trinity = Vehlein
Wife and 4 children. Wm Rankin
990b.
Nacogdoches   November 12, 1835
Received of Jorge Anto Nixon Comr
the titles of:
Mr. William Busby
James Rankin Senr
James Rankin Junr
Miles G. Stephens
William Winters
Michael Woods   [Sig]   Mat Hubert

991. HUEZAS, MARIA FALCONA [S]
Nacogdoches   6 April 1835
Certify Citizen Maria Falcona Huezas
is a resident of this Municipality
for many years, woman of good...
widow with family   Radford Berry
991a.
Nacogdoches   May 13, 1835
Major Nixon: Please deliver my
Title to W. Reagan
            Maria Falcona X Hueza
Witnesses
      Chas Taylor T.S. Barnes

992. HUFFMAN, JOHN   [S]
Nacogdoches   22 Sept 1835
Certify foreigner John Huffman is a
man of good...married with family...
            Radford Berry
[Rev] Accepted in Vehlein. A.Henrie

993. HUGHES, HIRAM   [E]
San Augustine   May 23, 1835
Hiram Hughes a native of Kentucky a
single man (a black- and gun-smith)
            R.C. McDaniel Sindico

994. HUGHES, DR. JAMES   [E]
District of Sabine   June 3, 1835
To Maj. George A. Nixon
Dr. James Hughes a native of Ohio,
now a citizen of the District...
recommend him as a practitioner of
Medicine and Surgery...location of
land.   B. Holt Comr

995. HUGHES, JAMES   [E]
District of Sabine   18 Sept 1835
I, James Hughes empower Owen Lindsey
to act for me in procuring an order
of survey   [Sig]   Jas Hughes

District of Sabine   Sept 18, 1835
James Hughes an old settler of Texas
and citizen of the District of Sabine, having immigrated in 1833...
            B. Holt Comr

996. HUGHES, ROBERT   [E]
Austin [de San F.]   20 July 1831
I have emigrated to this Colony...
Robert Hughes 40 years of age,
unmarried moved from Virginia and
arrived in June 1831.
            [Sig] Robt Hughes
[Note] Passport 16 June

93

997. HUGHES, THOMAS J. [S]
Nacogdoches   11 August 1835
Certify foreigner Thos J. Hughes is
a man of good...single without
family, resident of this State since
1832...   Radford Berry

998. HUGHES, WALTER   [E]
Precinct of Sabine   25 March 1835
Walter Hughes of Kentucky is now a
citizen of the District, family of
four perbons, a farmer...
                    B. Holt Comr
[Note] On 6 Mile Creek, near the
Sabine River. Surv. John A. Veatch

999. HUGHSON, JAMES   [E]
Austin   May 23, 1831
To Mr. S.F. Austin Empresario
I have emigrated to this Colony...
James Hughson 32 years of age
Temperance my wife 22 years of age
One male child. My family is in
Illinois and I shall remove them and
be here by the   1st Feby 1832.
            [Sig]   James Hughson

1000. HULING, THOMAS B.   [E]
San Augustine   Septr 22nd 1834
Thomas B. Huling is a native of
Pennsylvania, a man of family of two
persons...   Benjamin Lindsey Alc
1000a.
Zavala   Sept 30th 1835
G.A. Nixon Esqr.   Please let bearer
have my Land Title...
            [Sig] Thos B. Huling
G.A. Nixon Esqr.
Please send my Land Title by Mr.
T.B. Huling.   Sophia W. Dean
1000b.
[Field Notes] Beginning corner of
Thomas B. Huling's sitio on the E.
bank of Rio Angelina...
                Veatch Surveyor

1001. HUMBLE, JOHN
[Certificate of Character faded]
1001a.
Nacogdoches   Oct 13, 1835
I, John Humble appoint Benjamin F.
Wright my attorney to sell one
league and labor of land...
            John H--- [faded]
Witnesses
James C. Cain   A. McLaughlin
A.B. Davis   Franklin Fuller
94

1001b.
Nacogdoches   Oct 13, 1835
Sir: You are to survey the league &
labor which Mr.John Humble will
designate...   Geo W. Smyth

1002. HUMPHRYS, JAMES
Nacogdoches   Sept 18, 1835
Sir: You are to survey the sitio &
labor which Mr. James Humphrys will
designate...

1003. HUMPHRIES, WILLIAM (PELHAM)
San Augustine [E]   27 Sept 1834
William Umphries is a native of
Tennessee, a man of family of two
persons...Benjamin Lindsey Alcalde
1003b.
Nacogdoches   Oct 6, 1835
[Affidavit from Wm Umphreys that in
his Order of Survey the name Pelham
Umphreys incorrectly inserted; to
have it changed to William]

1004. HUNT, CHARLES S.   [E]
San Augustine   May 10, 1835
Charles S. Hunt is a native of Ken-
tucky, a single man...
            A. Hotchkiss Prmy Judge

1005. HUNT, NATHANIEL   [E]
San Augustine   22 Sept 1834
Nathaniel Hunt a native of Tennessee
a man of family of five persons...
            Benjamin Lindsey Alcalde
1005a.
[Field Notes] West bank of Ayish
Bayou for beginning corner of
Nathaniel Hunt sitio
1005b.
Received Comr Geo A. Nixon.
    Mr. B.H. Mudd Land Title
Nacogdoches   Charles S. Hunt

1006. HUNT, THOMAS   [S]
Nacogdoches   2 June 1835
Certify foreigner Thomas Hunt is a
man of good...single without family
Jn Egne Michamps Alcalde Interim
[Rev] Accepted in Zavala. A. Henrie

1007. HUNTER, ELIJAH   [E]
San Augustine   14 August 1835
E. Hunter a native of the U.S. a man
of family of three persons, emigrated to Tex-as in June 1834.
            R.C. McDaniel C.P.O.

1007a. Nacogdoches   Aug 14, 1835
Mr. Surveyor Sir: You are to survey
in Zavala's Grant the sitio which
Elijah Hunter will...
          Jorge Anto Nixon Comr
[Note] On the E side of River Neches

1008. HUNTER, RALPH   [E]
San Augustine   4 May 1835
Mr. Ralph Hunter a native of the
U.S. is a man of family of six per-
sons...emigrated to Texas in 1834
          R.C. McDaniel C.P.O.

1009. HUNTER, WILLIAM   [E]
Austin [de San F.]   Oct 4, 1832
To Mr. S.F. Austin Empresario
I have emigrated to this Country...
My name is William Hunter 32 years
of age, married. Elisa my wife 30
years of age.
3 Male 2 female children. From South
Carolina.   W. Hunter
[Note] Mr. Hunter's family is in
South Carolina to be here in one
year from date

1010. HUNTINGTON, J.   [E]
San Augustine   1 May 1835
Mr. J. Huntington of the U.S. is a
man of family of three persons...
emigrated to Texas in the Summer of
1834...   R.C. McDaniel C.P.O.
1010a.
Nacogdoches   Oct 4, 1835
Mr. Surveyor Sir: You are to survey in D.G. Burnett's Grant the
sitio which Mr. J. Huntington will
designate... Jorge Anto Nixon Comr

1011. HURD, NORMAN
[Field Notes] Commence W. bank of
River Nachas...Norman Hurd's sitio
                    Theo Cushing

1012. HUSTON, ALMANZON   [E]
San Augustine   Sept 23d 1834
Almanzon Huston a native of New York
a man of family of six persons...
          Benjamin Lindsey Alcalde
1012a.
[Field Notes] Commence at NE corner
of Savary's Survey for Almannon
Huston sitio   Burton Surveyor

1013. INGERSOLL, JOHN W.   [E]
San Augustine   30 June 1835
John W. Ingersul a native of the
U.S. is a man of family of three
persons...emigrated to this Country
in 1834...   R.C. McDaniel C.P.O.
[Rev] Accepted. A. Henrie
1013a.
Nacogdoches   Aug 7, 1835
Mr. Surveyor Sir: You are to
survey in Jose' Vehlein's Grant the
sitio which Mr. Jno W. Ingersull
will designate...
          Jorge Anto Nixon Comr
[Note] On Sandy Creek
[Reverse] John W. Ingersall

1014. INMAN, JOHN   [E]
San Augustine   August 19, 1835
John Inman a native of South Caroli-
na is a man of family of eight per-
sons...emigrated to the Country in
February 1831. Saml Thompson Alcd

1015. IRBY, JOHN H.   [S]
Nacogdoches   29 Oct 1835
Certify foreigner John H. Erby is a
man of good...single without family
resident of the Department since
1832...   Radford Berry

1016. IRION, ROBERT A.   [S]
Nacogdoches   29 Jany 1835
Certify foreigner Robert A. Irion is
a man of good...married with family
              Radford Berry
1016a.
Ncogdoches   Jany 29th 1835
Mr. Surveyor Sir: You are to survey in Vehlein's Grant the sitio
which Mr. Robt A. Irion will
designate... Jorge Anto Nixon Comr
[Note] Adjoining Peter Menard

1017. IRION, WILLIAM H.   [E]
Dept of Nacogdoches
[Precinct of Bevil ?]   4 Dec 1834
William H. Irons is a native of
Virginia, hath a family of four
persons...   John Bevil Alcalde
[Note] W.H. Irion wife and two
children   Zavala. The place where
he lives. Bluff Neches.   Burton

1018. IRVINE, JAMES T.P.   [S]
Nacogdoches   30 May 1835
Certify foreigner James T.P. Irvine
is a man of good...married with fam-
ily   Jn Egne Michamps Alclalde Int.
[Rev] Accepted A. Henrie
1018a.
District of Sabine   August 31, 1835
James T.P. Irvine is a native of
Tennessee has a family...emigrated
to Texas in 1830.   B. Holt Comr

1019. IRVINE, MRS. JANE   [E]
San Augustine   Sept 26, 1834
Mrs. Jane Irvine is a native of
North Carolina is a lady of family
of three persons
          Benjamin Lindsey Alcalde

1020. IRVINE, ROBERT B.   [E]
San Augustine   25 Sept 1834
R.B. Irvine is a native of Tennessee
a single man...
          Benjamin Lindsey Alcalde

1021. IRVINE, WILLIAM A.   [E]
San Augustine   Aug 18, 1835
William A. Irvine is a native of
Virginia a man of family of two
persons...emigrated to the Country
in 1822.   Saml Thompson Alcd

1022. ISAACS, ELIJAH   [E]
District of Bevil   Oct 10th 1834
Elijah Isaacks is a native of So.
Carolina, hath a family of four
persons...   John Bevil Alcalde

1023. ISAACS, WILLIAM   [E]
San Augustine   22 Sept 1834
William Isaacks a native of South
Carolina a man of family of seven
personss...
          Benjamin Lindsey Alcalde
1023a.
[Field Notes] Commence at corner of
W. Murphy's Survey for the beginning
of William Isaac sitio...

1024. IVES, ABRAHAM   [E]
San Augustine   Sept 22d 1835
Abraham Ives a native citizen is a
man of family of seven persons...
          Saml Thompson Alcd

1024a.
San Augustine   Sept 22, 1835
I, Abraham Ives appoint William
Inglish my attorney to petition for
one league & labor of land...
          [Sig] Abraham Ives
Witnesses
A.E.C. Johnson   C. Thompson
Saml Thompson Alcd
1024b.
Nacogdoches   Oct 9th 1835
Sir: You are to survey the sitio &
labor which Mr. Abraham Ives will
designate... Geo W. Smyth Comr

1025. JACK, PAT C.   [E]
Tenoxtitlan   24 March 1834
To Mr. S.F. Austin Empresario
I have emigrated to Texas...
I am unmarried. My age is twenty
five years.   Pat C. Jack

1026. JACK, WILLIAM H.   [E]
To Mr. S.F. Austin Empresario
I have emigrated to this Colony...
My name is William H.Jack.
Age 25 years, married.
My wife Laura H. age 17.
1 Female child. Moved from Alabama.
Arrived in this Colony 3 June 1830.
June 26, 1830   [Sig] Wm H. Jack

1027. JACKSON, CURTIS M.   [S]
Nacogdoches   16 June 1835
Certify foreigner Curtis M. Jackson
is a man of good...single without
family...
   Jn Egne Michamps Alcalde Interim
[Rev] Accepted in Burnett. A.Henrie

1028. JACKSON, JOHN   [S]
Nacogdoches   2 June 1835
Certify foreigner John Jackson is a
man of good...single without family
   Jn Egne Michamps Alcalde Interim

1029. JACKSON, THOMAS J.   [S]
Nacogdoches   16 June 1835
Certify foreigner Thomas J. Jackson
is a man of good...married with
family...
   Jn Egne Michamps Alcalde Interim
[Rev] Accepted in Burnet. A.Henrie
   On the waters of the Angelina

1030. JACOBS, JOHN   [S]
Nacogdoches   25 Aug 1835
Certify foreigner John Jacobs is a
man of good...single without
family...   Radford Berry
1030a.
Nacogdoches   25 Aug 1835
Mr. Thomas Golightly Sir:
You are to survey the third sitio
which   Mr. John Jacobs will designate...   Geo W. Smyth Comr
[Reverse] The within order has been
executed by Wm Brookfield Sur.

1031. JACOBS, JOHN   [S]
Nacogdoches   3 September 1835
Certify foreigner John Jacobs is a
man of good...single without family
                    Radford Berry
[Reverse] Accepted in Vehlein's.
                    Arthur Henrie
1031a.
Jorge Anto Nixon Esqr Sep 5, 1835
Sir: Please to let the Bearer Mr.
Jno Forbes have the Deed for my
quarter sitio. John X Jacobs
[Sig] John Forbes

1032. JACOBS, WILLIAM [E]
San Augustine   10th of June 1835
William Jacobs a native of the U.S.
is a man of family of three persons
emigrated to Texas in 1830...
                    R.C. McDaniel C.P.O.
1032a.
Nacogdoches   Aug 10, 1835
Mr. Surveyor Sir: You are to survey in Zavala's Grant the sitio
which Mr. W. Jacobs will designate
                    Jorge Anto Nixon Comr

1033. JAIME, VICENTA DIOS DE   [S]
Nacogdoches   21 October 1835
Certify citizen Vicenta Dios de
Jaime is a woman of very good...res-
ident of this Department since 1827
widow with family...has not obtained
land...   Radford Berry

1034. JAMES, JOSHUA   [S]
Nacogdoches   3 June 1835
Certify foreigner Joshua James is a
man of good...married with family...
          G. Pollitt Alcalde Interim
[Reverse] Accepted. Authur Henrie

1035. JAMESON, GEORGE   [E]
San Augustine   June 13, 1835
George Jameson a native of the U.S.
is a man of family consisting of
five persons emigrated to Texas in
1832.   R.C. McDaniel C.P.O.
1035a. Nacogdoches   Aug 11, 1835
Mr. Surveyor Sir: You are to survey in avala's Grant the sitio which
Mr. George Jameson will designate...
          Jorge Anto Nixon Comr

1036. JAMISON, ISAAC   [E]
Town of Austin [de San F.]
22 May 1830   I have emigrated to
this Colony...Isaac Jameison 31
years old married. Margaret my wife
28 years old   2 Male one female
children Occupation farmer. Moved
from Tennessee and arrived in this
Colony 10 Apl 1830 Isaac Jamieson

1037. JANEY, JOHN   [S]
Nacogdoches   3 Aug 1835
Certify foreigner John Ycean is a
man of good...single without family,
resident of this municipality since
1833...
Jn Egne Michamps Alcalde Interim
[On reverse: Young and Yancey]

1038. JETT, JAMES   [E]
Jurisdiction of Liberty Dec 21, 1834
James Jett of Louisiana is a man of
family consisting of his wife and
two children...
    G.A. Pattillo   Comr of Cow Bayou
[Rev] James Jett. Wife 2 children
Adjoining C. West on the northwest.
                    F. Hardin

1039. JETT, JOHN   [E]
Jurisdiction of Liberty Dec 20, 1834
Mr. John Jett a native of Louisiana
is a man of family consisting of
himself and wife...
          G.A. Pattillo Comr
[Note] Zavala's Grant
The place where he now lives on the
Sabine marsh between the mouth of
Snow River and Cow Bayou.
                    J.A. Veatch

1040. JETT, STEPHEN   [E]
Jurisdiction of Liberty Dec 20, 1834
Mr. Stephen Jett a native of Kentuc-

ky is a man of family consisting of
himself and one child...
G.A. Pattillo Comr
[Note] Zavala. The place that is
improved on Adams Bayou.
J.A. Veatch

1041. JEWEL, WINNEY   [E]
San Augustine   30 Aug 1835
Winney Jewel has taken the oath of
allegiance.   Nathan Davis Comr
1041a. [No place, no date]
Winney Jewel a native of North Caro-
lina is a woman of family consisting
of five persons...emigrated in the
year 1830.   Nathan Davis Comr
1041b.
San Augustine   30 Aug 1835
I, Winney Jewel appoint Edward O.
Legrand my attorney to petition for
one league & labor...being an old
settler in this county.
Winnie X Jewel
Witnesses: Peter C. Ragsdale
John Applegate   Richard Haley
Humphrey Chappell   Marke Haley

1042. JOHNS, WILLIAM   [E]
Liberty   27 Dec 1834
Wm Johns a native of Mississippi a
man of family consisting of himself,
his wife &   seven children...
James B. Woods
[Note] Wife & 7 ch Vehlein
Adjoining Benj J. Harper W. Corner
Franklin Hardin

1043. JOHNSON, A.E.C.   [E]
San Augustine   Sept 22d 1834
A.E.C. Johnson a native of Virginia
is a man of family consisting of
four persons
Benjamin Lindsey Alcalde
[Reverse] Achilles E.C. Johnson

1043a. Received of G.A. Nixon.
Robert Foots title, D.J. Woodlief
Title.   A.E.C. Johnson

1044. JOHNSON, ADAM   [S]
Nacogdoches   3 August 1835
Certify foreigner Adam Johnson is a
man of good...single without family
resident since 1832...
Jn Egne Michamps Alcalde Interim

1044a. Nacogdoches   August 3, 1835
Sir: You are to survey the 1/3 sitio
which Mr. Adam Johnson will
designate...   Geo W. Smyth
[Note] Waters of Sabine, North side

1045. JOHNSON, ALVEY R.   [S]
Nacogdoches   19 November 1834
Alvey R. Johnson is a man of good...
has five years in this county...
married with family...Vital Flores
[Note] Wife & 2 children
Burnet = one sitio of land =
Wm Brookfield
1045a.
Nacogdoches   Sept 5, 1835
Mr. Wm Brookfield Sir: You are to
survey the sitio & labor which Mr.
Alvey R. Johnson will designate...
Geo W. Smyth Comr
[Rev] The within order has been
executed by me.
Mr. William Brookfield Survyr
Surveyed Tuesday July 25th 1835

1046. JOHNSON, FRANCIS [S]
Nacogdoches   18 November 1834
Certify foreigner Francis Johnson is
a man of good...married with family
[Note] Wife   Vital Flores
3 Survey on the N. side of Hurricane
Bayou   Wm Robinson. Burnet
1046a.
Nacogdoches   Nov 18th 1834
Sir: You are to survey in Vehlein's
Grant the sitio which Mr. Francis
Johnson will...
Executed by Jeremiah Strode, Surv.

1047. JOHNSON HENRY A.   [S]
Nacogdoches   13 June 1835
Certify foreigner Henry A. Johnson
is a man of good...single without
family...
Jn Egne Michamps Alcalde Interim
[Rev] Accepted in Vehlein. A.Henrie

1048 JOHNSON, JAMES   [E]
San Augustine   Sept 26th 1834
James Johnson a native of Virginia a
man of family consisting of three
persons... Benjamin Lindsey Alcalde

1049. JOHNSON, JOHN   [E]
Jurisdiction of Liberty 24 Apr 1835
John Johnson a native of Louisiana a
man of family...Claiborne West Judge

98

1049a. Nacogdoches 12 September 1835
Certify foreigner John Johnson a man
of good...married with family and
resident of this Department since
1828... Radford Berry
1049b.
Nacogdoches Sept 12, 1835
Sir: You are to survey the sitio &
labor which Mr. John Johnson will
designate... Geo W. Smyth Comr

1050. JOHNSON, JOHN [E]
San Augustine June 15, 1835
John Johnson is a native of New
Jersey, a man of family of a wife...
A. Hotchkiss Primary Judge
[Rev] Accepted in Burnet. A.Henrie

1051. JOHNSON, JOHN D. [E]
District of Sabine 9 June 1835
John D. Johnson a citizen of the
District of Sabine has a family of
five persons...
B. Holt Commissioner
[Rev] Accepted in Zavala. A.Henrie
1051a.
[Field Notes] Beginning corner of
J.D. Johnson's sitio on east bank
Neches...Reported August 20th 1835
John A.Veatch

1052. JOHNSON, JOHN S. [E]
San Augustine Sept 23d 1834
John S. Johnson from evidence of two
witnesses a native of Virginia...man
of family consisting of five persons
Benjamin Lindsey Alcalde

1053. JOHNSON, NATHAN B. [S]
Nacogdoches 21 Sept 1835
Certify foreigner Nathan B. Johnson
is a man of good...widower with
family, resident of this Department
since Mar 1834... Radford Berry

1054. JOHNSON, SOLOMON [E]
San Augustine Octr 18th 1834
Sollomon Johnson is a man of family
consisting of six persons, a native
of Kentucky...
Benjamin Lindsey Alcalde

1055. JOHNSON, WILLIAM [S]
Nacogdoches 14 October 1834
Certify foreigner William Johnson is

a man of good...married with family
Luis Procela
[Note] 7 children = Burnets Colony

1056. JOHNSON, ZACHARIAH C. [E]
San Augustine Octr 18th 1834
Zachariah C. Johnson is a man of
family consisting of two persons & a
native of Kentucky...
Benjamin Lindsey Alcalde
[Note] Has only a wife. Zavala.
On Pine Island Bayou back of Hanks ;
Survey.

1057. JOHNSON, ELIZABETH [E]
Jurisdiction of Liberty 27 Dec 1834
Elizabeth Johnson a native of South
Carolina is a woman of family con-
sisting of herself and five children
J.B. Woods Alcalde

1058. JOHNSTON, HARRISON [E]
Jurisdiction of Liberty 8 June 1835
Harrison Johnston a native of Ken-
tucky is an unmarried man...
Wm Hardin Judge

1059. JOHNSTON, JOSEPH S. [E]
San Augustine April 4, 1835
Jos S. Johnston a native of Kentucky
is a single man... A.Hotchkiss
Primary Judge

1060. JOHNSTON SAMUEL P. [E]
District of Tennehaw 8 August 1835
Samuel P. Johnston is a native of
Georgia is a man of family consist-
ing of five persons...emigrated in
1834... Nathan Davis Comr
[Reverse] Accepted. A. Henrie

1061. JOHNSTON, WILLIAM [E]
San Augustine Sept 26th 1834
William Johnston a native of Ireland
a single man...
Benjamin Lindsey Alcalde

1062. JONES, B.F. [E]
District of Bevil Oct 3d 1835
Sir: You are to survey the sitio &
labor which Mr. B.F. Jones will
designate... Geo W. Smyth Comr

1063. JONES, CRAWFORD [E]
San Augustine Octr 5th 1835
Crawford Jones a native of South
Carolina is a man of family consist-

ing of 3 persons emigrated in 1830
                    Saml Thompson Alcd
1063a.
San Augustine   6th October 1835
I, Crawford Jones appoint James C.
Cain my attorney to petition for one
league & labor of land...
Witnesses   [Sig] C. Jones
E.O. Legrand
Morris May   E.W. Cullen
1063b.
Nacogdoches   Oct 12, 1835
Sir: You are to survey the sitio &
labor which Mr. Crawford Jones will
designate...   Geo W. Smyth Comr

1064. JONES, GEORGE W. [E]
San Augustine   Sept 23d 1834
George W. Jones a native of Tennessee a man of family of three
persons... Benjamin Lindsey Alcalde

1065. JONES, ISAAC
State of Illinois, Gallatin County
                    6th March 1832
We the subscribers have been inti-
mately acquainted with bearer Isaac
Jones Esq. for several years past
and do not hesitate to say...
[About 15 Illinois signatures]

1065a. Nacogdoches 13 Novr 1834
Certify Isaac Jones is a man of
good...has resided in this villa
for some time...   Vital Flores
[Note] Wife & 5 children in Vehlein.
Adjoining the upper line of Prentiss
11 league survey on the W bank of
the Trinity River = next to a league
adjoining it, if an order has already been issued for land claimed.
                    Jeremiah Strode
1065b.
James Dewits   April 19th 1835
Mr. Authur Henrie Esq. Dear Sir:
I have surveyed a sitio of land for
Mr. Jones above Prentiss upper line.
In looking for Prentiss line we
found a line which appeared not to
exceed 2500 varas above Prentiss
line & I run his line to agree with
that [further details of a survey
through Indian lands which apparent-
ly caused a question]   Wm Robinson

1065c.
Major Nixon Sir: August 29th 1835
I do hereby assertify that I was
present at the Coshatty Village when
Mr. Isaac Jones had his sitio of
land surveyed and that Ben Ashes
family and all of the ---? Indians
said they were perfectly willing
for him to survey there.
                    James H. Duncan

1066. JONES, JAMES T. [E]
Municipality of Tennehaw
                    12 August 1835
James T. Jones a native of Kentucky
a man of good...emigrated to this
Country in 1834 with his family of
three persons... Nathan Davis Comr

1067. JONES, JESSE R. [E]
By Thomas Bolling Robertson,
Governor of the State of Louisiana
Certify that Jesse R. Jones...was at
the time of signing the same and is
now Judge for the Parish of St.
Tammany... Fourth day of May 1822
                    Th B.Robertson
1067a.
Jurisdiction of Liberty 10 Sept 1835
Jesse R. Jones is a native of Ten-
nessee is a man of family consisting
of his wife and two children...
                    Wm Hardin Judge
[Rev] Accepted in Vehlein. A.Henrie

1068. JONES, JESSE T. [E]
Naches District   19 Jan 1835
I have been acquainted with Jesse T.
Jones for some time...is a man of
family and of good morals...
                    Wm Whitely Comr
[Note] Wife & 1 child. Burnet

1069. JONES, JOHN [E]
To Mr. S.F. Austin Empresario
I have emigrated to this Colony...
John Jones 38 years old. Married
Mary my wife 30. 4 Male 1 female 6
dependents. Arrived in April.
May 22, 1830   John Jones
1069a.   Austin [de San Felipe]
Mr. S.M. Williams Esq
Sept 12th 1831 From my acquaintance
with Mr. John Jones I believe him an
honorable man...receive a certifi-
cate as a settler...   N. Clay

Mr. S.M. Williams Esqr
Sept 12th 1831
I have been called upon by Mr.
Jones...from my acquaintance with
him I recommend him.   F.W. Johnson

1070. JONES, LEWIS [E]
San Augustine   Sept 22d 1835
Lewis Jones a native citizen of the
Country is a man of family of four
persons.   Nathl Thompson Alc
1070a.
San Augustine   23 Sept 1835
I, Lewis Jones appoint William Ing-
lish my attorney to petition for one
league & labor of land.
               [Sig] Lewis Jones
Witnsses
A.E.C. Johnson   Saml Thompson Alcd
1070b.
Nacogdoches   October 9th 1835
Sir: You are to survey the sitio &
labor which Mr. Lewis Jones will
designate...   Geo W. Smyth Comr

1071. JONES, PHINNEAS [E]
Town of Austin   17 May 1830
To Mr. S.F. Austin Empresario
I have emigrated to this Colony...
Phinneas Jones 23 years old.
Unmarried. Occupation farmer. Moved
from Pennsylvania and arrived in
March 1830.   [Sig] Phineas Jones
[Note] Wants land near Sutherland

1072. JONES, STEPHEN [E]
San Augustine   January 20th 1835
Stephen Jones a native of Virginia
is a man of family consisting of two
persons...   James S. Hanks Alcalde
[Note] Wife. At his improvement on
Bear Creek abt 3 miles above its
junction with the ---
               Zavala.   D. Brown

1073. JONES, WILLIAM [S]
Nacogdoches   3 June 1835
Certify foreigner William Jones ia a
man of good...single without family
Jn Egne Michamps Alcalde Interim
[Rev] Accepted in Burnet. A.Henrie

1074. JONES, WILLIAM [E]
District of Bevil   Octr 10th 1834
William Jones is a native of Geor-

gia...hath a family consisting of
two persons   John Bevil Alcalde
[Note] 2 children. Zavala.
     Where he lives.   D. Brown
1074a.
Mr George Anto Nixon Comr
Oct 4th 1835
You will please deliver to Geo W.
Smyth Esquire my title   Wm Jones

1075. JONES, WILLIS M.C.   [S]
Nacogdoches   16 May 1835
Certify foreigner Willys M.C. Jones
is a man of good...married with
family...   Radford Berry

1076. JORDAN, ELIZABETH
[Type script. "Original missing"]
[Order for Survey and Field Notes]
League and labor situated on the
right bank of the Atascoso...

1077. JORDAN, JAMES [S]
Nacogdoches   18 March 1835
Certify foreigner James Jordan is a
man of good...married with family...
               Radford Berry

1078. JORDAN, JAMES [S]
Nacogdoches   11 May 1835
Certify James Jordan is a man of
good... married with family...
               Radford Berry
1078a.
Mr. George A. Nixon   June 12th 1835
You will pleae deliver my title to
Robert W. Smith...[Sig] James Jordan
Witnesses T.D. Brooks W.F. Allison

1079. JORDAN, JOHN [S]
Nacogdoches   14 October 1834
Certify John Jordan is a man of
good... married with family...
               Luis Procela
1079a.
Major Nixon will please send the
deed for my land by C.M. Lewis
18 Jany 1835   [Sig] John Jordan

1080. JORDAN, JOSEPH   [E]
Municipality of Austin
December 20th 1834 Joseph Jordan is
a native of the U.S. a man of family
of three persons...
               Jesse Grimes   Judge

1080a.
George Anto Nixon Comr   Sir:
Please to send our deeds   by Mr.
Garison Greenwood.
April 20th 1835   Joseph Jordan
William Frost

1081. JORDAN, LEVI   [S]
Nacogdoches   8 September 1834
Certify foreigner Levi Jordan a man
of good...married with family...
Luis Procela Alcalde Interim
1081a.
Maj George Antonio Nixon Commissio-
er. You will please send my Grant by
Col. Strode...   Levi Jordan
February 4th 1835

1082. JORDAN, REDDEN A.   [E]
San Augustine   September 1st 1835
Redden Jordan a native of Tennessee
a single man...emigrated in 1831...
Saml Thompson Alcd
1082a.
San Augustine   Sept 6th 1835
I, Redden A. Jordain appoint Burwell
T. Thompson my agent for an order of
survey   Redding A. Jordan
Wit: A.E.C. Johnson   George H. Jones
Reddin A. Jordan took the oath
7 Sep 1835

1083. JOURDAN, WILLIAM   [E]
St. Augustine   Sept 23, 1834
William Jordan is a native of the
U.S. with a family consisting of six
persons   John Bevil Alc
1083a.
Dept of Nacogdoches October 5th 1835
William Jourdan is a native of South
Carolina and emigrated to Texas in
1825, hath a family consisting of
six persons...   Wm Williams Alcalde

1084. JOYNER, DANIEL   [S]
Nacogdoches   5 June 1835
Certify foreigner Daniel Joyner is a
man of good...married with family...
G. Pollitt Alcalde
[Rev] Accepted in Zavala. A. Henrie

1085. JUAREZ, VICTORIANO   [E]
[Field Notes] Survey of one league

and labor, No. 2, Class third, situated on the River Nueces, behind
the survey of Miguel del Gardo alias
Moria...

1086. KELLEM, LEVI   [E]
New Orleans   May 1, 1830
We the subscribers having known Mr.
Levi Kellem for a length of time...
[4 signatures in New Orleans]
1086a.
Town of Austin   May 24th 1831
Col. S.F. Austin   Sir:
I have emigrated to this Colony...
I am single, 18 years of age
Farmer by occupation, removed from
Louisiana and arrived in this Colony
2d April 1830.   Levi Kellem
[Note] An orphan

1087. KELLER, ANTONIO DANIEL   [S]
Nacogdoches   29 May 1835
Certify foreigner Antonio Daniel
Keller is a man...widower with four
children which are not married...
Jn Egne Michamps Alcalde Interim
[Reverse] Accepted. Arthur Henrie

1088. KELLER, FRANCIS   [E]
To Col. Stephen F. Austin Empresario
I have emigrated to this Colony...
My age is 29 years my wife Lavina
aged 28 years. Oldest child a female
Lucinda 16 months. I was born in the
State of Ohio, came to Texas in the
year 1825 and have been a resident
of your Colony since 12 November
1829 and am professed Roman Catholic
Apostolic and also my family.
March 1830   Francis G. Keller
[Note] Wants the league of land east
of Labaca adjoining above James Kerr
[Reverse]
Lavaca   3 Dec 1834
I have known Mr. F.G. Keller since
August 1825 and can say that his
character...   James Kerr

1089. KELLOGG, ALBERT G.   [S]
Nacogdoches   3 Dec 1834
Certify foreigner A.G. Kellogg is a
man of good...single man...
Vital Flores
[Note] Albert G. Kellogg. Adjoining

James Rowe's survey, Zavala.
                    J.A. Veatch
1089a.
Nacogdoches   Oct 8th 1837
Received of G.A. Nixon
Henery Williams   Wm M. Lumpkins
Owen Linsey   Thomas Linsey
           [by] A.G. Kellogg

1090. KENDRICK, ISAAC   [S]
Nacogdoches   28 May 1835
Certify foreigner Isaac Kendrick is
a man of good...married with family
Jn Egne Michamps Alcalde Interim

1091. KINNARD, MICHAEL   [E]
White Sulphur Springs July 29, 1835
Mr. Gale Borden   Sir:
I have transferred unto Messers.
Martin & Donoho my priviledge and
priority of location to one fourth
league of land adjoining the White
Sulphur Springs... Michael Kinnard
[Reverse]
Enter for Wm McCoy. 1/4 league

1092. KENNARD, WILLIAM S.   [S]
Nacogdoches   25 May 1835
Certify foreigner William S. Kennard
is a man of...married with family...
                    Radford Berry
1092a.
Nacogdoches   May 25, 1835
Mr. Surveyor   You are to survey in
Zavala's Grant the sitio of land
which Mr.   William S. Kenard will
designate... Jorge Anto Nixon Comr
[Note] On waters of Angelina about
40 miles NW Nacogdoches
[Reverse]
The Order changed and not taking up.

1093. KERBY, ISAIAH   [S]
Nacogdoches   25 May 1835
Certify foreigner Isaiah Kerby is a
man of good...married with family...
Jn Egne Michamps Alcalde Interim
[Rev] Burnet's Colony on the Waters
of the Angelina

1094. KENEDY, MARGARET   [E]
[No place or date. See Register]
A Memorandum from Mrs. Kenedy

Margaret Kennidy age thirty seven
moved to the Colony in June 1824.
From Atacapas one son and one daughter. [Atacapas = St.Martin Par. La.]

1095. KERBY, JOHN   [E]
Austin [de San Felipe] 4 April 1832
To Mr. S.F. Austin Empresario
I am desirous of being admitted as a
Colonist...My name is George Kerby
28 years of age. Sarah my wife 20
years. 2 Female children.
From Tennessee [Sig]   John Kirby
[Note] Contract of 1827
[Rev] John Kerby. 20 April 1829
1095a.
Nacogdoches   [S] 5 November 1834
Certify foreigner John Kerby is a
man of good...married with family...
           Vital Flores
[Note] John Kerby wife and three
children. On the Angelina east
branch on the Cherokee trace.
           Burnet. Jeremiah Strode

1095b.   July 25th 1835
Maj George Antonio Nixon
Sir: Please to send me my Grant for
my league of land by Jeremiah Strode
                    John X Kirby

1096. KILLILEY, MARK   [E]
[Field Notes]
Survey one league and labor of land
for Mark Killilly in two surveys.
The first...right bank of the Rio
Frio. The second on the right bank
of the Attascoso.

1097. KIMBALL, GEORGE   [E]
Town of Austin   25 June 1830
To Mr. S.F. Austin Empresario
I have emigrated to this Colony...
George Kimball 22 years of age un-
married. Moved from Luisiana and
arrived in Apr 1830
           [Sig]   George Kimball

1098. KIMBRO, LEMUEL   [E]
San Augustine   Aug 25, 1835
Certify that Lemuel Kimbro is a
citizen of this Country, a native of
Tennessee, a man of family of wife
and two children...emigratd in 1830.
           Saml Thompson Alcd

103

1099. KIMBRO, WILLIAM [E]
San Augustine   Feb 6, 1835
William Kimbro is a native of Tennessee a man of family consisting of
a wife and one child...
              A. Hotchkiss Primary Judge

1100. KINBROUGH, BUCKLY [S]
Nacogdoches   2 May 1835
Certify foreigner Buckly Kimbrough
is a man of good...married with
family...   Radford Berry

1101. KING, EDWARD   [S]
Nacogdoches   6 October 1835
Certify foreigner Edward King is a
man of good...married with family
          G. Pollitt Alcalde Interim
[Rev] Accepted. A. Hotchkiss Agent
for Joseph Vehlein

1102. KING, GRAY B.   [E]
Tenoxtitlan   29 April 1834
To Empresarios Austin and Williams
I have emigrated to Texas...
I am married. [Sig] George G. King
1102a.
Nacogdoches   Oct 9, 1834
Jurisdiction of Liberty
Gray B. King, a native of North
Carolina is a man of family consist-
ing of four in number...
              Wm Hardin Judge
1102b.
San Augustine   Sept 14, 1835
Gray B. King a native of No Carolina
a man of family of five persons...
emigrated to this Country in 1831...
          Saml Thompson Alcd
1102c.
Nacogdoches   Sept 1st 1835
Sir: You are to survey the sitio &
labor which Mr. Gray B. King will
designate...   Geo W. Smyth Comr

1103. KING, JONATHAN   [S]
Nacogdoches   28 September 1835
Certify foreigner Jonathan King is a
man of good...married with family...
     Jn Egne Michamps Alcalde Interim
[Rev] Accepted in Vehlein. A.Henrie

1104. KING, JOSIAH M.   [E]
District of Tenehaw   5 August 1835
Josiah M. King a native of Georgia
is a man of family consisting of

five persons, emigrated in 1834...
          Nathan Davis Comr

1105. KING, WILLIAM   [E]
San Augustine   August 18, 1835
William King is a native of Georgia
a man of family of a wife and four
children...emigrated to Texas in
1830...   A. Hotchkiss P. Judge

1106. KINKEAD, JOHN   [E]
Town of Austin   8 July 1830
I have emigrated to this Colony...
John Kincaid 33 years of age from
Kentucky. Occupation farmer. Arrived
in this Colony in Jany 1826. Swore
to the Constitution.
          [Sig] John Kinkead

1107. KIRBY, THOMAS M.   [E]
[No date or place]
Thomas H. Kirby a native of Missi
sippi is a man of family of two
persons... emigrated in 1830...
          Nathan Davis Comr

1108. KIRKHAM, JAMES   [E]
San Augustine   Sept 22, 1835
James Kirkham a native citizen is a
man of family of eight persons...
          Saml Thompson Alcd
1108a.
San Augustine   23 Sept 1835
I, James Kirkham appoint William
Inglish my attorney to petition for
one league & labor...
          James x Kirkham
Witnesses
A.E.C. Johnson   C. Thompson
Saml Thompson Alcd
1108b.
Nacogdoches   Oct 13th 1835
Sir: You are to survey the sitio &
labor which Mr. Jas Kirkham will
designate...   Geo W. Smyth Comr

1109. KIRKHAM, SPENCER   [E]
Jurisdiction of Liberty 10 Apr 1835
Spencer Kirkham a native of North
Carolina is a man of family of five
children...   Wm Hardin Judge

1110. KIVLAND, MARY BRIDGET
[Field Notes] Survey 1 lg for Mary
Bridget Kivland river Nueces...

1111. [Not found in file]

1112. KNEELAND, DAVID [E]
Town of Austin   3 June 1830
To Mr. S.F. Austin Empresario
I have emigrated to this Colony...
David Kneeland 45 years of age mar-
ried. Silence my wife 41 years.
One female child. Moved from Opelou-
sas and   arrived in the Colony in
May 1830.   [Sig] David Kneeland

1113. KNOWLES, DAVID [S]
Nacogdoches   16 July 1835
Certify foreigner David Knowles is a
man of good...married with family...
                    Radford Berry

1114. KOKERNOT, DAVID L. [E]
Austin   October 9, 1832
To Mr. S.F. Austin Empresario
I have emigrated with my family to
this Country...My name is David L.
Kokernot 23 years of age, a native
of Amsterdam. Am   married.my wife
Caroline 17 years of age. One female
child.   [Sig] D.L. Kokernot
1114a.
Jurisdiction of Liberty 23 Feb 1835
David L. Kokernot a native of Hol-
land is a man of family of his wife
and two children   Wm Hardin Judge

1115. KORN, JESSE [S]
Nacogdoches   9 October 1834
Certify resident of this Villa Jesse
Korn ia a man of good...married in
this Villa in Sor Nuestra Santa
Madre Church...   Luis Procela

1116. KUYKENDALL, ABRAHAM [E]
San Augustine   September 22, 1834
Abraham Kuykendall is a native of
North Carolina, a man of family of
eleven persons...
          Benjamin Lindsey Alcalde

1117. KUYKENDALL, ADAM [E]
Tenoxtitlan   20 Feby 1834
I have emigrated to Texas...
I am single. My age is 24.
          [Sig] Adam Kuykendall

1117a. Mill Creek   Octr 5th 1835
Dear Sir: I wish you to enter for
me a piece of land joining Philip
Right, William Kuykendall & Hill...
          Adam Kuykendall

1118. LACY, JOHN S. [S]
Nacogdoches   26 May 1835
Certify foreigner John S. Lacy is a
man of good...married with family...
Jn Egne Michamps Alcalde Interim
1118a.
J.A. Nixon Esq   Dec 9th 1835
Sir: You will please deliver the
Title for the League which I took on
order from your office to Doctor
J.A. Veatch.   J.S. Lacy

1119. LACY, MARTIN [S]
Nacogdoches   Sept 20, 1834
Certify Martin Lacy is a man of good
moral...Luis Procela Alcalde Interim

1120. LACY, MARTIN [E]
San Augustine   29 Aug 1835
Certify Martin Lacy is a citizen of
the Country, is a native of Mississippi... emigrated in 1831...
          Saml Thompson Alcd

1121. LADD, AMOS [S]
Nacogdoches   25 May 1835
Certify foreigner Amos Ladd is a man
of good...single without family...
Jn Egne Michamps Alcalde Interim

1122. LADD, WILLIAM J. [S]
Nacogdoches   7 May 1835
Certify foreigner William J. Ladd is
a man of good...single without
family...   Radford Berry

1123. LAFFERTY, BENIJHA [S]
Nacogdoches   15 April 1835
Certify foreigner Benijha Lafty is a
man of good...married with family...
          Radford Berry
1123a.
Recd. Nacogdoches   July 21,
1835 of J. Ant Nixon, Mr. Benajah
Lafferty Title...   John Engledow

1124. LAKEY, WILLIAM [E]
San Augustine   Sept 25th 1834
William Lakey a native of North
Carolina is a man of family of eight
persons... Benjamin Lindsey Alcalde
1124a.
G.A. Nixon Esq Dear Sir:
Sept 30th 1835 Please to let Mr.
T.B. Huling have my Land Title...
          [Sig] Wm Laky

1125. LAMB, GEORGE A.   [E]
George A. Nixon Commissioner
15 Sept 1835 We the undersigned do
certify that George A. Lamb is a
native of Kentucky and moved to this
Country in October 1834 of good
character...has a family seven in
number.
Joseph Lindley   Job S. Collard
Wm Ware   James H. Collard
Nat Robbins   E. Collard
Albert Gallatin   George W. Robinson
John B. Long   Wm Robinson
Shelton Allphin
B.B. Goodrich late Comr Precinct
Viesca
[Rev] Accepted in Vehlein. A.Henrie

1126. LANCASTER, ARCHIBALD   [S]
Nacogdoches   26 May 1835
Certify foreigner Archibald Lancaster is a man of good...single without
family...
     Jn Egne Michamps Alcalde Interim

1127. LANDRUM, ZACHARIAH   [E]
Town of Austin   27 May 1830
To Mr. S.F. Austin Empresario
I have emigrated to this Colony...
Zachariah Landrum 64 years old mar-
ried Lettice my wife 54 years old
Moved from Alabama and arrived 20th
Jany   1830.   [Sig] Z. Landrum

1128. LANE, JOHN S. [S]
Nacogdoches   28 May 1835
Certify foreigner John S. Lane is a
man of good...married with family...
     Jn Egne Michamps Alcalde Interim
1128a.
[Field Notes] South side of the
Bayou Pally Gotch for the beginning
corner of J.S. Lanes survey...
               D. Brown Surveyor
1128b.
25th Sept 1835 Recd of Maj Nixon
O.P. Bourlands Title. J.S. Lane
106

1129. LANGDON, L.R.   [E]
San Augustine   1 June 1835
L.R. Langdon is a native of the U.S.
a man of family of six persons that
he emigrated to Texas in 1831...
          R.C. McDaniel C.P.O.
1129a.
Nacogdoches   [No date]
Mr. Surveyor Sir: You are to survey in Zavala's Grant the sitio
which Mr. L.P. Langdon Will designate...   Jorge Anto Nixon Comr

1130. LANGFORD, ALFRED   [E]
San Augustine   7th July 1835
Alfred Langford is a native of Virginia, a man of family of three
persons, emigrated in June 1835...
          R.C. McDaniel C.P.O.
1130a.
Nacogdoches   Aug 15th 1835
Mr. Surveyor Sir: You are to survey in Zavala's Grant the sitio
which Mr. Alfred Langford will designate...   Jorge Anto Nixon Comr

1131. LANKFORD, GARRET M.   [E]
San Augustine   August 19, 1835
Garret M. Lankford a native of Tennessee is a man of family of eight
persons...emigrated in 1829...
     Saml Thompson Alcd

1132. LANKFORD, MARY   [E]
San Augustine   Sept 23d 1834
Mrs. Mary Lankford a native of Virginia is a widow woman of a family
of three persons
          Benjamin Lindsey Alcd

1133. LANIER, BENJAMIN   [S]
Dept of Nacogdoches Dec 19th 1834
Jurisdiction of Liberty
Benjamin Lanier is a native of Geor-
gia a man of family of seven per-
sons, his wife and five children...
          J.B. Woods Judge

1134. LARAMOORE, JOHN   [E]
San Augustine   Oct 20, 1835
John Larimore is a native of the
Territory of Arkansas that he is a
man of family of a wife...emigrated
to Texas in 1832...has taken the
oath.   A. Hotchkiss P. Judge
1134a.
Nacogdoches   Oct 22d 1835
Sir: You are to survey the sitio &

labor which Mr. John Larimore will designate... Geo W. Smyth Comr 1134b.
Nacogdoches   21 October 1835
I, James Laramoor appoint Thomas M. Smullin my attorney to receive an order of survey. [Sig] John Laramora
Witnesses
Enoch Frier   William Coote
Ephraim Talley   Shelby Corzine
A. Hotchkiss

1135. LARY, HENRY B. [S]
Nacogdoches   28 April 1835
Certify foreigner Henry B.Lary is a man of good...single...
Radford Berry

1136. LARY, SAMUEL [S]
Nacogdoches   28 April 1835
Certify foreigner Samuel Lary is a man of good...married with family...
Radford Berry

1137. LATHAM, JAMES [S]
Nacogdoches   27 May 1835
Certify foreigner James Latham is a man of good...married with family...
Jn Egne Michamps Alcalde Interim

1138. LATHAM, JOHN [E]
SanAugustine   August 19th 1835
John Latham is a native of North Carolina a man of family of wife and seven children emigrated to Texas in 1804...   A. Hotchkiss P. Judge

1139. LATHAM, KING [E]
San Augustine   August 19th 1835
King Latham a native of the Country is a man of family of five persons.
Saml Thompsoon Alcd

1140. LATHAM, LEWIS [E]
District of Sabine   May 17th 1835
Lewis Latham a native of Kentucky is now a citizen of the District, has a family of three persons...
B. Holt Comr

1141. LATHAM, LEWIS [S]
Nacogdoches   30 April 1835
Certify foreigner Lewis Latham a man of good...married with family...
Radford Berry

[Note] Married to a woman of the country   Radford Berry

1142. LATHAM, MASTIN [E]
District of Sabine   May 17, 1835
Mastin Latham a native of Kentucky now a citizen of the District, has a family of eight persons...
B. Holt Comr
To: Major Nixon, Nacogdoches

1143. LATHAM, SUSANNAH   [E]
San Augustine   May 19, 1835
Mrs. Susannah Latham is a woman of family of eight children...native of the U.States...that she is a citizen
A. Hotchkiss Primary Judge

1144. LATHER, ROBERT H.   [E]
District of Sabine   Oct 20th 1832
Robert H. Lather a native of Virginia, now a citizen of the Town of San Augustine, has a family of three persons...   B. Holt Commissioner
[Reverse] or Lowther

1145. LATHAM, JEREMIAH [E]
San Augustine   May 18, 1835
Jeremiah Latham is a man of family and a native of North Carolina...
John Bodine Alcalde pro tem

1146. LATTIN, A.D.   [E]
San Augustine   May 18, 1835
A.D. Lattin is a native of Vermont a man of family of a wife and one child... A. Hotchkiss Prmy Judge

1147. LAW, MARTIN   [E]
San Augustine   August 20th 1835
Martin Law a native of Pennsylvania is a single man...emigrated May 1832...   Saml Thompson Alcd

1148. LAW, ROSS
[Original faded. Taken from copy.]
Tennaha   Oct 10, 1835
Ross Law native of Virginia, family of 5 persons, emigrated in 1827.
1149. LAWHON, JUAN   [S]
Nacogdoches   21 November 1834
Certify foreigner Juan Lawhon is a

man of good...married in the Santa
Yglesia [Church]...   Vital Flores
[Note] Wife & 3 children. Zavala
Cane head on the W bank of Snow
River   Wm McFarland

1150. LAWSON, GEORGE P.   [E]
San Augustine   14 January 1835
George P. Lawson a native of Ohio is
a man of family of five persons...
emigrated in the year 1834...
                R.C. McDaniel C.P.O.
1150a.
Nacogdoches   Aug 12th 1835
Mr. Surveyor: You are to survey in
Zavala's Grant the sitio which Mr.
Geo P. Lawson will designate...
        Jorge Ant Nixon Comr

1151. LAWSON, JOHN P.   [E]
San Augustine   May 18, 1835
John P. Lawson is a native of Georgia...a man of family of a wife and
one child... A. Hotchkiss P. Judge

1152. LAZARIN, JULIO   [S]
Nacogdoches   15 August 1835
Certify citizen Julio Lazarin is a
man of good...resident of this Municipality since the year 1827...has
not obtained land... Radford Berry

1153. LAZARIN, MARCELINO   [S]
Nacogdoches   15 August 1835
Certify citizen Marcelino Lazarin is
a man of good...resident of the
Municipality since 1827...has not
obtained land... Radford Berry

1153a. Nacogdoches   August 15, 1835
Mr. George Aldrich   Sir:
You are to survey the sitio & labor
which Mr. Marcelino Lazarin will
designate... Geo W. Smyth Comr

1154. LEACH, RACHEL   [E]
San Augustine   May 23d 1835
Rachel Leach a native of Tennessee
is a widow woman of family of three
persons...   Nathan Davis Comr

1155. LEAL, FRANCISCO   [E]
[Field Notes] Survey of one league
and labor for Francisco Leal E. bank
Nueces between Thomas Pew and John
Canoles...

1156. LEAL, LUIS
[Field Notes] Survey of one third
for Luis Leal on East bank of Nueces
back of Francisco Leal...

1157. LEBARD, ELIJAH   [E]
Maj. Nixon will please send the deed
for my land... [Sig] Elijah LeBard
18th Jany 1835

1158. LEE, ISAAC   [S]
Nacogdoches   5 August 1835
Certify foreigner Isaac Lee is a man
of good...wants title to land he
settled...resided here since 1827,
married with family...
            Radford Berry
1158a. Nacogdoches   August 5th 1835
Mr. Brookfield Sir: You are to
survey the sitio & labor which Mr.
Isaac Lee will designate...
            Geo W. Smyth Comr
[Reverse]
The within order has been executed
by me.   William Brookfield

1159. LEE, ISAAC   [S]
Nacogdoches   20 September 1834
Certify foreigner Isaac Lee is a man
ofgood...   Vicente Cordova

1160. LEFTWICH, JESSE   [E]
Town of Austin   [no date]
To Mr. S.F. Austin Empresario
I have emigrated to this Colony...
Jesse Leftwich 55 years old.
Married. Sarah my wife 42 years old.
Merchant. Three male six female
children. Moved from Tennessee,
Maury County. Arrived in this Colony
April 1830. [Sig] Jesse Leftwich

1161. LEGRAND, EDWIN O.   [E]
San Augustine   December 3d 1834
Edwin O. Legrand a native of No
Carolina is a man of family of three
persons... E. Rains Acting Alcalde

1162. LEMOYN, GEORGE W.   [S]
Nacogdoches   17 September 1835
Certify foreigner George W. Lemoyn
is a man of good...single without
family...   Radford Berry
[Rev] Accepted in Vehlein. A.Henrie

1163. LEPURN, MICHAEL [E]
[Typescript: "Original Missing"]
Tenoxtitlan   22 May 1834
To Empresarios Austin & Williams
Application to be admitted as a
Colonist. I am unmarried my age 22
years   Miguel Lepurn
Who requested me to sign for him.
                    F.W. Johnson

1164. LESLEY, JAMES   [E]
District of Sabine   [no date]
Jas Lesley is a native of New York,
has a family of two persons...emi-
grated in 1833.   B. Holt Comr

1165. LESSLEY, LIMON D.   [E]
San Augustine   4 June 1835
Limon D. Lessley a native of Virginia is a man of family of four
persons...emigrated to the Country
in January 1835...
                    R.C. McDaniel C.P.O.
1165a.
Nacogdoches   .   Aug 20th 1835
Mr. Surveyor   Sir: You are to survey in Zavala's Grant the sitio
which Mr. Limon D. Lessley will
designate...Jorge Anto Nixon Comr
[Note] West side of the Neches

1166. LESTER, JOSIAH   [E]
Town of Austin   29th April 1830
I have emigrated to this Colony...
Josiah Lester 37 years old married
Solita my wife 33 years old
Four male children. Ocupation far-
mer. Moved from Louisiana and ar-
rived in Decr 1829
                [Sig] Josiah Lester

1167. LEWIS, BARBARA C.   [S]
Nacogdoches   October 9, 1834
Certify widow Barvara C. Lewis is a
woman   of very good...
                    Luis Procela

1168. LEWIS, H.K.   [E]
Town of Austin   21 May 1830
To Mr. S.F. Austin Empresario
I have emigrated to this Colony...
Henry K. Lewis 37 years old. Unmar-
ried. Moved from Kentucky and ar-
rived in this Colony in Feby 1829.
                [Sig]   H.K. Lewis

1169. LEWIS, JOHN T. [L?]   [E]
District of Ayish   12th Jany 1833
This day personally appeared John T.
Lewis late of Louisiana who removed
to this neighborhood Jany
1830...took the oath.
William McFarland Alcalde
1170. LEWIS, JOHN T.
District of Bevil   April 11th
1835   John T. Lewis of the U.S.
has a family of four persons...
Wm Williams Alcalde
1171. LEWIS, LORENO TAYLOR DE   [S]
Nacogdoches   24 April 1835
Certify foreigner Loreno Taylor de
Lewis is a woman of very good...with
family...   Radford Berry

1172. LEWIS, MARTIN B.   [E]
District of Bevil   April 11st 1835
Martin B. Lewis is a native of Indiana, hath a family of seven persons.
            Wm Williams Alcalde
1172a.
District of Ayish   12th January 1833
Martin B. Lewis who has resided in
this neighborhood since Jany 1830
who removed from Louisiana to this
place...took the oath.
        William McFarland Alcalde
[Note] M.B. Lewis, family of 7
persons   1830 August 30th.
Where he lives on Big Cow Creek.
            William McFarland

1173. LEWIS, PATSEY   [E]
San Augustine   September 23d 1834
Patsey Lewis a native of South Carolina is a widow of a family of four
persons... Benjamin Lindsey Alcalde

1174. LEWIS. SAMUEL L.   [E]
District of Bevil   April 11th 1835
Samuel L. Lewis a native of Tennessee hath a family of four persons...
        Wm Williams Alcalde
1174a.
District of Ayish   28 Jany, 1833
Saml L. Lewis Esqr who took the
oath...testimony of his servants and
other property being in Texas since
Jany 1830 and the final arrival of
himself and family in Texas between
the 1st and fifth of March 1832.
            Wm McFarland Alcalde

1175. LEWIS, WASHINGTON   [S]
Nacogdoches   28 March 1835
Certify foreigner Washington Lewis
is a man of good...widower with
family...   Radford Berry

1176. LEWIS, WILLIAM   [S]
Nacogdoches   18 June 1835
Certify foreigner William Lewis is a
man of good...married with famiily
Ene Egne Michamps Alcalde Interim
[Rev] Accepted in Zavala. A.Henrie

1177. LEWIS, WILLIE   [E]
San Augustine   Sept 22d 1835
Willie Lewis a native of the Country
is a man of family of seven persons
                Saml Thompson Alcd
1177a.
San Augustine 22d Sept 1835
I, Willie Lewis have appointed Wil-
liam Inglish my attorney to petition
for one league and labor...
                [Sig] Willie Lewis
Witnesses
A.E.C. Johnson
C. Thompson   Saml Thompson Alcd
1177b.
Nacogdoches   October 9th 1835
Sir: You are to survey the sitio &
labor which Mr. Willie Lewis will
designate...   Geo W. Smyth Comr

1178. LINVILLE, RICHARD   [S]
Nacogdoches   18 Dec 1834
Certify foreigner Ricardo Linbel is
a man of good...married with family
                Vital Flores
[note] On Lewis improvement adjoining Spears Survey on the Arroyo
upper line = four children =
Richard Linville.   Thos McFarland
[Rev] Accepted in Zavala. A.Henrie

1179. LINDLY, JONATHAN   [E]
San Jacinto   October 31st 1834
To the Alcalde at Nacogdoches
We certify that we have been acquainted with the Bearer Mr. Jonathan Lindly for some time past and
have no hesitation in recommend-
ing...   Joseph Lindly
                Nat Robbins
[Note] North side of Cushati trace
about 5 miles from his fathers survey...
110

1180. LINDLEY, JOSEPH   [E]
State of Tennessee, Henry County
                28th Jany 1827
We the undersigned...certify that we
are acquainted with Joseph Lindley.
[Signed by 3 Justices of the Peace]
[Note] At the place he has improved
=Vehlein = Rankin Wife & 4 children

1181. LINDLEY, SAMUEL   [E]
State of Illinois, Fayette Co.
                Sept 27, 1835
Mr. Samuel Lindley has resided in
this State about 20 years during
which time we have known him...
                [Officials signing]
[Note] Wife & 12 children. Vehlein
Abt 1-1/2 miles south Cooshatte
trace on branch of the San Jacinto

1182. LINDSEY, JAMES   [E]
Town of Austin   26 April 1830
To Mr. S.F. Austin Empresario
I have emigrated to this Colony...
James Lindsey 30 years old unmar-
ried. Occupation, carpenter & farm-
er. Moved from Kentucky and arrived
in Decr 1827. [Sig] James Lindsay

1183. LINDSEY, BENJAMIN   [E]
San Augustine   22 Sept 1834
Benjamin Lindsey a native of Tennessee is a man of family of eleven
persons...   E. Rains First Regidor

1184. LINDSEY, CHARLES   [E]
San Augustine   6 Sept 1835
Charles Linsey is a native of South
Carolina a man of family of seven
persons...emigrated to Texas in 1824
has taken the oath.
            Nathan Davis Commissioner
1184a.
San Augustine   September 1835
I, Charles Linsey appoint Wm Jones
my attorney to obtain an order of
survey... [Sig] Charles Lindsey
Witness: J.S. Johnston
[Note] The order of survey to call
for his improvements where he lives

1185. LINDSEY, ISAAC   [E]
San Augustine   November 30th 1834
Isaac Lindsey a native of Georgia

a man of family of three persons...
James W. Bullock Alcalde pro tem
[Note] Wife and one child. Zavala
On Taylors Bayou. G.Smyth Surveyor

1186. LINDSEY, ISAAC [E]
San Augustine   26 Sept 1834
Isaac Lindsey...a native of South
Carolina is a man of family of five
persons... Benjamin Lindsey Alcalde
The above named party has been duly
sworn.

1187. LINDSEY, JOHN [S]
Nacogdoches   1 November 1834
Certify foreigner John Lindsey is a
man of good...married with family...
                        Vital Flores
[Note] Wife and six children.Vehlein
On the Trinity west to Hardins.
                        Hirom Sur.

1188. LINDSEY, OWEN [E]
San Augustine   Sept 27th 1834
Owen Lindsey a single man and native
of Louisiana...
           Benjamin Lindsey Alcalde

1189. LINDSEY, PENNINGTON [E]
San Augustine   6 Sept 1835
Pennington Linsey a native of South
Carolina is a man of family of two
persons...emigrated to Texas in 1824
taken the oath.
           Nathan Davis Commissioner
1189a.
San Augustine   12 September 1835
I, Pennington Linsey appoint Wm
Jones my attorney to obtain an order
of survey...[Sig] Pennington Lindsey
Witness: J.S. Johnston

1190. LINDSEY, THOMAS [E]
District of Ayish September 17, 1835
Thos Lindsey a native of Louisiana
has a family of two persons...emi-
grated to Texas in 1824...
B. Holt Comr of the Sabine District
1190a.
District of Sabine   17 Sept 1835
I, Thomas Lindsey of the District of
Ayish Buyo empower W.H. Landrum to
act for me in procuring an order of
survey...   [Sig] Thomas Lindsey
Witness: B. Holt Comr
Wm Earl   Larkin Gross

1191. LINDSEY, THOMAS [E]
San Augustine   22 Sept 1834
Thomas Lindsey a native of Louisiana
is a single man...
           Benjamin Lindsey Alcalde

1192. LINNEY, HENRY [E]
Town of Austin   5 June 1830
To Mr. S.F. Austin Empreario
I have emigrated to this Colony...
Henry Linney 50 years of age. Widow-
er. 2 Male 1 female children.
Occupation farmer. Moved from the
State of Kentucky arrived in the
Country in 1823 and in this Colony
in May 1830.   Henry X Linney

1193. LINEY (LUNEY), PATSY [E]
San Augustine   May 19, 1835
Patsy Luney is a woman of family of
two children...
           A. Hotchkiss Prmy Judge
[Reverse] Patsey Luney.
Accepted in Zavala. A. Henrie
[Note in pencil: Liney]

1194. LINSEY, MICAJAH [E]
San Augustine   6 Sept 1835
Micajer Linsey a native of South
Carolina a man of family of two
persons...emigrated to Texas in
1824, has taken the oath...
           Nathan Davis Comr
1194a.
San Augustine   12th Sept 1835
I, Micajah Linsey have appointed Wm
Jones my attorney to obtain an order
of survey   [Sig] Micajer Linsey
Witness: J.S. Johnston

1195. LITTLE, DYER B. [S]
Nacogdoches   28 April 1835
Certify foreigner Dyer Blithe is a
man of good...single...
           Radford Berry

1196. LITTLE, HIRAM [E]
San Jacinto   18 Aug 1835
Hiram Little is a native of Illinois
is a man of family of four persons
B.B. Goodrich Comr Prect of Viesca
[Rev] Accepted in Vehlein. A.Henrie

1197. LITTLE, JOHN [S]
Nacogdoches   19 Sept 1834
Certify foreigner Jno Little is a
                                   111

man of good...
                Luis Procela Alcalde Interim
[Reverse]   John Little
1197a.
Mr.a G.A. Nixon Dear Sir:
Please deliver my title to Mr. Jos
Durst   Jany 25th 1835
            [Sig] John Litle

1198. LITTLE, WALTER   [E]
Jurisdiction of Liberty May 13,1835
Certify that Walter Little is a
citizen of this Colony, a man of
family of himself & wife and three
children...   Edwd Tanner
Primary Judge in the 3d Instance

1199. LITTLE, WILLIAM   [S]
Nacogdoches   11 Sept 1835
Certify foreigner William Little is
a man of good...married with family
                      Radford Berry
[Rev] Accepted in Vehlein. A.Henrie

1200. LLOYD, WILLIAM M.   [E]
San Augustine   August 18th 1835
William M. Lloyd a native of Tennessee is a single man...emigrated in
1828...   Saml Thompson Alcd

1201. LOBAN, THOMAS   [E]
San Augustine   Sept 1st 1835
Thomas Lobar a native of South Car-
olina a man of family of two per-
sons, emigrated in 1831...
            Saml Thompson Alcd
[Reverse]   Thomas Loban

1202. LOCK, JOHN   [E]
San Augustine   Oct 10th 1835
John Lock a native of Tennessee a
man of family of five persons...
emigrated in 1829
            Saml Thompson Alcd
1202a.
San Augustine   Oct 10th 1835
I authorize Samuel Stivers to peti-
tion for one league and labor...
            [Sig] John Lock
Witnesses: E.O. Legrand
           Saml Thompson, Alcd

1203. LOCKHART, SAMUEL   [E]
San Felipe de Austin July 14, 1830
To Mr. S.F. Austin Empresario
I have emigrated to this Colony...
My name is Samuel Lockhart aged 45
112

years. My wife Winey aged 34. One
male child. Removed from Louisiana.
Arrived in this Colony in June 1830.
Occupation farmer.
            [Sig] Samuel Lockhart

1204. LOCKRIDGE, NICHOLAS   [E]
Clinton   Nov 17, 1829
Col. S. Austin   Dear Sir:
The Bearer Nicholas Lockridge is an
inhabitant of Louisa and I take the
liberty of introducing him to you.
His object in visiting Texas...
                Ed. W. Ripley
1204a.
San Felipe de Austin   6 July 1830
To Mr. S.F. Austin Empresario
I have emigrated to this Colony...
My name is Nicholas Lockridge aged
53 years. My wife Alsey aged 45
years. Five male children, five
female children. One servant.
Removed from Louisiana. Arrived in
this Colony in April last.
            [Sig] N. Lockridge

1205. LOGAN, WILLIAM   [S]
Nacogdoches   30 October 1834
Certify a resident of this Munici-
pality Guillermo G. Logan is a man
of good...married with family...
                Vital Flores
[Note] On the waters of the San
Jacinto adjoining Mr. Briscoes
survey.   S.C.Hirom
1205a.
Nacogdoches   Decr 1st 1835
Recd of Geo Anto Nixon
Copies of the titles of Miguel Cor-
tinas, Juan Carmon, Miguel Tores,
Manuel Tascan & Luterio Lopez.
                Wm G. Logan

1206. LOGAN, WILLIAM M.   [E]
Jurisdiction of Liberty 7 Apr 1835
Wm M. Logan is a native of Tennessee
is an unmarried man..Wm Hardin Judge
[Rev] Accepted Vehlein. A.Henrie

1207. LONGBOTHAM, ROBERT B.   [S]
Nacogdoches   14 Oct 1834
Certify foreigner R.B. Longetcham is
a man of good...married with family
                Luis Procela
[Reverse] Robert B. Longbotham
Adjoining N. Robbins survey. Vehlein
Wife and 7 children

1208. LOPEZ, FELICIANO [S]
Nacogdoches   8 September 1835
Certify citizen Feliciano Lopez is a
man of good...resident of this Municipality since 1828...married with
family...has not obtained land...
            Radford Berry

1209. LOPEZ, JOSE LEONICIO [S]
Nacogdoches   6 April 1835
Certify citizen Jose Leonicio Lopez
is a resident of this Municipality
for many years...married with family
has not obtained land...
            Radford Berry

1210. LOPEZ, JUAN   [S]
Nacogdoches   31 July 1835
Certify citizen Juan Lopez is a
resident of this Municipality for
many years...arried with family...
has not obtained land
            Radford Berry

1211. LOPEZ, PEDRO   [S]
Nacogdoches   15 August 1835
Certify citizen Pedro Lopez is a
man of good...resident of this Municipality since 1825...single without
family, has not obtained land...
            Radford Berry

1212. LORCHE, SEVERAN   [E]
State of Louisiana, Par. of Ouachita
                     Sept 28th 1831
To the Honble Stephen F. Austin,
Texas. I have known Mr. Saverin
Lorche the bearer for twenty years,
he being raised a near neighbor...
Oliver Jeleongon   Par. Judge
1212a.
Monroe, La.   October 1831
Col. Stephen F. Austin   Dear Sir:
I have taken the liberty of making
known to you Mr. Sovern Lorche, a
native of the parish who goes to
your colony in my company with a
view of making a permanent settle-
ment.   J.W. Mason
1212b.
Town of Austin   19 Octr 1831
To Mr. S.F. Austin Empresario
Having emigrated to this Country...
Severan Lorche 21 years of age.
Married. Moved from Luisiaia and
arrived in the Colony Octr 183-
[blank]   [Sig] Severin Larche

1213. LOSOYA, DOMINGO
[Field Notes] One league for Domingo Losaya situated on the south
side of the Medina River, below the
Rio Grande road in McMullin's Colony

1214. LOUT, PINCKNEY   [E]
San Augustine   November 1sr 1834
Pinckney Lout is a native of Indiana
a man of family of four persons...
            Benjamin Lindsey Alcalde
[Note] Pinckney Lout wife and two
children East side of Neches the
place improved by Platiller. Zavala.
            J.A. Veatch

1215. LOVE, WILLIAM   [E]
San Augustine   May 19, 1835
William Love is a native of South
Carolina, a single man...
            A. Hotchkiss Primary Judge

1216. LOW, ELI   [E]
Presink of Sabine   14 December 1834
Eli Low a native of Tennessee a man
of family of eight persons...
            Elbert Hines Commissioner
1216a.
Mr. G.A. Nixon Sir:
Let Mr. Isaac Low have my land title
August 15th 1837   [Sig] Eli Low

1217. LOW, ISAAC   [E]
We the undersigned citizens of
McNairy & Hardin Counties, Tennessee, have been personally acquainted
with Isaac Low (a farmer)...
25 May 1828
            [50 signers in Tennessee]
1217a.
Sabine District   26 April 1830
Mr. Isaac Low from Tennessee emigrated to this District in August 1828,
with family   David Hines Alcalde

1218. LOWRY, JOHN   [E]
Tunahaw District   Sept 26, 1835
John Lowry a native of Louisiana is
a single man...emigrated in 1821...
            Nathan Davis Commissioner
1218a.
Tunahaw District   Sept 26th 1835
I authorize Richard Hala to apply
for an order of survey...
            John X Lowry

1219. LUCAS, JOHN   [E]
San Augustine   April 3 1835
John Lucas a native of New Jersey is
a man of family of seven persons...
        A. Hotchkiss Prmy Judge

1220. LUCAS, ROBERT   [E]
San Augustine   June 12, 1835
Robert Lucas a native of New Jersey
a man of family of nine children...
        A. Hotchkiss Prmy Judge
[Rev] Accepted in Zavala. A.Henrie

1221. LUCE, WILLIAM   [S]
Nacogdoches   3 November 1834
Certify foreigner William Luce a man
of good...married with family...
                Vital Flores
[Note] Wife and five children
1221a.
Nacogdoches   18th May 1835
Mr. George A. Nixon Esq
You will please send my title by
Martin Lacy.   [Sig] William Luce

1222. LUMBRERA, ANISETA   [S]
Nacogdoches   20 June 1835
Certify citizen Aniseta Lumbrera is
a res   ident of this Municipality
for many years, woman of good...
widow with family...has not received land...   G. Pollitt Alcalde
1222a.
Nacogdoches   Sept 10, 1835
Sir: You are to survey the sitio &
labor which Mrs. Aneseta Lumbrera
will designate   Geo W. Smyth Comr

1223. LUMPKIN, WILLIAM   [S]
Nacogdoches   21 November 1834
Certify foreigner William Lumpkin is
a man of good...married with family
                Vital Flores
[Note] Wife & four children.
E. Line Weekes survey =
                Burnet = J.Strode

1224. LUMPKIN, WILLIAM M.   [S]
Nacogdoches   9 Oct 1835
Certify foreigner Wm M. Lumpkin is a
man of good...married with family...
resident of this Department since
1832...   Radford Berry

1225. LUNA, GERTRUDIS   [S]
Nacogdoches   6 April 1835
Certify citizen Gertrudis Luna a
resident of this Municipality and
born here, widow with family, has
not obtained land...Radford Berry

1226. LUNA, MANUEL DE
[Field Notes] Survey number 3, class
one, for Manuel de Luna. Situated on
the south side of the Medina River,
about 14 miles from Bexar in
McMullin's Colony...
[Rev] Manuel de la Luna 1 league

1227. LUND, OLIVER   [E]
Naches   October 1, 1835
I have been acquainted with Oliver
Lund for some considerable time...
without any family, a house carpen-
ter by occupation...Wm Whiteley
        Comr for the Naches Precinct
[Note] Emigrated to this State in
1833
[Reverse] Recd of Geo W. Smyth the
Order of Survey of Oliver Lund.
October 14, 1835   W.S. McDonald

1228. LUSK, GEORGE V.   [E]
San Augustine   May 25, 1835
George V. Lusk a native of So Caro-
lina a man of family of four persons
                Nathan Davis Comr
1228a.
San Augustine   23 Feb 1834
George V. Lusk [takes the oath of
allegiance]
        A. Hotchkiss Primary Judge

1229. LUSK, ROBERT O.   [E]
San Augustine   August 30, 1835
Robert O. Lusk a native of Kentucky
a man of family of two persons...
emigrated to this Country in 1833...
        Nathan Davis Commissioner
1229a. San Augustine   30 Aug 1835
Robert O. Lusk has taken the oath of
allegiance.   Nathan Davis Comr
1229b. San Augustine   30 Aug 1835
I, Robert O. Lusk appoint Edward O.
Legrand my attorney to petition for
one league and labor...
                Robert O. Lusk
Witnesses
Richard Haley   Archibald Smith
Jess Amason   John Haley

1230. LUSTER, THOMAS [E]
Austin   15 March 1833
I have emigrated to this Country...
Thomas Lester 33 years of age
Sarah my wife 21 years of age
2 Male 1 female children
Moved from Ohio and arrived this
month   [Sig] Thomas Luster

1231. LYNCH, STEPHEN [S]
Nacogdoches   8 Sept 1835
Certify foreigner Stephen Lynch is a
man of good...widower with family
and resident of this Department
since 1825...has not   obtained
land...   Radford Berry
1231a.
Nacogdoches   Sept 9, 1835
Sir: You are to survey the sitio &
labor which Mr. Stephen Lynch will
designate...   Geo W. Smyth Comr

1232. LYON, JAMES M.   [S]
Nacogdoches   28 April 1835
Certify foreigner James M. Lynch a
man of good...married with family...
                    Radford Berry

1233. MABBITT, L.H.   [E]
San Augustine   24 Sept 1834
L.H. Mabbitt is a native of Arkansas
Territory, a single man...
                    John Bevil Alcd
1233a.
San Augustine   24 Sept 1834
Mr. Surveyor: You are to survey in
Zavala's Grant the sitio which Mr.
Leonard H.Mabbitt will designate...
                 Jorge Anto Nixon Comr
[Note] At the place described by M.
                    G.W. Smyth

1234. MACKEY, NAOMI   [E]
Precinct of Sabine October 1st 1834
Naomi Mackey is a native of Georgia,
a woman of family of six persons...
                  Elbert Hines Comr

1235. MADDEN, JAMES   [E]
Naches   June 8th 1835
I certify that I have been acquainted with James Madden for some time
say three or four years...a man of
family...   William Whiteley
                  Comr Naches Precinct

1236. MADRIGAL, FELIPE   [E]
San Augustine   August 19, 1835
Feilie Madregal is a man of family
consisting of three children...a
native Mexican.
             A. Hotchkiss P. Judge

1237. MAGINNIES, JOHN   [E]
San Augustine   April 3d 1835
John Maginnies a native of Virginia
is a man of family of five persons.
             A. Hotchkiss Pmy Judge

1238. MAHAN, TIMOTHY   [E]
San Augustine   August 20, 1835
Timothy Mahan is a native of Kentucky a man of family consisting of two
children, came into Texas in 1824.
             A. Hothkiss P. Judge
1238a.
San Augustine   August 20, 1835
Sir: You are to survey the sitio &
labor which Mr. Timothy Mahan will
designate...   Geo W. Smyth Comr

1239. MAIN, MICHAM   [E]
Naches   May 9, 1835
I have been acquainted with Micham
Main for some considerable time. He
is a man of family and has been in
the Country about two years. He is a
farmer...   William Whiteley
             Comr for the Naches Pct

1240. MALLOY, JOHN THOMAS
[Field Notes] Survey one league and
one labor for John Thomas Malloy in
two surveys...between the forks of
the head waters of Aransas Creek...

1241. MALONE, JOHN   [S]
Nacogdoches   26 May 1835
Certify foreigner John Malone is a
man of good...single without family
   Jn Egne Michamps Alcalde Interim
1241a.
Mr. George A. Nixon   Dear Sir:
Please to send me my title by the
bearer Mr. W.F. Alleson...
June 13th 1835   John X Malone
Witnesses
Thos D. Brookes
Robt W. Smith

115

1242. MALONE, WILLIAM T.   [E]
San Augustine   August 19, 1835
W.T. Malone is a native of Mississippi a man of family of wife and
two children...emigrated to Texas in
1812...   A. Hotchkiss P. Judge

1243. MALY, JULIANA   [E]
Jurisdiction of Liberty 23 Feb 1835
Juliana Maly is a woman of family of
two children...   Wm Hardin Judge
[Reverse] Grant the order for this.
                    Nixon

1244. MANCHACA, FRANCISCO   [S]
Nacogdoches   21 July 1835
Certify citizen Francisco Manchaca
is a man of good...single without
family...has not obtained land...
                    Radford Berry

1245. MANENT, JACQUE & GABRIEL [E]
Town of Austin   6 July 1830
To Mr. S.F. Austin Empresario
I have emigrated to this Colony...
Gabriel Manent native of France 26
years of age. Unmarried. Arrived in
this Colony June 1830. Removed from
France.   [Sig] G. Manent
Town of Austin   6 July 1830
To Mr. S.F. Austin Empresario
I have emigrated to this Colony...
Jacque Manent native of France 24
years of age unmarried. Moved from
France and arrived in June 1830.
              [Sig] J. Manent
[Witness?] Bertrand Manent

1246. MANING, STEPHEN
We the undersigned certify that we
have been acquainted with Mr. Stephen Maning for several years while
he lived in the neighborhood where
he now lives...
Brooklyn   Augt 13, 1831
[About 60 signatures]
[Note] Wife & 5 children at the
mouth of Nelson's Creek. Vehlein.
                    Wm Rankin

1247. MANLOVE, BARTHOLOMEW   [E]
Austin   April 26, 1832
To Mr. S.F. Austin Empresario
I am desirous of becoming a colon-
ist...My name Bartholomew Manlove 57
years of age. Married. Moved from
Kentucky where his family resides.
116

Abarella. Two [?] sons, five
daughters   [Sig] B. Manlove
Passport dated 2d April

1248. MANN, LEVI   [S]
Nacogdoches   28 May 1835
Certify foreigner Levi Mann is a man
of good...single without family...
Jn Egne Michamps Alcalde Interim
[Rev] Accepted. Arthur Henrie

1249a. MANSFIELD, ISAAC   [E]
Austin   15 September 1832
To Mr. S.F. Austin Empresario
I have emigrated to this Country...
Isaac Mansfield 46 years of age,
single. Native of Connecticut and
arrived in this Colony in June 1832.
          [Sig] Isaac Mansfield

1250. MANSOLA, JUAN BAUTISTA   [S]
Nacogdoches   18 July 1835
Certify citizen Juan Bautista Mansola is a man of good...single without
family...has not received land...
                    Radford Berry
1250a.
Nacogdoches   August 4, 1835
Sir: You are to survey the 1/3
sitio which Mr. Juan Bautista Mansola will designate...
              Geo W. Smyth Comr

1251. MANSOLA, JOSE MARIA   [S]
Nacogdoches   25 August 1835
Certify citizen Jose Maria Mansola
is a man of good...resident of this
Municipality and born here...has not
received land...   Radford Berry

1252. MANSOLO, ANTONIO   [S]
Nacogdoches   7 September 1835
Certify citizen Antonio Mansolo is a
man of good...resident of this Municipality and born here...married
with family....   Radford Barry

1253. MANWARING, WILLIAM   [E]
Nacogdoches   June 4th 1833
Messrs Austin & Williams
Villa of Austin
Gentlemen: William Manwaring a na-
tive of England, unmarried...thirty
five...wishes to settle in your
Colony...Mr. Manwaring has lived
with me for the last four months
as a gardner...   Adolfo Sterne

1253a. Nacogdoches   20 April 1835
Certify foreigner William Manwaring
is a man of good...single without
family...   Radford Berry

1254. MARDEZ, ABNER   [E]
Jurisdiction of Liberty 10 Sep 1835
Abner Mardez is a native of Virginia
a man of family of his wife and
seven chldren...   Wm Hardin Judge
[Rev] Accepted in Vehlein. A.Henrie

1255. MARIOTINY, MARY ANN   [S]
Nacogdoches   10 May 1835
Certify foreigner Mary Ann Mariotiny
is a woman of very good...widow with
family...   Radford Berry

1256. MARIWATHER, JOHN   [E]
District Of Tenehaw   Aug 12th 1835
John Mariwather is a native of No
Carolina a man of family of nine
persons...emigrated in 1833...
            Nathan Davis Comr

1257. MARSHALL, JOHN   [E]
Town of Austin   4 March 1830
To Mr. S.F. Austin Empresario
I have emigrated to this Colony...
John Marshall 48 years old, married.
Leah my wife 44. Occupation farmer
Five male, one female children
Moved from Arkansas and arrived in
this Colony in Jany 1830.
            [Sig] John Marshal

1258. MARSHALL, SAMUEL B.   [S]
Nacogdoches   29 April 1835
Certify foreigner Samuel B. Marshall
is a man of good...married with
family...   Radford Berry

1259. MARSHALL, WILLIAM   [S]
Nacogdoches   3 August 1835
Certify foreigner William Marshall
is a man of good...single without
family...resident of this Municipality since 1827...
Jn Egne Michamps Alcalde Interim

1260. MARTIN, DANIEL   [S]
Nacogdoches   13 October 1835
Certify foreigner Daniel Martin is a
man of good...married with family
and resident since 1833...
            Radford Berry

1261. MARTIN, EDMOND H.   [S]
[Passport] New Orleans 9 June 1832
To Edmund H. Martin native of the
U.S. to go on the Am. Schooner Bras-
oria, to Brasoria on personal
business.

1262. MARTIN, ENRIQUE   [S]
Nacogadoches   19 November 1834
Certify Mr. Enrique Martin is a man
of good...married with family...
            Vital Flores
[Note] Wife = Vehlein = 8 miles
beyond his fathers survey.
            Wm Robinson

1263. MARTIN, HENRY   [E]
District of Sabine   27 May 1832
Mr. Henry Martin who emigrated to
this District with his family from
Alabama in March 1822. Wishing to
remove to Austin's Colony...
            Jas Gaines Alcalde
[Note] Wife and 5 children.
Burnet's Col. Three Cabin Bayou abt
15 miles from the road. Wm Robinson
1263a.
Nacogdoches   Nov 7th 1834
Mr. Wm Robinson, Surveyor Sir:
You are to survey in David G. Bur-
net's Grant the sitio which Mr.
Henry Martin will designate...
        Jorge Anto Nixon Comr
[Note] On 3 Cabin Bayou about 15
miles above the St. Antonio road

1264. MARTIN, PHILIP   [S]
Nacogdoches   4 April 1835
Certify foreigner Felipe Martin is a
man of good...married with family...
            Radford Berry
1265. MARTIN, NIEL   [S]
Nacogdoches   3 Sept 1834
Certify Mr. Niel Martin came to this
jurisdiction in 1827...living in
this Municipality as a resident
since that year...a man of good...
            Luis Procela

1266. MARTIN, TOLLIVER   [E]
Town of Austin   26 May 1830
To Mr.S.F.Austin Empresario
I have emigrated to this Colony...
Toliver Martin 36 years old married
Elisabeth my wife. Moved from South
Carolina and arrived in this Colony
in Feby 1830.   Tolliver Martin

1267. MARTINEZ, DIONISIO
[Field Notes] Survey number one, in
class one of one league for Dionisio
Martinez on the south side of the
Medina below the Rio Grande Road...

1268. MARTINEZ, JOSE MARIA   [S]
Nacogdoches   29 April 1835
Certify citizen Jose Maria Martinez
is a man of good...married with
family...has not obtained land...
                    Radford Berry
1268a.
Nacogdoches   May 14, 1835
Mr. Nickeon will please deliver to
Mr. R.W. Smith my title.
          Hosea Mirea x Martinez
Witnesses Jesse H. Chambers
          Wm Reagan

1269. MARTINES, JUANA
Received of the Comr Jorge Antonio
Nixon Title of a league of land
belonging to Juana Martinez situated
in Zavala's Colony
  A. Sterne agent for Juana Martinez

1270. MASCORO, MARIA GRACIA   [S]
Nacogdoches   9 April 1835
Certify citizen Maria Gracia Mascoro
resident of this Municipality for
many years is a widow with family...
has not obtained land...
                    Radford Berry

1271. MASON, JAMES   [E]
Presink of Sabine   14 December 1834
James Mason a native of South Carolina a man of family of seven
persons...   Elbert Hines Comr
[Note] James Mason wife and five
children. Adjoining south of McNealy's survey. Zavala.   T. McFarland

1272. MASON, JAMES   [E]
San Augustine   Sept 2, 1835
James Mason a native of South Carolina a man of family of wife and
four children...emigrated in 1830.
          A. Hotchkiss P.Judge
1272a.
Nacogdoches   Oct 22d 1835
This day before me Mr. George W.
Smyth came James Mason by his attorney Thomas Smullin and made protest
against the survey made by [blank]
Hoffman on a tract of land lying on
118

the Patroon in the neighborhood of
James Mason's settlement, said tract
situated on the claim of said Mason.

1273. MASON, JAMES Y.   [E]
San Augustine   Oct 6, 1835
James Y. Mason a native of Virginia
is a man of family of three persons
emigrated in 1829, has taken the
oath.   Saml Thompson Acld
1273a.
San Augustine   6 October 1835
I, James Y. Mason appoint James C.
Cain my attorney to petition for one
league and labor...
          [Sig] James Y. Mason
Witnesses   E.O. Legrand
Moris May   E.W. Cullen

1274. MASON, JOHN   [E]
San Augustine   27 September 1835
John Mason a native of South Carolina...emigrated in 1830 a man of
family of eight persons...took the
oath.   Saml Thompson Alcd
1274a.
San Augustine   Sept 28th 1835
Mr. Commissioner: Mr. Thomas M.
Smullin is by me authorized to receive from you an order of survey
for league & labor...
          [Sig] John Mason
Witness: George English

1275. MASTERS, JACOB SR.   [S]
Nacogdoches   30 October 1834
Certify foreigner Jacob Mosbers is a
man of good...married with family...
                    Vital Flores
[Note] Masters. Wife and 2 ch.
[Reverse]   Jacob Masters Sr.

1276. MASTERS, JACOB JR.   [S]
Nacogdoches   30 October 1834
Certify foreigner Jacob Mosbers,
son, is a man of good...married with
family...   Vital Flores
[Note] Wife and 3 children.
                    Wm Robinson
[Reverse]   Jacob Masters, Jr.

1277. MATHEWS, JOHN   [S]
Nacogdoches   9 Oct 1835
Certify foreigner John Mathews is a

man of good...married with family
and resident of this Department
since 1833.   Radford Berry
1277a.
Sir: You are to survey the sitio &
labor which Mr. John Mathews will
designate...   Geo W. Smyth Comr

1278. MAY, GEORGE   [S]
Nacogdoches   4 May 1835
Certify foreigner George May is a
man of good...married with family...
                    Radford Berry

1279. MAY, MORRIS   [S]
Nacogdoches   7 March 1835
Certify foreigner Morris May is a
man of good...married with family...
                    Radford Berry
1279a.
San Augustine   August 20th 1835
Morris May a native of Georgia is a
man of family of three persons...
emigrated to this Country in 1828...
        Saml Thompson Alcd

1280. MAYES, ANDREW   [E]
Austin   June 2, 1832
To Mr. S.F. Austin Empresario
I have emigrated to this Country...
My name is Andrew Mayse. I am mar-
ried 32 years of age. My wife Mary
Anne 22 years of age. 1 Male 2 fe-
male children. Moved from Alabama
and arrived in this Colony 2d June
1831.   [Sig] Andrew Mayes

1281. MAYES, WILLIAM D.   [E]
Town of Austin   June 17, 1830
To Mr. S.F. Austin Empresario
I have emigrated to this Colony...
William D. Mayes 24 years old, un-
married. Occupation farmer. Moved
from Mississippi and arrived in this
Colony in Jan [?] 1830
              [Sig] W.D. Mayes

1282. MAYFIELD, ALFRED   [E]
San Augustine   Oct 6, 1835
Alfred Mayfield a native of Mississippi is a man of family of five
persons...emigrated in 1830...
           Saml Thompson Alcd

1282a.
San Augustine   6th October 1835
I, Alfred Mayfield appoint James C.
Caincy attorney to petition for one
league and labor...
        [Sig] Alfred Mayfield
Witnesses   E.O.Legrand
E.W. Cullene   Morris May

1283. MAYFIELD, JOHN E.   [E]
Jurisdiction of Liberty 1 Feb 1835
John E. Mayfield a native of Kentucky is a man of family of his wife
and two children   Wm Hardin Judge

1284. MAYO, JOHN W. ´ [E]
San Felipe de Austin   Feb 26th 1830
Col S.F. Austin Sir:
We have been for some length of time
acquainted with Mr. John W. Mayo...
an honest and industrious man...
          Joshua Fletcher
          J. White
1285. MAXWELL, THOMAS   [E]
San Augustine   March 28, 1835
Thomas Maxwell a native of Tennessee
a man of family of six persons...
          R.C. McDaniel Sindico

1286. MEANS, RACHEL   [E]
District of Sabine   June 5th 1835
I the undersigned, a citizen of the
Sabine District, appoint William
Meanes (my son) to act for me...my
Title for a league of land...not
knowing how to write...
B. Holt Comr.   Rachel X Meanes
1286a.
District of Sabine   June 6th 1835
Rachel Meanes a native of Georgia
now a citizen of this District, has
a family of three persons...
              B. Holt   Comr

1287. MEANS, WILLIAM   [E]
[District of Sabine]   [No date]
William Meanes a native of Georgia
has a family of four persons,
farmer...   B. Holt Comr
[Note] Accepted in Zavala. A.Henrie

1288. MEDINA, JUAN JOSE   [S]
Nacogdoches   4 April 1835
Certify citizen Juan Jose Medina a
resident of this Municipality for

many years, married with family...
not received land... Radford Berry

1289. MELTON, ELIZABETH   [E]
San Augustine   Sept 1st 1835
Elizabeth Melton a native of Georgia
is a widow woman of family of three
persons...emigrated in 1824...
              Saml Thompson Alcd

1290. MELTON, WILLIAM   [S]
San Augustine   Oct 18, 1835
William Melton a native of Alabama
is a man of family of two persons...
emigrated in 1830...
              John Chumney 2 Regidor

1291. MENARD, MICHAEL B.   [E]
Jurisdiction of Liberty Octr 8, 1834
Mr. Michael B. Menard a native of
Canada is a man of family and good..
              Wm Hardin Prim. Judge

1292. MENARD, PETER J.   [E]
Jurisdiction of Liberty 5 Decr 1834
Peter J. Menard is a native of Illinois is a man of family of himself
and wife...   Wm Hardin Judge

1293. MENCHACA, JOSE NASARIO [S]
Nacogdoches   11 May 1835
Certify citizen Jose Nasario Menchaca is a resident of this Municipality and born here, single...has not
received land...   Radford Berry

1294. MENCHACA, MARIA SOLEDAD   [S]
Nacogdoches   7 April 1835
Certify citizen Maria Soledad Menchaca is resident of this Municipal=
ity for many years and a woman of
very good...widow with family, has
not received land.. Radford Berry

1295. MENDEZ, CATALINA   [S]
Nacogdoches   7 September 1835
Certify citizen Catalina Mendez is a
man of good...resident of this Municipality since 1825...married with
family, has not received land...
              Radford Berry

1296. MERCER, GEORGE R.   [S]
Nacogdoches   Sept 12, 1835
Certify foreigner George R. Mercer

is a man of good...married with
family, resident in this Department
since October 1833   Radford Berry
[Rev] Accepted in Vehlein. A.Henrie

1297. MERCHANT, LITTLEBERRY   [E]
San Augustine   August 19th 1835
Littleberry Merchant a native of
Tennessee a single man...emigrated
1st March 1832 Saml Thompson Alcd

1298. MERCHANT, EDWARD A.   [E]
San Augustin   August 19th 1835
Edward A. Merchant a native of South
Carolina a man of family of six
persons...emigratd in 1829.
              Saml Thompson Alcd

1299. MERCHANT, JOHN DILLER   [E]
San Augustine   August 19th 1835
John D. Merchant a native of South
Carolina a man of family of eight
persons...emigrated Feruary 1832.
              Saml Thompson Alcd

1300. MERRY, JOHN   [E]
Jurisdiction of Liberty 24 Apr 1835
John Merry a native of Virginia is a
man of family of four children...
              Wm Hardin

1301. MESENHAMA, JACOB   [E]
San Augustine   Sept 23d 1835
Jacob Mesenhama a native of Germany
is a man of family of eight persons
emigrated in 1830...
              Saml Thompson Alcd
1301a.
San Augustine   23d Sept 1835
I, Jacob Mesenhama appoint William
Inglish my attorney to petition for
one league & labor...
              Jacob X Mesenhama
Witnesses   C. Thompson
A.E.C. Johnson Saml Thompson, Alcd
1301b.
Nacogdoches   October 9th 1835
You are to survey the league and
labor which Mr. Jacob Mesenhama will
designate   Geo W. Smyth Comr

1302. MESSENHAMA, JOHN   [E]
San Augustine   Sept 23d 1835
John Mesenhama a native of Germany
is a man of family of two persons...
emigrated in 1830...
              Saml Thompson Alcd

1302a. San Augustine 23d Sept 1835
I, John Mesenhama do appoint William
Inglish my attorney to petition for
one league & labor...
                    John X Mesenhama
1302b.
Nacogdoches   October 1835
Sir: You are to survey the sitio &
labor which Mr. John Mesenhama will
designate...   Geo W. Smyth Comr

1303. MICHAEL, JAMES   [E]
Dept. of Sabine   7 June 1835
James Michael is a native of Alabama
now a citizen of this Department...
                    B. Holt Comr
[Rev] Accepted in Zavala. A.Henrie

1304. MICHAMPS, JUAN EUGENE   [S]
Nacogdoches   29 May 1835
Certify Mr. Juan Eugene Michamps 1st
Regidor and Alcalde Interim for
this Municipality is a man of good
widower with family...
    G. Pollitt 1st Regidor
    Antonio Menchaca Sindico
[Rev] Accepted. Arthur Henrie

1305. MIDDLETON, J.F.   [E]
San Augustine   15th May 1835
J.F. Middleton a native of the U.S.
is a man of family of five persons
emigrated in 1829...
              R.C. McDaniel C.P.O.
[Reverse] Accepted. A. Henrie
1305a.
Nacogdoches   August 9, 1835
Mr. Surveyor Sir: You are to survey in Zavala's Grant the sitio
which Mr. J.F. Middleton will
designate... Jorge Anto Nixon Comr

1306. MIDKIFF, CANDIS   [S]
Nacogdoches   3 December 1834
Certify Mrs. Candis Midkiff is a
woman of good...widow with children...   Vital Flores
[Note] Candis Midkiff widow 3 children. Adjoining his[sic] brothers
league.   Burnet

1307. MIDKIFF, ISAAC J.   [S]
Nacogdoches   3 December 1834
Certify foreigner Isaac J. Midkiff
is a man of good...married with
family...   Vital Flores
[Note] Isaac J. Midkiff. Wife and

child. Burnett. West side of the
Trinity about 12 miles above Robbins
about 6 miles from the river
                    J. Strode

1308. MIGUEL, JOSE SAN   [S]
Nacogdoches   15 June 1835
Certify citizen Jose San Miguel is a
resident of this Municipality and
born here...single without family...
not obtained land
    Jn Egne Michamps Alcalde Interim
[Rev] Accepted in Burnet. A.Henrie

1309. MILHOMME, DAVID   [S]
Nacogdoches   4 December 1835
Certify foreigner David Milhomme is
a man of good...married with family
    Jn Egne Michamps Alcalde Interim
[Rev] Accepted in Vehleins Grant.
A. Hotchkiss Atty for Joseph Vehlein

1310. MILLARD, ROBERT F.   [S]
Nacogdoches   18 April 1835
Certify foreigner Robert F. Millard
is a man of good...married with
family...   Radford Berry

1311. MILLER, CHARLES B.   [S]
Nacogdoches   1st May 1835
Certify foreigner Charles B. Miller
is a man of good...single without
family...   Radford Berry

1312. MILLER, EDWARD   [E]
San Augustine   9 March 1835
Mr. Edward Miller a native of Ken-
tucky is a man of family of five
persons, that he emigrated in Janu-
ary 1835...   R.C. McDaniel C.P.O.
[Reverse] Accepted. A. Henrie
1312a.
Nacogdoches   August 12, 1835
Mr.Surveyor   You are to survey in
Zavalas Grant the sitio which Mr.
Edwd Miller will designate...
                    Jorge Anto Nixon Comr

1313. MILLER, FREDERIC   [E]
Jurisdiction of Liberty 12 Jan 1835
Frederic Miller a native of Louisiana a man of family his wife and
seven children   John Stewart
    Comr Precinct Cow Bayou
[Note] On the Spring Gullies = 6
miles from the Neches E side.
                    Zavala

1314. MILLER, J.B.   [E]
[No place or date]   Mr. Williams
Dear Sir: You will please put the
name of James Clark on the land adjoining the McNeals, on the east
side of the Bernard he has examined
as you directed me to inform him to
do and is much pleased with.
                    J.B. Miller
1315. MILLER, JOHN   [E]
District oBevil   October 6th 1834
John Miller is a native of Tennessee
hath a family of twelve persons...
                    John Bevil Alcalde

1316. MILLER, LEROY   [E]
San Augustine   October 23d 1834
Leroy Miller is a native of Alabama
a single man...
        Benjamin Lindsey Alcalde
[Note] Leroy Miller adjoining Solo-
mon Millers's Survey. Zavala.
                    D. Brown

1317. MILLER, MATHEW S.   [E]
San Augustine   October 23d 1834
Mathew S. Miller a native of Alabama
a single man...
        Benjamin Lindsey Alcalde
[Note]   Head waters of Cow Bayou.
Zavala   Adjoining Henry's Survey.
                    D. Brown
1317a.
Recd of Majr Nixon Comr
Mathew S. Miller's Title.
Decr 8, 1835   Solomon Miller

1318. MILLER, PHILIP   [E]
Jurisdiction of Liberty 26 Dec 1834
Philip Miller a native of Kentucky a
man of family of his wife and two
children...   Wm Hardin Judge

1319. MILLER, RUTHY   [E]
Municipality of Austin   Jan 2d 1835
Mrs. Ruthy Miller is a native of the
U.S. a widow woman of family of
seven persons   Jesse Grimes Judge
[Note] 7 child. Vehlein. Rankin.
Department of the Brasos on the E
Branch of San Jacinto below Prentis'
claim.

1320. MILLER, SOLOMON   [E]
San Augustine   Sept 22d 1834
Solomon Miller a native of the U.S.
a single man...Benjamin Lindey Alc
122

1321. MILLER, WILLIAM   [S]
Nacogdoches   26 September 1835
Certify foreigner William Miller is
a man of good...married with family
                    Radford Berry
[Rev] Accepted in Burnet. A.Henrie

1322. MILLS, GRANVILLE   [S]
Nacogdoches   28 July 1835
Certify foreigner Granville Mills is
a man of good...married with family.
                    Radford Berry
[Reverse] Granville Mills.
                    Arthur Henrie

1323. MILLSPAUGH, WILLIAM   [E]
Precinct of Cow Bayou 3d Dec 1834
Mr. William Millspaugh a native of
New York is a Mechanic of the Black-
smith trade   E.A. Pattillo Comr
[Note] Wm Milspaugh. Single. Zavala
The place called hackberry on Cow
Bayou, 4th sitio.   F. Hardin

1324. MILTON, FRANCIS   [S]
Nacogdoches   17 Sept 1834
Certify citizen Francis Milton is a
resident of very good...married in
Santa Madre Church...
        Luis Procela Alcalde

1325. MILTON, MINISTER L.   [E]
San Augustine   24 September 1834
Minister L. Milton a native of Ohio
a single man...
        Benjamin Lindsey Alcalde

1326. MILTON, WILLIAM K.   [E]
San Augustine
Wm K. Milton is a native of Georgia
a man of family of [blank] persons
        A. Hotchkiss Primary Judge
[Note] About eleven miles above the
San Antonio Crossing of Naches at
Williamses on the East side of
Naches River
[Note added on the same sheet]
Admitted on the 25th of February &
refused Cook, although he has been
settled 18 mo in the Country &
raised a crop. Also refused the Rev.
Reed who came in Oct last into the
Country and said that his instruc-
tions did not allow him to receive
anyone henceforth...without his pay-
ing a premium, so the R.R. told me.
If so why why did he admit Melton?

1327. MITCHELL, ELIZABETH   [E]
San Augustine   Sept 1st 1835
Elizabeth Mitchell a native of Virginia is a widow woman of family of
two persons...emigrated in 1830...
                Saml Thompson Alcd

1328. MITCHELL, JAMES   [S]
Nacogdoches   22 Sept 1834
Certify foreigner James Mitchell is
a man of good...married with family
          Luis Procela Alc Int

1329. MITCHELL, JAMES   [E]
Naches   March 19, 1835
I have been acquainted with James
Mitchell for some time he is a man
of good character. He is a man of
family. His occupation is farmer...
          William Whiteley Comr
          for the Naches District
1329a.
Nacogdoches   March 21st 1835
Mr. Surveyor Sir: You are to sur-
vey in Burnet's Grant the sitio
which Jas Mitchel will designate...
          Jorge Anto Nixon Comr
[Note] Adjoining James Box on the
  Trinity

1330. MIX, NATHANIEL   [E]
District of Bevil Sep 28th 1835
Nathaniel Mix a native of Pennsyl-
vania is a single man...
          Wm Williams Alcalde
[Rev] Accepted in Zavala in place of
John Lewis who has declined taken
land as a Colonist by the former
from the applicant. 1/4 Sitio.
          Arthur Henrie

1331. MOLINA, CARMEN
[Field Notes] Survey of one league
and one labor for Carmen Molina on
the right bank of En Medio Creek...

1332. MOLINA, JUAN
[Field Notes] Survey of one league &
labor for Juan Molina on the right
bank of the En Medio Creek...

1333. MOLINA, JUAN DE DIOS
[Field Notes] Survey of one league &
labor for Juan de Dios Molina...
right bank of the En Medio Creek...

1334. MOLINA, TORIBIO
[Field Notes] Survey of one league &

labor for Toribio Molina on the left
bank of Nueces River...
1334a.
[Field Notes] Survey for Theodoro
Molina of one league & labor on the
right bank of En Medio Creek...

1335. MONETT, NARCESSE   [E]
District of Sabine Sept 15, 1835
Narcesse Monett a native of Louisi-
ana...emigrated in 1829...
               B. Holt Comr
[Note] P.S. and has a family of
          three persons.
1335a. District of Sabine 16 Sep1835
We, Ramsey Christy & Narcece Monett
of the District of Sabine empower
W.H. Landrum to act for an order of
survey...   Ramsey X Christy
Witness   Narcece X Mone tt
B. Holt   Jas Hughes

1336. MONROE, AUGUSTUS G.   [E]
San Augustine   Sept 5, 1835
Augustus G. Monroe a native of Vir-
ginia is a man of family of four
children... A. Hotchkiss P. Judge
[Rev] Accepted in Vehlein. A.Henrie

--   MONSON, LEWIS C.
[Typescript "Original Missing"]
Brazoria   9 November 1833
Lewis C. Monson took the oath before
me this day.   Henry Smith

1337. MONTGOMERY, DENNIS C.   [E]
San Augustine   12 May 1835
Dennis C. Montgomery a native of the
U.S. and emigrated in 1834 that he
has a family of five persons...
          R.C. McDaniel C.P.O.
1337a.
Nacogdoches   Aug 8, 1835
Mr. Surveyor You will survey in
Zavala's Grant the sitio which Mr.
Dennis C. Montgomery will designate
          Jorge Anto Nixon Comr
[Not] On the west side of the River
  Neches

1338. MOONEY, RICHARD   [E]
District of Tenehaw Sept 3d 1835
Richard Mooney a native of Mississippi is a man of family of four
persons...emigrated 1830...
          Nathan Davis Comr

1339. MOORE, D.S.D.   [E]
San Augustine   April 23, 1835
D.S.D. Moore is a citizen and was as
early as 1826...
          A. Hotchkiss Prmy Judge

1340. MOORE, JOHN
[Field Notes] Beginning corner of
John Moore's sitio on the Sabine
River north of G.S. Bowl survey...
          Pennington Surveyor

1341. MOORE, JOHN   [E]
Town of Austin   3 July 1830
To Mr. S.F. Austin Empresario
I have emigrated to this Colony...
John Moore 54 years of age. Widower.
Occupation farmer. 2 Female 1 male
children. Moved from Louisiana and
arrived in the Colony in Apr 1830.
          [Sig] John Moore

1342. MOORE, JOHN   [E]
San Augustine   26 September 1834
John Moore is a native of N. Caroli-
na a man of family of eight persons
          Benjamin Lindsey Alcalde
[Note] 6 Children.Vehlein's Grant
About 6 miles from Mr. Townson

1343. MOORE, JOHN   [S]
Nacogdoches   28 May 1835
Certify foreigner John Moore is a
man of good...married with family...
Jn Egne Michamps Alcalde Interim

1344. MOORE, JOHN
[Field Notes] Beginnig corner of
John Moore's sitio...waters of
Heusing Bayou...on the waters of
Bear Creek...

1345. MOORE, JOHN   [E]
San Augustine   Sept 27th 1834
John Moore is a native of Virginia a
man of family of three persons...
          John Bevil Alcalde

1346. MOORE, URIAH   [S]
Nacogdoches   14 October 1834
Certify Foreigner U. Moore is a man
of good...married with family...
          Luis Procela
[Note] Uriah Moore has wife and two
children. Place where he has improved.

124

1347. MOORE, URIAH   [E]
To the Empresarios Austin & Williams
I have emigrated to Texas...
I am married. My wife's name is
Ester and have three children. My
age 26 my wife 23 years.
          [Sig] Uriah Moore
1347a.
Major Nixon will please send the
deed for my land.
3d March 1835 [Sig] Uriah Moore

1348. MOORE, VINSON   [S]
Nacogdoches   18 Sept 1834
Certify foreigner Vinson Moore is a
man of good...married with family...
          Luis Procela Alcalde Interim
1348a.
Nacogdoches   Nov 27, 1835
Recd of G.A. Nixon Commissioner for
Burnett's Grant the Title belonging
to Vinson Moor for one sitio of
land.   John D--ts

1349. MORA, ESTEBAN   [S]
Nacogdoches   6 April 1835
Certify citizen Esteban Mora is
resident of the Municipality, born
here, married with family...has not
received land...   Radford Berry

1350. MORA, ESTEBAN   [S]
Nacogdoches   28 August 1835
Certify citizen Esteban Mora is a
man of good...resident of this Municipality...married with family...
not received land... Radford Berry
1350a. Nacogdoches   29 August 1835
Sir: You are to survey the sitio
and labor which Stephen Mora will
designate...   Geo W. Smyth Comr

1351. MORA, FRANCIS X. DE
Nacogdoches   Dec 6th 1834
Mr. Jeremiah Strode Sir: You are
to survey in Vehlein's Grant the
sitio which Mr. Francis X. de Mora
will designate...
          Jorge Anto Nixon Comr
[Note] West side of the Trinity
joining Menard & McKenneys seven
league tract

1352. MORALES, ANDRES   [S]
Nacogdoches   6 June 1835
Certify citizen Andres Morales is a
man of good...resident of this

Municipality for many years, married
with family...has not received
land...   G. Pollitt Alcalde
[Reverse]   Accepted in Vehlein as he
lives there   A. Henrie

1353. MORELAND, ISAAC N.   [E]
Jurisdiction of Liberty 26 Decr 1834
Isaac N. Moreland is a native of
Georgia is an unmarried man...
          Wm Hardin Judge

1354. MORELAND, JOHN W.   [S]
Nacogdoches   2 May 1835
Certify foreigner John W. Moreland
is a man of good...married with
family...   Radford Berry

1355. MORENO, YNES   [S]
Nacogdoches   27 October 1835
Certify citizen Ynes Moreno ia a man
of good...resident of this Department since 1831...single without
family...has not received land...
          Radford Berry

1356. MORGAN, CHARLES   [E]
Jurisdiction of Liberty 24 Nov 1834
Mr. Charles Morgan a native of Ten-
nessee is a man of family of himself
and wife...   Wm Hardin Judge
[Note]   On the Sabine at Powers
Bluff. Zavala.   Franklin Hardin

1357. MORGAN, HENRY   [E]
San Augustine   August 29th 1835
Henry Morgan native of New York is a
single man...emigrated in 1829...
          Saml Thompson Alcd

1358. MORGAN, HUGH   [S]
Nacogdoches   19 May 1835
Certify foreigner Hugh Morgan is a
man ofgood...married with family...
          Radford Berry

1359. MORGAN, JAMES   [S]
Nacogdoches   16 January 1835
Certify foreigner James Morgan is a
man of good...married with family...
          Radford Berry
[Note]   Floating ord. Vehlein
Wife 2 ch.   Hiroms

1360. MORGAN, JOSEPH   [S]
Nacogdoches   13 December 1834
Certify foreigner Josef Morguen is a
man of good...married with family...
          Vital Flores
[Note]   Joseph Morgan. Wife and one
child. On the Cushatti Trace about
half way to from the Trinity to the
Alabama Village. Vehlein.
          S.C. Hiroms

1361. MORRIS, ALFRED   [E]
San Augustine   August 20, 1835
Alfred Morris is a native of Georgia
has family of a wife and one child.
Emigrated in 1833...
          A.Hotchkiss Prmy Judge

1362. MORRIS, ELISHA   [E]
San Augustine   22 Sept 1834
Elisha Morris a native of Alabama a
man of family of three persons...
          Benjamin Lindsey Alcalde
[Note]   Wife and one child. About 5
or 10 miles above Ashworth's Ferry
on the Nueces   J.A. Veatch
1362a.
Recd of Maj Nixon   Dec 10th 1835
The title of Elijah Morris.
          Geo W. Smyth

1363. MORRIS, RITSON   [E]
Austin   Novr 12, 1832
To Mr. S.F. Austin Empresario
I have emigrated in this Country...
My name is Ritson Morris 32 years of
age. Am married. My wifes name Min-
erva 23 years of age. I have two
female children.
          [Sig]   Ritson Morris

1364. MORRIS, SHADRACK   [E]
Presink of Sabine October 5th 1834
Shadrack Morris a native of Kentucky
is a man of family of nine persons.
          Elbert Hines Commissioner
[Note]   Wife and 7 children.
          Adjoining McRim
1364a.
Sabine District   May 10th 1835
Maj Nixon Sir: Have the goodness
to send my title by John A. Veatch.
          [Sig]   Shadrack Morris

1365. MORRIS, WILLIAM [E]
Precinct of Viesca   Novr 30th 1834
We certify that we are acquainted
with William Morris. Mathew Hubert
   James Foster Comr Pct Viesca

1366. MORRISSON, EDMOND [E]
District of Bevil   Feb 7th 1835
Edmund Morrisson native of Maryland
hath a family of six persons...Mr.
E. Morrisson it is believed came
into the Country in January 1825.
      Wm Williams Alcalde
[Note] Unfinished

1367. MORSE, HENRY [E]
Town of Austin   17 May 1830
To Mr. S.F.Austin Empresario
I have emigrated to this Colony...
Henry Morse aged 34 years married
Elisa W my wife 28 years. Two male
one female children. Three depend-
ents. Moved from Mississippi and
arrived in this Colony in April
1830.   [Sig] Henry Morse

1368. MORTON, DAVID S. [E]
[A list with no place or year]
Octr 20-Octr 31
David S. Morton Ala 23 years Farmer
Mary his wife 17 years
Martha Stanback widow 50 years
Susan Ann Anderson widow 19 years 1
male.   Wm Wright wife & family
Thomas Wright wife & family
[This list was copied into Austin's
"Register of Families" for Octr 20-
31, 1835]

1369. MORTON, JOHN [E]
Sulphur Fork Prairie, Dept of Texas
Mr. George W. Smyth Sir: [no date]
Dr. Rowe Surveyor acting under your
orders has without my knowledge or
consent surveyed a league for James
Smith in which he has included my
house & farm...He has also tres-
passed on a survey made for Cavan-
augh...I therefore protest...
            John Morton

1370. MORVAN, JOSEPH [S]
Nacogdoches   26 May 1835
Certify foreigner Joseph Morvan is a
man of good...married with family...
Jn Egne Michamps Alcalde Interim

1371. MORROW, THOMAS [E]
Tenoxtitlan   31 March 1834
To Empresarios Austin & Williams
I have emigrated to Texas...
I am a widower. My age 74 years.
   [Sig] James Morrow

1372. MORROW, THOMAS [E]
Tenoxtitlan   28 Feby 1834
To the Empresarios Austin & Williams
I have emigrated to Texas...
I am married my wifes name is Eliza-
beth and have four children. My age
32 my wife 28. [Sig] Thomas Morrow

1373. MOSELEY, ROBERT J. [E]
State of Tennessee
Nashville   Feby 28, 1830
I am informed that Doctor Socrates
S. Moseley and his brother Mr. Robert J. Moseley are about to visit
the Mexican Province of Texas. These
young gentlemen have been raised to
the vicinity of this place...
   Wm Carroll Governor of Tennessee
1373a.
To Mr. S.F. Austin Empresario [no
date] I have emigrated to this
Colony...Robert J. Moseley 24 years
old. One dependant. Moved from Tennessee and arrived in this Colony in
April 1830. [Sig] Robert J. Moseley
[Note] Has a pass from 26 for a year
to remove from Tennessee

1374. MOSELEY, SOCRATES S. [E]
To Mr. S.F. Austin   May 17, 1830
I have emigrated to this Colony...
Socrates S. Moseley 27 years of
age. Unmarried. Physician moved from
Tennessee and arrived in this Colony
in April 1830. [Sig] S.S. Moseley

1375. MOSS, JAMES [E]
San Augustine   October 23rd 1834
James Moss a native of Virginia is a
single man...   Benjamin Lindsey
              Alcalde
1376. MOSS, MARK [E]
Austin   August 20, 1832
To the Empresarios Austin &
Williams   I have emigrated to
this Country...My name is Mark Moss

My name is Mark Moss by birth an
Englishman. My age 30 years. Unmarried. I arrived in this Colony July
22, 1832.   [Sig] Mark Moss

1377. MOSS, NATHANIEL   [E]
Jurisdiction of Liberty 27 Dec 1834
Nathaniel Moss a native of Virginia
is a man of family of his wife and
two children   Wm Hardin Judge
[Note] Unfinished

1378. MOTT, FRANKLIN   [E]
District of Bevil October 2d 1835
Franklin Mott a native of Alabama
and emigrated 1833, hath no family
                 Wm Williams Alcalde
[Note] Unfinished

--   MOST (MAST), JACOB   [S]
Nacogdoches   4 April 1835
Certify foreigner Jacob Maste is a
man of good...married with family...
                       Radford Berry

1379. MOTT, JOSEPH   [E]
District of Bevil Oct 10th 1834
Joseph Mott a native of S. Carolina
hath a family of seven persons...
              John Bevil Alcalde
[Note] Wife and five children.
Zavala   Head of Little Village
Creek.   J.A.Veatch

1380. MOTT, PARTHENIA   [E]
District of Bevil   October 2d 1835
Parthenia Mott or Coursey is a
native of Georgia and emigrated in
1833, hath a family of three persons
                 Wm Williams Alcalde
[Reverse] Parthenia Coursy

1381. MUDD, B.H.   [E]
San Augustine   22 Sept 1834
B.H. Mudd native of the U.S. is a
man without a family and a man of
good... Benjamin Lindsey Alcalde

1381A. MULLEN, JAMES   [S]
Nacogdoches   June 6, 1835
Mr. Surveyor. You are to survey in
Vehlein's Grant the quarter sitio

which Mr. James Mullen will designate...   Jorge Anto Nixon Comr
[Note] On Angelina

1382. MULLEN, PATRICK   [E]
San Augustine   Sept 22d 1834
Mr. Surveyor Sir: You are to survey in Zavala's Grant the sitio
which Mr. Patrick Mullen will designate...   Jorge Anto Nixon Comr
[Note] The place where he lives

1383. MUNDAY (MONDAY), SAMUEL   [E]
San Augustine   Oct 4th 1835
Samuel Munday a native of N. Caroli-
na is a man of family of three per-
sons...emigrated in 1831...
                Nathan Davis Comr
1383a.
San Augustine   7 Oct 1835
I, Samuel Monday appoint Franklin
Fullervmy attorney to petition for
a league and labor...
              [Sig] Saml Mondy
Witnesses   Joseph Harper
E.O. Legrand   Robert Strange
Thomas Thrasher   Thomas Hawkins

1384. MURCHISON, MARTIN   [S]
Nacogdoches   8 November 1834
Certify foreigner Martin Muchrison
is a man of good...married with
family...   Vital Flores

1385. MURPHY, PETER   [S]
Nacogdoches   19 Sept 1835
Certify citizen Peter Murphy is a
man of good...resident of this Department since 1812...married without family...has not received land
              Radford Berry

1386. MURPHY, SYLVESTER   [E]
Town of Austin   Oct 11, 1831
To Mr. S.F. Austin Empresario
I have emigrated to this Colony...
Sylvester Murphy 37 years of age
Anne my wife 37 years of age.
One female child. Occupation farmer.
Move from Georgia and arrived in
this Colony 2 Feby 1831.
              [Sig] Sylvester Murphy

1387. MURPHY, WILLIS   [E]
San Augustine   Sept 23d 1834
Willis Murphy a native of Mississip-
pi a man of family of nine persons
            Benjamin Lindsey Alcalde

1388. MURPHY, SAMUEL   [E]
San Augustine   Oct 5, 1835
Samuel Murfrey a native of the U.S.
is a man of family of two persons...
emigrated in 1829...
            Nathan Davis Comr
1388a.
I authorize Franklin Fuller to peti-
tion for one league and labor..
            Samuel X Murphrey
Witnesses   E.O. Legrand
Jesse Singleton   A.B. Davis
E.M. Fuller   W. Morgan

1389. MUSE, K.H.
Lewis Holloway   John Daugherty
John C. Walling   Caleb Holloway
John Roland   Mat Doyal
Wm P. Chisum   Danl Holloway
Wm M. Lumpkin   Simpson Holloway
Received Houston 19th December 1838
From the General Land Office the
foregoing Orders of Survey as issued
by G.W. Smyth Commissioner.
      K.H. Muse Agent for Walling
[Reverse] Agent for John Walling

1390. MUSSETT, WILLIAM S.   [S]
Nacogdoches   6 June 1835
Certify foreigner William S. Mussett
is a man of good...single without
family...
      G. Pollitt Alcalde Interim
[Rev] Accepted Zavala. A.Henrie 1/4

1391. MYERS, ELIAS G.   [E]
San Augustine   Octr 26, 1834
Elias G. Myers a native of Tennessee
a man of family... Benjamin Lindsey
[Note] Wife and one child on the
Trinity east side about 30 miles
above the Road.

1392. MYERS, HENRY   [S]
Nacogdoches   4 June 1835
Certify foreigner Henry Myers is a
man of good...single without family
  Jn Egne Michamps Alcalde Interim
[Rev] Accepted in Burnet. A.Henrie

1393. McADAMS, JAMES   [E]
San Augustine   August 18, 1835
James McAdams a native of North
Carolina a man of family of a wife
and three children...emigrated in
1832.   A. Hotchkiss P. Judge

1394. McADAMS, JOHN   [E]
San Augustine   August 18, 1835
John McAdams a native of Alabama...
emigrated in 1832, a man of family
of eight persons...
            A. Hotchkiss, P. Judge

1395. McCELVEY, JAMES   [E]
Augustine   August 18, 1835
James McCelvey a native of Tennessee
a man of family of a wife and no
children...emigrated to Texas in
1824...   A. Hotchkiss P. Judge

1396. McCELVEY, JESSE   [E]
San Augustine   August 17, 1835
Jesse McCelvey is a native of Tennessee is a single man...emigrated
in 1825...   A. Hotchkiss P. Judge

1397. McCLANE, WILLIAM   [E]
Tenoxtitlan   23 May 1834
To the Empresarios Austin and
Williams   I have emigrated to
Texas...I am unmarried. My age 30
years.   [Sig] Wm McClane

1398. McCLOUD, ALEXANDER   [S]
Nacogdoches   3 March 1835
Certify foreigner Alexander McCloud
is a man of good...married with
family...   Radford Berry
1398a.
Nacogdoches   March 3, 1835
Sir: You are to survey in Zavala's
Grant the sitio which Mr. Alexander
McCloud will designate...
            Jorge Anto Nixon Comr
[Note] On Pine Island Bayou adjoin-
ing Hezekiah Williams north line.

1399. McCORMICK, JOHN   [S]
Nacogdoches   24 October 1835
Certify foreigner John McCormick is
a man of good...single without family and resident of this District
since 1832...
            G. Pollitt Alcalde Interim

1400. McCOY, DAVID   [E]
San Augustine   26 Sept 1834
David McCoy a native of Virginia a
man of family of twelve persons...
        Benjamin Lindsey Alcalde

1401. McCRARY, CYRENY   [E]
San Augustine   August 30th 1835
Cyreny McCrerey a native of Kentucky
is a woman of family of five persons
emigrated in 1822...
        Nathan Davis Comr
1401a.
San Augustine   30 August 1835
Cyreny McCrery has taken the oath of
allegiance...   Nathan Davis Comr
1401b.
San Augustine   30 August 1835
I, Cyreny McCrery appoint Edward O.
Legrand my attorney to petition for
one league and labor ...
        Cyreny McCrery
Witnesses
Peter C. Ragsdale   Arabel Smith
Jesse Henderson   John Haley
Charles Haley
1401c.
San Augustine   Sept 1, 1835
Mr. Sydn Pennington Sir:
You are to survey the sitio & labor
which Cyreny McCrary will designate
        Geo W. Smyth Comr

1402. McCUNE, JAMES   [S]
Nacogdoches   1 July 1835
Certify foreigner James McCune is a
man of good... married with family
Jn Egne Michamps Alcalde Interim

1403. McDANIEL, JAMES   [E]
Jurisdiction of Liberty July 7, 1835
I have been acquainted with James
McDaniel a native of Ireland, a man
of good...   Jno A. Williams
I am acquainted with Mr. Jas McDan-
iel and hold him...   Wm Duncan
[Rev] Accepted in Vehlein. A.Henrie

1404. McDANIEL, ROBERT C.   [E]
San Augustine   25 Sept 1834
Robert C. McDaniel a native of Vir-
ginia a man of family of three per-
sons...   Benjamin Lindsey Alcalde
[Note] Chambers Bluff above on the
        W. Bank

1404a. Recd of G.A. Nixon Commissioner R.C. McDonalds Title
Sept 7, 1835   Henry Teal

1405. McDONALD, DANIEL   [E]
To Mr. S.F. Austin Empresario
I am desirous of locating myself in
the Colony...
Daniel McDonals 32 years old
Mary Anne my wife 29
One male two female children
        [Sig] Daniel McDonald
[Dated March 1830 in Austin's
Register]

1406. McDONALD, DONALD   [E]
San Augustine September 24th 1834
Donald McDonald is a native of upper
Canada a man of family of five per-
sons...
        Benjamin Lindsey Lindsey Alcalde

1407. McDONALD, HUGH JR   [E]
To Mr. S.F. Austin Empresario
I am desirous of locating myself in
this Colony...
Hugh McDonald Jr 28 years old
Mary my wife   22 years old
        Hugh McDonald Jr

1408. McDONALD, THOMAS   [S]
Nacogdoches   1 June 1835
Certify foreigner Thomas McDonald a
man of good...married with family...
Jn Egne Michamps Alcalde Interim
[Rev] Accepted in Burnet. A.Henrie

1409. McDONALD, THOMAS   [E]
San Augustine   Sept 22, 1834
Thos McDonald a native of the U.S. a
man of family of eight persons...
        Benjamin Lindsey Alcalde

1410. McDONALD, WILLIAM   [E]
Jurisdiction of Liberty 25 Apr 1835
William McDonald a native of South
Carolina a man of family...
        Claiborne West Judge

1411. McDONALD, WILLIAM   [S]
Nacogdoches   14 October 1834
Certify foreigner Wm McDonald a man
of good...married with family...
        Luis Procela
[Note] Wm McDonald. Has a wife and

three children. 3 miles from Wm
Robinson the Surveyor who is to be
the surveyor in this case. Vehlein

1412. McDONALD, W.S. [S]
Nacogdoches   3 June 1835
Certify foreigner W.S. McDonald is a
man of good...married with family...
Jn Egne Michamps Alcalde Interim

1413. McDOWEL, MILLS   [E]
             May the 30th 1831
Mills McDowel wishing to become a
citizen and obtain land in Austin's
Colony he being unacquainted with
the proper office...hath applied to
us for a certificate...has supported
the character of... Jesse Grimes
                    Francis Holland

1414. McELROY, PHILIP   [E]
Austin   July 23d 1832
A list of Philip McElroys family
Philip McElroy aged 33 years
Almyra McElroy his wife aged 22
years   3 Male children
4 Female children
Above is a list of my family and
with which I have moved to this
Colony.   [Sig] Philip McElroy

1415. McFADDEN, JONATHAN   [E]
San Augustine   August 19, 1835
Jonathan McFaddin a native of Louisiana a single man...emigrated in
1822...   Saml Thompson Alcd

1416. McFADEN, SAMUEL   [E]
San Augustine   August 19th 1835
Samuel McFaden a native of Kentucky
a man of family of seven persons...
emigrated in 1822...
            Saml Thompson Alcd

1417. McFADDIN, WILLIAM   [S]
Jurisdiction of Liberty Nov 24, 1834
Wm McFaddin a native of Tennessee is
a man of family of his wife and
three children   Wm Hardin Judge
[Note] Adjoining King & Harper -- on
the N. on Long Creek. F. Hardin
Vehlein
[Note] Adjoining King & Harper
On the N. on Long Creek
F. Hardin   Vehlein

1418. McFADDIN, WILLIAM   [E]
San Augustine   Sept 1st 1835
William McFadden a native of Louisiana a man of family of three persons...emigrated in 1833...
            Saml Thompson Alcd

1419. McFARLAND, SAMUEL P.   [E]
San Augustine   July 27, 1835
Samuel P. McFarland is a native of
Indiana a single man...
            A. Hotchkiss P. Judge
[Rev] Accepted in Vehlein 1/4 sitio
                    Arthur Henrie

1420. McFARLAND, THOMAS S.   [E]
San Augustine   March 14th 1835
Thos S. McFarland is a native of
Indiana a single man...
            A. Hotchkiss P. Judge

1421. McFARLAND, WILLIAM   [S]
Nacogdoches   17 Sept 1834
Certify William McFarland is a man
of good morals...widower with chil-
dren...Luis Procela Alcalde Interim
1421a.
Recd of Comr Nixon   [No date]
The Title of Charles S. Hunt, John
Shears, Abraham Kuykendall, S.D.
Moore & William Caldwell.
                    Wm McFarland

1422. McFARLANE, DUGALD   [E]
To Mr. S.F. Austin Empresario
I have emigrated to this Colony...
Dougal McFarlane 33 years old
Elisa my wife   27
One male one female [children]
Moved from Alabama and arrived in
this Colony 10 May 1830.
            [Sig] Dugald McFarlane

1423. McGAFFEY, JOHN   [E]
Jurisdiction of Liberty Dec 20, 1834
Mr. John McGaffey a native of New
Hampshire a man of family of himself
and wife and three children...
            G.A. Pattillo Comr
[Not] John McGaffey. Zavala
Wife 3 children. On the coast at
Locust Grove. F. Hardin

1424. McGAHEY, BENJAMIN   [E]
San Augustine   May 19, 1835
Benjamin McGahey is a native of
South Carolina a man of family of a
wife...   A. Hotchkiss Prmy Judge

1425. McGAHEY, JAMES S. [E]
Jurisdiction of Liberty Apr 30, 1835
James S. McGahey a native of North
Carolina is at present a resident of
this Jurisdiction a man of family of
himself & wife   W. Duncan 2d Judge

1426. McGALIN, THOMAS   [E]
San Augustine   September 24, 1834
Thomas McGalin is a native of Vir-
ginia a man of family of eight per-
sons...   Benjamin Lindsey Alcalde
1426a.
[Field Notes] Beginning corner of
Thomas McGalin sitio on the west
bank of the River Angelina...
                    J.A. Veatch
1426b.
Mr. George Anto Nixon Esqr, Comr
Sir: Please to deliver to Benjamin
Lindsey the title to my land.
                Thomas X McGalin

1427. McGEE, ANTHONY   [E]
San Augustine   May 23, 1835
Anthony McGee a native of Tennessee
a man of family of a wife and three
children...A. Hotchkiss Prmy Judge

1428. McGEE, JESSE   [E]
San Augustine   May 24, 1835
Jesse McGee a native of Indiana a
man of family of a wife and one
child... A. Hotchkiss Prmy Judge

1429. McGEE, JOHN   [E]
San Augustine   Sept 22, 1834
John McGee a native of the Mexican
Government is a man of family of
three persons...
           Benjamin Lindsey Alcalde

1430. McGEE, RALPH   [S]
Nacogdoches   2 February 1835
Certify foreigner Ralph McGee a man
of good...married with family...
 Jn Egne Michamps Alcalde Interim
[Note] Wife 7 ch = w. side of Trini-
ty   One league Wm Rankin. Vehlein

1431. McGILL, HENRY   [E]
San Augustine   20 August 1835
Henry McGill a native of Louisiana a
man of family of four persons...emi-
grated in August 1834...
           R.C. McDaniel C.P.O.

1431a. Nacogdoches   Aug 7, 1835
Mr. Surveyor Sir: You are to survey in Zavala's Grant the sitio
which Mr. Henry McGill will designate...   Jorge Anto Nixon Comr
[Note] On the west shore of the
              Neches

1432. McGLOIN, EDWARD J.
[Field Notes] Survey of one league
for Edward McGloin on the bank of
the River Nueces...

1433. McGLOIN, JAMES
[Field Notes] Three surveys to
James McGloin on the Nueces ...

1434. McGLOIN, JOHN
[Field Notes] Survey of one third
of a league to John McGloin on the
Attascosa...

1435. McGLOIN, PATRICK
[Field Notes] Survey of one league
to Patrick McGloin on the Nueces...

1436. McGOWAN, DENNIS
[Field Notes] Survey of one league
for Dennis McGowan on the Nueces...

1437. McGREGOR, JOHN   [E]
Naches   June 6th 1835
I have been acquainted with John
McGregor for some considerable time
is a good citizen...a single man a
farmer...   Wm Whiteley
     Comr for the Naches Precinct

1438. McHANK, HORATIO   [E]
District of Bevil October 2d 1834
Horatio McHanks a native of Kentucky
a single man... John Bevil Alcalde
[Note] His improvement on Sabine Bay
              D. Brown Surv

1439. McILWAIN, WILLIAM   [S]
Nacogdoches   30 September 1835
Certify foreigner Wm McIlwain...
single without family and a resident
of this Department since September
1832 [?]   Radford Berry

1440. McINTYRE, ELIZABETH   [E]
San Augustine   Sept 1st 1835
Elizabeth McIntyre a native of Vir-

ginia is a widow of nine persons in family...emigrated in 1829...
Saml Thompson Alcd

1441. McINTYRE, THOMAS [E]
San Augustine   Sept 1st 1835
Thomas McIntyre a native of Tennessee a single man...emigrated in 1829...   Saml Thompson Alcd

1442. McKELVEY, HEZEKIAH [E]
San Augustine   Sept 1st 1835
Hezekian McKelvey a native of Tennessee a man of family of six persons...emigrated in 1824...
Saml Thompkins Alcd

1443. McKELVEY, SUSANNAH [E]
San Augustine   Sept 1st 1835
Susannah McKelvey native of Virginia is a widow woman of family of three persons...emigrated in 1824...
Saml Thompson Alcd

1444. McKENZIE, M.A. [S]
Nacogdoches   11 June 1835
Certify foreigner M.A. McKenzie is a man of good...married with family...
Jn Egne Michamps Alcalde Interim
[Rev]·Accepted in Zavala. A.Henrie

1445. McKENZIE, REUBEN [S]
Nacogdoches   10 November 1834
Certify foreigner Reuben McKenzie is a man of good...married with family
Vital Flores

1446. McKIM, JAMES [E]
San Augustine   Sept 27th 1834
James McKim a native of Louisiana... hath a family of eight persons...
John Bevil Alcd ·

1447. McKINNEY, JAMES [S]
Nacogdoches   14 Decr 1835
Certify foreigner James McKinney is a man of good...married with family, resident of this Department since 1824...   Radford Berry

1448. McKINNEY, THOMAS F.
Quintana   Augt 24, 1835
Mr. Spencer H. Jack San Felipe
Dear Sir: This will be handed to

you by Messrs Atkinson & Loony both of whom... They have been with me for some time & I can confidently recommend them...They are requested to select land for Stephens & Wesly...   Thomas F. McKinney

1449. McKINNEY, WILLIAM [S]
Nacogdoches   14 December 1835
Certify foreigner Wm C. McKinney is a man of good...married with family, citizen of this Department since 1824...   Radford Berry

1450. McKINSEY, DANIEL [S]
Nacogdoches   16 May 1835
Certify foreigner Daniel McKinsey is a man of good...married·with family
Radford Berry

1451. McKINZA, C.T. [S]
Nacogdoches   13 May 1835
Certify foreigner C.T. McKinza is a man of good...married with family...
Radford Berry

1452. McLAREN, JOHN [E]
Town of Austin   12 July 1830
I have emigrated to the Colony...
John McLaren 36 years old single
Moved from Virginia and arrived in Feby 1825.   [Sig] John McLaren

1453. McLAUGHLIN, ALFRED [S]
Nacogdoches   21 September 1835
Certify foreigner Alfred McLaughlin is a man of good...single without family...   Radford Berry
[Note] Unfinished
[Rev] Accepted in Zavala. A.Henrie

1454. McLAUGHLIN, ARCHIBALD [S]
Nacogdoches   8 July 1835
Certify resident Archibald McLaughlin is a man of good...single...
Jn Egne Michamps Alcalde Intrim

1455. McLAUGHLIN, STEPHEN [S]
Nacogdoches   8 July 1835
Certify foreigner Stephen McLaughlin is a man of good...single...
Jn Gene Michamps Alcalde Interim
[Note] Unfinished

1456. McLEAN, DANIEL [S]
Nacogdoches   7 Jany 1835
Certify foreigner Daniel McLane is a
man of good...married with family...
                    Radford Berry
1456a.
Nacogdoches   20 Nov 1835
Have received of Citizen Jose' Car-
vajal...the documents of a concession to me as a citizen of a sitio
of land...   Daniel McLean

1457. McLAIN, JAMES [S]
Nacogdoches   14 September 1835
Certify foreigner James McLean is a
man of good...widower with family
and resident of the Department since
1830...   Radford Berry
1457a.
Nacogdoches   Sept 14th 1835
Sir: You are to survey the sitio &
labor which Mr. James McLain will
designate...   Geo W. Smyth Comr
[Rev] The within order has been ex-
ecutd by me.   Wm Brookfield Surv

1458. McLEOD, JOHN [E]
Sabine   June 9th 1835
John McLeod a citizen of the Dis-
trict...sustains an industrious...
                B. Holt Comr
[Rev] Accepted in Zavala. A.Henrie

1459. McMAHAN, JAMES [S]
Nacogdoches   30 May 1835
Certify foreigner James McMahan is a
man of good...married with family...
     Jn Egne Michamps Alcalde Interim
[Reverse] Accepted. A.Henrie

1460. McMAHON, SAMUEL D. [E]
San Augustine   Sept 23d 1834
James D. McMahon a native of Tennessee is a man of family of seven
persons... Benjamin Lindsey Alcalde

1461. McMULLEN, JOHN
[Field Notes] Survey of a tract for
John McMullen situated on the River
Nueces...

1462. McMULLEN, JOHN
[Field Notes] Survey of one league
for John McMullen...Nueces River...

1463. McMULLEN, PATRICK R.
District of Tennehaw 10 Aug 1835
Patrick R. McMullen a native of
Ireland is a man of family of two
persons...emigrated in 1834...
                Nathan Davis Comr
[Note] Un.

1464. McNAULTY, SARAH [S]
Nacogdoches   18 May 1835
Certify foreigner Sarah McNaulty is
a widow with family...Radford Berry
[Note] McAnulty

1465. McNEAL, JOHN [E]
San Augustine   May 17, 1835
John McNeal a native of South Carolina a man of family of wife and ten
children... A. Hotchkiss Prmy Judge

1466. McNEALY, J.B. [E]
Major Nixon will please send the
Deed for my land to me by C.H. Sims
2d March 1835   J.B. McNealy

1467. McNEIL, ANGUS [S]
Nacogdoches   7 Sept 1835
Certify foreigner Angus McNeil is a
man of good...married with family...
                    Radford Berry
[Rev] Accepted in Vehlein. A.Henrie

1468. McNEILL, HENRY C. [S]
Certify foreigner Henry C. McNeill
is a man of good...single without
family...   Radford Berry
[Rev] Accepted in Vehlein.A.Henrie

1469. McRAE, ALEXANDER [S]
Nacogdoches   5 June 1835
Certify foreigner Alexander Mackrae
is a man of good...married with
family...
     G. Pollitt Alcalde Interim
[Rev] Accepted in Zavala. A.Henrie

1470. McVAY, POLLY [E]
San Augustine   Sept 1st 1835
Polly McVay a native of Tennessee is
a widow woman of family of two persons...emigrated in 1829...
          Saml Thompson Alcd

1471. McWLLIAMS, FRANCIS A. [E]
San Augustine   Dec 26th 1834
Francis A. McWilliams a native of
Virginia is a man of family of six
persons...E. Rains Acting Alcalde

1472. NASH, DAVID R. [E]
Matagorda   December 1, 1833
To Col. S.F. Austin, Empresario
[At] San Felipe, Texas
I am now in Texas with your Colony
I have a family consisting of a wife
& one child. I expect my family in
the Country in a short time. I wish
to be received by you as a Colonist.
          [Sig]   David R. Nash

1473. NASH, JOHN D. [S]
Nacogdoches   28 May 1835
Certify foreigner John D. Nash is a
man of good...married with family...
Jn Egne Michamps Alcalde Interim
[Rev] Accepted. Arthur Henrie

1474. NASH, WILLIAM [E]
San Augustine   Sept 22d 1834
William Nash a native of Tennessee
is a man of family of four persons
          Benjamin Lindsey Alcalde
[Note] Wife 3 children = Zavala
North of Almr Houston Survey
Isaac W. Burtin = Mr. Nash wishes
Mr. B to survey his lands. Can he be
appointed. No

1475. NATIONS, JOSEPH [E]
San Augustine   Aug 17, 1832 [sic]
Joseph Nations a native of Georgia
is a single man of good...emigrated
in 1832 Nov   Saml Thompson Alcd

1475a. Nacogdoches 11 December 1834
Certify Mr. Joseph Nations is a man
of good...single... Vital Flores
[Rev] Accepted in Burnet.
          1/4 A.Henrie
1475b.
San Augustine   August 17th 1835
Sir: You are to survey the third
sitio which Mr. Joseph Nations will
designate   Geo W. Smyth Comr

1476. NAVARRO, J.A. [S]
Mr. Stephen F. Austin
Bexar   24 June 1830

[Two page letter from J. Antonio
Navarro re affairs in Texas]

1477. NAVARRO, MARIA CONCEPCION [S]
Nacogdoches   2 Sept 1835
Certify citizen Maria Concepcion
Navarro native of Bexar is a woman
of very good...resident of this
Municipality since 1810...widow with
family...3 children...has not re-
ceived land...   Radford Berry

1478. NEALY, JOHN M. [E]
San Augustine   Sept 22d 1834
John M. Nealy a native of South Carolina a man of family of eight
persons... Benjamin Lindsey Alcalde

1479. NEILL, GEORGE [S]
Nacogdoches   10 June 1835
Certify foreigner George Neill a man
of good...married with family...
Jn Egne Michamps Alcalde Interim
[Rev] Accepted in Burnet. A. Henrie

1480. NELSON, JOSHUA [E]
San Felipe   May 26, 1830
To Col. S.F. Austin Empresario
Sir: Having been in this Colony
since the 20th of January 1829...I
am desirous of becoming a citizen...
I have no family. My native Country
the State of New York, my age is 39
years. My occupation a school
teacher.   [Sig]   Joshua Nelson

1481. NELSON, O.C. [E]
San Augustine   11th Feb 1835
O.C. Nelson a native of the U.S. is
a man of family of three persons...
emigrated in February 1835.
          R.C. McDaniel C.P.O.
[Reverse] Accepted. A. Henrie
1481a.
Nacogdoches   Aug 7, 1835
Mr. Surveyor You are to survey in
Zavala's Grant the sitio which Mr.
O.C. Nelson will designate...
          Jorge Anto Nixon Comr
[Note] On the Neches on the West
          side

1482. NELSON, SAMUEL [E]
San Augustine   Oct 7, 1834
Samuel Nelson a native of Tennessee,
a single man...
          Benjamin Lindsey Alcalde

1482a. District of Sabine
May 2d 1835   Mr. Hotchkiss
Dear Sir: You will please make out a
bill of expenses due on my Title for
a quarter...I have authorized Mr.
Holt to pay you...[Sig] Saml Nelson

1483. NEVAN, PATRICK
[Field Notes] Survey of one league
for Patrick Nevan situted on the
right margin of the Nueces...

1484. NEVILLE, JAMES   [S]
Nacogdoches   25 September 1835
Certify foreigner James Neville is a
man of good...married with family...
                     Radford Berry
[Rev] Accepted in Vehlein. A.Henrie

1485. NEWELL, STEUART   [S]
Nacogdoches   28 July 1835
Certify foreigner Stuart Newel is a
man of good...married with family...
                     Radford Berry
[Rev] Accepted in Zavala A. Henrie

1486. NEWLON, WILLIAM   [E]
San Augustine   29 August 1835
William Newlon a native of Virginia
is a man of family of two in number
emigrated in October 1832, took the
oath...   Saml Thompson Alcd

1487. NEWMAN, THOMAS   [E]
Jurisdiction of Liberty 21 Dec 1834
Thomas Newman a native of Louisiana
and now a resident citizen of this
Jurisdiction is a man of family of
wife and three children...
                     J.B. Woods Alcalde
[Reverse] Thomas Newman
           Hannah Newman

1488. NEWTON, JOEL   [E]
San Augustine   9th March 1835
Mr. Joel Newton is a native of Ala-
bama is a man of family of nine
persons, that he emigrated in the
summer of 1834...
                     R.C. McDaniel C.P.O.
1408a.
Mr. Surveyor You are to survey in
Zavala's Grant the sitio which Mr.
Joel Newton will designate...
           Jose Anto Nixon Comr

1489. NEXSEN, GEORGE W.   [E]
To Mr. S.F. Austin Empresario...
I am desirous of being admitted...
My name is George W. Nexsen aged 31
years. My wife Katharine Mary.
One male, one female children.
Removed from New York.
           [Sig] Geo W. Nexsen

1490. NICHOLSON, STEPHEN   [E]
Jurisdiction of Liberty 22 Feb 1835
Stephen Nichelson a native of England is a man of family of himself
and wife...   Wm Hardin Judge

1491. NICHOLS, HENRY   [E]
San Augustine   22 Sept 1834
Henry Nichols a native of Mississip-
pi a man of family of four persons
           Benjamin Lindsey Alcalde
1491a. [Field Notes]
Commence at SW corner of Williams
Survey for beginning of Henry
Nukolds sitio at his improvement on
Houson Bayou...

1492. NICHOLS, WILLIAM   [E]
Department of Bevil Oct 3d 1835
William Nichols emigrated in 1826
was from the State of Louisiana...
hath a family of six persons...
           Wm Williams Alclalde

1493. NICHOLSON, RODERICK   [E]
To Mr. S.F. Austin Empresario
I desire to locate in the Colony...
Roderick Nicholson 28 years old
Mary Anne my wife 18 years old
One male one female children
           [Sig] Roderick Nickoson

1494. NELSON, WILLIAM   [E]
State of Illinois, Sangamon County
We the undersigned having been acquainted with William Nelson a number of years...Springfield, Illinois
October 2d 1834
[about 80 signers from Springfield]

1495. NIXSEN, CALVIN   [E]
I relinquish right & title to a
quarter sitio numbered (8) to Wil-
liam Latham.
Dec 26, 1835   [Sig] Calvin ---
Witness   James P. Wallace
[Rev] Relinquishment Calvin Nixsen
[--- cannot be read as Nixsen. Ed]

135

1496. NOBLIT, JOHN [S]
Nacogdoches   29 July 1835
Certify foreigner John Noblit is a
man of good...single without famiily
                     Radford Berry
[Rev] Accepted in Zavalas. A.Henrie

1497. NORBECK, NICHOLS [S]
Nacogdoches   25 Aug 1835
Certify foreigner Nicholas Norbeck
is a man of good...married to a
woman of the Country with a family
of three persons, resident of this
Municipality since 1830.
                     Radford Berry
[Reverse]
Nacogdoches   25 Aug 1835 [E]
This day appeared ...Nicholas Nor-
beck and took the oath...
                     Radford Berry

1498. NORRIS, JOHN   [E]
San Augustine   Sept 1st 1835
John Norris a native of the Country
is a man of family of six persons...
                     Saml Thompson Alcd

1499. NORRIS, SARAH H.   [E]
San Augustine   Sept 1st 1835
Sarah H. Norris a native citizen is
a widow woman with a family of four
persons...   Saml Thompson Alcd
1499a.
San Augustine   1st Sept 1835
I, Sarah H. Norris appoint John
Norris my attorney to petition for
one league and labor of land...
                     Sarah H. Norris
Saml Thompson   by John Norris

1500. NORRIS, THOMAS   [E]
San Augustine   Sept 1, 1835
Thomas Norris a native of Maryland
is a man of family of six persons...
emigrated in 1803...
                     Saml Thompson Alcd

1501. NORTHCROSS, JAMES   [E]
Town of Austin   19 June 1830
To Mr. S.F. Austin Empresario
I have emigrated to this Colony...
James Northcross 28 years old unmar-
ried farmer. Moved from Alabama and
arrived in Aug 1829. Jas Northcross
[Note] Wants his land joining
   Wilbarger either above or below

1502. NORTON, JAMES   [E]
To Mr. S.F. Austin Empresario
I have emigrated to this Colony...
James Norton age 38 years. Emigrated
from New Orleans in Louisiana and
arrived in this Colony in October
1827   [Sig] Norton

1503. NORWELL, LIPSCOMB   [S]
Nacogdoches   16 May 1835
Certify foreigner Lipscomb Norwell
is a man of good...married with
family...   Radford Berry

1504. NOWLAN, DANIEL   [S]
Nacogdoches   April 21, 1835
It my duty as Comr to administer to
you the oath on the Holy Bible to
cause you to respect the Constitution of Mexico and no religion is
admitted but the Roman Catholic
religion will you swear to support
the above.   Jorge Anto Nixon Cmor
[Reverse]
Nacogdoches   April 21st 1835
I was born a Roman Catholic, all my
relations are Roman Catholic, and I
have taken the oath as requested on
the Bible by the Commissioner Jorge
Anto Nixon of the within paper.
                     Daniel Nowlan
1504a.
Nacogdoches   23 April 1835
Certify foreigner Daniel Nowlan is a
man of good...single...Radford Berry

1506. NUGENT, CINCINATUS   [S]
Nacogdoches   1 September 1835
Certify foreigner Quintus Cincinatus
Nujent of the State of Mississippi
is a man of good...married with
family, resident of this Municip.
since 1825... Radford Berry [Note]
Two in family
[Reverse]
Nacogdoches   1 Sept 1835
This day appeared before me Cincina-
tus Nujent and took the oath...
                     Radford Berry

1507. NUTELL, ROBERT   [S]
Nacogdoches   16 July 1835
Certify foreigner Robert Nutell is a
man of good...married with family...
                     Radford Berry
[Rev] Accepted in Vehlein or Burnet

1508. OBAN, THOMAS   [E]
San Augustine   Oct 1st 1835
Thomas Oban a native of South Caro-
lina a man of family of nine persons
emigrated in 1822...Nathan Davis Com
1508a.
7th October 1835 I hereby authorize
Franklin Fuller to petition for one
league and labor...
                [Sig]   Thomas Oband
Witnesses   E.O. Legrand
W.L. Scott   Thomas Fuller
A.B. Davis   James Jones

1509. O'BOYLE, DANIEL
Refugio   Nov 21, 1834
Appeared before me Daniel O'Boyle
and Juan O'Boyle natives of Ireland,
first married and the second single
here for a month intending to join
league and one quarter
            Power & Hewetson Colony
1509a.
[Field Notes] Survey of one third of
a league, League No. 2 for Daniel
O'Boyle on the right bank of the
Attascoso Creek...

1510. O'BOYLE, EDWARD
[Field Notes] Survey of one league
and one labor for Edward O'Boyle on
the east bank of Attascoso Creek,
League No. 7...

1511. O'BOYLE, MICHAEL
[Field Notes] Survey of 1/3 league
part of League No. 7 for Michael
O'Boyle on left bank of Rio Frio...

1512. O'BOYLE, PATRICK
[Field Notes] Survey of one league
and one labor for Patrick O'Boyle,
League No. 1 on the west bank of
Aransas...

1513. O'BOYLE, RODERICK
[Field Notes] Survey of one third
of a league for Roderick O'Boyle...
on the left bank of the Rio Frio...

1514. O'BRYANT, PETER   [E]
District of Tenahaw   Aug 15th 1835
Patrick O'Bryant a native of Tennes-
see is a man of family of five
persons...emigrated in 1832...
            Nathan Davis Comr
[Peter written over Patrick]

1515. ODELL, BENJAMIN   [E]
San Augustine   September 1st 1835
Benjamin Odle a native of Tennessee
a single man...emigrated in 1825...
            Saml Thompson Alcd

1516. ODELL, SARAH   [E]
San Augustine   27 Sept 1834
James Odle a native of Tennessee is
a man of family of six persons...
            Benjamin Lindsey Alcalde
[Note] Sarah Odell widow. 4 children
Adjoining her father on the west and
north. Zavala
[Reverse]
I Sarah Odell invest my father Eli
Gilliland to get out an order of
survey for my self and children as
my Husband is dead.
            [Sig]   Sarah Odell

1517. ODLUM, BENJAMIN
[Field Notes] Survey of one third
of a league for Benjamin Odlum of
Survey No. 9 on the right bank of
the Rio Frio...

1518. O'DOCHERTY, GEORGE
[Field Notes] Survey of one league
and one labor for George O'Docherty,
League No 2, west margin of the east
fork of the Aransas...

1519. O'DOCHERTY, WILLIAM
[Field Notes] Begin on right bank
of the Nueces at corner of James
McGloin land, one league for William
O'Docherty...

1520. ODOM, KINCHING   [E]
Nueces   January 30th 1835
I have been acquainted with Kinching
Odom for some time say for one year
or more. He is a man of good report
and has a family   Wm Whiteley
            Comr for the Naches Precinct

1521. ODUM, BRITAIN   [E]
District of Sabine   June 6th 1835
Britain Odum a native of Georgia now
a citizen of the District aforesaid,
has a family of five persons...
            B. Holt Comr
[Rev]   Accepted Zavala. A.Henrie

1522. OGDEN, OLIVER W. [S]
Nacogdoches   1 June 1835
Certify foreigner Oliver W. Ogden a
man of good...married with family...
    Jn Egne Michamps Alcalde Interim
[Rev] Accepted in Z. Arthur henrie

1523. OLIVER, ALFRED [S]
Nacogdoches   23'May 1835
Certify foreigner Alfred Oliver is a
man of good...married with family...
    Radford Berry

1524. ORSMENT, WASHINGTON [E]
San Augustine   Sept 1st 1835
Washington Orsment is a native of
Massachusetts a single man...emi-
grated 1831...
    Saml Thompson Alcalde

1525. OSBOURNE, SPENCER [E]
San Augustine   May 1st 1835
Spencer Osbourne a native of Illi-
nois a man of family of five persons
emigrated in 1834...
    R.C. McDaniel C.P.O.
1526a.
Nacogdoches   Aug 14, 1835
Mr. Surveyor   You will survey in
Zavala's   Grant the sitio which Mr.
Spencer Osbourne will designate...
Jorge Anto Nixon Comr

1526. OSBURN, WALTER [S]
Nacogdoches   27 April 1835
Certify foreigner Walter Osburn is a
man of good...married with family...
    Radford Berry

1527. OWEN, JOHN [E]
Town of Austin   1 June 1830
To Mr. S.F. Austin Empresario
I have emigrated to this Colony...
John Owen 21 years old
Christine my wife 21 years old
Occupation farmer. Moved from Lui-
siana and arrived in the Colony in
1822.   John X Owen

1528. PACE, HARDY [E]
District of Bevil   Dec 14th 1834
Hardy Pace a native of Georgia hath
a family of seven persons...
    John Bevil Alcalde
[Note] Wife & 5 ch. Pine Bayou lower
end of Davis' Prairie. Hiroms.
Zavala
138

1529. PACE, JAMES R. [E]
Town of Austin   24 June 1830
To Mr. S.F. Austin Empresario
James Robert Pace, William Carrol
Pace, minors over 14 years of age
and Albert Gallatin, Wesley Walker,
Polly Jones, Dempsey Council, Mary
Anne Elizabeth & Gideon P. Pace,
minors under 14 years of the late
Gideon Pace, request to be admit--
ted... James R. Pace for himself &
brothers & sisters

1530. PACE, WILLIAM [E]
Jurisdiction of Liberty Dec 27, 1834
William Pace a native of Virginia a
man of famiily of his wife and eight
children...   Wm Hardin Judge
1530a.
Jany 26th 1835   Mr. Saml C. Hiroms
Surveyor Sir:
You are to survey in Vehlein's Grant
the sitio which Mr. Wm Pace will
designate...   Jorge Anto Nixon Comr
[Note] Nearby adjoining Henty's
line on Trinity Pine. 2 miles below
the Long King's village (at his
improvement)

1531. PACE, WILLIAM [E]
District of Sabine   Sept 8th 1835
William Pace who has a family of
eight persons and resident of this
District nine years an immigrant
from Louisiana in 1826...
    B. Holt Comr

1532. PADILLA, AUGUSTIN [S]
Nacogdoches   8 May 1835
Certify citizen Augustin Padilla is
a man of good...single without fami-
ly...has not received land...
    Radford Berry
[Note] Unf.

1533. PADILLA, MARIA ESTEFANA [S]
Nacogdoches   6 April 1835
Certify citizen Maria Estefania Padilla is a resident of this Municipality and born here, a woman of
very good...abandoned by her husband
about eight years ago, with a large
family...considered as a widow...has
not obtained land... Radford Berry
[Reverse] Admitted L. de Zavala,
By his attorney Arthur Henrie

1534. PADON, JOHN [E]
SanAugustine   May 18, 1835
John Padon a native of the North of
Ireland is a single man...
        A. Hotchkiss Primary Judge

1535. PAGE, DAVID [S]
Nacogdoches   1 November 1834
Certify foreigner David Page a man
of good...married with family...
        Vital Flores

1536. PAIT, JOHN W. [S]
Nacogdoches   17 June 1835
Certify foreigner John W. Pait a man
of good...married with family...
Jn Egne Michamps Alcalde Interim
[Rev] Accepted Burnet. Arthur Henrie

1537. PALVADO, JOSEPH [S]
Nacogdoches   11 May 1835
Certify foreigner Joseph Palvado is
a resident of this Municipality for
many years, married with family to
a woman of this Country...
        Radford Berry

1538. PAMPLIN, WILLIAM [E]
San Augustine   Sept 26, 1834
William Pamplin a native of Virginia
hath a family of six persons...
        John Bevil Alcd

1539. PANTELEON, BERNARDO [E]
San Augustine   March 30, 1835
Burnardo Pantalion is a citizen of
the Country, a native of Louisiana,
a man of family of a wife and four
children...
        A. Hotchkiss Primary Judge

1540. PANTALEON, EUSIBIO YUIR [S]
Nacogdoches   12 Feb 1835
Citizen Eusebio Your Pantaleon is a
man of good...married in Sor Nuestra
Santa Madre Church to a woman of the
Country...   Juan Mora

1541. PARKER, ARGALUS G. [E]
District of Bevil   Sept 30th 1834
Argales G. Parker a native of North
Carolina hath a family of two
persons...   John Bevil Alcalde
[Note] Argalus G. Parker

1542. PARKER, CHRISTOPHER ADAMS
Nacogdoches   [S] 7 September 1835
Certify foreigner Christopher Adams
Parker a man of good...single with-
out family...   Radford Berry

1543. PARKER, DANIEL JR [S]
Nacogdoches   3 June 1835
Certify foreigner Daniel Parker Jr a
man of good...single without family
Jne Egne Michamps Alcalde Interim
1543a.
Recd of the Comr George Anto Nixon
the title for one league for Michael
Main.
Sept 15th 1835   Daniel Parker

1544. PARKER, DICKERSON [S]
Nacogdoches   18 May 1835
Certify foreigner Dickerson Parker
is a man of good...single...
        Radford Berry
1544a.
Please send my title by the bearer
July 20th 1835   Dickerson Parker
[Reverse]
Mr. Garrison Greenwood has paid the
fees on Mr. Dickason Parkers title
in my presents.   A. Henrie
Sixteen dollars fifty cents
Received by me. Jorge Anto Nixon
        Land Comr

1545. PARKER, IRA [E]
San Augustine   April 1st 1835
Ira Parker a native of No Carolina a
man of family of six persons...
        John Bodine Alcalde pro tem

1546. PARKER, ISAAC [E]
State of Illinois, Vandalia
27 Sept 1833   The bearer hereof
Isaac Parker Esqr a resident at this
time of this State was before his
departure from Cole County an Acting
Justice of the Peace of said County
He is about to emigrate to Texas.
        John Reynolds   Gov of Illinois
1546a.
Nacogdoches   March 18th 1835
Mr. Saml C. Hiroms Surveyor Sir:
You are to survey in Joseph Veh-
lein's Grant the sitio which Mr.
Isaac Parker will designate...
        Jorge Anto Nixon Comr
[Note] On Long King's Creek

139

1547. PARKER, ISAAC G.   [S]
Nacogdoches   18 April 1835
Certify foreigner Isaac G. Parker is
a man   of good...single without
family...   Radford Berry

1548. PARKER, J.W.   [E]
Tenoxtitlan   22 May 1834
To the Empresarios Austin & Williams
I have emigrated to Texas...
I am married my wifes name Patsy and
have   5 children. My age 37, my
wifes age 37.   [Sig]   J.W. Parker

1549. PARKER, JESSE Y.   [S]
Nacogdoches   25 October 1834
Certify foreigner Jessey Parker is a
man of good...married with family...
                Vital Flores

1550. PARKER, JOHN   [E]
Naches   March 19, 1835
I have been acquainted with John
Parker for some time...a single man
a farmer...   Wm Whiteley
        Comr for the Naches Precinct

1551. PARKER, SILAS M.   [E]
Tenoxtitlan   22 May 1834
To Empresarios Austin & Williams
I have emigrated to Texas...
I am married my wife name is Lucinda
and have 4 children. My age 32 my
wifes age 23   Silas M. Parker

1552. PARKER, WILEY   [S]
Nacogdoches   25 October 1834
Certify foreigner Wiley Parker is a
man of good...married with family...
                Vital Flores

1553. PARMER, ISHAM   [E]
San Augustine   Sept 26, 1834
Isham Parker a native of Missouri...
a single man...
        Benjamin Lindsey Alcalde
1553a.
San Augustine   Septr 18th 1837
Mr. G.A. Nixon Sir:
Please deliver to the bearer Mr.
Benjamin Anderson my Title to a
quarter league.   Isom Parmer

1554. PARMER, JOHNSON JR   [E]
San Augustine   [no date]
Johnson Palmer Junior a native of
the U.S. is a man of family of four
persons...emigrated in 1828...
            R.C. McDaniel C.P.O.
[Reverse] Johnson Parmer
1554a.
Nacogdoches   Aug 9, 1835
Mr. Surveyor Sir: You are to survey in Zavala's Grant the sitio
which Mr. Johnson Parmer Junr will
designate...
        Jorge Anto Nixon Commissioner

1555. PARMER, JOHNSON SR   [E]
San Augustine   20 June 1835
John Parmer of Alabama is a man of
family of three persons...emigrated
in 1834...   R.C. McDaniel C.P.O.
[Reverse] Johnston Parmer
1555a.
Nacogdoches   Augt 16th 1835
Mr. Surveyor Sir: You are to survey in Zavala's Grant the sitio
which Mr. Johnston Parmer will designate...   Jorge Anto Nixon Comr
[Note] On River Angelina

1556. PARMER, THOMAS   [E]
Precinct of Cow Bayou Dec 20th 1834
Thomas Parmer a native of Missouri
is a man of family of himself and
wife... G.A. Pattillo Commissioner
[Note] Zavala's Grant = Wife
On the Sabine adjoining on the north
of Powers Bluff =
        William McFarland Surveyor

1557. PARSONS, SAMUEL M.   [E]
Precinct of Tenahaw   May 22, 1835
Saml M. Parsons is a sittesn of said
district, a native of New York...two
family   Nathan Davis Commissioner
[Note] Unf.

1558. PARTIN, JOHN C.   [E]
Given this 8th day of Decr 1829
Certify that I have known John C.
Partin from the time he landed in
the Country...
Jesse   Thos M. Duke
John Huff   Peter Demos
Freeman George   John Demoss
Ralph Wright   Lewis Demoss
William Duty   William Demoss

I do certify that I have been acquainted with Mr. J.C. Partin for
several months...
Dec 10th 1829   W.C. Finley [?]

1559. PASQUASIN, SILVERA [S]
Nacogdoches   11 Sept 1835
Certify citizen Silvera Pasquasin is
a woman of very good...widow with
family, resident of this Municipality since 1832. Has not obtained
land...   Radford Berry

1560. PATRICK, GEORGE M.
Nacogdoches   Oct 10th 1835
Christian Smith Jr   Jas McGahey
Edward King   Geo White
John Merry   Mosley Baker
Stephen Nicholson   John R. Rhea
John R. Falk   Geo Ellis
Gilbert Brooks   Hannah Nash
Henry White   Jas Morgan
Received the land titles of the
above named individuals from Office.
                      Geo M. Patrick

1561. PATTERSON, G.H. [E]
San Augustine   17 August 1835
G.H. Patterson a native of Virginia
a man of family of a wife and six
children...emigrated in 1824.
            A. Hotchkiss P. Judge
1561a.
San Augustine   August 17th 1835
Sir: You are to survey the sitio &
labor which Mr. G.H. Patterson will
designate... Geo W. Smyth

1562. PATTERSON, JOHN [S]
Nacogdoches   9 Oct 1835
Certify foreigner John Patterson is
a man of good...single without family...resident of this Department
since 1830...   Radford Berry
1562a.
Nacogdoches   October 13, 1835
Sir: You are to survey the third of
a sitio which Mr. John Patterson
will designate...Geo W. Smyth Comr

1563. PATTILLO, GEORGE A. [E]
Precinct of Cow Bayou 4th Jan 1835
Certify George A. Pattillo a native
of Georgia a man of family of his

wife and nine children...
            John Stewart Comr
[Note] Including his improvement,
three plantations on Cow Bayou.
Zavala

1564. PATTON, COLUMBUS R. [E]
To Mr. S.F. Austin Empresario
I am desirous of being admitted...
Columbus R. Patton 19 years of age.
Moved from Kentucky and arrived in
this Colony 1831. Columbus R. Patton

1565. PATTON, JAMES [E]
Naches   September 10th 1835
I have been acquainted with James
Patton for some considerable time...
man of family and farmer...
                  Wm Whiteley
Comr for the Precinct of the Naches
[Rev] Accepted in Vehlein. A.Henrie

1566. PATTON, MOSES L. [S]
Nacogdoches   2 May 1835
Certify foreigner Moses L. Patton is
a man of good...single without fami-
ly...   Radford Berry
1566A.
Nacogdoches   December 8, 1835
Received of Comr George A. Nixon
Mr. Robert Patton land title one
league   Moses L. Patton

1567. PATTON, ROBERT S. [S]
Nacogdoches   May 2d 1835
Certify foreigner Robert S. Patton
is a man of good...married with
family...   Radford Berry

1568. PATTON, WILLIAM H. [E]
Austin   Nov 2, 1832
To Mr. S.F.Austin Empresario
I have emigrated to this Country...
My name is William Patton 25 years.
Unmarried, arrived in this Colony 27
Novr 1831. [Sig] William H. Patton

1569. PAULEY, ANDREW [E]
Austin   Jany 17, 1832
I have emigrated to this Colony...
Andrew Pauley 31 years of age
Margaret my wife 20 years of age
One female child. Family residing in
the State of Tennessee.
                  Andrew Pauley

1570. PAYNE, GEORGE T.   [E]
San Augustine   25 Aug 1835
George T. Payne a native of Georgia
a man of family of two persons
emigrated in the Spring of 1834..
R.C. McDaniel C.P.O.
1570a.
Nacogdoches   Aug 8, 1835
Mr. Surveyor You are to survey in
Zavala's Grant the sitio which Mr.
Geo T. Payne will designate...
                Jorge Anto Nixon Comr

1571. PAYNE, JOHN C.   [E]
San Augustine   August 17, 1835
John C. Payne a native of Tennessee
a single man...emigrated in 1825...
A. Hotchkiss Primary Judge

1572. PAYNE, THOMAS   [E]
San Augustine   Sept 22d 1834
Thomas Payne native of Tennessee is
a man of family of seven persons...
Benjamin Lindsey Alcalde

1573. PAYNE, W.H.   [E]
San Augustine   Nov 2, 1835
Walton H. Payne a native of Georgia
a man of family of wife and four
children...emigrated in 1833...
A. Hotchkiss P. Judge

1574. PEACOCK, WILLIAM
State of La., Parish of Washington
I have been acquainted with Mr.
William Peacock, the bearer, for
many years past, a citizen of said
Parish for a number of years...
planting or farming his occupation
contemplates exploring the Province
of Texas...   17 February 1830
Thos C. Warner Par Judge

1575. PECK, SOLOMON R.   [S]
Nacogdoches   18 April 1835
Certify foreigner Solomon R. Peck is
a man of good...single without
family...   Radford Berry

1576. PIER, THOMAS
[Field Notes] Survey of one league
and labor on the east bank of River
Nueces adjoining John Carroll...
[Typescript "Original missing"]

1577. PEMBERTON, JOHN J.   [E]
[Precinct of Bevil] Decr 29th 1834
John J. Pemberton a native of Ten-
nessee hath a family of six persons
                John Bevil Alcalde
[Note] Unf.
[Reverse] Mr. Pemberton has taken
the oath that the Law requires
January 28, 1835   Nixon Comr

1578. PENA, MARIA VELANDA   [S]
Nacogdoches   19 June 1835
Certify citizen Maria Velarda Pena a
resident of this Municipality and
born here, woman of very good...
widow with family...has not received land...
Jn Egne Michamps Alcalde Interim
1578a.
Nacogdoches   August 12th 1835
Sir: You are to survey the sitio &
labor which Mrs. Ma Velarda Pena
will designate   Geo W. Smyth Comr

1579. PENA, ROSALIO
[Field Notes] Survey of one league
and labor for Rosalio Pena on the
left bank of En Medio Creek...

1580. PENNINGTON, SYDNEY O.   [E]
San Augustine   [no date]
Sydney O. Pennington a native of
Kentucky is a single man...emigrated
in 1831   [Remainder missing]
1580a.
San Augustine   Oct 12th 1835
To the Honl G.W. Smyth Dear Sir:
Myself with J.T. Johnson & Wm F.
Clark, old settlers that are entitled to land in Texas have made
selection on Lake Cass, near the Red
River...to Mr. Syd O. Pennington
which he agreed to survey. But in
consequence of the present difficulties was stopped from so doing.
Consequently selections are endan-
gered and we would beg that you...
stop the sd land from being surveyed
until the present difficulties are
settled... By Sydn O. Pennington

1581. PEOPLES, JEHU   [S]
Nacogdoches   20 May 1835
Certify foreigner Jehu Peoples of
good... married with family...
                Radford Berry

1582. PEPIN, VICTOR   [E]
Town of Austin   12 July 1830
I have come to the Colony...
My name is Victor Pepin 49 years of
age. Married. My family consists of
2 sons & 2 daughters that are now in
the U.S.   [Sig] V. Pepin

1583. PERKINS, B.H.   [E]
Texana   21st Jany 1836
Mr. G. Borden Jr.   Dear Sir:
Major B.H. Perkins wishes to enter
the league of land below Coxes...and
has requested me to address you on
the subject...Anything that you may
do for him...   James Kerr

1584. PERKINS, JAMES   [E]
San Augustine   Aug 20, 1835
James Perkins a native of Virginia a
man of family of a wife and one
child...emigrated in 1830.
              A. Hotchkiss P.Judge

1585. PERKINS JAMES   [S]
Nacogdoches   15 September 1834
Certify foreigner Santiago Puerquens
[faded and cannot be read]
              Vicente Cordova

1586. PERKINS, JOHN   [E]
Precinct of Cow Bayou 9 Jan 1835
John Perkins a single man of Louisiana has charge of a family consisting of his mother and his four
sisters...   John Stewart Comr

1586. PERRY, JAMES F.   [E]
State of Missouri,
County of Washington
I, John Brickey, presiding Justice
of the County Court of said county
certify I have been personally
acquainted with the bearer James
F. Perry in the county aforesaid for
about thirteen years...
20 March 1830   John Brickey
1586a.
Hazlewood [Mo]   April 10, 1830
The bearer Mr. James F. Perry is
well known to me...
              William Carr Judge
1586b.
Given in New Orleans 13 June 1831
Passport given to Mr. James Perry of
Potosi' in the State of Missouri,

with his wife and five children of
both sexes and one niece, to estab-
lish land with the Empresario S.F.
Austin.   Fran. Pizarro Martinez
[Mexican Consul in New Orleans, La.]

1588. PERRY, WILLIAM M.   [E]
To the Empresarios Austin & Williams
I have emigrated to Texas...
I am a married man my wife name is
J. Ann I have four children 3 males
& 1 female. My age 33 my wife 28
years   [Sig] Wm M. Perry

1589. PETERS, GEORGE R.
Nacogdoches   2d February 1835
Certify foreigner George R. Peters
is a man of good...single...
  Jn Egne Michamps Alcalde Interim
[Note] 1/4 West side of Trinity
       above Jas Garner

1590. PETERS, L.K.   [E]
San Augustine   27 April 1835
L.K. Peters a native of the U.S. a
man of family of five persons emi-
grated in 1824
              R.C. McDaniel C.P.O.
1590a.
Nacogdoches   Aug 11, 1835
Mr. Surveyor   You are to survey in
Zavala's Grant the sitio which Mr.
L.K. Peters will designate...
              Jorge Anto Nixon Comr

1591. PETERS, WILLIAM   [E]
Austin   September 8, 1832
To Empresarios Austin & Williams
I have emigrated to the Country...
My name is William Peters was born
in Hamburg. Am 31 years of age, am a
widower with one child which is now
in the States. [Sig] William Peters

1592. PETERSON, OLIVER   [E]
Sant Augustene   April 28, 1835
Ollever Peterson a native of Swede-
land and a man of family of a wife
and one child...
       John Bodine Alcalde pro tem
1592a.
Nacogdoches   May 1, 1835
Mr. Surveyor Sir: You are to survey the sitio which Mr. Oliver Peterson will designate...
              Jorge Anto Nixon Comr

1593. PETTUCK, GEORGE
[Field Notes] Survey of one league
and one labor for George Pettuck on
the west bank of the Rio Frio between Matthew Buirn and James
Garman...

1594. PETTUCK, JAMES
[Field Notes] Survey of one third
league for for James Pettuck on the
left bank of the Rio Frio adjoining
Roderick O'Boyle...

1595. PETTIT, WALKER   [E]
San Augustine   May 23d 1835
Certify Walker Pettit a native of
Kentucky a man of family of six
persons...   Nathan Davis Comr
[Reverse] Accepted. A.Henrie

1596. PEW, THOMAS
[Field Notes] Survey of one league
and labor for Thomas Pew on the left
bank of the River Nueces adjoining
John Carroll...

1597. PEYTON, WILLIAM   [S]
Nacogdoches   30 September 1835
Certify foreigner William Peyton a
man of good...single without family
resident of this Dept. since 1829...
                Radford Berry

1598. PHARIS, DANIEL   [E]
San Augustine   Sept 22d 1834
Certify Daniel Pharis a native of
Mississippi a man of family of five
persons... Benjamin Lindsey Alcalde

1599. PHARIS, SAMUEL   [E]
San Augustine   Sept 23d 1834
Certify Samuel Pharis a native of
the U.S., a man of family of three
persons...   John Bevil Alcalde

1600. PHARISH, JOHN   [S]
District of Bevil   March 21, 1835
John Pharish a native of South Carolina and a family of eight
persons...   Wm Williams Alcalde

1601. PHARISS, WILLIAM   [E]
San Augustine   December 26th 1834
Certify William Phariss a native of
South Carolina is a man of family of
eight persons...
    James W. Bullock Alcalde pro tem
144

1602. PHILLIPS, REUBEN   [S]
Nacogdoches   10 August 1835
Certify foreigner Reuben Phillips is
a man of good...married with family
                Radford Berry
[Note] 11 in fambley
[Rev] Accepted in Vehlein. A.Henrie

1603. PHILLIPS, SAMUEL   [S]
Nacogdoches   12 October 1835
Certify foreigner Samuel Philips is
a man of good...single without
family...   Radford Berry
[Reverse] Accepted. A. Hotchkiss
attorney for Joseph Vehlein

1604. PEARSON (PIERSON), J.W.G.
Austin   [E]   5 December 1832
To Mr. S.F. Austin Empresario
I have emigrated to this Country...
J.W.G. Pearson 37 years of age
Elizabeth my wife 27   do
4 Male children. Moved from Kentucky
& arrived in this Colony Oct 1831
            [Sig]   J.W.G. Pierson

1605. PILEBURN, JOHN   [S]
Nacogdoches   22 June 1835
Certify foreigner John Pileburn is a
man of good...married with family...
    G. Pollitt Alcalde Interim
[Rev] Accepted in Burnet. A.Henrie

1606. PINCKNEY, JOHN T.   [S]
Nacogdoches   9 February 1835
Certify foreigner John T. Pinckney
is a man of good...married with
family...   Radford Berry Alc

1607. PITTS, JONATHAN C.   [S]
Nacogdoches   Aug 7th 1835
Mr. Surveyor Sir: You are to survey in Joseph Vehlein's Grant the
sitio which Mr. Jonathan C. Pitts
will designate...
        Jorge Anto Nixon Comr
[Note] On the waters of S. Jacinto

1608. PIVETOT, MICHAEL   [E]
[District of Bevil] Decr 10, 1834
Certify Michael Pivertaun [Pivetot
written above] a native of Louisiana
hath a family of eight persons...
        John Bevil Alcalde

[Reverse] Accepted in Zavala where
he now lives. A. Henrie

1609. PLAKEY, THOMAS   [E]
To Mr. S.F. Austin Empresario
I have emigrated to this Colony...
Thomas Plakey 56 years of age
Nancy   47   do
4 Male 4 female chilren. Moved from
Kentucky and desirous of being
admitted...   May 8, 1832
                Thomas Plakey
[Note] Passport dated 20"April. Cer-
tificate issued. Took the oath be-
fore John Austin.
[Reverse] Thomas Blakey

1610. PLUMMER, LUTHER T.M.   [E]
Tenoxtitlan   22 May 1834
To the Empresarios Austin & Williams
I have emigrated to Texas...
I am married my wife is name Rachael
and my age 22 my wife 16.
                Luther T.M. Plummer

1611. POE, AARON   [E]
San Augustine   Oct 6, 1835
Certify Aaro Poe a native of Loui-
siana is a man of family of ten
persons...emigrated in 1831 and has
taken the oath... Nathan Davis Comr
1611a.
San Augustine   2 Oct 1835
I hereby authorize Franklin Fuller
to petition for one league and
labor...   [Sig] Aaron Poe
Witnesses E.O. Legrand
Daniel Fuller   A.B. Davis
Samuel Tenniel? Thos H. Garner

1612. POTTITT, GEORGE   [S]
Nacogdoches   10 Feb 1835
Certify foreigner George Pottitt is
a man of good...married with family.
                Radford Berry
[Reverse] George Pettitt

1613. POLVADORE, JUAN   [E]
San Augustine   Sept 1st 1835
Certify John Polvadore a native of
France is a man of family of seven
persons...Emigrated about 50 years
since...   Saml Thompson Alcd
[Note] Unf.

1614. POLVADOR, MARIA HONORIA
Nacogdoches   31 June 1835
Certify citizen Ma Honoria Polvadora
is a resident of this Municipality
and born here, a widow with family.
has not   obtained land...
        Jn Egne Michamps Alc Int
1614a.
Nacogdoches   Sept 18th 1835
Sir: You are to survey the sitio &
labor which Maria Honoria Palvador
will...

1615. POOL, BEVERLY   [S]
Nacogdoches   2 January 1835
Certify foreigner Beverly Pool is a
man of good...married...
        Radford Alcalde Alc
[Note] On the Navasoto north of
Bejar Road wife & 4 children,
        Brookfield. Burnet

1616. POOL, JOHN   [E]
San Augustine   9 May 1835
Certify John Pool a native of Pen-
nsylvania a single man...
        John Bodine Alcalde pro tem

1617. POOL, JEREMIAH C.   [S]
Nacogdoches   1 November 1834
Certify foreigner Jonathan C. Pool
is a man of good...married with
family...   Vital Flores
[Note] Wife and five children.
Vehlein On the Twelve Mile Creek on
the Labiah road. Mr. Robinson

1618. POOL, WALTER T.   [S]
Nacogdoches   20 May 1835
Certify foreigner Walter T. Pool is
a man of good...married with family
                Radford Berry
1618a.
Recd of Major G. Nixon
Walter T. Poole Title to his land
4 Oct 1835   C.A. Lewis

1619. POOR, IROE ,   [E]
Department of Texas, Sulphur Fork
Prairie   To George W. Smyth Esqr
Through Benjn Tennill a Surveyor
acting under your instruction I
protest against survey made by...
Rowe. Said survey includes at least
hakf of the league on which I have
an improvement...
30 Novr 1835   Ira Poor

145

1620. PORTER, ALEXANDER H.   [E]
District of Bevil   25 March 1835
Certify Alexander H. Porter a native
of Virginia hath a family of three
persons...   Wm Williams Alcalde

1621. PORTER, JOHN JONES   [S]
Nacogdoches   18 March 1835
Certify foreigner J.J. Porter a man
of good...married with family...
[Reverse] John James Porter

1622. PORTER, SAMUEL   [E]
San Augustine   August 25, 1835
Certify Samuel Porter a native of
Virginia that he is a man of family
of wife and four children...emigra-
ted in 1831.
          A. Hotchkiss Primary Judge
1622a.
San Augustine   25 Aug 1835
I, Samuel Porter appoint Edwin O.
Legrand my attorney to petition
for one league & labor...
              Samuel X Porter

1623. POTTER, ROBERT   [S]
Nacogdoches   8 July 1835
Certify foreigner Robert Potter a
man of good...widower with family...
              Radford Berry
[Note] Unf.

1624. POWEL, ISAAC   [E]
District of Sabine   22 Dec 1834
Certify Isaac Powel a native of No
Carolina, is a man of family of
three personss Elbert Hines Comr
[Note] Isaac Powel wife and one
child. Adjoining North of John S.
Smith Survey near the Sabine.
          Zavala J.A. Veatch

1625. PRADO, JOSE ANTONIO
Nacogdoches   Sept 22d 1834
Mr. Wm Brookfield Sir: You are to
survey in Vehlein's Grant the sitio
which Mr. Jose Anselmo Prado will
designate... Jorge Anto Nixon Comr
[Reverse] The within order has been
executed by me. William Brookfield
[Also has] Jose' Anto Prado

1626. PREWITT, JACOB   [S]
Nacogdoches   4 December 1834
Certify foreigner Jacob Pruet is a
146

man of good...married with family...
              Victor Flores
[Note] Jacob Prewit. He does not
sign. Wife and 2 children. Burnet
The place where he now lives. Strode
1626a.
Naches District   March 19, 1835
G.A. Nixon Esqr, Commissioner
Sir: Please to let Leonard Williams
have my deed...   Jacob X Prewett
Witness Wm Whiteley

1627. PRICE, GEORGE W.   [S]
Nacogdoches   27 April 1835
Certify George W. Price a man of
good...single..   Radford Berry

1628. PRICHARD, JOSEPH   [S]
Nacogdoches   22 April 1835
Certify foreigner Joseph Prichard a
man of good...single without
family...   Radford Berry

1629. PRICHARD, WILLIAM B.   [E]
Austin   April 20, 1832
To Mr. S.F. Austin Empresario
I have emigrated to this Colony...
William B. Pritchard 25 years of
age, unmarried. Moved from Alabama.
[Sig] William B. Prichard
Passport 2 April 1832

1630. PRINCE, J.R.   [E]
San Augustine   27 June 1835
Certify J.R. Prince a native of N.
York is a man of family of seven
persons, that he emigrated in the
fall of 1834...R.C. McDaniel C.P.O.
1630a.
Nacogdoches   August 12, 1835
Mr. Surveyor Sir: You are to sur-
vey in Zavala's Grant the sitio
which Mr.R.Prince will designate...
              Jorge Anto Nixon Comr
[Note] On east side of Rio Alabama

1631. PRISCICK, WILLIAM   [S]
Nacogdoches   24 April 1835
Certify foreigner William Priscick a
man of good...married with family...
              Radford Berry

1632. PROSELO, GERTRUDIS [E]
San Augustine   Sept 1, 1835
Certify Atruis Procell is a native
citzen and a widow woman of family
of six persons Saml Thompsoon Alcd
[Reverse] Gertrudis Procelo
1632a.
San Augustine
I authorize Peter Stockman to apply
for an order of survey...
                    Atruis X Procell
Witnesses   Hosea X Francisco
Joseph Polvadore Saml Thompson Alcd

1633. PRU, MARIA JOSEFA   [S]
Nacogdoches   20 June 1835
Certify citizen Maria Josefa Prou is
a woman of very good...widow with
family...has not received land...
Jn Egne Michamps Alcalde Interim
[Rev]   Ma Josefa Pru
1633a.
Nacogdoches   August 4th 1835
Sir: You are to survey the sitio &
labor which Ma Josefa Pru will
designate...   Geo W. Smyth Comr

1634. PRUET, JOSIAH   [S]
Nacogdoches   13 June 1835
Certify foreigner Josiah Pruet is a
man of good...Widower with family...
Jn Egne Michamps Alcalde Interim

1635. PRUITT, JOHN   [S]
Nacogdoches   28 May 1835
Certify foreigner John Pruitt is a
man of good...married with family...
Jn Egne Michamps Alcalde Interim
[Reverse] Acceptd. Arthur Henrie

1636. PRY, PETER B.   [E]
District of Bevil   Sept 30, 1834
Certify Peter B. Pry a native of
Kentucky hath a family of three
persons...   John Bevil Alcd

1637. PUNCHARD, JOSEPH H.   [E]
Austin   Decr 14, 1832
To Mr. S.F. Austin Empresario
I have emigrated to this Country..My
name is Joseph H. Punchard 51 years
of age. Dorcas my wife. 2 Male 4
female children. Moved from
Mississippi.   Joseph H. Punchard

1638. PUNCHARD, WILLIAM   [E]
Austin   Decr 14, 1832
To Mr. S.F. Austin Empresario
I have emigrated to this Country...
My name is William Punchard 45 years
of age. Unmarried. Moved from Mis-
sissippi. [Sig] Wm Punchard

1639. PURDOM, HENRY   [E]
Tenoxtitlan   29 April 1829
To the Empresarios Austin & Williams
I have emigrated to Texas...
I am a widower & have 2 children.
My age 49.   [Sig] Henry Purdom

1640. PURDY, LITSOM   [E]
Tenoxtitlan   8 June 1834
To the Empresarios Austin & Williams
I have emigrated to Texas...
I am married. My wifes name Mary and
2 children. My age 31. My wifes 28
years.   [Sig] Letsom Purdy

1641. QUINILTY, JOHN L.   [S]
Nacogdoches   11 September 1835
Certify foreigner John L. Quilnity
is a man of good...married with
family to a woman of the Country...
                    Radford Berry
[Rev] Accepted im Vehlein. A.Henrie
For one quarter on account of his
marrying a Mexican having already
got a league.

1642. QUINTERO, TEODORO   [S]
Nacogdoches   2 September 1835
Certify citizen Teodoro Quintero is
a man of good...resident of this
Municipality since 1818...has not
obtained land...   Radford Berry

1643. QUIRK, HENRY N.[M] [E]
San Augustine   Sept 1st 1835
Certify Henry M. Quirk is a native
citizen and a married man of two in
family...   Saml Thompson Alcd

1644. RAFFERTY, JAMES   [E]
San Augustine   4 May 1835
Certify James Rafferty a native of
Kentucky is a man of family of seven
persons that he emigrated March 1835
                R.C. McDaniel C.P.O.

1644a.
Nacogdoches   Augt 7, 1835
Mr. Surveyor You are to survey in
Zavala's Grant the sitio which James
Rafferty will designate...
               Jorge Anto Nixon Comr
[Note] On the west side of River
Neches

1645. RAGLAND, WILLIAM [E]
San Augustine   May 10, 1835
Certify William Ragland a single man
a native of Tennessee...
               A. Hotchkiss P.Judge

1646. RAGUET, HENRY [S]
Nacogdoches   11 May 1835
Certify foreigner Henry Raguet a man
of good...married with family...
               Radford Berry
1646a.
Nacogdoches   May 25, 1835
Received of G.A. Nixon Commissioner
the copy of the Title of Francisco
Martinez as his agent. Henry Raguet

1647. RAIMOND, SAMUEL [E]
District of Tenahaw   July 21, 1835
Certify Samuel Raimond a native of
Tennessee a man of family of five
persons...emigrated in 1831 and has
taken the oath.   Nathan Davis Comr

1648. RAINES, C.B. [E]
Tenoxtitlan   22 April 1834
I have emigrated to Texas...
I am unmarried my age 28 years.
               [Sig] C.B. Raines

1649. RAINES, SAMUEL M.   [E]
San Augustine   August 18, 1835
Certify Samuel M.Raines a native of
Louisiana a man of family of wife
and one child...emigrated in 1831...
               A. Hotchkiss Prmy Judge

1650. RAINS, EMERY [E]
San Augustine   22 Sept 1834
Certify Emery Rains a native of
Tennessee is a man of family of nine
persons... Benjamin Lindsey Alcalde
1650a.
George A. Nixon Comr   April 1st 1835
Pleas to deliver the title to my
land to Benjamin Linsey Esqr
               E. Rains

148

1651. RALPH, SAMUEL [S]
Nacogdoches   2 December 1834
Certify foreigner Samuel Ralph is a
man of good...married with family...
               Vital Flores
[Note] Wife & 1 ch. 2 mi above the
town of Zavala on the Angelina.
               David Brown

1652. RAMIRES, JESUS [S]
Nacogdoches   22 Aug 1835
Certify citizen Jesus Ramires is a
man of good...resident of this Municipality and born here...has not
obtained land...   Radford Berry

1653. RAMIRES, JOSE [S]
Nacogdoches   8 Sept 1835
Certify citizen Jose Ramires is a
man of good...resident of this District and born here...single without
family...has not obtained land...
               Radford Berry
1653A.
Nacogdoches   31 Oct 1835
Certify citizen Jose Ramirez ...a
resident of this Dept. since 1813,
married with family, has not obtained land...   Radford Berry

1654. RAMIREZ, MARIA DAMACIA [S]
Nacogdoches   8 Sept 1835
Certify Maria Damacia Ramirez is a
woman of very good...widow with
family, resident of this Municipality since 1811... has not obtained
land...   Radford Berry

1655. RAMIRES, MEREJILDO [S]
Nacogdoches   8 Sept 1835
Certify citizen Merejildo Ramirez is
a man of good...married with family,
resident of the Municipality since
1829...has not obtained land...
               Radford Berry

1656. RAMSDALL, FRANCIS   [S]
Nacogdoches   15 May 1835
Certify foreigner Francis Ramsdall
is a man of good...married with
family...   Radford Berry

1657. RANDOLPH, ROBERT   [S]
Nacogdoches   5 October 1835
Certify Robert Randolph a man of
good... single without family...
               Radford Berry
[Note] Unfinished title

1658. RANEY, JOHN [E]
To Mr. S.F. Austin Empresario
I have emigrated to this Country...
John Raney 50 years of age native of
England. Nancy 51 years of age.
2 Female children. Arrived in this
Country in April 1830. John Raney

1659. RANKIN, FREDERICK [S]
Nacogdoches   13 November 1834
Mr. Frederick Rankin is a man of
very good...married with family...
                    Vital Flores

1660. RANKIN, JAMES [E]
San Felipe de Austin June 10, 1830
To Mr. S.F. Austin Empresario
I have emigrated to this Colony...
My name is James Rankin. Age 22
years. Single. My father is dead and
I have no parent in this Country to
represent me. I removed from Ala-
bama, arrived in this Colony in
1827. Occupation farmer.
            [Sig] James Rankin Jr
1660a.
Nacogdoches   Nov 13, 1834
To Mr. Wm Robinson Surveyor Sir:
You are to survey in Jos Vehlein's
Grant the sitio which Mr. James
Rankin Jr. [this name written over
"Fred. Rankin"] will designate...
      Jorge Anto Nixon Comr
[The above Order was crossed out]
[Rev] Returned by Mr. Hubert and
changed to James Rankin Jur.

1661. RANKIN, JAMES [E]
Municipality of Austin Nov 3d 1834
I certify James Rankin a native of
Kentucky a man of family of two
persons...
Jesse Grimes Primary Judge , Austin

1662. RANKIN, ROBERT [E]
Municipality of Austin Nov 3d 1834
I certify Robert Rankin a native of
Virginia a man of family of four
persons...
Jesse Grimes Primary Judge, Austin

1663. RANKIN, WILLIAM [E]
To Mr. S.F. Austin Empresario
[no date] I have emigrated to this
Colony...William Rankin 21 years
old. Unmarried. An Orphan. From

Alabama and arrived in this Colony
in 20 Jany 1830.   Wm Rankin

1664. RANKIN, WILLIAM M. [E]
To Mr. W.F. Austin Empresario
May 27, 1830 I have emigrated to
this Colony...Wm M. Rankin 43 years
old. Married. Sarah my wife 33. 2
Male 2 female children Moved from
Alabama. Arrived 20 Jany 1830.
      [Sig] W.M. Rankin

1665. RANSOM, GEORGE [S]
Nacogdoches   15 May 1835
Certify foreigner George Ransom is a
man of good...single without family
[Note] Unf. title   Radford Berry

1666. RATLIFF, A.G. [W.D.]
Mr. George A. Nixon   30 June 1835
Please give the title papers of my
land to Mr. Thomas S. McFarlan
            Montgomery B. Thomas
      by W.D. Ratliff A.G.

1667. RATLIFF, ELISHA [S]
Naogdoches   15 Nov 1834
Certify Elisha Ratliff is a man of
good...married with family...
                    Vital Flores
[Note] Wife & 4 children
1667a.
Fort Teran   March 1835
Mr. Jorge Anto Nixon, Comr,
Nacogdoches Sir:
Deliver my title to M.B. Menard
Witness   Elisha X Ratliff
Robt O.W. McManus

1668. RATLIFF, WILLIAM D. [S]
Nacogdoches   31 Dec 1834
Certify foreigner William D. Ratliff
is a man of good...married with
family...   Vital Flores
[Note] Unfinished title
[Rev] Accepted in Burnet. A.Henrie

1669. RAWLINGS, JOHNSON [E]
San Augustine   15 Sept 1835
I, Johnson Rawlings appoint William
English my attorney to petition for
one league and labor to which I am
entitled as an old settler...
          [Sig] Johnson Rawlings
Witnesses George English
      E. Rains   R.A. Berry
                              149

1670. RAY, JONATHAN D. [E]
San Augustine   May 23d 1835
Certify Jonathan D. Ray a native of
Tennessee is a man of family of two
persons   Nathan Davis Comr
[Reverse] Accepted. Arthur Henrie

1671. RAYDON, JOHN [E]
District of Tenahaw August 20, 1835
Certify John Raydon a native of
Georgia is a man of family of three
persons...that he emigrated in 1830
and has taken the oath
                Nathan Davis Comr

1672. RAYMOND, ALFRED [E]
San Augustine   Sept 22, 1835
Alfred Raymond a native citizen is a
man of family of five persons...
                Saml Thompson Alcd
1672a.
San Augustine   22 Sept 1835
I, Alfred Raymond appoint William
English my attorney to petition for
one league & labor...
        [Sig] Alfred Raymond
Witnesses .
A.E.C. Johnson C.Thompson
Saml Thompson Alcd
1672b.
Nacogdoches   October 9, 1835
Sir: You are to survey the sitio &
labor which Mr. Alfred Raymond will
designate... Geo W. Smyth Comr

1673. RAYMOND, JOHN [E]
San Augustine   Sept 22, 1835
Certify John Raymond a native citi-
zen and a man of family of eleven
persons... Saml Thompson Alcd
1673a.
San Augustine   22 Sept 1835
I, John Raymond appoint William
Inglish my attorney to petition for
one league & labor...
        [Sig] John Raymond
Witnesses
A.E.C. Johnson Saml Thompson Alcd
1673b.
Nacogdoches   October 9, 1835
Aie: You are to survey the sitio &
labor which Mr. John Raymond will
designate... Geo W. Smyth Comr

150

1674. READ, JOHN C. [E]
Jurisdiction of Liberty 28 Dec 1834
Certify John C. Read a native of
Kentucky a man of family of his wife
and one child   Wm Hardin Judge

1675. REAGAN, WILLIAM [S]
Nacogdoches   13 April 1835
Certify foreigner William Reagan is
a man of good...married with family
                Radford Berry

1676. REAL, DANIEL [S]
Nacogdoches   4 May 1835
Certify foreigner Daniel Real is a
man of good...married...
                Radford Berry

1677. REAL, HENRY [S]
Nacogdoches   4 May 1835
Certify foreigner Henry Real is a
man of good...single...
                Radford Berry

1678. REAL, JAMES [S]
Nacogdoches   4 May 1835
Certify foreigner James Real is a
man of good...single without
family... Radford Berry

1679. REAS (RIOS), SIMON DEL [E]
Recd of Major Nixon
Simon del Reas title for the owner
                Arthur Henrie

1680. REAVES, GREEN [E]
San Augustine   Sept 1st 1835
Certify Green Reaves a native of
Kentucky a man of family of five
persons...emigrated in 1830.
                Saml Thompson Alcd
[Note] Unfinished title

1681. REDLICK, AUGUST CHARLES [S]
Nacogdoches   28 May 1835
Certify foreigner August Charles
Redlickis a man of good...married
with family...
Jn Egne Michamps Alcalde Interim
[Rev]: Accepted. Arthur Henrie

1682. REDMOND, ZACHARIAH [E]
San Augustine   22 Sept 1834
Certify Zachariah Redmond a native
of South Carolina a man of family of
three persons...
                Benjamin Lindsey Alcalde

1683. REED, BENJAMIN S. [E]
Municipality of Tennehaw 18 Aug 1835
Certify Benjamin S. Reed a native of
Georgia a man of family of four
persons...emigrated in 1832...
Nathan Davis Comr
[Note] Unfinished title

1684. REED, ISAAC [S]
Nacogdoches 21 January 1835
Appeared before me Radford Berry,
foreigner Isaac Reed, origin the
U.S., age 59, married, farmer and
stockraiser, wants to settle...
Radford Berry
Witnesses James Carter Henry Awalt
John Egne Michamps

1685. REED, ISAAC H. [S]
Nacogdoches 24 January 1835
Certify foreigner Isaac H. Reed is a
man of good...married with family...
Radford Berry Alc
[Note] Wife & ch

1686. REED, WILLIAM B. [S]
Nacogdoches 16 May 1835
Certify foreigner William B. Reed is
a man of good...married with family
Radford Berry

1687. REED, WILLIAM B. [S]
Nacogdoches 21 May 1835
Certify foreigner William B. Reed is
a man of good...married with family
Radford Berry

1688. REEL, DANIEL, HENRY & JAMES
Mr. George Antono Nixon
May 10th 1835 Sir: You will please
deliver the three titles for land
coming to us the undersigned, to
Mr. R.W. Smith.
Witness present   Daniel Reel
Levi Jordan   Henry Reel
Joseph Durst   James Reel

1689. RENFRO, DAVID [E]
District of Sabine [no date]
Certify that David Renfro of this
District of Sabine has a family of
five persons being a citizen of this
place since 1827.
B. Holt Comr for District of Sabine

1690. RENFRO, ISAAC [E]
District of Sabine [no date]
Certify that Isaac Renfro a native
of Missouri has a family...emigrated
in 1825 B. Holt Comr
[Note] Unfinished title

1691. RESENDIS, LUCIANA
[Field Notes] Survey of one league
and one labor for Luciano Resendis
on Enmedio Creek (on the left bank)
opposite the survey of Cannan Molina

1692. REYES, JUAN JOSE DE LOS [S]
Nacogdoches 8 April 1835
Certify citizen Juan Jose de los
Reyes is a resident of this Munici-
pality and born here, married with
family, has not obtained land...
Radford Berry
1692a.
Nacogdoches 28 Decr 1835
Recd of G.A. Nixon the title of Juan
Josen Reyes. Juan Santos Coy

1693. REYNOLDS, ALBERT G. [S]
[Certificate of Reception]
Villa de Austin 20 April 1831
Certify that Albert G. Reynolds is
one of the Colonists...arrived in
this Colony 1 April 1831; married
with family of 6 persons...
Empresario Samuel M. Williams
[Reverse]
New Orleans Feb 29, 1832
Presented for going to Brasoria on
the American schooner of the same
name, Captain Rowland.
[by the Mexican Consul]

N. Orleans June 6, 1832
Return to Brasoria on the ship above
with his wife and five children.

1694. REYNOLDS, JAMES
[Certificate of Reception]
Villa of Austin 1 April 1831
Certify James Reynolds is one of the
Colonists...has six months to arrive
after the above date...
Estevan F. Austin

1695. REYNOLDS, JOSEPH [S]
Nacogdoches 18 September 1835
Certify foreigner Joseph Reynolds is
a man of good...single without fami-
151

ly, resident of this Department
since 1833... Radford Berry
[Note] Unf. title

1696. RHEA, JOHN R. [E]
Jurisdiction of Liberty 24 Feb 1835
Certify that John R. Rhea a native
of Pennsylvania is a man of family
of wife and five children...
Wm Hardin Judge

1697. RICARDO, GUADALUPE [S]
Nacogdoches 4 April 1835
Certify citizen Guadalupe Ricardo is
a resident of this Municipality for
many years, widower with family, has
not obtained land... Radford Berry

1698. RICE, CLINTON [E]
San Augustine August 18th 1835
Certify Clinton Rice a native of
Tennessee is a man of family of
three persons...emigrated in 1826...
Saml Thompson Alcd
[Note] Unfinished title

1699. RICE, JOSEPH [E]
San Augustine August 20, 1835
Certify Joseph Rice a native of
Tennessee is a man of family of five
persons...emigrated in 1826...
Saml Thompson Alcd
[Note] Unfinished title

1700. RICHARDS, CHARLES [S]
Nacogdoches 28 October 1834
Certify by two residents A.C. Allen
and Genere Fil that foreigner
Charles Richal is of good morality
Vicente Cordova
[Note] Unfinished title

1701. RICHAL, SANTIAGO (JAMES RICHARDS)
Nacogdoches 28 October 1834
Certify by two residents A.C. Allen
and Genere Fil that foreigner San-
tiago Richal is of good morality...
Vicente Cordova
[Note] Unfinished title

1702. RICHARDS, WILLIAM [E]
San Augustine Sept 1, 1835
Certify Wm Richards a native of
Tennessee a single man...emigrated
in March 1834...
A. Hotchkiss P.Judge
[Rev] Accepted in Vehlein. A.Henrie
152

1703. RICHARDSON, BENJAMIN [E]
District of Bevil October 12, 1834
Certify Benjamin Richardson a native
of Georgia hath a family of ten per-
sons... John Bevil Alcalde
[Note] Zavala = on the E side of
Neches on his improvement.
Wife & 3 ch.
[Note] Unfinished title

1704. RICHARDSON, FELIX A. [S]
Nacogdoches 29 April 1835
Certify foreigner Felix A. Richard-
son is a man of good...married with
family... Radford Berry
[Note] Unfinished title

1705. RICHARDSON, WILLIAM [S]
Nacogdoches 7 September 1835
Certify foreigner William Richardson
is a man of good...single without
family... Radford Berry
[Rev] Accepted in Vehlein. A.Henrie
1705a.
Nacogdoches 1 Decr 1835
Wm Richardson has lost or mislaid an
order of survey issued from the
office of Comr. Jorge Anto Nixon in
favor of R.C. Rogers No. 440
Vehlein. William Richardson
1705b.
Receipt for Order of Surveys
May 15, 1838
No. 391 Mrs. Hana Damacia Ramires
375 Mr. Antonio Mensola
319 J.B. McNeely
374 Mr. Cateleno Mendes
392 Mrs. Isbell Gutierez
436 Manuel Flores
The above orders were handed to
Commissioner Smith and sent by him
to the Genl Land Office. Recd the
above orders of Survey. S)
W. Richardson

1706. RICHEY, HIRAM [E]
Jurisdiction of Liberty 24 Apr 1835
Certify Hiram Richey a native of
Louisiana, a man of family...
Claiborne West Judge
[Note] Unfinished title

1707. RICHEY, JOSEPH [E]
Jurisdiction of Liberty 24 Apr 1835
Certify Joseph Richey a native of
Louisiana and a single man...
Claiborne West Judge

1707a. J.A. Nixon Comr
April 24, 1835   Dear Sir: Please
send me the title to my land per
David Garner.   Joseph X Richey

1708. RICHEY, UEL   [E]
Jurisdiction of Liberty 24 Apr 1835
Certify Uel Richey a native of Lou-
isiana, a single man...
           Claiborne West Judge
1708a.
J.A. Nixon Comr   April 25, 1835
Dear Sir: Please send me the title
to my land per David Garner...
              Uel X Richey

1709. RILEY, JAMES   [S]
Nacogdoches   27 October 1834
Certify foreigner Santiago Riley a
man of good...married with family...
              Vital Flores
[Note]. Riley. Wife & 5 children
1709a.
Nacogdoches   Sept 8, 1835
Received of Jorge Anto Nixon a title
of land for Jaime Riley.
           J. Roberts for J. Riley

1710. RIOS, MANUELA DEL   [S]
Nacogdoches   13 June 1835
Certify citizen Manuela del Rio is a
resident of this Municipality for
many years woman of very good...
widow with family...wants land...
     Jorge Egne Michamps Alc. I.
[Note] Unfinished title
[Reverse] Accepted. A. Henrie

1711. RIO, PEDRO DEL   [S]
Nacogdoches   30 June 1835
Certify citizen Pedro del Rio is a
man of good...resident of this Muni--
cipality and born here, married, has
not obtained land
     Jn Egne Michamps Alcalde Interim
1711a.
Nacogdoches   August 3d 1835
Sir: You are to survey the sitio &
labor which Mr. Pedro del Rio will
designate...   Geo W. Smyth Comr
[Note] On the Sabine

1712. RIO, SIMON DEL   [S]
Nacogdoches   15 April 1835
Certify citizen Simon del Rio is a
resident of this Municipality for
many years, man of good...single

without family. Has not obtained
land...   Radford Berry

1713. RISENHOOVER, BENSON   [S]
Nacogdoches   28 April 1835
Certify foreigner Benson Risenhoover
is a man of good...married with
family...   Radford Berry
[Note] Unfinished title

1714. RITTER, EVERETT   [E]
San Augustine   18 August 1835
Certify Everett Ritter is a citizen
of the Municipality of San Augustine
a native of Tennessee & emigrated in
1831...   Nathan Davis Comr
[Note] Unfinished title

1715. RITTER, GEORGE W.   [S]
Nacogdoches   17 September 1835
Certify foreigner George W. Ritter
is a man of good...married with
family and resident of this Department since 1832...   Radford Berry
[Note] Unfinished title

1716. RIVERS, JOHN   [E]
Maj Nixon   March 3, 1835
Dear Sir: Please deliver my title to
Mr. Merchison.   John X Rivers
A. Henrie

1717. RIVERIE, JUAN LA   [S]
Nacogdoches   24 January 1835
Certify foreigner Juan La Riviere is
a man of good...married with family
              Radford Berry

1718. ROADS, THOMAS   [E]
Precinct of Tenahaw 17 August 1835
Certify that Thomas Roads a native
of Georgia a man of family of fore
persons   Nathan Davis Comr
[Note] Unfinished title

1719. ROARK, JOHN   [S]
Nacogdoches   23 April 1835
Certify foreigner John Roark is a
man of good...married with family...
              Radford Berry

1719. ROARK, JOHN   [S]
Nacogdoches   23 April 1835
Certify foreigner John Roark a man
of good...married with family...
              Radford Berry

1720. ROARK, RUSSELL [S]
Nacogdoches   20 July 1835
Certify foreigner Russell Roark a
man of good...single without family
                    Radford Berry
[Rev] Accepted om Vehlein 1/4 sitio
1720a.
Sir: Novr 2d 1835
Please to let the bearer have my
title.   Russel Roark
J.A. Nixon Esqr

1721. ROARK, WILLIAM [S]
Nacogdoches   4 December 1834
Certify foreigner Wm Roark is a man
of good...married with family...
                    Vital Flores
1721a.
Recd of George Antonio Nixon Comr
the title of Wm H. Steel for one
fourth sitio in David G. Burnet's
Grant.
5th Sept 1835   Recd per Wm Roark

1722. ROBERSON, JAMES [E]
San Augustine   Oct 5th 1835
Certify James Roberson a native of
Kentucky a man of family of five
persons...emigrated 1831 and has
taken the oath of allegiance.
                    Nathan Davis Comr
1722a.
San Augustine   Oct 7, 1835
I, James Robertson appoint [blank]
to petition for one league & labor
Witnesses   [Sig] James Roberson
E.O. Legrand
Wm T. Hatton   James Moran
A.B. Davis   John Ware

1723. ROBERTS, CHARLES [E]
San Augustine   August 22d 1835
Certify Charles Roberts a native of
Georgia a man of family of six per-
sons...emigrated February 1832, has
taken the oath   Saml Thompson Alcd
[Note] Unf title
1723a.
San Augustine   August 22d 1835
I, Charles Roberts appoint S.W.
Blout my attorney to petition for

one league and labor as an old settler... [Sig] Charley Roberts
Witness Saml Thompson Alcd

1723A. ROBBINS, THOMAS [S]
Nacogdoches   17 July 1835
Recd of Major G.A. Nixon the follow-
ing titles:
        Jose' Maria Sanchez
        Cesario Chamar
        William Skinner
        Manuel Plummer
        James M. Lyon
        [By] Thomas Robbins

1724. ROBERTS, CHARLES L. [S]
Nacogdoches   23 March 1835
Certify foreigner Charles L. Roberts
a man of good...single without
family...   Radford Berry

1725. ROBERTS, ELISHA
[10 Documents in this file]
Parish St. Tammany, Louisiana
                    29 April 1822
Elisha Roberts Esqr of this Parish,
having intention to travel...evi-
dence of good character. Elisha
Roberts has resided in the Parish
for upwards of seven years...
[Nine names of the Parish]

San Augustine   20th August 1835
To George W. Smyth Comr. Greetings:
Whereas Elisha Roberts is about
applying to you for title to the
land whereon he now lives known as
the Lugan[?] Claim. This is to ad-
vise you not to make any such title
as the said Roberts is an intruder
and I have the only legal title to
the land...by a title given me by
the Spanish Gov...I do protest.
C. Thompson   B.J. Thompson

To George W. Smyth Comr
The petition of Elisha Roberts...en-
titled to a league and labor...he
settled the land he now occupies in
1822 and has resided on the same
since...made improvements...has made
application for a sitio and the same
has been conceded...further repre-
sents that one Burrel Thompson with
Lewis Holloway...have prayed of you

not to expedite a title to your
petitioner pretending they have a
legal claim and have presented old
papers for the purpose. [4 pages;
older Spanish grants etc]
  Thos J. Rusk Pro Elisha Roberts

Nacogdoches   Sept 9th 1835
Having taken into consideration...I
have arrived at the following con-
clusion:
1st That the petitioner Elisha
Roberts has remained in peacable
possession of the land for thirteen
years.
2nd. That the General Govt has ap-
proved and put him in possession.
[Further summarises conclusions]
to the petitioner Elisha Roberts a
title for the land.   Henry Rueg

San Augustine   September 25, 1835
To George W. Smyth Comr Dear Sir:
William N. Siglar who laid in a
protest against me have had a survey
made by Mr. Casine without notifying
me and have been across the line of
the land which you made the title to
me and I protest...Mr. Siglar has
done all this to vex me.
               Elisha Roberts

1726. ROBERTS, ISAAC [S]
Nacogdoches   9 October 1834
Certify foreigner Isaac Roberts is a
man of good...married with family...
[Note] Unf. title   Luis Procela
1726a.
Recd of Comr G.A. Nixon
Newton C. Hodges and Isaac Barnets
titles July 24th 1837   I. Roberts

1727. ROBERTS, JOHN [S]
Nacogdoches   7 October 1835
Certify that resident of this Villa
Juan S. Roberts is of good...married
in this Villa in Nuestra Santa Madre
Church...   Luis Procela

1729. ROBERTS, JOSEPH [E]
Jurisdiction of Liberty 21 Nov 1834
Certify that Joseph Roberts a native
of Prussia a man of family of three
[Note] Unf. title   Wm Hardin Judge
1729a. Nacogdoches   27 May 1835
Certify foreigner Joseph Roberts is

a man of good...married with family
   Jn Egne Michamps A.I.
[Note] Unfinished title

1730. ROBERTS, NATHANIEL   [S]
Nacogdoches   15 September 1834
Certify foreigner Nathaniel Robes
living on the Trinity is an old
resident of this Jurisdiction...
            Vicente Cordova
[Reverse] Nathaniel Roberts

1731. ROBERTS, NOEL   [E]
San Augustine   August 1835
Certify Noel Roberts a native of
Louisiana is a man of family of
three persons emigrated in 1824...
            Saml Thompson Acld
1731a.
Ayish Bayou   25 September 1835
To George W. Smyth Comr Dear Sir:
This is to notify you that a certain
William N. Siglar have without
giving notice to me have had a Sur-
vey made by a Surveyor by the name
of Cosine [Corzine] and have taken
taken into his Survey the labor of
land which you made a title for.
Now I do solemnly protest...
               Noel G. Roberts

1732. ROBERTS, NOEL J.   [E]
San Augustine   Sept 27th 1834
Certify Noel J. Roberts a native of
Louisiana a man of family of two
persons...Benjamin Lindsey Alcalde
[Note] Unfinished title

1733. ROBERTS, WILLIAM   [E]
San Augustine   Nov 25th 1834
Certify William Roberts a native of
Virginia a man of family of six
persons... Benjamin Lindsey Alcalde
[Note] Wife and four children.
Zavala The place where he lives.
            David Brown

1734. ROBERTS, WILLIAM   [E]
Certify Mr. William Roberts emi-
grated early in the year 1826 and
was present when I published the
Constitution of the State as Alcalde
and administered the oath to him...
Samuel --- Witness Jas Gaines
[Note] Unfinished title

1735. ROBERTSON, ARTHUR [E]
Austin   30 Septem 1831
To Mr. S.F. Austin Empresario
I have emigrated to this Country...
My name is Arthur Robertson. My age
21 unmarried   Arthur Robertson

1736. ROBERSON, EDWARD [E]
San Augustine   Oct 10, 1835
Certify Edward Robison a native of
Virginia a man of family of nine
children...came to Texas in 1831 as
said by Mr. Watson, and he has taken
the oath...   A. Hotchkiss P.Judge
[Note] Unf. title
1736a.
San Augustine   9 October 1835
I, Edward Roberson appoint Richard
Haley my attorney to petition for
one league & labor...
               Edward X Robison
[Reverse] Edward Robinson

1737. ROBERTSON, EDWIN [E]
San Augustine   29 April 1835
Certify Mr. Edwin Robertson a native
of the U.S. a man of family of four
persons emigrated in Sept 1834...
         R.C. McDaniel C.P.O.
[Reverse] Accepted. A. Henrie
1737a.
Nacogdoches   August 12, 1835
Mr. Surveyor You are to survey in
Zavala's Grant the sitio which Mr.
E. Robertson will designate...
               Jorge Anto Nixon

1738. ROBERTSON, LARKIN [S]
Nacogdoches   4 May 1835
Certify foreigner Larkin Robertson
is a man of good...married with
family...   Radford Berry

1739. ROBINETT, C.C. [S]
Nacogdoches   13 June 1835
Cerify foreigner Calvin C. Robinett
a man of good...married with family
   Jn Egne Michamps Alcalde Interim

1740. ROBINSON, BENJAMIN W. [S]
Nacogdoches   14 October 1834
Certify foreigner Benjamin W. Robin-
son a man of good... Luis Procela
[Note] Wife and two children.

8 Miles above his father on the San
Jacinto. Vehlein. Brookfield
1740a.
Nacogdoches   August 19th 1835
Received of George A. Nixon
Mr. William Meirs title
       [Sig] Benjamin W. Robinson

1741. ROBINSON, GEORGE W. [E]
To Empresarios Austin & Williams
Tenoxtitlan   15 June 1834
I have emigrated to Texas...
I am married. My wifes name Eliza
and have 1 child. My age 25 my wife
16.   [Sig] George W. Robinson

1742. ROBINSON, JAMES W. [S]
Nacogdoches   Sept 27, 1835
Certify foreigner James W. Robbinson
is a man of good...married with
family...   Radford Berry
[Rev] Accepted in Vehlein. A.Henrie

1743. ROBINSON, JEREMIAH S. [E]
Lavaca   16th April 1830
To Stephen F. Austin Esq. Empresario
I have emigrated to this Colony...
Jeremiah S. Robinson My age is 23
years, born in the State of Missis-
sippi and emigrated from that state
to this Department and arrived in
this Colony in 1830. Am unmarried.
1743a.
Morral Hill, Lavaca   17 Apl 1830
Col. Stephen F. Austin Esq
Dear Sir: Permit me to introduce
Mr. Jeremiah Robinson late of Mis-
sissippi, a young man with ...all
the qualifications and worth...wish
to settle on the East side of the
Navidad...   James Kerr
   Navidad. Date above.
The above named Jeremiah Robinson...
I think him a worthy young Gentleman
                 Jno Andrews

1744. ROBINSON, JOEL [E]
District of Bevil   Octr 8th 1834
Certify Joel Robinson a native of
Virginia is a single man of good...
         John Bevil Alcalde

1744a. Mr. Geo A. Nixon Comr
Sir: You will please deliver to
George W. Smyth my title...
Joel Robeson   April 27th 1835

1745. ROBINSON, JOHN G.
[Old File Jacket? No documents]
Testimonio of the original Title
issued to John G. Robinson in Austin
& Williams Colony for 1 League of
land. Government dues paid. See
receipt within.
[Added note] Illegal, originally
granted to E. Cotton.

1746. ROBINSON, SAMUEL   [E]
San Augustine   August 31st 1835
Certify Samuel Robinson a native of
Kentucky a single man...emigrated in
1831...   Saml Thompson Alcd
[Note] Unf. title

1747. ROBINSON, WILLIAM   [E]
Arkansas Territory, Co. of Lawrence
William Robinson wishing to migrate
to Texas...to have a recommendation
I have been acquainted with said
William Robinson Esq. for four years
and upwards he has been an Acting
Justice of the Peace...
        Peyton R. Pitman Judge
6th December 1821

Arkansas Territory, Lawrence County
William Robbenson wishing to migrate
to Texas, therefore certify he has
resided in this place for eleven
years which time I have lived in the
same settlement...
7th December 1821   William Russel
[Reverse]
December the 7th 1821
I certify that I have been acquainted with William Robbenson from 1812
to this time.   Edward M'Donald
        a Justice of the Peace
[Notation] Wm Robinson. Certificate
Sept 18th 1834

1748. ROBLEAU, HONORE   [S]
Nacogdoches   30 May 1835
Certify foreigner Honori Robleau a
man of good...married to a daughter
of the Country...
 Jn Egne Michamps Alcalde Interim
[Reverse] Accepted. A.Henrie
1/4 League. Married a Mexican

1749. ROBSON, MATTHEW   [E]
Precinct of Tennahaw Sep 10th 1835
Certify Mathew Robeson a native of
England emigrated 1831...a wife and
3 children...   Nathan Davis Comr
[Reverse]
Sept 14th 1835. I hereby certify
that the within Mathew Robeson has
taken the oath...Nathan Davis Comr
1749a.
San Augustine   Sept 19th 1835
I hereby authorise John Inman to
apply for an order of survey...
        Mathew X Robson
Witnesses D. Jerome Woodlief
        John D. Merchant

1750. ROCKWALL, CHESTER   [E]
San Augustine   August 17, 1835
Certify Chester Rockwill is a native
of New York...a single man...emigra-
ted 1833   A. Hotchkiss P. Judge
[Note] Unfinished title

1751. RODDY, HALL   [S]
Nacogdoches   [no date]
Certify foreigner Hall Roddy is a
man of good...single without family,
resident of the State since 1832...
        Radford Berry

1752. RODGERS, ROBERT   [S]
Nacogdoches   25 May 1835
Certify foreigner Robert Rodgers a
man of good...married with family...
 Jn Egne Michamps Alcalde Interim

1753. RODGERS, SAMUEL   [S]
Nacogdoches   24 April 1835
Certify foreigner Samuel Rodgers a
man of good...married with family...
        Radford Berry

1754. RODGERS, ESTEVAN   [S]
Nacogdoches   19 November 1834
Certify Estevan Rodgers a man of
good...married with family...
        Vital Flores
[Note] Wife & 6 children. At the
Grasshouse Prairie on the San Pedro
Creek.

1755. RODRIGUEZ, DAMIEN   [S]
Nacogdoches   8 September 1835
Certify citizen Damien Rodriguez is

a man of good...resident of this Municipality since 1813...has not received land... Radford Berry
[Note] Unfinished title

1756. RODRIGUEZ, JOSE ANTONIO [E]
Nacogdoches   3 April 1835
Mr. David Brown, Surveyor   Sir:
You are to survey in Vehlein's Grant the sitio which Mr. Jose Anto Rodriguez will designate...
        Jorge Anto Nixon Comr
[Note] On Big Sandy Creek between Trinity and Nachez
[Reverse]
Nacogdoches   18 August 1835
For the present renounce all my rights in the Colony of Empresario Jose Vehlein...sign with a cross because I cannot write.
        Jose Antonio X Rodriguez
Witness: Adolfo Sterne
[Note] Returned by Mr. Stern and vacant for another.

1757. RODRIGUES, JUAN   [S]
Nacogdoches   16 July 1835
Certify citizen Juan Rodrigues is a man of good...single without family
        Radford Berry
[Note] Unfinished title

1758. ROEBUCK, ELIZABETH   [E]
Precinct of Sabine 18 Oct 1834
Certify Elizabeth Robuc a native of Georgia a woman of family of five persons...   Elbert Hines Comr
[Note] Elizabeth Roebuck four children. Next survey to Morris on the Naches. Zav.   Unfinished title

1759. ROGERS, BETHANY   [S]
Nacogdoches   11 December 1834
Certify Mrs. Bethany Rogers is a woman of good...widow whose husband lived all the time in this town...
        Vital Flores
1759a.
San Augustine [E] Aug 17th 1835
Certify Bethany Rogers native of South Carolina a widow woman of family of six persons...emigrated in Nov 1832...   Saml Thompson Alcd
1759b. San Augustine Aug 17, 1835
Sir: You are to survey the sitio &

labor which Mrs. Bethany Rogers will designate   Geo W. Smyth Comr

1760. RODGERS, ROBERT JR.   [E]
San Augustine   Dec 14th 1834
Certify Robert Rogers a native of Tennessee a man of family of nine persons...E.Rains Alcalde Interim

1761. RODGERS, ROBERT C.   [S]
Nacogdoches   10 September 1835
Certify foreigner Robert C. Rodgers a man of good...married with family...   Radford Berry
[Rev] Accepted in Vehlein. A.Henrie

1762. ROGERS, STEPHEN   [E]
Tenoxtitlan   27 February 1834
To the Empresarios Austin & Williams
I have emigrated to Texas...
I am married. My wife's name is Rebecca and have seven children. My age 2[?]8 my wife 23.
        [Sig]   Stephen Rogers

1763. ROJO, FRANCISCO DE   [E]
San Augustine   August 20, 1835
Certify Francisco de Rojo is a native of Nacogdoches a man of family of three children...
        A. Hotchkiss P.Judge
1763a.
San Augustine   August 18th 1835
Sir: You will survey the sitio & labor which Mr. Francisco de Rojo will designate Geo W. Smyth Comr

1764. ROLLAND, JOHN   [S]
Nacogdoches   9 Oct 1835
Certify foreigner John Rolland is a man of good...single without family...   Radford Berry

1765. ROLLINS, ELITHALIT   [S]
Nacogdoches   26 January 1835
Certify foreigner Elithalet Rollins is a man of good...married with family...   Radford Berry
[Note] Widower 6 children. On vacant land near the Sabine about 3 miles from it adjoining Cobbs & Gibsons

158

1766. ROMERO, MANUEL ANTONIO [S]
Nacogdoches   4 August 1835
Certify citizen Manuel Anto Romero
is a resident of this Municipality
married with family and resident of
this Department since 1831...
              Radford Berry
1766a.
Nacogdoches   August 1835
Mr. Roark Sir: You are to survey
the sitio & labor which Mr. Manuel
Antonio Romero will designate...
              Geo W. Smyth Comr

1767. ROSALES, PEDRO [S]
Nacogdoches   24 August 1835
Certify citizen Pedro Rosales is a
man of good...resident of this Municipality and born here...single
without family...has not received
land...   Radford Berry

1768. ROSE, JOHN E. [E]
San Augustine   Octr 5, 1835
Certify John E. Rose a native of
Tennessee man of family of five per-
sons...emigrated 1826 and has taken
the oath...   Saml Thompson Alcd
1768a.
San Augustine   6 October 1835
I, John E. Rose appoint James C.
Cain my attorney to petition for one
league & labor... [Sig] John E. Rose
Witnesses   E.O. Legrand
       Morris May   E.W. Cullene
1768b.
Sir: You are to survey the sitio &
labor which Mr. John E. Rose will
designate...   Geo W. Smyth Comr

1769. ROTH, JACOB [S]
Nacogdoches   25 May 1835
Certify foreigner Jacob Roth is a
man of good...married with family
Jn Egne Michamps Alcalde Interim

1770. ROWE, JAMES [S]
Nacogdoches   3 December 1834
Certify foreigner James Rowe is a
man of good...single... Vital Flores
[Note] Single. 4th of sitio near
Santa Ana adjoining J.A. Veatch's
Survey. Zavala
1770a.
Geo Anto Nixon Comr   Oct 3, 1837
Dear Sir: You will send me the title

to my land by the bearer...
              James Rowe

1771. ROWE, JOSEPH [E]
San Augustine   Sept 26th 1834
Certify Joseph Roe is a native of No
Carolina a man of family of two
persons... Benjamin Lindsey Alcalde
[Note] Unfinished title

1772. ROWE, ROBERT [E]
San Augustine   January 22d 1835
Certify Robert Rowe a native of
North Carolina a man of family of
nine persons... James S. Hanks Alcd
1773. ROWLAND, JOHN G. [S]
Villa de Brasoria   17 March 1832
To Citizen John Austin Alcalde of
the Jurisdiction of Austin
17 March 1832   Certify Mr. John
Rowland obedient to the laws and
observant of the customs...asks admission as a Colonist in the Contract of Empresario Austin.
              Juan Austin

1774. ROZELL, ASHLEY B. [S]
Nacogdoches   2 May 1835
Certify foreigner Ashley B. Rozell a
man of good...married with family
              Radford Berry
1774a.
Nacogdoches   Oct 27, 1835
Recd of J.A. Nixon Commissioner
Ashley B. Rozell Title
              Arthur Henrie

1775. ROZELL, T. [S]
Nacogdoches   2 May 1835
Certify foreigner T. Rozell a man of
good...married with family...
              Radford Berry

1776-1779 [Not in file]

1780. RUDDELL, GEORGE [S]
Nacogdoches   5 December 1834
Certify foreigner George Ruddell a
man of good...widower...Vital Flores
[Note] George Ruddell. 3 children.
The place where he lives. Burnet.
J. Strode
1780a.
Mr. George Antonio Nixon
July 3d 1835 Sir: Please send my
Grant by Jeremiah Strode who will
pay you...   George Ruddell

159

1781. RUDDELL, ISAAC [S]
Nacogdoches   14 September 1835
Certify foreigner Isaac Ruddell a
man of good...single without family
                    Radford Berry
[Note] Unfinished title
[Rev] Accepted in Vehlein. A.Henrie

1782. RUGG, SARAH [E]
San Augustine   Oct 10, 1835
Certify Sarah Rugge a widow...family
of two children, that she is a native of Georgia...emigrated in 1833
as said to me by Mr. Haley and Mr.
Adams and that she has taken the
oath.   A.Hotchkiss P.Judge
[Note] Unfinished title
1782a.
San Augustine   Oct 10, 1835
I, Sarah Rugg appoint Richard Haley
my attorney to petition for one
league and labor... Sarah X Rugge
A. Holtchkiss Primary Judge

1783. RUMMEL, JOHN [E]
San Augustine   25 Sept 1834
Certify J.S. Rummel a native of
Pennsylvania is a single man...
                    John Bevil Alcd
[Note] Unfinished title

1784. RUNNELS, JOHNSON [E]
San Augustine   Sept 17th 1835
Certify Johnson Runnels a native of
Kentucky a man of family of four
persons...emigrated in 1812...
       Wm McFarland Primary Judge

1785. RUNNELS, LINA [E]
Jurisdiction of Liberty 13 Feb 1835
Certify Lina Runnels a native of
Louisiana a woman of family of her-
self and five children...
       John Stewart Commissioner
       for the Precinct of Cow Bayou

1786. RUNNELS, MATILDA [E]
San Augustine   May 23d 1835
Certify Matilda Runnels a native of
Tennessee a widow woman of family of
seven persons... Nathan Lewis Comr
[Reverse] Accepted. Arthur Henrie

1787. RUSK, JOSEPH [E]
San Augustine   August 11th 1835
Certify Mr. Joseph Rusk a native of
Virginia is a man of family of six
persons, that he emigrated in 1834
             R.C. McDaniel C.P.O.
1787a.
Nacogdoches   Augt 13th 1835
Mr. Surveyor Sir: You are to sur-
vey in Zavala's Grant the sitio
which Mr. Jos Rusk will designate...
       Jorge Anto Nixon Commissioner
[Note] On Village Creek

1788. RUSK, THOMAS J. [S]
Nacogdoches   23 May 1835
Certify foreigner Thomas J. Rusk a
man of good...married with family...
                    Radford Berry

1789. RUSSELL, ALEXANDER [E]
Tenoxtitlan   22 April 1834
To the Empresario Austin & Williams
I have emigrated to Texas...
I am unmarried. My age 35 years.
                    Alexr. Russell

1790. RUSSELLL, AURELIA [E]
District of Sabine   5 June 1835
Certify Aurelia Russel a native of
Connecticut has a family of three
persons...   B. Holt Comr

1791. RUSSEL, EDWARD [S]
Nacogdoches   4 April 1835
Certify foreigner Edward Russel a
man of good...married with family...
                    Radford Berry

1792. RUSSELL, ELI [S]
Nacogdoches   6 June 1835
Certify foreigner Eli Russel a man
of good...married with family....
       Geo Pollitt Alcalde Interim
[Rev] Accepted in Burnet. A.Henrie

1793. RUSSELL, JESSE [S]
[San Augustine?] 20 September 1835
Certify Jesse Russell a native of
North Carolina emigrated in 1833 is
a man of family of three persons...
took the oath...
       A. Hotchkiss Pry Judge
[Note] Unfinished title

160

1793a.
San Augustine   Oct 2d 1835
Mr. Commissioner: I hereby authorize
Thomas M. Smullin to acquire from
you an Order of Survey in my name...
          Jesse X Russell

1794. RUSSELL, JONATHAN   [E]
San Augustine   Sept 1st 1835
Certify Jonathan Russell a native of
Tennessee a man of family of four
persons...emigrated 1833...
          Saml Thompson Alcd
[Note] Unfinished title

1795. RUSSELL, MARGARET   [E]
San Augustine   2 October 1835
Certify Margaret Russell widow of
James Russell is a native of Virgin-
ia...emigrated in 1833...a lady of
family of four persons...took the
oath...   Saml Thompson Alcd
[Note] Unfinished title
1795a.
San Augustine   October 2d 1835
Mr. Commissioner: I hereby authorize
Thomas M. Smullin to receive from
you an Order of Survey for me...
          Margaret X Russell
Witneaa: William Coote

1796. RUSSELL, ROBERT W.   [E]
District of Bevil   March 15, 1835
Certify R.W. Russill a native of
Penselvania hath a family of three
persons...   Wm Williams Alcalde
1796a.
G.A. Nixon Esqr   Sir:
Please let T.B. Huling have my land
title   Sept 30th 1835
          Robert W. Russell

1797. RUSSEL, REUBEN R.   [S]
Nacogdoches   2 December 1834
Certify foreigner Reuben R. Russel a
man of good...married with family...
          Vital Flores
[Note] Vehlein. Jeremiah Strode
Wife 3 children. On Rose's Creek 4
miles south E of Jacob Martins

1798. RUSSELL, ROBERT   [E]
District of Sabine   [no date]
Certify Robert Russell a native of
Connecticut now a citizen of the
District...   B. Holt Commissioner

1799. RUSSEL, THOMAS J.
[Typescript "Original Missing"]
Nacogdoches   23 May 1835
Thomas J. Russel is married with a
family   Radford Berry

1800. RYAN, EDWARD
[Field Notes] Survey of one third
for Edward Ryan on the left bank of
Postele Creek on the head waters of
the Aransas

1801. RYAN, JOHN
[Field Notes] Survey one league and
labor to John Ryan on the east bank
of the Aransas adjoining George
O'Docherty...

1802. RYAN, JUAN F. [S]
Nacogdoches   9 February 1835
Certify foreigner Juan F. Ryan is a
man of good...single without family
[Note] Unfinished title
          Radford Berry

1803. RYAN, SIMON
[Field Notes] Survey of one league
and labor for Simon Ryan on the left
bank of Rio Frio...

1804. RYLANDER, NILS   [E]
To Mr. S.F. Austin Empresario
I have emigrated to this Colony...
Niles Ralander 27 years old. Swede
by birth. Arrived this Colony
December 1831.[Sig] Nils Rylander

1805. SACO, MIGUEL   [S]
Nacogdoches   5 Sept 1835
Certify foreigner Miguel Saco is a
man of good...married with family,
resident of this Municipality since
1827...   Radford Berry
1805a.
Nacogdoches   Sept 5th 1835
Mr. Roark   Sir: You are to survey
the sitio and labor which Mr. Miguel
Saco will designate...
          Geo W. Smyth Comr
[Note] Where he lives on the east

side of the Bayou Terrero, adjoining the land of Skelton, Joseph Durst, Juan Tobar, Manuel Santos & road leading from Nacogdoches to Bexar

1806. SADLER, JOHN [E]
San Augustine   September 25, 1834
Certify John Sadler a native of Tennessee is a man of family of four persons...Benjamin Lindsey Aalcalde
[Note] Wife & 2 chn = Vehlein
Next to Saml Lindley. Wm Rankin

1807. SALAZAR, ANTONIO [S]
Nacogdoches   10 August 1835
Certify citizen Anta Salaza is a man of good...single without family, resident of this Municipality and born here...   Radford Berry
[Note] Antonio Salazar
1807a.
Nacogdoches   August 15th 1835
Sir: You are to survey the sitio which Mr. Antonio Salaza will designate... Geo W. Smyth Comr

1808. SALAZAR, MAXIMO [S]
Nacogdoches   9 April 1835
Certify citizen Maximo Salazar is a resident of this Municipality for many years and married with family has not received land...
                Radford Berry

1809. SALINAS, JOSE MARIA
[Field Notes] One league of land for Jose Maria Salinas on the NE side of the Atascoso Creek in McMullins Colony, about thirty miles from Bexar...

1810. SANCHES, JOSE [S]
Nacogdoches   Aug 17, 1835
Sir: You are to survey the third part of a sitio which Mr. Jose' Sanches will designate...
                Chas S. Taylor

1811. SANCHES, JOSE ANTONIO [S]
Nacogdoches   19 July 1835
Certify citizen Jose Anto Sanches is a man of good...single without family...has not received land...
                Radford Berry

1812. SANCHES, JOSE FRANCISCO [E]
San Augustine   Sept 1st 1835
Certify Hosa Francisco Sanchez is a native citizen and a single man...
                Saml Thompson Alcd

1813. SANCHES, JOSE MARIA [S]
Nacogdoches   7 May 1835
Certify citizen Jose Maria Sanchez is a man of good...resident of this Municipality and born here, married with family, has not received land...   Radford Berry
[Note] Widower one child

1814. SANCHES, JUAN JOSE [S]
Nacogdoches   5 April 1835
Certify citizen Jose Sanchez is a resident of this Municipality and born here, married with fámily...has not received land.   Radford Berry

1815. SANCHES, JULIAN BAZILIO [S]
Nacogdoches   2 May 1835
Certify citizen Sahan Bazilio Sanches is a resident of this Municipality and born here...single without family, has not received land...
                Radford Berry

1816. SANCHES, MARIA TRINIDAD [S]
Nacogdoches   9 Julio 1835
Certify citizen Maria Trinidad Sanches is a woman of good...widow with family...   Radford Berry
[Rev] Accepted in Burnet. A.Henrie

1817. SANDERS, GEORGE [E]
San Augustine   Sept 22d 1835
Certify George Sanders a native citizen of the Country is a man of family of two persons...
                Saml Thompson Alcalde
1817a.
San Augustine   23d Sept 1835
I, George Sanders appoint William Inglish my attorney to petition for one league and labor...
                George Sanders
Witnesses   A.E.C. Johnson
C. Thompson   Saml Thompson Alcalde
1817b.
Nacogdoches   Oct 9th 1835
Sir: You are to survey the sitio & labor which Mr. George Sanders will designate... Geo W. Smyth Comr

1818. SANDERS, JAMES C.   [E]
San Augustine   August 24, 1835
Certify James C. Sanders a native of
Tennessee a single man...emigrated
1832...   Saml Thompson Alcd

1819. SANDERS, JOHN   [E]
San Augustine   Sept 17th 1835
Certify John Sanders a native of the
Country is a man of family of three
persons...W. McFarland Primary Judge
1819a.
San Augustine   18th September 1835
I, John Sanders have appointed William English my attorney to petition
for one league and labor...
                John --- by Wm Inglish
1819b.
Nacogdoches   Sept 21, 1835
Sir: You are to survey the sitio &
labor which Mr. John Sanders will
designate...   Geo W. Smyth Comr

1820. SANDERS, LEVI   [E]
San Augustine   September [blank]
I certify Levi Sanders a native of
Tennessee...a single man...emigrated
in 1831.   Saml Thompson Alcd

1821. SANDERS, WILLIAM   [E]
San Augustine   Sept 22d 1835
Certify William Sanders a native
citizen and a man of family of six
persons...   Saml Thompson Alcd
1821a.
San Augustine   23d Sept 1835
I, William Sanders appoint William
Inglish my attorney to petition for
one league and labor...
        [Sig] William Sanders
Witnesses   A.E.C. Johnson
C. Thompson   Saml Thompson Alcd
1821b.
San Augustine   Oct 10th 1835
James Kirkham by his official P/A
made me his agent...and William
Sanders has done the same...I hereby
appoint David Brown my substitute...
                Wm Inglish
Witness J. Blair

1821c. San Augustine Oct 10th 1835
Mr. George W. Smyth Comr Sir:
Please deliver the Orders of Survey
that I left in your possession to
Mr. David Brown   Wm Inglish
Witness J. Blair
1821d.
Sir: You are authorized to survey
the sitio and labor which Mr. Wm
Sanders will designate...
        Geo W. Smyth

1822. SANDERSON, WILLIAM H.   [S]
Nacogdoches   17 August 1835
Certify citizen William H.Sanderson
is a man of good...resident of this
State since 2d August 1832, single
without family... has not obtained
land...   Radford Berry
[Reverse]
Nacogdoches   17 Agt 1835
Personally appeared before me Wil-
liam H. Sanderson and took the oath
                Radford Berry

1823. SAN PATRICIO DE HIBERNIA
[Field Notes of Town tract]
Survey of four leagues for the Town
Tract of San Patricio de Hibernia in
McMullen and McGloin's Colony...
Nueces River...

1824. SANTOS, CORNELIUS   [E]
San Augustine   [no date]
I certify Cornelius Santos a native
of Texas and a single man of good...
                Nathan Davis Comr
1824a.
San Augustine   [no date]
Certify that Cornelius Santos has
taken the oath...Nathan Davis Comr
1824b.
San Augustine   30 August 1835
I, Cornelius Santos appoint Edward
O. Legrand my attorney to petition
for one third...
        Cornelius X Santos
Witnesses   Humphrey T. Chappell
Richard Haley   Peter C. Ragsdale
John Applegate   Mark Haley

1825. SANTOS, JOSE   [E]
San Augustine   August 19, 1835
Certify Jose Santos is a native of
old Spain, a man of family of a wife
and four children...came to the

163

Country when a child...
A. Hotchkiss P.Judge

1826. SAUL, JOHN [E]
District of Bevil October 8th 1834
John Saul is a native of Georgia...
hath a family of eight persons...
John Bevil Alc
[Note] Wife & 6 children. At his
improvements adjoining Mr. Watts
lower line on the Indn Creek.
Geo W. Smyth = Zavala

1827. SAVERY, ASAHEL [E]
[District of Bevil] Novr 17th 1834
Certify Asahel Savary is a native of
Vermont, hath a family of four
persons... John Bevil Alcalde

1828. SAVERY, HARVEY P. [E]
[District of Bevil] Nov 17th 1834
Certify Harvey P. Savery is a native
of Missouri is a single man...
John Bevil Alcalde
[Note] Wife 2 child = Zavala
W of Charles Williams & S of Almanson Houston. Near the mouth of Pine
Isle Bayou Isaac Burton

1829. SCANLIN, CHRISTOPHER
[Field Notes] Survey of one third
league for Christopher Scanlin on
the right bank of the Atascoso
adjoining Elizabeth Jordan's Survey

1830. SCANLIN, JERRY
[Field Notes] Survey of one league
and labor for Jerry Scanlin on the
left bank of the River Nueces above
the junction of the Rio Frio...

1831. SCATES,, JOSEPH W. [E]
Jurisdiction of Liberty 24 Feb 1835
Certify Joseph W. Scates a native of
Kentucky a man of family of his wife
and one child... Wm Hardin Judge

1832. SCHRIERS, JOHN [E]
District of Bevil Sept 30th 1834
Certify John Scriers a native of
Louisiana hath a family of six
persons... John Bevil Alcalde
[Note] Schrier. Wife and four children. The place he has improved.
Zavala

1833. SCOTT, ALEXANDER A. [S]
Nacogdoches 27 April 1835
Certify Alexander A. Scott man of
good...singl... Radford Berry

1834. SCOTT, JAMES [E]
San Augustine 22d September 1834
Certify James Scott a native of New
York is a man of family of six
persons... Benjamin Lindsey Alcalde

1835. SCOTT, JOHN [S]
Nacogdoches 27 April 1835
Certify foreigner John Scott a man
of good...married with family...
Radford Berry

1836. SCOTT, WILLIAM JOSEPH [S]
Nacogdoches 16 May 1835
Certify foreigner W.J.L. Scott a man
of good...married with family...
Radford Berry
1836a.
I the undersigned Pastor of Austin's
Colony and Vicar General of all the
foreign colonies of Texas Do certify
that William Joseph Scott has been
baptised according to the Rites...
Church. His Godfather Joseph Dugat
on the 12th January 1832.
Michael Muldoon

1837. SCRITCHFIELD, HENRY [E]
San Augustine August 17, 1835
Certify Henry Scrutchfield a native
of Louisiana a single man...came to
Texas in 1822...
A. Hotchkiss P. Judge

1838. SCRITCHFIELD, JOHN [E]
San Augustine May 18, 1835
Certify John Scritchfield a native
of Virginia a man of family of wife
and six children...
A.Hotchkiss Prmy Judge

1839. SCRITCHFIELD, POLLY [E]
San Augustine May 18, 1835
Certify Polly Scritchfield a widow
woman of family of 5 children a
native of Ohio
A. Hotchkiss Prmy Judge
1839a.
Nacogdoches July 21st 1835
Recd from the hands of Major Nixon
on account of A. Hotchkiss the fol-

164

lowing Titles
Polly Scritchfield, Bernard Pantaleon, and Isaac Simpson.
    [by]   Charles S. Taylor

1840. SCRUGHAM, EDWARD W.
[Field Notes] Survey of one league
and labor for Edward W.B. Scrugham
on the east bank of the Rio Frio...
opposite Michael Heley's Survey...

1841. SCURLOCK, WILLIAM   [E]
San Augustine   August 20th 1835
Certify William Scurlock a native of
No Carolina a single man...emigrated
February 1834... Saml Thompson Alcd

1842. SEETS, PRECIOUS   [E]
Certify Precious Seets a native of
Tennessee is a widow of family of
two persons...emigrated February
1834...   Saml Thompson A

1843. SEGUIN DE CASANOBO,
       MARIA MANUELA
Nacogdoches   6 April 1835
Certify citizen Maria Manuela Sequin
de Casanobo is a resident of the
Municipality and born here, is a
woman of very good...has been abandoned about eight years by her husband, with a very numerous family,
and is to be considered a widow. Has
not received land... Radford Berry
[Note] Deserted by her husband
[Revere] Accepted. Arthur Henrie

1844.   SEGURA, MARCELINO
[Field Notes] Survey of one league
and labor for Marcelino Segura in
the forks of the head waters of
Attascoso Creek...

1845. SELSER, NIMROD   [E]
San Augustine   22 Sept 1834
Certify Nimrod Selser a native of
the U.S. a man of family of eighteen
persons   Benjamin Lindsey Alcalde
1845a.
San Augustine   Sep 1834
Mr. Surveyor Sir: You are to survey
in Zavala's Grant the sitio which
Mr. Nimrod Selser will designate...
    Jorga Anto Nixon Comr
[Note] Wolf Creek, where he lives
[Rev] District of Bevil Feby 20 1835
I certify I have transferred all my

right to the within survey to Mr. N.
Allen...   N.R. Selser
Give Mr. Allen the Order. Nixon

1846. SERVANTES, AGAPITO [S]
Nacogdoches   4 August 1835
Certify citizen Agapito Cervantes is
an old settler and resident of this
Municipality married with family,
has not received land...
      Radford Berry
1846a.
Nacogdoches   August 4th 1835
Sir: You are to survey the sitio &
labor which Mr. Agapito Servantes
will designate   Geo W. Smyth Comr
[Rev] The within order has been executed. Wm Brookfield Surveyor

1847. SERVANTES, JOSE   [S]
Nacogdoches   Oct 9, 1835
Sir: You are to survey the sitio &
labor which Jose Servantes will
designate...   Geo W. Smyth Comr

1848. SESSUM MICHAEL   [E]
Tenoxtitlan   22 May 1834
To the Empresarios Austin &
Williams   I have emigrated to
Texas...I am unmarried, my age 22
years   Michael Sessom
Who wishes me to sign for him.
      F.W. Johnson

1848a. SETTLE, WILLIAM H. [S]
Consul of the U.S. of Mexico, New
Orleans Passport to Mr. William H.
Settle native of these states to go
on the American Schooner Brasoria,
Captain Rowland, pass to Brasoria on
personal business. Given in New
Orleans, 6 June 1832.
    Francisco Pizarro Martinez
[Signed] William H. Settle

1849. SEWALL, WILLIAM   [E]
San Augustine August 29th 1835
Certify William H. Sewall native of
Georgia a man of family of two per-
sons...emigrated in 1826...
    Saml Thompson Alcd

1850. SEXTON, WILLIAM   [E]
Town of Austin   May 21, 1830
To Mr. S.F. Austin Empresario
I have emigrated to this Colony...

William Sexton, 24 years old
unmarried occupation farmer moved
from Louisiana and arrived in this
Colony 5 Jany 1830. 3 dependents
[Sig] Wm Sexton

1851. SHANNON, JOHN   [E]
To the Illustrious Ayuntamiento of
Austin   Being solicited by Mr.
John Shannon...I have been personal-
ly acquainted with Mr. Shannon eight
years...I sincerely wish we had many
such to emigrate...
Jany 27th 1831   Francis Holland

1852. SHANNON, OWEN   [E]
[Repeat above, naming Owen Shannon]

1853. SHANNON, WILLIAM T.   [S]
Nacogdoches   30 May 1835
Certify foreigner William T. Shannon
is a man of good...married with
family...
Jn Egne Michamps Alcalde Interim

1854. SHELDON, JOHN P.   [E]
San Felipe de Austin   24 Feb 1832
I have emigrated to this Colony...
My name is John P. Sheldon aged 40
years Eliza my wife 33 years
3 Male children 4 female children
Removed from Michigan Territory. I
agree to remove my family...within
one year...   Jno R. Sheldon

1855. SHELTON, JACOB   [E]
San Augustine   14 May 1835
Certify Jacob Shelton a native of
the U.S. a man of family of three
persons...emigrated in 1834...
R.C. McDaniel C.P.O.
1855a.
Nacogdoches   Augt 11, 1835
Mr. Surveyor Sir: You are to sur-
vey the sitio which Mr. Jacob Shel-
ton will designate...
Jorge Anto Nixon Comr

1856. SHEPHERD, HUGH   [S]
Nacogdoches   16 May 1835
Certify foreigner Hugh Shepherd of
good...   Radford Berry

1857. SHEPHERD, WILLIAM
The State of Alabama, Perry County
August 2d 1839.   Whereas William
Shepherd of the State and County...
166

intends removing to the Province of
Texas that he may obtain land...we
believe him to be a worthy citizen
[About 12 Alabama signers]

1858. SHERMAN, WILLIAM   [S]
Nacogdoches   17 Aug 1835
Certify foreigner William Shearman
is a man of good...married with
family...resident of this Municipality since 1829...   Radford Berry
1858a.
To Wm Robinson Surveyor Sir: You
are to survey in Vehlein's Grant the
sitio which Mr. Wm Serman will
designate... Jorge Anto Nixon Comr
[Note] Adjoining Mr. Jos C.
Teague's Survey on Hickory Creek
[Reverse] I hereby renounce all
right title and interest I have to
this order or as a Colonist in the
Colony of Jose Vehlein.
[Sig] Wm Sherman

1859. SHIELDS, GILBERT   [E]
San Augustine   20 April 1835
Certify Gilbert Shields, native of
the U.S. a man of family of four
persons, emigrated in 1834...
R.C. McDaniel C.P.O.
[Reverse] Accepted. A.Henrie
1859a.
Nacogdoches   August 15th 1835
Mr. Surveyor Sir: You are to survey in Zavala's Grant the sitio
which Mr. G. Shields willl
designate...Jorge Anto Nixon Comr

1860. SHIELDS, WILLIAM   [S]
Nacogdoches   29 May 1835
Certify foreigner William Shields a
man of good...single without family
Jn Egne Michamps Alcalde Interim
[Rev] Accepted in Burnetts. A.Henrie

1861. SHIP, JOSEPH   [E]
San Augustine   Sept 22d 1834
Certify Joseph Ship a native of
South Carolinad a man of family of
nine persons...
Benjmain Lindsey Alcalde

1862. SHIPMAN, DANIEL   [E]
Mr. Gale Borden Jr.   Jany 8th 1836
Dear Sir: After my best respects to
you & family, I wish you to examine

in the office and see if you can
ascertain if that League of land
ever has been deeded to Mr. John
Trobough or any other person, it
lies on Syms Bayou bounded by...John
R. Harris...Please give my brother
all information on the subject.
                    Danl Shipman
[Addressed] Mr. Gale Borden Jr
                    San Felipe de Austin
by Mr. J.M. Shipman

1863. SHIPMAN, EDWARD   [E]
Town of Austin   18 June 1830
To Mr. S.F. Austin Empresario
I have emigrated to this Colony...
Edward Shipman am unmarried 26 years
of age. Moved from Arkansas and
arrived in this Colony in 1823.
          [Sig] Edward Shipman

1864. SHIPP, WILLIAM   [E]
San Augustine   January 24th 1835
Certify William Shipp a native of
Kentucky a man of family of two
persons... James S. Hanks Alcalde

1865. SHIRES, MICHAEL   [S]
Nacogdoches   20 May 1835
Certify Michael Shires a man of very
good...married with family...
              Radford Berry

1866. SHOEMAKER, EVANS   [E]
San Augustin   May 3d 1835
Certify Evans Shoemaker a native of
Tennessee a man of family of seven
persons...Nathan Davis Commissioner
[Reverse] Accepted. Arthur Henrie

1867. SHULTZ, CHRISLEY   [E]
San Augustine   May 18, 1835
Certify Crisley Shultz a man of
family of a wife & six children a
native of Tennessee...
          A. Hotchkiss Prmy Judge

1868. SIDEX, BATTESE   [E]
Austin Colony, Lost Creek
5th Feby 1834
[To] Mr. Saml Williams Sir:
If I can be permitted to take a
Quarter League and obtain a Title...
              Battese Sidex
[Reverse] J.B. Sidex

1869. SIGLER, WILLIAM N.   [E]
Dept. of Nacogdoches Nov 19th 1834
Certify William N. Sigler a native
ofNorth Carolina hath a family of
seven persons...John Bevil Alcalde
[Note] Wm N. Sigler. Wife and 5
chidren North side of Taylors Bayou.
Burton
1869a.San Augustine   Sept 4th 1835
To George W. Smyth Comr. Sir:
I am informed by Elisha Roberts that
he does intend having a title to
part of the land whereon I now live
which will appear according to field
notes. The land whereon I live, the
land has been settled seven or eight
years and occupied by John Haley,
and transferred to me by the said
Haley, and I now hold the Power of
Attorney to act for Haley...
[Two pages of protest against making
a Title to Roberts] Wm N. Sigler
We the subscribers do hereby certify
that all the facts set forth [are
true]: A.E.C. Johnson M. Cartwright
Ramond Dailey   Saml Thompson
A.D. Bateman   Charles Gates
George H. Jones   E.O. Legrand
1869b.   San Augustine
To Geo W. Smyth Commissioner
The petition of Wm N. Sigler repre-
sents that he has been appointed the
lawful agent of Haley and Susannah
Haley to obtain a title to four
labors which they have long since
settled...they have obtained an
order of survey from your Honor
on which they intend having laid on
their old claim...Elisha Roberts had
made a survey on the claim...
Wm N. Sigler Atty for Haley & wife

1870. SIMMONS, HENDERSON   [E]
District of Tenahaw July 15th 1835
Certify that Henderson Simmons a
native of Mississippi a man of family of six persons emigrated in 1832
and has taken the oath.
              Nathan Davis Comr
[Reverse] Accepted. A.Henrie

1871. SIMMONS, JAMES   [E]
Precinct of Cow Bayou   2 Feby 1835
Certify James Simmons Senr a native
of Louisiana man of family of himself and two children...
              John Stewart Comr

1872. SIMMONS, RICHARD [E]
District of Bevil   Octr 12th 1834
Certify Richard Simmons a native of
South Carolina hath a family of four
persons... John Bevil Alcalde
[Note] Wife and 2 children. The
place he has improved. Zavala
                       G.W.S.
1872a. Bevil   Oct 3d 1835
Sir: You are to survey the sitio &
labor which Mr. Richard Simmons will
designate.. Geo W. Smyth

1873. SIMPSON, B.H. [E]
San Augustine   August 18th 1835
Certify B.H. Simpson a native of
Tennessee a man of family of seven
persons...emigrated in 1831...
           Saml Thompson Alcd

1874. SIMPSON, DINSMORE [E]
San Augustine   August 20th 1835
Certify Dinsmore Simpson a native of
Tennessee a man of family of six
persons...emigrated in 1831...
           Saml Thompson Alcd
1874a.
Nacogdoches   Sept 4th 1835
Sir: You are to survey the sitio &
labor which Mr. Dinsmore Simpson
will designate   Geo W. Smyth Comr

1875. SIMPSON, ISAAC [E]
Nacogdoches   March 31, 1835
Certify Isaac Simpson a man of fami-
ly a native of the U.S. that he is a
citizen...A. Hotchkiss Primary Judge
[Note] Northeast of Col Beans Sur-
       vey.   Burnetts Colony
[Reverse] Isaac Simpson

1876. SIMPSON, JOHN J. [S]
Nacogdoches   16 Sept 1834
Certify citizen John Simpson is a
man of very good...married...
     Luis Procela Alcalde Interim
1876a.
Nacogdoches   May 16, 1837
Received of the Comr Geo A. Nixon
Alexander W. Beckman Land Title for
one league.   Jno J. Simpson

1877. SIMS, B.
Delapplan   League No. 35
L. McNeel   46
Nicholas Herron   1/4 Lg   8
Burnapp   League   34
Self   "   5
do   "   6
S.W.Sweney   "   14
B.W. Strodder   "   26
The above list is selected by men
that is in the Country with thar
Familys and Mr. McNeal clears out
League No. 24.   B. Sims
[Reverse] A list of selections
1877a.
No. 2 On the San Antonio Road is
       taken by D.C. Barret
 "   37 On the waters of Plum & Peach
 "   Creek. D. Barrett
 "   41 On the waters of G-- Creek
        G. Merrell
 "   51 Back of T.J. Gasly is taken by
        Mr. Pease
 "   52 E of 51 & S No.9 by R.O.Hul-
        bert
1/4 No. 18 E of No. 13 (Thompsons)
        E.M. Pease
Mr. Borden: May 7th 1835
The above Nos are selected by the
gentlemen as named which you will be
so good as to respect.   B. Sims
[Reverse] Entered on book

1878. SIMS, CHARLES H. [S]
Nacogdoches   29 November 1834
Certify resident Carlos Simes is a
man of very good... Vital Flores
[Note] Single. 4th sitio adjoining
Minchie's Survey, Joseph Vehlein
Hardin Surveyor

1879. SIMS, CHARLES H. [S]
Nacogdoches   10 August 1835
Certify foreigner Charles H. Sims a
man of good...married with family,
resident of this Municipality since
1829...   Radford Berry

1880. SIMS, RICHARD [E]
San Augustine   May 30, 1835
Certify Richard Sims a native of
Georgia a man of family of a wife
and six children..
     A. Hotchkiss Primary Judge
[Rev] Accepted. Arthur Henrie

1881. SINCLAIR (ST. CLAIR),
                    WILLIAM [E]
San Augustine   September 1st 1835
Certify William Sinclair a native of
South Carolina a man of family of
ten persons...emigratd in 1830...
            Saml Thompson Alcd
[Reverse] Wm St. Clair

1882. SINGLETON, GEORGE W.   [E]
To the Empresario S.F. Austin
I have been a citizen of this Colony
for the last eight years and having
lately married, I request admission. My name is George W. Singleton
aged 23. My wife Elizabeth aged 24.
One female   child. Occupation
farmer & raising stock
Jany 9th 1832   Geo W. X Singleton
Has selected the land on the Yegua,
south west side between Clokeys &
the Yegua. It is not yet surveyed.

1883. SKELTON, JUAN   [S]
Nacogdoches   18 September 1834
Certify foreigner Juan Skelton is a
man of good...   Vicinte Cordova

1884. SKERRETT, GEORGE W.   [E]
Tenoxtitlan   27 April 1834
To Empresarios Austin & Williams
I have emigrated to Texas...
I am married my wife (Mary) Maria &
2 children. My age 34 my wifes 22
            Geo W. Skerrett

1885. SKILLERN, ISAAC C.   [S]
Nacogdoches   9 Oct 1835
Certify foreigner Isaac C. Skellein
a man of good...married with family
and resident of this Department
since 1833...   Radford Berry
1885a.
Nacogdoches   Oct 10th 1835
Sir: You are to survey the sitio &
labor which Mr. Isaac Skellon will
designate...   Geo W. Smyth Comr

1886. SKINNER, JAMES H.   [E]
Town of Austin   3 June 1830
To Mr. S.F. Austin Empresario
I have emigrated to this Colony...
James H. Skinner 35 years of age.
Unmarried. Moved from Louisiana and
arrived in this Colony in May 1830.
            James H. Skinner

1887. SKINNER, MANUEL   [S]
Nacogdoches   28 April 1835
Certify foreigner Manuel Skinner a
man of good...widower with family...
            Radford Berry

1888. SKINNER, WILLIAM   [S]
Nacogdoches   18 May 1835
Certify foreigner William Skinner is
a man of good...married with family
            Radford Berry

1889. SLAUGHTER, GEORGE   [E]
San Augustine   Oct 10, 1835
Certify George Slaughter a native of
Mississippi a single man...emigrated
in 1826   A. Hotchkiss P. Judge
1889a.
San Augustine   9th Oct 1835
I George Slaughter appointed Richard
Haley my attorney to petition for
one third league...
            [Sig] George Slaughter

1890. SLAUGHTER, SAMUEL   [E]
San Augustine   Oct 10, 1835
Certify Samuel Slaughter a native of
Mississippi a single man...emigrated
in 1826...   A. Hotchkiss P. Judge
1890a.
San Augustine   9 Oct 1835
I, Samuel Slaughter appoint Richard
Haley my attorney to petition for
one third... Samuel X Slaughter

1891. SLAUGHTER, WILLIAM T.   [E]
San Augustine   20 June 1835
Certify William T. Slaughter a native of Kentucky a man of family of
four persons, emigrated in May 1832
            R.C. McDaniel C.P.O.
1891a.
Nacogdoches   Aug 6th 1835
Mr. Surveyor Sir: You are to survey in Zavala's Grant the sitio
which Mr. W.T. Slaughter will
designate... Jorge Anto Nixon Comr
[Note] On the west bank of R. Neches

1892. SMALL, JAMES   [E]
Jurisdiction of Austin Dec 6th 1829
We the undersigned citizens of the
Jurisdiction of Austin certify that
we have been acquainted with James

Small...recommend as a Colonist...
James Whiteside   Walter C. White
Oliver Jones   Thomas Davis
John York
[Reverse]
Jurisdiction of Austin
Petitioner is the head of a family
two female dependents, one being
twenty four years of age and named
Rhody, the other only six years of
age and called Emeline. Your petitioner is thirty four years of
age, by occupation a farmer...early
emigrated to the wilderness without
yet obtaining land...

1893. SMITH, ABRAHAM   [E]
San Augustine   August 18th 1835
Certify Abraham Smith a native of
Tennessee a man of family of four
persons...came in 1831...
        Saml Thompson Alcd

1894. SMITH, ALEXANDER   [S]
Nacogdoches   2 Feby 1835
Certify foreigner Alexander Smith a
man of good...single...
    Jn Egne Michamps Alcalde Interim
[Note] 1/4 Vehlein

1895. SMITH, ALEXANDER W.   [E]
San Augustine   22 July 1835
Certify Mr. Alexander W. Smith a
native of   Alabama a man of family
of two persons...   emigrated in
1834...   R.C. McDaniel C.P.O.
1895a.
Nacogdoches   Aug 8th 1835
Mr. Surveyor You are to survey in
Zavala's Grant the sitio which Mr.
Alexander W. Smith will designate...
        Jorge Anto Nixon Comr

1896. SMITH, AMOS [E]
District of Bevil   Octr 11th 1834
Certify Amos Smith a native of Vir-
giñia...hath a family of four
personss...   John Bevil Alcalde

1897. SMITH, ARCHIBALD   [E]
San Augustine   August 18th 1835
Certify Archibald Smith a native of
Louisiana a man of family of a wife
and three children...emigrated in
1822...   A. Hotchkiss Prmy Judge

1898. SMITH, EDWIN [E]
San Augustine   September 1st 1835
Certify Edwin Smith a native of
Mississippi a man of family of five
persons...emigrated in 1833...
        Saml Thompson Alcd

1899. SMITH, EDWIN   [S]
Nacogdoches   3d February 1835
Certify foreigner Edwin Smith a man
of good...married with family...
        Radford Berry
[Note] Wife & 3 ch = on the west
side of the Neches, above Clear Cr

1900. SMITH, ELIZABETH   [E]
Town of Austin   29 June 1830
I have emigrated to this Colony...
Elisabeth Smith 64 years old widow
2 Children 1 male 1 female
Moved from Louisiana and arrived in
this Colony 1st May 1830.
        Elisabeth Smith

1901. SMITH, HENRY   [E]
Brasoria   9th Novmr 1933
I, Henry Smith Alcalde of the Muni-
cipaltyof Brasoria do hereby certify
that Lewis C. Manson took the oath
        Henry Smith

1902. SMITH, JAMES   [S]
Nacogdoches   30 March 1835
Certify foreigner James Smith a man
of good...married with family...
    Jn Egne Michamps Alcalde Interim

1903. SMITH, JAMES   [E]
San Augustine   August 18, 1835
Certify James Smith a native of
North Carolina a man of family of
wife and five children...emigrated
1831...   A. Hotchkiss Prmy Judge

1904. SMITH, JAMES   [E]
San Augustine   June 10, 1830
To Mr. S.F. Austin Empresario
I have emigrated to this Colony...
My name is James Smith age 25 years.
Single. Removed to Texas in 1826.
Occupation farmer. Removed from
Louisiana.   [Sig] James Smith

1905. SMITH, JEREMIAH [E]
Nacogdoches   Nov 22, 1834
Mr. Surveyor   Sir: You are to
survey in Joseph Vehlein's Grant the
sitio which Mr. Jeremiah Smith will
designate... Jorge Anto Nixon Comr
[Note] Adjoining Wm Smith on the
    Trinity

1906. SMITH JOHN   [E]
San Augustine   Sept 27th 1834
Certify John Smith a native of Vir-
ginia a man of family of three per-
sons...   Benjamin Lindsey Alcalde
1906a.
Sabine District   April 25, 1835
To Maj Nixon Comr   Nacogdoches
Dear Sir: Please to deliver to
William D. Smith a Title for my
league.   John Smith

1907. SMITH, JOHN W.   [E]
Town of Austin   July 3, 1830
To Mr. S.F. Austin Empresario
I have emigrated to this Colony...
John W. Smith 37 years of age. Far-
mer. Sarah my wife 26. 2 Male 2
female children Arrived in this
Colony in Jany 1830. Wife and family
in Ohio and expected to arrive soon.
        [Sig] John Smith

1908. SMITH, JOSEPH   [E]
District of Sabine Oct 12th 1835
Certify Joseph Smith a native of
South Carolina has a family...emi-
grated in 1830. B. Holt Comr

1909. SMITH, LUTHER   [E]
Naches Precinct   February 3, 1835
Certify that I have been acquainted
with Luther Smith for two or three
years...a   farmer.
        Wm Whiteley Commissioner
1909b.
Nacogdoches   14 Sept 1835
Certify foreigner Luther Smith is a
man of good... widower with family,
resident of this Department since
1828...   Radford Berry

1910.   SMITH, M.W.   [E]
Tenoxtitlan   19 April 1834
To Empresarios Austin & Williams
I have emigrated to Texas...
I am unmarried. My age 27 years
        [Sig] M.W. Smith

1911. SMITH, MAJOR   [E]
San Augustine   Sept 23d 1834
Certify Major Smith a native of No
Carolina a man of family of five
persons...Benjamin Lindsey Alcalde

1912. SMITH,MARY   [E]
San Felipe de Austin 10 June 1830
To Mr. S.F. Austin Empresario
I have emigrated to this Colony...
My name is Mary Smith, widow.
One male child, two female.
Removed to this Colony in Novr 1829,
from Louisiana. Occupation stock
raising.   [Sig] Mary Smith

1913. SMITH, MAURICE   [S]
Nacogdoches   1st May 1835
Certify foreigner Maurice Smith is a
man of good...married with family...
        Radford Berry

1914. SMITH, MENEN   [E]
San Augustine   August 17th 1835
Certify Menen Smith native of Louisiana man of family of four persons
emigrated in 1822...
        Saml Thompson Alcd

1915. SMITH, NIMROD   [E]
San Augustine   Sept 1st 1835
Certify Nimrod Smith a native of
Kentucky man of family of three
persons...emigrated in 1826...
        Saml Thompson Alcd

1916. SMITH, ROBERT H.   [S]
Nacogdoches   21 April 1835
Certify foreigner Robert H. Smith a
man of good...single without
family...   Radford Berry

1917. SMITH, R.W.   [S]
Nacogdoches   13 April 1835
Certify foreigner R.W. Smith a man
of good...single without family...
        Radford Berry

1918. SMITH, SION   [E]
San Augustine   Sept 27th 1834
Certify Sion Smith a native of North
America hath a family of six persons
        John Bevil Alcd

1919. SMITH, THOMAS [S]
Nacogdoches   6 June 1835
Certify foreigner Thomas Smith a man
of good...married with family...
    G. Pollitt Alcalde Interim
[Rev] Accepted. Vehlein where he
    lives
1919a.
Nacogdoches   June 6, 1835
Mr. Surveyor   You are to survey in
Vehlein's Grant the sitio which Mr.
Thomas Smith will designate...
        Jorge Anto Nixon Comr

1920. SMITH, WILLIAM [S]
Nacogdoches   30 May 1835
Certify foreigner William Smith is a
man of good...single without family
    Jn Egne Michamps Alcalde Interim
[Reverse] Accepted 1/4 Sitio Zavala

1921. SMITH, WILLIAM [S]
Nacogdoches   22 Nov 1835
Certify William Smith is a man of
good...married with family...
        Vital Flores
[Note] Cleared by Wm Cunningham

1922. SMITH, WILLIAM [S]
Nacogdoches   9 Oct 1834
Certify foreigner William Smith is a
man of good...married with family...
        Luis Procela

1923. SMITH, WILLIAM [S]
Nacogdoches   4 Decr 1834
Certify foreigner Wm Smith is a man
of good...married with family...
        Vital Flores
[Note] Wife & 5 children = Zavala
Gaytors Bayou west side of Kerrs
Survey   J.A. Veatch

1924. SMITH, WILLIAM [E]
Town of Austin   25 June 1830
To Mr. S.F. Austin Empresario
I have emigrated to this Colony...
William Smith 28 years old, single.
Occupation farmer. Moved from Geor-
gia and arrived in this Country 1st
April 1830.   [Sig] William Smith
[Note] Selected his land back of the
land belonging to J.E. Phelps

1925. SMITH, WILLIAM [E]
Nacogdoches   Nov 22d 1834
Mr. William Brookfield Surveyor
Sir: You will survey in Vehlein's
Grant the sitio which Mr. Wm Smith
will designate...
        Jorge Anto Nixon Comr
[Note] The 1st Survey above Wm Pace
on Trinity

1926. SMITH, WILLIAM [E]
San Augustine   Sept 29, 1835
Certify William Smith a native of
Tennessee a man of family of wife
and two children...emigrated 1830...
        A. Hotchkiss P. Judge
1926a.
San Augustine   28 Sept 1835
I, William Smith Junr appoint Madi-
son Fuller my attorney to petition
for one league and labor...
        William X Smith jr

1927. SMITH, WILLIAM D. [S]
Nacogdoches   29 December 1834
Certify foreigner Wm D. Smith is a
man of good...married with family...
        Vital Flores
[Note] Wife and three children. The
selection made on Trinity Bay.
Vehlein   F. Hardin

1928. SMITH, WILLIAM [E]
San Augustine   Aug 25, 1835
Certify William Smith a citizen of
this Country, a man of family of a
wife and one child...native of Tennessee, emigrated in 1831...
        Saml Thompson Alcd
[Reverse] Wm D. Smith

1929. SMITH, WILLIAM [E]
Tenoxtitlan   26 Feby 1834
To the Empresarios Austin & Williams
I have emigrated to Texas...
I am unmarried. My age [blank]
        Wm H. Smith
1929a. Liberty   Octr 1st 1834
Certify William H. Smith a native of
Louisiana, a man of family of
three...   Wm Hardin Judge

1930. SMITH, WILLIAM L. [E]
To Mr. F. Hardin Surveyor
You are to survey the sitio which
Mr. Wm L. Smith will designate...
        A.Hotchkiss

[Note] Near the mouth of Trinity east side improvement made by Mr. Mil--

1931. SMITHER, LANCELOT   [E]
Town of Austin   7 Augt 1830
To Mr. S.F. Austin Empresario
I have emigrated to the Colony...
Lancelot Smither 27 years of age
unmarried farmer. Moved from Alabama
and arrived in this Colony in April
1828.   L. Smither

1932. SMITHSON, JOHN P.   [E]
Tenoxtitlan   5 April 1834
To the Empresarios Austin & Williams
I have emigrated to Texas...
I am unmarried. My age 25.
              [Sig] John P. Smithson

1933. SMITHWICK, NOAH   [E]
Town of Austin   9th July 1830
To Mr. S.F. Austin Empresario
I have emigrated to this Colony...
Noah Smithwick 22 years of age.
Moved from Tennessee and arrived in
this Colony in 1827. Occupation Gun
Smith.   [Sig] Noah Smithwick

1934. SMYTH, GEORGE W.   [E]
San Augustine   23d Sept 1834
Certify George W. Smyth a native of
the U.S. from Alabama a man with a
family of two persons...
          John Bevil Alcalde
1934a.
[To] A. Henrie   Dec 17th 1834
Dear Sir: Inclosed I send you the
return of a few Surveys. By examining the notes of Hiram Brown's Survey you will find it does not con-
tain quite a league which is all
that could be had in that place. Mr.
Hanks who acted as his agent wishes
to add marsh to complete the sitio
I expect to be in Nacogdoches by the
18th of January.   Geo W. Smyth
P.S. Hesekiah Williams & Hesekiah
Reines Williams have each an order
for one sitio which you will per-
ceive by examining the order but
being single men they are only entitled to 1/4 sitio which I have
surveyed for them.   GWS
I send you Hanks order the return
for which I already made.

1934b. Mr. Geo A. Nixon Comr
April 29th 1835 Sir: You will
please deliver our Titles to Geo W.
Smyth:
Ephraim Thompson   Peter Pry
Hesekiah Williams   John Skeers
Charles Williams   Salley Glenn
Hesekiah Williams   Nathaniel Grigsby
Joseph Grigsby   Hesekiah R.Williams

1935. SNIVELY, JACOB   [S]
Nacogdoches   6 July 1835
Certify foreigner Jacob Snively is a
man of good...single without family
Jn Egne Michamps Alcalde Interim
1935a.
440 Bautista Cherena   l & l
445 Francisco Manchaca   1/3
442 Antonio Calderon   1/3
 "   Santiago Chevana   1/3
 "   J.M. Servantes   1/3
     Pedro Resalles   1/3
503 Santos Garcia   1/3
 59 Marcus Garcia   [deleted]
     P. Servants   1/3
     J.W. Mansola   1/3
     Maria Beele   l & l
     Francisco Dias   1/3
307 T. Quintero   l & l
     M.C. Navaro   "
     Ventura Guerra   "
441 Augustus Dias   1/3
The above orders were handed to Comr
Smyth and sent by him to the Commr
Genl Office
Recd the above orders of Survey
Apl 7th 1838   J. Snively

1936. SPAIN, ELIHU D.   [E]
San Augustine   Sept 26, 1835
Certify Elihu D. Spain is a native
of Tennessee a man of family of wife
and one child...emigrated in 1831...
          A. Hotchkiss P. Judge
1936a.
San Augustine   26 Sept 1835
I, Elihu D. Spane have appointed
Franklin Fuller my attorney to peti-
tion for league & labor...
          [Sig] Elihu DSpain

1937. SPAIN, RANDOLPH D.   [S]
Nacogdoches   20 May 1835
Certify foreigner Randolph D. Spain

a man of good...single without family Jn Egne Michamps Alcalde Interim

1938. SPARKS, JAMES   [S]
Nacogdoches   18 May 1835
Certify foreigner James Sparks a man
of good...married with family...
                    Radford Berry

1939. SPARKS, JAMES   [S]
Nacogdoches   18 May 1835
Certify foreigner James Sparks a man
of good...married with family...
                    Radford Berry

1940. SPARKS, RICHARD   [S]
Nacogdoches   24 February 1835
Certify foreigner Richard Sparks a
man of good...married with family...
                    Radford Berry
1940a.
Nacogdoches   Sept 25, 1837
Received of G.A. Nixon the within
titles being finished previous to
the closing of the Land Office.
  Jeremiah Latham   Jehu Prophets
  Redmond Coates   Morton Latham
  John Taylor   Henry Awalt
  George Price   Elias Myers
       [by] Richard Sparks

1941. SPARKS, WILLIAM F.   [S]
Nacogdoches   5 December 1835
Certify foreigner William F. Sparks
a man of good...married with family
  Jn Egne Michamps Alcalde Interim

1942. SPEER, ANDREW   [S]
Nacogdoches   1 December 1834
Certify Foreigner Andrew Speer a man
of good...married with family...
                    Vital Flores
[Note] Andrew Speer. Zavala
Wife and four children. McFarland
At place where he lives.

1943. SPEARS, JOHN   [S]
Nacogdoches   6 June 1835
Certify foreigner John Spears a man
of good...single without family...
  G. Pollitt Alcalde Interim
[Rev] Accepted. Zavala   1/4 sitio

1944. SPEER, THOMAS   [S]
Nacogdoches   18 June 1835
Certify foreigner Thomas Speer a man
of ood...married with family...
  Jn Egne Michamps Alcalde Interim
[Rev] Accepted in Zavala. A.Henrie
1944a.
[Field Notes] Commencing at a cor-
ner in a lake on the west side of
the Naches for the beginning corner
of Thomas Speer sitio
1944b.
Recd of Geo Anto Nixon the title of
Thomas Speer. Sept 26th 1835
                    Geo W. Smyth

1945. SPLANNE, THOMAS M.
To Mr. S.F. Austin Empresario
I have emigrated to this Colony...
Thos M. Splanne 39 years of age
Margaret my wife 35 years of age
2 Male 4 female children. Moved from
Kentucky and arrived in this Colony
in 1831.   [Sig] T.M. Splane

1946. SQUIRES, JOSEPH   [E]
San Augustine   Apl 8, 1835
Certify Joseph Squyars is a man of
family of ten persons, a native of
South Carolina
              A. Hotchkiss P. Judge

1947. STAGNER, HENRY   [E]
District of Bevil   Octr 10th 1834
Certify Henry Stagner a native of N.
Carolina hath a family of three
persons...   John Bevil Alcalde

1948. STALLINGS, JACOB   [S]
Nacogdoches   11 December 1835
Certify foreigner Jacob Stallings a
man of good...married with family,
resident of this Department since
1819...   Radford Berry

1949. STANLEY, STEPHEN   [S]
Nacogdoches   1 December 1834
Certify foreigner Stephen Stanley a
man of good...married with family...
                    Vital Flores
[Note] Stephen Stanley. Wife & 3
children. The place he has improved
on the Angelina south side. Zavala
[Field Notes] West bank of the Angelina for beginning Stephen Stanleys
sitio...   Smyth Surveyor

1950. STANLEY, STEPHEN J. [S]
Nacogdoches   28 February 1835
Certify Stephen J. Stanley a man of
good...married with family...
                    Radford Berry
[Note] Zacharia C. Johnson has known
him for 2 years. Wife.

1951. STANLEY, WILLAFRED [S]
Nacogdoches   1 December 1934
Certify foreigner Willafred Stanley
a man of good...married with family
                    Vitlal Flores
[Note] Willafred Stanley wife and 3
children on the south side of Angelina, the place he has improved.
     Vehlein   G.Smyth

1952. STANLEY, WILLIAM C. [S]
Nacogdoches   12 September 1835
Certify foreigner Wm C. Stanley a
man of good...single without family
                    Radford Berry
[Rev] Accepted in Vehlein. A.Henrie

1953. STEEL, WILLIAM H. [S]
Nacogdoches   22 April 1835
Certify foreigner William H. Steel a
man of good...single without family
                    Radford Berry

1954. STEINSON, JOHN [E]
District of Sabine   May 26th 1835
Certify John Steinson a native of
South Carolina man of family of five
persons, a Mechanic to occupation
whom I recommend... B. Holt Comr

1955. STEPHEN, AMOS [E]
San Augustine   Oct 10, 1835
Certify Amos Stephens a native of
Virginia a man of family of eight
persons, emigrated in 1829...
              Saml Thompson Alcd
1955a.
San Augustine   Oct 10, 1835
I authorize Samuel Stivers to peti-
tion for one league & labor...
              [Sig] Amos Stephens
Witnesses E.O. Legrand
Saml Thompson Alcd
1955b.
Nacogdoches   Oct 13th 1835
Sir: You are to survey the sitio &
labor which Mr. Amos Stephens...
              Geo W. Smyth

1956. STEPHENS, THOMAS [S]
Nacogdoches   31 January 1835
Certify foreigner Thomas Stephens a
man of good...married with family...
                    Radford Berry

1957. STEPHENSON, ANDREW [E]
San Augustine   4 June 1835
Certify Andrew Stephenson a native
of Georgia a man of family of six
persons...emigrated May 1835...
              R.C. McDaniel C.P.O.
1957a.
Nacogdoches   Augt 12, 1835
Mr. Surveyor You are to survey the
sitio which Mr. Andrew Stephenson
will designate
              Jorge Anto Nixon Comr

1958. STEPHENSON, HENRY [E]
San Augustine   February 9th 1835
Certify Henry Stephenson a native of
Virginia a man of family of five
persons... James S. Hanks Alcd

1959. STEPHENSON, WILLIAM
Mr. Nixon and Mr. Hodgekiss
You will pleas send my Title by the
bearer February 1st 1835
              [Sig] Wm Stephenson

1960. STERNE, ADOLPHUS [S]
Nacogdoches   10 October 1834
Certify citizen Adolfo Sterne is a
man of very good..,married in this
Villa in Nuestra Santa Madre Church
                    Luis Procela
1960a.
Nacogdoches   March 21, 1835
Mr. Surveyor You are to survey in
David G. Burnet's Grant the sitio
which Adolphus Sterne will designate
              Jorge Anto Nixon Comr
[Note] Comanchy Trace adjoining
                    Joseph Hertz.
[Reverse] I hereby resign all my
right title and interest in and to
the within order, or any claim as a
Colonist in the said Grant.
                    Adolfo Sterne
Nacogdoches   August 18th 1835
1960b.
Received Nacogdoches Aug 12th 1835
From the Comr George A. Nixon the
following titles...
     Philip Martin in Burnet's Colony
     Wm Burleson in   ditto

Gregorio Garcia in Zavala
                              Adolphe Sterne
1960c.
Received the Title of Jose Damacio y
Garcia and the title of Gregorio
Garcia to be copied.
                              Adolphus Sterne
1960d.
[The following is a fragment]
Cow Bayou   January
Mr. William Ashworth Dear Sir:
Call at the Land Office
and get a title to my L[and]
the Cow Bayou fronting
Surveyed by Doct Vea[tch]
money for the same

1961. STERNES, JOHN   [S]
Nacogdoches   8 June 1835
Certify foreigner John Sternes a man
of good...married with family...
    Jn Egne Michamps Alcalde Interim
[Rev] Accepted in Zavala. Henrie

1962. STERRETT, A.B.   [E]
Town of Austin   19 Feby 1831
To Mr. S.F. Austin Empresario
I have emigrated to this Colony...
A.B. Sterret 33 years of age
Martha my wife 22 years of age
2 Male children. Occupation farmer.
Moved from Luisiana and arrived 1st
Dec 1830.   [Sig] A.B. Sterrett

1963. STEVENS, CORBIT   [S]
Nacogdoches   10 June 1835
Certify foreigner Corbit Stevens a
man of good...single without family
    Jn Egne Michamps Alcalde Interim

1964. STEVENS, MILES G.   [S]
Nacogdoches   20 November 1834
Certify Miles G. Stevens a man of
good...married with family...
                  Vital Flores
[Note] Wife & 1 child. 3d Survey
for the Baptist Village = Vehlein.
Rankin

1965. STEVENSON, GILBERT   [E]
Jurisdiction of Liberty Nov 27, 1834
Certify Gilbert Stevenson a native
of Louisiana a man of family of wife
and one child...   Wm Hardin Judge
[Note] Gilbert Stevenson. Wife and

one child. The place where he has
improved on the east bank of the
Neches.

1966. STEVENSON, JOHN SENR   [E]
Jurisdiction of Liberty Nov 27, 1834
Certify John Stevenson Senr a native
of Virginia a man of family of wife
and ten children... Wm Hardin Judge
[Note] John Stevenson. Zavala
Wife and ten children

1967. STEVENSON, JOHN JR.   [E]
Jurisdiction of Liberty Nov 28, 1834
Certify John Stevenson Junr a native
of Louisiana a man of family and of
good...   Wm Hardin Judge

1968. STEVENSON, WILLIAM   [E]
Jurisdiction of Liberty Nov 28,1834
Certify William Stevenson a native
of Louisiana man of family of his
wife and two children...
        Wm Hardin Judge
[Reverse] perhaps Stephenson

1969. STEWART, JOHN   [E]
Jurisdiction of Liberty Nov 24, 1834
Certify John Stewart a native of
Pennsylvania a man of family of wife
and four children... Wm Hardin Judge
[Note] South of Wm Hardin's Survey
on the W side of Trinity River,
within one mile above the Coushatta
Village.   F. Hardin = Vehlein

1970. STEWART, WILLIAM   [E]
Tenoxtitlan   22 May 1834
To the Empresarios Austin & Williams
I have emigrated to Texas...
I am married. My wife's name Sarah
Anne and have 6 children. My age 33
my wifes 33   William Stewart

1971. STIVERS, SAMUEL   [E]
San Augustine   Sept 23d 1834
Certify Dr. Samuel Stivers a native
of New Jersey a man of family of
eight persons...
        Benjamin Lindsey Alcalde

1972. STOCKMAN, PETER   [E]
San Augustine   August 20, 1835
Certify Peter Stockman a native of
Luisiana and a man of family of

three persons...emigratd to the above in 1810...Saml Thompson Alcd

1973. STOCKTON, STEPHEN [E]
San Augustine   17 March 1835
Certify Stephen Stockton a man of family of eight persons...emigrated in 1834...   R.C. McDaniel C.P.O.
1973a.
Nacogdoches   Augt 12th 1835
Mr. Surveyor Sir: You are to survey in Zavala's Grant the sitio which Mr. Stephen Stockton will designate
          Jorge Anto Nixon Comr

1974. STODDARD, DAVID [E]
Town of Austin   16 July 1830
I have emigrated to this Colony... David Stoddard 35 years of age unmarried. From Massachusetts. Arrived in this Colony in August 1829. Occupation farmer.
          David Stoddard

1975. STODDARD, JESSE W. [S]
Nacogdoches   22 Sept 1834
Certify foreigner J.W. Stoddard a man of good...married with family...
          Luis Procela
[Note] Jesse W. Stoddard. Wife and two children. Place where he lives in Burnet's   Colony

1976. STONE, R. JR. [E]
San Augustine   26 Feb 1835
Certify R. Stone jr. a native of Kentucky is a man of family of seven persons...emigrated in the fall of 1833...   R.C. McDaniel C.P.O.
1976a.
Nacogdoches   Aug 20th 1835
Mr. Surveyor You are to survey in Zavala's Grant the sitio which Mr. R. Stone will designate...
          Jorge Anto Nixon Comr

1977. STOUT, ISAAC L. [E]
San Augustine   15 July 1835
Certify Isaac L. Stout a native of the U.S. a man of family of four persons...emigrated in Spring of 1835...   R.C. McDaniel C.P.O.
1977a.
Nacogdoches   Augt 9, 1835
Mr. Surveyor You are to survey in

Zavala's Grant the sitio which Mr. Isaac L. Stout will designate...
          Jorge Anto Nixon Comr

1978. STOUT, WILLIAM [E]
San Augustine   August 19th 1835
Certify William Stout a native of Tennessee is a widower without children...emigrated in 1827...
          Saml Thompson Alcd

1979. STRANGE, JOHN [E]
San Augustine   Octr 5th 1835
Certify John Strange a native of No Carolina is a man of family of eight persons, emigrated in 1827...
          Saml Thompson Alcd
1979a.
San Augustine   6th October 1835
I, John Strange have appointed James C. Cain my attorney to petition for one league & labor... John Strange
Witnesses   E.O. Legrand
     E.W. Cullene   Morris May
1979b.
Nacogdoches   Octr 12, 1835
Mr. J. Snively, Surveyor Sir: You are to survey the sitio & labor which John Strange will designate...
          Geo W. Smyth Com

1980. STRICKLAND, DAVID [E]
Precinct of Tunahaw July 14th 1835
Certify David Strictland is a citizen of this Country & an old settler a native of Kentucky...a man of family of seven persons...
          Nathan Davis Commissioner

1981. STRICKLAND, SAMUEL [E]
San Augustine   August 20, 1835
Certify Samuel Strickland is a native of Kentucky a man of family a wife and three children...emigrated in 1821...took the oath in 1828 in presence of Col. Jose De Los Piedras... A. Hotchkiss Prmy Judge

1982. STRODE, JEREMIAH
Nacogdoches   July 24th 1835
Received, Wm Heath Grant for 1/4 league of land also Pedro Bermellas Grant for 1/4 league of land. Received of Comr Mr. George Antonio Nixon the above Grants.
          Jeremiah Strode

177

1983. STRONG, THERON [E]
Jurisdiction of Liberty Nov 24, 1834
Certify Theron Strong a native of
New York a man of family of two
persons...   Wm Hardin Judge
[Note] Wife and child. Zavala.
F.Hardin   The place where he lives
on the Sabine.

1984. STUART, JAMES [E]
To Mr. S.F. Austin Empresario
James Stewart 29 years old
Zillah Anne 22 years old.
2 Female children, Moved from Mississippi and arrived in this Colony
in Novr 1829.   May 25, 1830
        [Sig] James Stuart

1985. STUBBLEFIELD, JOHN J.   [S]
Nacogdoches   29 Decr 1834
Certify John J. Stubblefield a man
of good...married with family...
                Vital Flores
[Note] John J. Stubblefield. Wife
and two children. At the mouth of
the first creek below the Kichi
Crossing on the Neches west side.
Vehlein

1986. STUBBLEFIELD, WOODROUGH [S]
Nacogdoches   7 Oct 1835
Certify Woodraugh Stublifield a man
of good...married with family...
                Radford Berry
[Reverse] Accepted. A.Hotchkiss
        attorney for Joseph Vehlein.

1987. SUBLETT, PHILLIP A.   [E]
San Augustine   26 Sept 1834
Certify Philip A. Sublett a native
of Kentucky a man of family of three
persons... Benjamin Lindsey Alcalde
1987a.
San Augustine   Aug 17, 1835
Certify Phillip Sublett a native of
Kentucky is a man of family of a
wife and one child...emigrated in
1820...   A. Hotchkiss P. Judge

1988. SULLINS, JESSE   [E]
San Augustine   August 18, 1835
Certify Jesse Sullins a native of
Tennessee a man of family of a wife
amd one child...emigrated in 1832...
        A. Hotchkiss P. Judge

1989. SULLIVAN, JOHN   [E]
To Mr. S.F. Austin Empresario
I am desirous of locating myself and
family in this Colony...
John Sullivan 38 years old
Eunice my wife 37 years old
Three male and two female children.
Feby 20, 1830 [Sig] John Sullivan

1990. SUTHERLAND, WILLIAM   ]E]
Town of Austin   15 May 1830
To Mr. S.F. Austin Empresario
I have emigrated to this Colony...
William Sutherland 30 years old,
married Susan my wife 30
Moved from Luisiana and arrived in
this Colony in April 1830.
        [Sig] William Sutherland

1991. SWAIN, WILLIAM L.   [E]
Tenoxtitlan   23 May 1834
To the Empresarios Austin & Williams
I have emigrated to Texas...
I am unmarried. My age 29 years
        [Sig] W.L. Swain

1992. SWEENY, WILLIAM B.   [E]
Austin   Feby 7, 1832
To Mr. S.F. Austin Empresario
I have emigrated to this Colony...
Wm B. Sweeny 22 years of age
Elisabeth M 18   do
One male child. My family are resid-
ing in Tennessee and arrived in this
Colony 20th Jany 1832. W.B. Sweeny
Passport dated 31 Decr 1831

1993. SWEET, SIDNEY A.   [S]
Nacogdoches   12 May 1835
Certify foreigner Sidney A. Sweet a
man of good...married with family...
        Radford Berry
1993a.
Maj. Nixon Sir   Sept 30th 1837
Please deliver to Mr. Lord my Land
Title   Sidney A. Sweet

1994. SWEETENBURG, F.   [E]
San Augustine   August 18, 1835
Certify F. Sweetenburg a native of
South Carolina single man...emi-
grated May 1832.
        Saml Thompson Alcd

1995. SWIFT, SITH   [S]
Nacogdoches   28 July 1835
Certify foreigner Sith Swift a man
of good...married with family...
                    Radford Berry
[Rev] Accepted in Zavala. A.Henrie

1996. SWISHER, JAMES G.   [E]
Tenoxtitlan   27 May 1834
To the Empresarios Austin & Williams
I have emigrated to Texas...
I am married my wifes name Elizabeth
and have six children. My age 39 my
wifes age 36 years.
        [Sig]   James G. Swisher

1997. TAILOR, JOHN   [E]
San Augustine   Octr 4, 1835
Certify John Tailor a native of
Georgia a man of family of four
persons...emigrated in 1831 and has
taken the oath. Nathan Davis Comr
1997a.
San Augustine   7 Octr 1835
I authorize Franklin Fuller to peti-
tion for one league & labor
            [Sig] John Tailor
Witnesses   E.O. Legrand
A.B. Davis   W.L.Scott
Thomas Williams   Simpson Fuller

1998. TALBOT, WILLISTON   [S]
Nacogdoches   2 June 1835
Certify foreigner Williston S. Tal-
bot a man of good...single without
family...
    Jn Egne Michamps Alcalde Interim
[Rev] Accepted in Z.   A.Henrie
1998a.
Precinct of Tunnahaw Sepr 14, 1835
Certify Williston P. Talbot a native
of Virginia a man of family of too
persons...immigrated in 1828...
Nathan Davis Comr
[Reverse] Williston J. Talbot.
            Fraudulent

1999. TALLEY, EPHRAIM   [S]
Nacogdoches   28 May 1835
Certify foreigner Ephraim Talley a
man of good...single without family
    Jn Egne Michamps Alcalde Interim
[Reverse] Accepted. Arthur Henrie

2000. TANNEHILL, JESSE C.   [E]
Town of Austin   22 June 1830
To Mr. S.F. Austin Empresario

I have emigrated to this Colony...
Jesse C. Tannehill 32 married
Jane my wife 26. One male and one
female children. Occupation farmer.
Moved from Tennessee and arrived in
this Colony April 1828.
        [Sig] J.C. Tannehill

2001. TANNER, GEORGE   [E]
San Augustine   Sept 22, 1835
Certify George Tanner a native citi=
zen a man of family of seven persons
            Saml Thompson Alcd
2001a.
San Augustine   23d Sept 1835
George Tanner has appointed William
Inglish my attorney to petition for
one league & one labor...
        [Sig] George Tanner
Witnesses   A.E.C. Johnson
C. Thompson   Saml Thompson Alcd
2001b.
Nacogdoches   October 9th 1835
Sir: You are to survey the sitio &
labor which Mr. George Tanner will
designate... Geo W. Smyth Comr

2002. TANNER, THOMAS   [E]
District of Bevil   June 6, 1835
Certify Thomas Tanner a native of
South Carolina hath a family of
seven persons...came in 1831...
        Wm Williams Alcalde

2003. TAYLOR, CHARLES S.   [S]
Nacogdoches   July 24, 1835
Received of Comr J.A. Nixon the
following Titles:
  George Anding   George Clark
  A.D. Lathin   Walker Pettitte
  T.H. Garner   Elizth Groce
  E.W. Gilleland   in all seven titles
            Chas S. Taylor

2004. TAYLOR, JAMES   [S]
Nacogdoches   5 Augt 1835
Certify foreigner James Taylor a man
of good...single without family...
resident this Municipality since
1820...   Radford Berry
2004a.
Nacogdoches   August 5, 1835
Sir: You are to survey the third
sitio which Mr. James Taylor will...
            Geo W.Smyth

2005. TAYLOR, MRS. JANE   [E]
Jurisdiction of Liberty Dec 26, 1834
Certify Mrs. Jane Taylor a native of
Mississippi is a woman of family of
seven   chidren... Wm Hardin Judge
2005a.
Liberty   August 11th 1835
G.A. Nixon Esqr Dear Sir:
Please let Mr. Joseph Bryan have my
title   Jane X Taylor
Witness Wm M. Logan

2006. TAYLOR, JOHN   [S]
Nacogdoches   20 May 1835
Certify foreigner John Taylor a man
of good...married with family...
                    Radford Barry

2007. TAYLOR, JOHN B.   [E]
Columbia   January 3, 1836
Mr. Bordon   Sir:
Please to enter my name down to a
peas of land joining Mr. Clarey land
at H. Leags old place on the Colori-
dua which I believe is vacant when
the land office is opened and you
will oblige me very much.
                    John B. Taylor
N.B. I have just arrived from Bexar
[To] Mr. Bordin, Land Office,
San Filipe

2008. TAYLOR, JOHN M.   [E]
District of Bevil   Sept 30th 1834
Certify John M. Taylor a native of
Tennessee a single man.
                    John Bevil Alcalde

2009. TAYLOR, JOHN R.   [S]
Nacogdoches   20 Sept 1834
Certify foreigner John R. Taylor is
a man of good...
               Luis Procela Alcd Interim

2010. TAYLOR, OWEN   [E]
San Augustine   Sept 23d 1834
Certify Owen Taylor a native of the
U.S. a man of family of nine
persons...   John Bevil Alcalde
2010a.
Nacogdoches   October 3d 1835
Certify Owin Taylor a native of
Georgia...emigrated in 1829 hath a
family of six persons...
               Wm Williams Alcalde

2011. TAYLOR, WILLIAM   [E]
San Augustine   August 20th 1835
Certify William Taylor a native of
England a man of family of a wife
and nine children...emigrated in
1833.   A. Hotchkiss P. Judge

2012. TAYLOR, WILLIAM B.   [S]
Nacogdoches   Oct 5, 1835
Certify foreigner William B. Taylor
a man of good...married with family
                    Radford Berry
[Rev] Accepted in Zavala. A.Henrie
In place of No. 156 in name of Wil-
liam Guthrie

2013. TAYLOR, WILLIAM H.   [E]
Town of Austin   7 May 1830
To Mr. S.F. Austin Empresario
I have emigrated to this Colony...
William H. Taylor 41 years old.
Widower. Occupation farmer. Moved
from Luisiana and arrived in Texas
in 1821 and in this Colony in April
1829.   [Sig] Wm H. Taylor

2014. TEAGUE, JOSEPH C.   [S]
Nacogdoches   9 Nov 1834
Certify foreigner Joseph C. Teague a
man of good...married with family...
                    Vital Flores

2015. TEAL, EDWARD   [E]
San Augustine   August 19, 1835
Certify Edward Teal a native of
Maryland a man of family of three
children...emigrated in 1824...
          A. Hotchkiss P. Judge

2016. TEAL, HENRY   [S]
Nacogdoches   17 January 1835
Certify foreigner Henry Teal is a
man of good...single without family
          Jn Egne Michamps Alcalde Interim

2017. TEAL, JOHN   [E]
Tenoxtitlan   24 May 1834
To Empresarios Austin & Williams
I have emigrated to Texas...
I am married my wifes name Polly and
have 4 children. My age 38 my wife
age 27 yr   [Sig] John Teal

2018. TEEL, PETER [S]
Nacogdoches   26 May 1835
Certify foreigner Peter Teel is a
man of good...married with family...
  Jn Egne Michamps Alcalde Interim
2018a.
Major Nixon will oblige the under-
signed by delivering his Title to
Mr. Samuel Lindley
May 26th 1835   Peter Teel

2019. TEJERA, VENTURA   [S]
Nacogdoches   1 June 1835
Certify citizen Ventura Tijera a man
of good... resident of this Munici-
pality for many years, married with
family...has not obtained land...
  Jn Egne Michamps Alcalde Interim
[Rev] Accepted in Burnet. A.Henrie
2019a.
Nacogdoches   Oct 14th 1834
Mr. William Brookfield Sir: You
are to survey in Joseph Vehlein's
Grant the fourth of a sitio which
Mr. Ventura Tijera will designate...
        Jorge Anto Nixon Comr
[Note] One fourth of a sitio adjoin-
ing   Mrs. Mary Jaca Chamar

2020. TERY, JESSE   [S]
Nacogdoches   1 Novr 1834
Certify foreigner Jese Tery is a man
of good...married with family...
        Vital Flores
[Note] Jese Terry. Vehlein
        Next to Mr. Lindsey
2021. TEVIS, GEORGE W.   [E]
Dept of Nacogdoches   Decr 4, 1834
Certify George W. Tevis a native of
Louisana is a single man...
        John Bevil Alcalde
[Note] Single. Adjoining David B---
Survey on the Neches. 4th. Zavala.
        D. Brown
2022. TEVIS, NOAH   [E]
Dept of Nacogdoches   4th Decr 1834
Certify Noah Tevis a native of Mary-
land hath a family of eleven persons
        John Bevil Alcalde
[Note] Wife and seven children.
Zavala   The place where he lives
Neches.   D.Brown

2023. THOMAS, AMOS   [S]
Nacogdoches   12 Dec 1834
Certify foreigner Amos Thomas a man
of good...single...   Vital Flores

[Note] Single. 4th sitio. At head
of Old River on the north side.
        Zavala.
2024. THOMAS, G.S.   [E]
Liberty   Octr 12th 1834
Certify G.S. Thomas a native of
North Carolina a man of family of
three... Wm Hardin, Primary Judge

2025. THOMAS, HEZEKIAH   [E]
San Augustine   August 18, 1835
Certify Hezekiah Thomas a native of
North Carolina a man of family of a
wife and four children...emigrated
in 1831... A. Hotchkiss Prmy Judge

2026. THOMAS, IREDELL D.   [E]
San Augustine   May 20, 1835
Certify Iredell D.Thomas a native of
North Carolina a man of family of
wife and two children...
        A. Hotchkiss Primary Judge

2027. THOMAS, JAMES   [E]
San Augustine   August 18, 1835
Certify James Thomas a native of
North Carolina a single man...
emigrated 1831...
        A. Hotchkiss Prmy Judge

2028. THOMAS, JAMES   [S]
Nacogdoches   7 Sept 1835
Certify foreigner James Thomas a man
of good...married with family...
        Radford Berry
[Rev] Accepted in Zavala. A.Henrie

2029. THOMAS, JAMES J.   [S]
Nacogdoches   30 May 1835
Certify foreigner James J. Thomas a
man of good...married with family...
  Jn Egne Michamps Alcalde Interim

2030. THOMAS, JOHN   [E]
To Mr. S.F. Austin Decr 29, 1831
I have emigrated to this Colony...
John Thomas 29 years of age. Unmar-
ried   Moved from Luisiana and
arrived in this Colony October 1831.
        [Sig] John Thomas

2031. THOMAS, JOHN   [E]
San Augustine   13 May 1835
Certify Mr. John Thomas a native of
jorge and was born in the county of

Worn and is a man of family...
  John Bodine Alcalde pro tem
[Rev] Accepted in Vehlein. A.Henrie

2032. THOMAS, JOSIAH   [S]
Nacogdoches   26 Oct 1835
Certify foreigner Josiah Thomas a
man of good...married with family
and resident of this Department
since 1832...   Radford Berry
2032a.
Nacogdoches   Oct 26th 1835
Mr. J. Snively Sir: You are to
survey the sitio & labor which Mr.
Josiah Thomas will designate...
  Geo W. Smyth Comr

2033. THOMAS, MRS. MARY   [E]
San Augustine   May 18, 1835
Certify Mrs. Mary Thomas a native of
Nor Carolina a woman of family of
nine children...   A. Hotchkiss
                  Primary Judge

2034. THOMAS, MONTGOMERY B.   [S]
Nacogdoches   1 June 1835
Certify foreigner Montgomery B.
Thomas a man of good...single with--
out family...
Jn Egne Michamps Alcalde Interim
[Rev] Accepted in Burnet. A.Henrie

2035. THOMAS, SHADRACK D.   [S]
Nacogdoches   1 May 1835
Certify citizen Shadrick D. Thomas a
man of good...married with family...
                  Radford Berry
2035a.
Nacogdoches   May 1, 1835
Mr. Surveyor You are to survey in
Joseph Vehlein's Grant the sitio
which Mr. Shadrach D. Thomas will
designate...
[Note]   North of Menard's Survey

2036. THOMAS, THEOPHILUS   [S]
Nacogdoches   21 April 1835
Certify foreigner Theophilus Thomas
a man of good...single without
family...   Radford Berry
2036a.
Nacogdoches   April 21, 1835
Mr. S.C. Hiroms Surveyor
You are to survey in Zavala's Grant
the quarter sitio which Mr. Theophilus Thomas will designate...
        Jorge Anto Nixon Comr

182

[Note] Near the head of Big Sandy
about 9 miles above the Road from
Nacogdoches to Trinity adjoining
Bartolo Escobeda

2037. THOMAS, WILEY S.   [E]
San Augustine   April 16, 1835
Certify W.S. Thomas a native of
North Carolina... a single man...
  A. Hotchkiss Prmy Judge
2037a.
Nacogdoches   Apl 13, 1835
Mr. Surveyor You are to survey in
Joseph Vehlein's Grant the 1/4 sitio
which Mr. Wiley S. Thomas will
designate... Jorge Anto Nixon Comr
[Note] Adjoining John J. Simpsons
sitio on Trinity

2038. THOMPSON, PETER S.   [E]
Dept of Tenahaw   Sept 17th 1835
Certify Peter S. Thompson a native
of Ohio a man of family of seven
persons...emigratd 1832 has taken
the oath.   Nathan Davis Comr

2039. THOMPSON, CREED T.   [S]
Nacogdoches   3 October 1835
Certify foreigner Creed T. Thompson
a man of good...married with family
and resident of this Department
since 1833...   Radford Berry
2039a.
Nacogdoches   October 30th 1835
Sir: You are to survey the sitio &
labor which Creed T. Thompson will
designate...   Geo W. Smyth Comr
[Rev] U.S.A. mar[ried] 8 person

2040. THOMPSON, CYRUS W.   [E]
Jurisdiction of Liberty 2 June 1835
Certify Cyrus W. Thompson a native
of New York an unmarried man...
  Wm Hardin Judge
[Reverse] Accepted in Vehlein on Big
Sandy 1/4 sitio. A. Henrie
2040a.
Nacogdoches   June 10, 1835
Mr. Surveyor You are to survey in
Jose' Vehlein's Grant the quarter
sitio which Mr. Cyrus W. Thompson
will designate...
        Jorge Anto Nixon Comr
[Note] On Big Sandy

2041. THOMPSON, EPHRAIM [E]
District of Bevil   Sept 30th 1834
Certify Ephraim Thompson a native of
Kentucky hath a family of eleven
persons...   John Bevil Alcalde

2042. THOMPSON, JAMES [E]
Precinct of Viesca   15th Aug 1835
Certify James Thompson a man of
family of eight persons a native of
South Carolina B.B. Goodrich Comr
[Rev] Accepted in Vehlein. A.Henrie

2043. THOMPSON, SAMUEL [E]
San Augustine   Aug 19th 1835
Certify Samuel Thompson a native of
N. Carolina a man of family of two
persons...emigrated in 1826.
A. Hotchkiss P. Judge

2044. THOMPSON, J. ORVILLE [E]
Jurisdiction of Liberty 2 June 1835
Certify J. Orville Thompson a native
of New York is an unmarried man...
Wm Hardin Judge
[Reverse] Acceptd in Vehlein on his
improvement. 1/4 sitio. A.Henrie

2045. THOMSON, Z.L. [Z.S.] [S]
Nacogdoches   4 May 1835
Certify foreigner Z.S.Thomson is a
man of good...married with family...
Radford Berry

2046. THORN, COL. F. [E]
July 17, 1835
Received from the Office of Major
Nixon, at the request of Com Sparks,
the following Land Titles, viz.
David McKenzie   Reden Garner
Sarah McNulty   Willis Curry
Isaac H. Reed   William B. Reed
Hugh Shepherd
Making together seven in number.
F.Thorn

2047. THORN, JOHN S. [S]
Nacogdoches   5 May 1835
Certify foreigner John S. Thorn a
man of good...single without family
Radford Berry

2048. THORNBURGH, ALEXANDER C. [E]
San Augustine   August 24th 1835
Certify Alexander C. Thornburgh a

native of No Carolina a man of family of fivepersons...emigrated 1829.
Saml Thompson Alcd

2049. THOUVENIN, ARNOLD [S]
Nacogdoches   23 April 1835
Certify foreigner Arnold Thouvenin a
man of good...single...
Radford Berry

2050. TILLEY, JOSIAH [E]
To S.F. Austin Empresario [no date]
I am desirous of being admitted...
Josiah Tilley 44 years of age.
Widower 2 Male 5 female children.
Moved from Alabama and arrived in
this Colony in May 1831.
[Sig] Josiah Tilley

2051. TIMMONS, JAMES F. [S]
Nacogdoches   9 October 1834
Certify foreigner James F. Timmons a
man of good...single...
Luis Procela

2052. TIMMONS, THOMAS [S]
Nacogdoches   20 September 1834
Certify foreigner Thomas Timins a
man of good...   Vicente Cordova

2053. TIMMONS, THOMAS G. [S]
Nacogdoches   23 September 1835
Certify foreigner Thomas G. Timmins
a man of good...married with family
and resident of this Department
since 1831...   Radford Berry
2053a.
Nacogdoches   Sept 23d 1835
Sir: You are to survey the sitio &
labor which Mr. Thos G.Timmins will
designate...   Geo W. Smyth Comr

2054. TODD, CONRAD [E]
San Augustine   27 August 1835
Certify Mr. Conrad Todd a native of
the U.S. a man of family, emigrated
in Spring 1835...
R.C. McDaniel C.P.O.
[Reverse] Accepted. A. Henrie
2054a.
Nacogdoches   August 14, 1835
Mr. Surveyor   You are to survey in
Zavala's Grant the sitio which Mr.
Conrad Todd will designate...
Jorge Anto Nixon Comr

2055. TODD, JACKSON   [S]
Nacogdoches   2 June 1835
Certify foreigner Jackson Todd a man
of good...single without family...
   Jn Egne Michamps Alcalde Intermim

2056. TODD, WILLIAM   [E]
Precinct of Tunahaw May 21st 1835
Certify William Todd a citizen of
this Country a native of Georgia, a
man of family of thirteen persons...
   Nathan Davis Commissioner

2057. TOLBERT, JOHN   [E]
Naches District   May 2d 1835
Certify I have been acquainted with
John Tolbert for a considerable
time. He is a man of family...a
farmer...   Wm Whiteley
   Comr for the Naches District
[Reverse]   John Talbert
2057a.
Mr. Nixon will please deliver my
title to Jonathan S. Collard...
May 18th 1835   John Talbert

2058. TOMLINSON, THERESA   [S]
Nacogdoches   29 August 1835
Certify foreigner Theresa Thombleston of Louisiana...widow with family
of 5 children, resident of this
Municipality since 1824...has not
obtained land...   Radford Berry
2058a.
San Augustine   Sept 4th 1835
Sir: You are to survey the sitio &
labor which Mrs. Teresa Tomlinson
will designate   Geo W. Smyth Comr

2059. TONAGE, SHELLY   [E]
San Augustine   Aug 29th 1835
Certify Shelly Tonage a native of
Tennessee is a single man...emigrat-
ed in 1831...   Saml Thompson Alcd

2060. TONGE, JUAN B.   [S]
Nacogdoches   18 November 1834
Certify foreigner Juan B. Fang a man
of good...single...   Vital Flores
[Note] At his improvements on the
waters of Thompson's Creek. Single
man.   Robertson
[Reverse]   Juan B. Tonge

2061. TORRES, JOSEFA   [S]
Nacogdoches   4 April 1835
Certify foreigner Josefa Torres is
resident of this Municipality for
many years, widow with family and
has not obtained land...
   Radford Berry

2062. TORRES, MARIA DEL PILAR [S]
Nacogdoches   23 June 1835
Certify citizen Maria Del Pilar
Torres is a woman of good...resident
of this Municipality and born here,
widow with family...has not obtained
land...   G. Pollitt Alcalde Interim
2062a.
Nacogdoches   Sept 11th 1835
Sir: You are to survey the sitio &
labor which Mrs. Maria del Pillar
Torres will designate...
   Geo W. Smyth Comr

2063. TORRES, MIGUEL   [S]
Nacogdoches   4 April 1835
Certify citizen Miguel Torres a
resident of this Municiapality for
many years, married with family, has
not obtained land... Radford Berry

2064. TORRES, PATRICIO DE   [S]
Nacogdoches   8 Sept 1835
Certify citizen Patricio de Torres
is a man of good...married with
family, resident of this Municipality since 1801, has not obtained land
   Radford Berry

2065. TOVAR, JUAN F.F.   [S]
Nacogdoches   3d April 1835
Mr. David Brown, Surveyor. You are
to survey in Joseph Vehlein's Grant
the sitio which Mr. Juan F.F. Tovar
will designate
   Jorge Anto Nixon Comr
[Note] On the Mansola Road between
Neches & Trinity on Big Sandy Creek
[Reverse]
Nacogdoches   August 11th 1835
Surveyor returned this order because
there was no vacant land at the
place designated. Consequently all
pretension to said League of Land
and the right to any other in the
said Colony are hereby waived.
   Juan F.F. Tobar per Adolfo Stena

184

2066. TOWNES, DAVID   [S]
Nacogdoches   8 August 1835
Certify foreigner David Towns is a
man of good...widower with family
resident of   this of this Municipality since 1826...
                    Radford Berry

2067. TOWNSEND, MRS. ISABELLA [E]
San Augustine   Sept 1st 1835
Certify Mrs. Isabella Townsend is a
native of England,widow, family of
one son... A. Hotchkiss P. Judge
[Rev] Accepted in Vehlein A.Henrie

2068. TOWNSEND, JACOB   [S]
Nacogdoches   29 December 1834
Certify foreigner Jacob Townsend is
a man   of good...single...
                    Vital Flores
[Note] Vehlein. Single. Adjoining
east of Mr. Bloodgood's survey.
                    F. Hardin

2069. TOWNSEND, THOMAS R.   [S]
Nacogdoches   14 October 1834
Certify foreigner Thomas R. Townsend
a man of good...married with family.
                    Luis Procela
[Note] Thomas Townsend wife and four
children. Burnet. The place where he
lives
2069a.
Nacogdoches   October 29, 1835
Received of the Comr George A. Nixon
Mr. Francisco Johnson Land Title 1
league   [Sig] Thomas R. Townsend
2069b.
Nacogdoches   October 30th 1835
Received of Geo A. Nixon Comr
Mr. James Neville Title for one
league [Sig] Thomas R. Townsend

2070. TREDWELL, TIMOTHY   [S]
Nacogdoches   1st June 1835
Certify foreigner Timothy Tredwell a
man of good...single with family...
     Jn Egne Michamps Alcalde Interim
[Rev] Accepted in Zavala. A.Henrie

2071. TRENARY, JOHN B.   [E]
Naches   September 5th 1835
I have been acquainted with John B.
Trenary for some time. He is a man
of family, farmer... Wm Whiteley
                Comr Pct of Naches
[Rev] Accepted in Vehlein. A.Henrie

2072. TREVINO, JOSE LIONISIO   [S]
Nacogdoches   19th July 1835
Certify citizen Jose Lionisio Trevino a man of good...married with
family...has not obtained land...
                    Radford Berry

2073. TREVINO, ROMALDO [S]
Nacogdoches   15 May 1835
Certify citizen Romaldo Trevino is a
resident of this Municipality for
many years, single without family...
                    Radford Berry

2074. TROUTMAN, HIRAM B.   [S]
Nacogdoches   25 May 1835
Certify foreigner Hiram B. Troutman
is a man of good...married with
family...   Radford Berry

2075. TUCKER, JAMES B.   [E]
San Augustine   August 17, 1835
Certify James B. Tucker a native of
Virginia a man of family of eight
children...settled in Texas in
1834... A. Hotchkiss Primary Judge

2076. TURNER, JOHN
[Field Notes] Survey of one league
and one labor for John Turner on the
west bank of the Rio Frio adjoining
Michael Haley's Survey...

2077. TURNER, JONATHAN   [E]
San Augustine   27 May 1834
Certify Jonathan Tanner a native of
Indiana a man of family of two per-
sons, emigrated in 1834...
               R.C. McDaniel C.P.O.
[Reverse] Accepted. A.Henrie
2077a.
Nacogdoches   Aug 11, 1835
Mr. Surveyor You are to survey in
Zavala's Grant the sitio which Mr.
Jonathan Turner will designate...
          Jorge Anto Nixon Comr

2078. TURNER, JOSEPH W.   [S]
Nacogdoches   13 January 1835
Certify foreigner Joseph W. Turner a
man of good...married with family...
                    Radford Berry
[Note] wife & 1 child = Pine Island
Adjoinig Jno Gilchrist. Jno A.Veatch

2079. TURNER, RUFIN [E]
District of Bevil October 10th 1834
Certify Rufin Turner a native of N.
Carolina hath a family of four per-
sons...   John Bevil Alcalde

2080. TUTT, CLEMENT [E]
San Augustine   September 25th 1834
Certify Clement Tutt a native of
South Carolina...a man of family of
nine persons
            Benjamin Lindsey Alcalde
2080a.
San Augustine   August 20th 1835
Certify Clement Tutt a native of
South Carolina man of family of nine
persons...emigrated in 1827...
            Saml Thompson Alcd

2081. USSERY, JOHN [E]
San Augustine   August 19, 1835
Certify John A. Ussery a native of
Virginia a single man...emigrated
1832...   A. Hotchkiss P. Judge

2082. USSERY, MARYWEATHER [E]
San Augustine   Sept 1st 1835
Certify Maryweather Usery a native
of Tennessee a single man...emigra-
ted Feb 1832... Saml Thompson Alcd

2083. USSERY, M.S. [E]
San Augustine   May 25, 1835
Certify M.S. Ussery a native of
Virginia a man of family of two
persons... R.C. McDaniel Sindico

2084. USSERY, NANCY [E]
San Augustine   May 26, 1835
Certify Nancy Ussery a native of
Virginia is a widow woman of family
of five persons
            R.C. McDaniel Sindico

2085. VACOCU, BAPTISTE ANDRES [S]
Nacogdoches   26 May 1835
Certify foreigner Baptiste Andres
Vacocu a man of good...married with
a woman of the Country...
            Jn Egne Michamps Alc Int

2086. VAIL, DANIEL A. [E]
San Augustine   August 17, 1835
Certify Daniel H.Vail a native of
Connecticut a man of family of a
wife, emigrated April 1831...
            A. Hotchkiss P. Judge
186

2087. VALLANOVA, FRANCO JACINTO
Nacogdoches [S] 14 August 1835
Certify citizen Fco Jacinto Ballano-
va a man of good...resident of this
Municipality and born here...married
with family...has not received land
            Radford Berry
2087a.
Nacogdoches   August 14th 1835
Mr. William Brookfield Sir:
You are to survey the sitio which
Mr. F.J. Vallanova will designate...
            Geo W. Smyth Comr

2088. VALLE, SANTIAGO DEL [S]
Nov 6, 1824   [Decree from the
President of Mexico establishing per
diems and honorariums for the Depu-
ties and Senators of the future
Congress of the Republic of Mexico]
A Copy   Santiago del Valle

2089. VAN, MASON [E]
Precinct of Tunnahaw Aug 19, 1835
Certify Mason Van a native of South
Carolina a man of family of eight
persons... emigrated 1822...
            Nathan Davis Comr

2090. VANMETER. S.K. [E]
San Augustine   5 Aug 1835
Certify S.K. Vanmeter a native of
Kentucky man if family of four per-
sons...emigrated in 1834...
            R.C. McDaniel C.P.O.
2090a.
Nacogdoches   August 3d 1835
Mr. Surveyor   You are to survey in
Zavala's Grant the sitio which   Mr.
S.K. Vanmeter will designate...
      Jorge Anto Nixon Comr
[Note] On River Neches

2091. VANNORDSTAND, ABRAHAM [E]
Jurisdiction of Liberty 5 Sep 1835
Certify Abraham Vannordstand a na-
tive of New Jersey a man of family
of his wife and three children...
            Wm Hardin Judge
[Rev] Accepted in Vehlein. A.Henrie

2092. VANNOY, JOSEPH [E]
San Augustine   Sept 1st 1835
Certify Joseph Vannoy a native of
Kentucky a married man a wife and
two children...emigrated March 1832
            Saml Thompson Alcd

2093. VAN SIKELL, BENJAMIN [S]
Nacogdoches   19 January 1835
Certify foreigner Benjamin Vansikel
a man of good...single...
Jn Egne Michamps Alcalde Interim

2094. VANWICK (VANWINKE), MARIA [S]
Nacogdoches   Oct 26, 1835
Certify citizen Mary Vanwinke is a
woman of good...widow with family
and resident of this Department
since 1832...   Radford Berry

2095. VARGOS, JUAN   [S]
Nacogdoches   13 April 1835
Certify citizen Juan Vargas a resi-
dent of this Municipality for many
years, married with family and has
not received land... Radford Berry
2095a.
Nacogdoches   May 13th 1833
Major Nixon will please deliver my
title to William Reagan.
                   Juan X Vargas
Witnesses
Robert Smith   Jesse H. Chambers

2096. VAUGHAN, GEORGE   [E]
San Augustine   Sept 22, 1835
Certify.George Vaughan a native
citizen a man of family of four
persons...Saml Thompson Alcalde
2096a.
San Augustine   22 Sept 1835
I, George Vaughan appoint William
Inglish my attorney to petition for
one league and labor...
            [Sig] George Vaughan
Witnesses   A.E.C. Johnson
C. Thompson   Saml Thompson Alcd
2096b.
Nacogdoches   October 9th 1835
Sir: You are to survey the sitio &
labor which Mr. George Vaughan will
designate...   Geo W. Smyth Comr

2097. VAUGHN, JOHN   [S]
Nacogdoches   20 September 1834
Certify foreigner John Vaughan a man
of good...married with family...
                Luis Procela Alcd Int
2097a.
Major Nixon will send the deed for
my land by C.M. Lewis
18th Jany 1835   John Vaughn

2098. VEATCH, JOHN A.   [E]
San Augustine   Sept 22d 1834
Certify John A. Veatch a native of
Kentucky a man of family of four
persons...
        Benjamin Lindsey Alcalde
[Reverse] John Veitch
2098a.
Nacogdoches   6 April 1835
Certify foreigner John A. Veitch is
a man of good...married with
family...   Radford Berry
2098b.
Nacogdoches   Nov 30th 1835
Received of Mr. G.A. Nixon, G.A.
Pattillos land title.
              John A. Veatch

2100. VICKERS, JOHN A.   '[E]
San Augustine   10th June 1835
Certify John A. Vickers a native of
the U.S. a man of family of six
persons, emigrated in 1834...
           R.C. McDaniel C.P.O.
2100a.
Nacogdoches   Augt 17th 1835
Sir: You are to survey in Zavala's
Grant the sitio which Mr. Jno A.
Vickers will designate...
           Jorge Anto Nixon Comr

2101. VIDAL, LOUIS ALEJANDRO   [S]
Bexar   13 December 1832
Empresario S.F. Austin and Williams
I am European by birth, married with
a Mexican in the City of Bexar, wish
admission as a Colonist...My name is
Luis Alexandro Vidal, native of
France, Canton of Marseille, of the
Department of Boca del Vonne, age 41
years. My wife Da Victorina Vidal,
born de la Baume, native of Nacog-
doches and of age 26 years.   Vidal
              Victorina Vidal
[Note] Certificate given 22 December
1832,in Bejar.   Austin
[Certificate]
Bejar   22 December 1832
Estevan F. Austin y Samuel M.
Williams   Empresarios.
Certify that Luis Alexander Vidal
native of France and married to a
Mexican is seated among the families
Estevan F. Austin
        by   Samuel M. Williams

                                  187

2102. VIDALES, MANUEL   [S]
Nacogdoches   21 August 1835
Certify citizen Manuel Vidales is a
man of good...resident of this Municipality since 1827...has not received land...   Radford Berry
2102a.
Nacogdoches   August 21, 1835
Sir: You are to survey the third
sitio which Manuel Vidales will
designate...   Geo W. Smyth Comr

2103. VINA, JUANA COMUNIS DE LA
Nacogdoches   [S]   9 July 1835
Certify citizen Juana Comunes de la
Vina a woman of good...widow with
family...   Radford Berry

2104. VINA, POLANIO LA   [S]
Nacogdoches   23 July 1835
Certify citizen Polonio la Vina is
resident of this Municipality and
born here, a man of good...single
without family...has not received
land...   Radford Berry
2104a.
Nacogdoches   Sept 7, 1835
Sir: You are to survey the third
sitio which Mr. Polanio la Vina will
designate   Geo W. Smyth Comr

2105. VINTON, OLIVER MILLS   [S]
Nacogdoches   29 May 1835
Certify foreigner Oliver Mills Vin-
ton a man of good...married with
family...
 Jn Egne Michamps Alcalde Interim
[Rev] Accepted. A.H.   One sitio

2106. WADE, JOHN   [S]
[Passport]
Consul of U.S. of Mexico in New
Orleans Passport to Mr. John Wade,
native of Ireland, to go on the
American schooner Brasoria, Rowland
her Captain, to Brasoria with his
wife, on personal business. Given in
New Orleans, 9 June 1832
          Francisco Pizarro Martinez
[Signed] John Wade
2106a.
Nacogdoches   6 October 1835
Certify foreigner John Wade a man of
good...married with family...
          Radford Berry

[Reverse] Accepted, A. Hotchkiss
          agent for Joseph Vehlein

2107. WADE, NATHAN   [S]
Nacogdoches   24 September 183
Certify foreigner Nathan Wade a man
of good...single without family...
          Radford Berry
[Reverse] Accepted in Vehlein. 1/4

2108. WAGNER, JOHN A.   [S]
Nacogdoches   8 June 1835
Certify foreigner John A. Wagner a
man of good...single without family
 Jn Egne Michamps Alcalde Interim
[Rev] Accepted in Zavala 1/4 sitio

2109. WAKEFIELD, ROBERT   [E]
San Augustine   9 May 1835
To Robert Wakefield a native of N.
Jersey a man of family of two per-
sons...emigrated in 1834...
          R.C. McDaniel C.P.O.
2109a.
Nacogdoches   Augt 18th 1835
Sir: You are to survey in Zavala's
Grant the sitio which Mr. Robt Wake-
field will designate...
     Jorge Anto Nixon Comr
[Note] On the waters of Big Alabama

2110. WAKEFIELD, UZZIEL   [E]
Austin   19 October 1832
To Mr. S.F. Austin Empresario
I have emigrated to this Colony...
Uzziel Wakefield 30 years of age
Eliza my wife 20 years of age
One female child. Moved from Ala-
bama.   [Sig] Uzziel Wakefield

2111. WALDROP, WILEY   [S]
Nacogdoches   19 Sept 1835
Certify foreigner Wiley Waldrop is a
man of good...married with family,
resident of this Department since
1827...   Radford Berry

2112. WALKER, CLAIBORNE   [E]
San Augustine   August 17, 1835
Certify Claiborne Walker a native of
Tennessee a single man...emigrated
in February 1832...
          Saml Thompson Alcd

2113. WALKER, FIELDING [E]
Department of Bevil October 2d 1835
Certify Fielding Walker a native of
Kentucky and emigrated 1833, hath no
family   Wm Williams Alcalde

2114. WALKER, HIRAM [S]
Nacogdoches   29 January 1835
Certify foreigner Hiram Walker a man
of good...married with family...
                Radford Berry

2115. WALKER, JOEL [E]
San Augustine   Sept 25, 1834
Certify Joel Walker a native of No
Carolina a man of family of five
persons...Benjamin Lindsey Alcalde

2116. WALKER, JOHN [S]
Nacogdoches   11 October 1834
Certify foreigner John Walker a man
of good...married with family...
                Luis Procela

2117. WALKER, JOSEPH [E]
Precinct of Sabine   March 29, 1835
Certify Joseph Walker is now a citizen of the District of Sabine, has a
family of nine persons and residing
here since 1833, a farmer and Black-
Smith.   B. Holt Commissioner

2118. WALKER, LEWIS [E]
San Augustine   Feb 2, 1835
Certify Lewis Walker a man of family
of a wife and three children, a
native of Alabama...
        A.Hotchkiss Primary Judge

2119. WALKER, PHILLIP [S]
Nacogdoches   28 September 1835
Certify foreigner Phillip Walker is
a man of good...single without
family...
  Jn Fgne Michampo Alclalde Interim
[Recent Note] Native of Chester
S.C. Born March 11, 1815. Father
James Walker, mother Martha
Telford W. 4/9/28 JHW
[Rev] Accepted in Vehlein. A.Henrie

2120. WALLACE, ELISHA H.R. [S]
Nacogdoches   4 May 1835
Certify foreigner Elisha H.R. Wallace is a man of good...married
with family... Radford Berry

2121. WALLING, JESSE [S]
Nacogdoches   9 Oct 1835
Certify foreigner Jesse Walling a
man of good...widower with family
and resident of this Department
since 1833... Radford Berry

2122. WALLING, JESSE [E]
Orders of Survey in the General Land
Office, City Houston. Copies to be
sent to Nacogdoches County by mail
to the care of Jesse Walling & three
orders was obtained from George W.
Smyth office in the year 1835.
    1 Henry Whitesides
    2 Lewis Holloway
    3 Simpson Holloway
    4 Daniel Holloway
    5 Caleb Holloway
    6 Mathew Dyal
    7 William M. Lamkin
    8 John Rolland
    9 John Dorrity
   10 William P. Chisum
   11 John C. Walling
   12 James Taylor

2123. WALLING, JOHN [S]
Nacogdoches   17 Sept 1834
Certify foreigner John Walling a man
of good...married with family...
        Luis Procela Alc Interim
2123a.
Nacogdoches   August 14, 1835
Mr. William Brookfield Sir: You
are to survey the sitio & labor
which John Walling will designate...
        Geo W. Smyth Comr

2124. WALLING, JOHN C. [S]
Nacogdoches   9 Oct 1835
Certify foreigner John C. Walling a
man of good...single without family.
resident of this Department since
1833...   Radford Berry

2125. WALTERS, LEMUEL S. [E]
San Augustine   January 25, 1835
Certify Lemuel S. Walters a native
of No Carolina a man of family of
ten persons...
        James S. Hanks Alcalde

2126. WARD, JAMES S. [S]
Nacogdoches   23 March 1835
Certify foreigner James S. Ward a

man of good...married with family...
Radford Berry

2127. WARE, HARDY [S]
Nacogdoches   3 Octr 1835
Certify foreigner Hardy Ware a man
of good...widower with family and
resident of this Department since
1824...   Radford Berry

2128. WARE, JAMES [E]
Austin   May 4, 1832
To Mr. S.F. Austin Empresario
I have emigrated to this Colony...
James Ware 44 years of age
Georgeanne 42   do
7 Male 3 female [children]
My family reside in Kentucky & I
shall move them to this Country by
the 1st Decmr next.   Jas Ware
Passport dated 23 Feby 1832

2129. WARREN, LEWIS [E]
Precinct of Sabine   27 Oct 1834
Certify Lewis Warin a native of
Virginia a man of no family...
Elbert Hines Comr
[Note] Single. In Zavala. McFarland
Place where he lives
[Reverse] Lewis Warren

2130. WASHBURN, NEVELS [S]
Nacogdoches   3 Octr 1835
Certify foreigner Nevels Washburn a
man of good...married with family...
Radford Berry
[Rev] Accepted Vehlein. A.Henrie

2131. WATKINS, JAMES E. [S]
Nacogdoches   14 September 1835
Certify foreigner James E. Watkins a
man of good...single without family
Radford Berry
[Rev] Accepted in Vehlein. A.Henrie

2132. WATSON, G.W. [S]
Nacogdoches   8 Decr 1834
Certify foreigner G.W. Watson a man
of good...married with family...
Vital Flores
[Note] George W. Watson. Zavala
Veatch   Wife and one child.
Forks of Taylor Bayou and double
point east of ---

2133. WATSON, HARRISON E. [E]
San Augustine   April 4th 1835
Certify Harrison E. Watson a native
of Virginia a man of family of four
persons A. Hotchkiss Primary Judge

2134. WATSON, LEMUEL [E]
San Augustine   9th May 1835
Certify Mr. Lemuel Watson a native
of the U.S. man of family of four
persons...emigrated in 1834...
R.C. McDaniel C.P.O.
2134a.
Nacogdoches   Augt 9, 1835
Mr. Surveyor You are to survey the
sitio in Zavala's Grant which Mr.
Lemuel Watson will designate...
Jorge Anto Nixon Comr
[Note] On the River Neches

2135. WATSON, WILLIAM [E]
San Augustine   August 20th 1835
Certify William Watson a native of
Kentucky a single man...emigrated in
November 1832... Saml Thompson Alcd

2136. WATSON, WILLIS B. [E]
San Augustine   May 23d 1835
Certify Willis B. Watson a native of
Tennessee a man of family of eight
persons...   Nathan Davis Comr
[Reverse] Accepted. Arthur Henrie

2137. WATTS, JOHN [E]
District of Bevil   Octr 13th 1834
Certify John Watts a native of Mis-
sissippi hath a family of seven
persons...   John Bevil Alcalde
[Note] Wife 5 ch

2138. WATTS, THOMAS [E]
District of Bevil   Octr 13th 1834
Certify Thomas Watts a native of
Ireland hath a family of nine
persons...   John Bevil Alcalde
[Note] Wife & 7 children = At his
improvements on the Indian Creek.
G.W. Smyth.   Zavala's Grant

2139. WAUGH, JOHN [S]
Nacogdoches   12 October 1835
Certify foreigner John Waugh is a
man of good...married with family...
Radford Berry
[Reverse] Accepted. A. Hotchkiss
Attorney

2140. WEBB, WILLIAM [E]
San Augustine   Sept 23d 1834
Certify William Webb a native of
Virginia a man of family of two
persons...
        Benjamin Lindsey Alcalde

2141. WEEKS, JOHN   [E]
Precinct of Tenahaw 17 August 1835
Certify John Weeks a native of New
Jersey hath a family of seven per-
sons...   Nathan Davis Alcalde
[Reverse] John Weekes

2142. WEEKES, JOSE   [S]
Nacogdoches   20 September 1834
Certify foreigner Jose Weekes is
according to Jose Dorte, Pedro Ellis
Bean, Juan Escovet a man of good...
        Vicente Cordova

2143. WEIR, WILLIAM [E]
San Jacinto   Novr 11th 1834
We have been acquainted with the
bearer Mr. William Weir for a con-
siderable time
        Joseph Lindley
        Elijah Collard
        Lemuel M. Collard
[Certified by] James J. Foster
        Commissioner for the
        Precinct of Viesca
[Note] Wife & 3 children. At his
improvements adjoining Jos. Lindley
= Vehlein   Wm Rankin

2144. WELCH, CHARLES P.   [E]
Jurisdiction of Liberty Jun 30, 1835
Certify Charles C.P. Welch a native
of South Carolina emigrated 1824, a
man of family has a wife and two
children...and is Acting Commissioner of the Precinct of Cedar Bayou.
        Wm Hardin Judge

2145. WELLS, SAMUEL G.   [E]
Naches   9 May 1835
Certify I have been acquainted with
Samuel G. Wells for some consider-
able time, a man of family...farmer
        William Whiteley
        Comr for Naches Precinct
2145a.
To Mr. George Anto Nixon Comr Sir:
Please send my deed that is in the
office by Mr. Garrison Greenwood.
20th April 1835   Samuel G. Wells

2146. WELCH, GEORGE W.   [S]
Nacogdoches   24 September 1835
Certify foreigner George W. Welch a
man of good...single without family
        Radford Berry
[Rev] Accepted in Vehlein. 1/4
        Henrie

2147. WELSH, GROSS   [E]
Town of Austin   11 May 183-
To Mr. S.F. Austin Empresario
I have emigrated to this Colony...
Groce Welsh 29 years old. Single.
Occupation farmer. Moved from Lui-
siana and arrived in May 1830.
        [Sig] Gross Welsh

2148. WELSH, HENRY P.   [E]
Town of Austin   17 May 1830
To Mr. S.F.Austin Empresario
I have emigrated to this Colony...
Henry P. Welsh 23 years of age.
Unmarried. Moved from Luisiana and
arrived in this Colony 15 May 1830.
        [Sig] Henry P. Welsh

2149. WELCH, JOHN   [E]
Jurisdiction of Liberty 31 May 1835
Certify John Welch a native of Ire-
land a man of family of his wife and
three children...   Wm Hardin Judge
[Reverse] Accepted in Vehlein for
No. 5 Survey for Genl Russel

2150. WEST, BERRY   [E]
District of Bevil   May 12th 1835
Certify Berry a native of Mississip-
pi hath a family of six persons...
        Wm Williams Alcalde

2151. WEST, CLAIBOURN   [E]
Jurisdiction of Liberty Dec 11, 1834
Certify that the Honorable Claibourn
West is a man of family of his wife
and four children...Wm Hardin Judge
[Note] Claibourne West. Zavala
The place where he lives. F.Hardin

2152. WEST, GADEI   [E]
District of Bevil   October 4th 1835
Certify Gadei West came 1829, a
native of Mississippi hath a family
of eight persons
        Wm Williams Alcalde

2153. WEST, JORDAN [E]
Jurisdiction of Liberty 25 May 1835
Certify Jordan West a native of
Mississippi man of family of his
wife and five children...
            Wm Hardin Judge
[Reverse] Accepted. A. Henrie
          The place where he lives

2154. WESTFALL, ANDREW E.   [S]
Nacogdoches   4 July 1835
Certify foreigner Andrew E. Westfall
is a man of good...married...
    Jn Egne Michamps Alcalde Interim
[Rev] Accepted in Vehlein. A.Henrie

2155. WESTERN, THOMAS G.
[Without date. See Register]
            Thomas G. Western
            40 years of age. Single
            & native of New York

            Alvan Wetherby
            28 years of age. Single
            & native of Boston
These are to be included after 15th
Decr if there is room and Western in
particular   S.F. Austin

2156. WHARTON, WILLIAM H.   [E]
To Mr. S.F. Austin Empresario
I have emigrated to this Colony...
William H. Wharton 25 years of age
Sarah Anne my wife 22   do
One child male. Moved from Tennessee
and arrived in this City in November
1827.   [Sig] Wm H. Wharton

2157. WHITAKER, BENJAMIN   [S]
Nacogdoches   22 May 1835
Certify foreigner Benjamin R. Whitaker is a man of good...married with
family...   Radford Berry

2158. WHITAKER, M.G.
Nacogdoches   August 10, 1835
Recd of Jorge Anto Nixon Comr
2 Land Titles, one for Gertrudis
Luna, the other for Maria de Cantun.
            [Sig] M.G. Whitaker
Attest John Forbes

2159. WHITAKER, WILLIAM   [E]
Town of Austin   1 May 1830
To Mr. S.F. Austin Empresario
I have emigrated to this Colony...
William Whitaker 27 years old.
Married Nancy my wife 24 years old
Two male children. Occupation farmer
Moved from Luisiana and arrived in
this Colony in 1822...
            [Sig] William Whitaker

2160. WHITCOMB, DR. JOSEPH   [S]
Nacogdoches   10 October 1835
Certify resident of this Villa,
Dotor Joseph Whitcomt is a man of
good...   Luis Procela

2161. WHITCOMB, JOSEPH
[Field Notes] Joseph Whitcomb's
sitio between Oyster Bayou and
Double Bayou...

2162. WHITE, ALEXANDER   [S]
Nacogdoches   10 August 1835
Certify foreigner Alexander White is
a man of good...married with family,
resident of this Municipality since
1828...   Radford Berry
2162a.
Nacogdoches   10th August 1835
Mr. Benjamin Tennell Sir: You are
to survey the sitio & labor which
Mr. Alexr White wil designate...
            Geo W. Smyth Comr

2163. WHITE, ARCHIBALD S.   [E]
Town of Austin   27 May 1830
To Mr. S.F. Austin Empresario
I have moved to this Colony...
Archibald White 59 years old.
Married Margaret my wife 53 years
old Four male three female child-
ren. Moved from Tennessee and ar-
rived in this Colony Feby 1830.
            [Sig] A. White

2164. WHITE, ARMSTEAD   [S]
Nacogdoches   26 May 1835
Certify foreigner Armstead White is
a man of good...single without
family...
    Jn Egne Michamps Alcalde Interim

2165. WHITE, BENJAMIN   [E]
District of Sabine Aug 20th 1835
Certify Benjamin White native of

Luisiana is a man of good...emi-
grated 1823 to this District...
      B. Holt Comr
2165a.
Sabine District   Sept 1st 1835
I, Benjamin White of the District
appoint William Earl of the District
in procuring an Order of Survey for
my sitio...   [Sig] Bénjamin White
Witnesses James T. White
          Thomas C. Holt

2166. WHITE, DAVID [E]
San Augustine   Sept 27th 1834
Certify David White a native of
Louisiana a single man...
      Benjamin Lindsey Alcalde

2167. WHITE, ELIZABETH   [E]
District of Sabine August 20th 1835
Certify Elizabeth White a native of
Louisiana, a citizen of the District
emigrated to this place in 1823, has
a family of five persons...
          B. Holt Comr
2167a.
Personally appeared 25th April 1835
Elizabeth White a citizen of the
District of Sabine, authorized Wil-
liam H. Landrum to act for her for
an Order of Survey...titles to lands
which I claim as an old settler & a
Mexican citizen...
      Elizabeth X White
Witnesses S.D. Mcgee   Wm Johnston

2168. WHITE, GEORGE [E]
Jurisdiction of Liberty 22 Feb 1835
Certify George White a native of
Louisiana is a man of family of his
wife and three children...
      Wm Hardin Judge

2169. WHITE, HENRY [E]
Jurisdiction of Liberty 23 Feb 1835
Certify Henry White a native of
Louisiana is a single man...
      Wm Hardin Judge

2170. WHITE, JAMES T. [E]
San Augustine   August 18th 1835
Sir You are to survey the sitio &
labor which Mr. James T. White will
designate... Geo W. Smyth Comr
[Note] Where he lives

2171. WHITE, JESSE [E]
Jurisdiction of Liberty 23 Feb 1835
Certify Jesse White a native of
Louisiana is a single man...
      Wm Hardin Judge

2172. WHITE, MARTIN   [E]
San Augustine   October 29th 1834
Certify Martin White a native of
Louisiana a man of family of six
persons...Benjamin Lindsey Alcalde
[Note] Martin White wife and four
children On Bear Creek. Zavala.
Adjoining Thomas Lindsey's Survey.
        D. Brown
2172a. Mr. George Anto Nixon Esqr
Comr Sir: Please deliver to Ben-
jamin Lindsey the Title to my land
and oblige.   May 9th 1835
    [Sig] Martin White

2173. WHITE, SAMUEL A.   [E]
To Mr. S.F. Austin Empresario
I have emigratd to this Colony...
Saml A. White 26 years of age.
Unmarried Moved from Tennessee and
arrived in this Colony 20 Feby 1830.
    [Sig] S.A. White

2174. WHITE, WILLIAM
Nacogdoches   28th May 1835
Received of J.A. Nixon Comr
Wm White Title. A.P. Cunningham

2174A. WHITE, WILLIAM   [S]
Nacogdoches   2 Decr 1834
Certify foreigner Wm White a man of
good...married with family...
      Vital Flores

2174B. WHITE, WILLIAM
Jurisdiction of Liberty 23 Feb 1835
Certify William White a native of
Louisiana is a single man...
      Wm Hardin Judge

2175. WHITE, WILLIAM M. [E]
Jurisdiction of Liberty 27 Dec 1834
Certify William M.White a native of
Mississippi a single man...
      Wm Hardin Judge
[Note] Unfinished title

2176. WHITEHEAD, EPHRAIM [E]
Town of Austin   1 Novem 1831
To Mr. S.F. Austin Empresario
I have emigratd to this Colony...
                    193

I am a native of Ireland. My name is Ephraim Whitehead 60 years of age. Widower and have 1 male 2 female children. Moved from Luisiana and arrived in this Colony in Aug last. [Sig] E. Whitehead

2177. WHITELY, WILLIAM [S]
Nacogdoches   12 January 1835
Certify foreigner William Whitely is a man of good...single...
        Radford Berry

2178. WHITESIDES, HENRY [E]
San Augustine   August 10th 1835
Certify Henry Whitesides a native of Kentucky a man of family a wife and two children...lived in Texas six years commencing in 1824...
        A. Hotchkiss P. Judge
2178a.
Nacogdoches   August 14th 1835
Mr. William Brookfield Sir: You are to survey the sitio & labor which Henry   Whitesides will designate...   Geo W. Smyth Comr

2179. WHITING, HERVEY [E]
Jurisdiction of Liberty 28 Dec 1834
Certify Hervey Whiting a native of Connecticut a man of family of wife and six children...Wm Hardin Judge
[Reverse] Harvey Whiting

2180. WHITING, SAMUEL [E]
Jurisdiction of Liberty Oct 1, 1834
Certify Samuel Whiting a native of Connecticut a man of family of twenty one...
        Wm Hardin Primary Judge

2181. WIGGINS, HARBARD L. [E]
San Augustine   August 17, 1835
Certify Harbard L. Wiggins a native of North Carolina man of family of wife and one child...emigrated 1830...   A. Hotchkiss P. Judge

2182. WIGGINS, RODERICK [E]
San Augustine   Sept 22d 1834
Certify Roderick Wiggins a native of Kentucky a man of family of four persons...Benjamin Lindsey Alcalde

2183. WILBORNE, KITCHEN A. [S]
Nacogdoches   17 September 1835
Certify foreigner Kinchene A. Wil-
194

borne a man of good...married with family...   Radford Berry
[Rev] Accepted in Vehlein. A.Henrie

2184. WILBURN, DANIEL [S]
Nacogdoches   20 Sept 1834
Certify foreigner Daniel Wilburn a man of good...married with family...
        Luis Procela Alcalde Interim

2185. WILBURN, WILLIAM [E]
Jurisdiction of Liberty 27 Dec 1834
Certify William Wilburn a native of Louisiana a man of family of himself and his wife and one child...
        J.B. Woods
[Note] Wm Willburn = Cypress Cr. North of Burrel Blackman = Vehlein = F. Hardin

2186. WILKINSON, DAVID [E]
San Augustine   18th Aug 1835
Certify David Wilkerson a citizen of this Municipality, a native of South Carolina a man of family of eight persons...emigrated in about 1822...
        Nathan Davis Comr
[Rev] David Wilkinson

2187. WILLIAMS, BROOKS [S]
Nacogdoches   29 May 1835
Certify foreigner Brooks Williams is a man of good...married with family
Jn Egne Michamps Alcalde Interim
[Reverse] Accepted. A.Henrie

2188. WILLIAMS, CHARLES [E]
San Augustine   Octr 27th 1834
Certify Charles Williams a native of Louisiana...a man of family of five persons... Benjamin Linsey Alcalde
[Note] Wife and 3 children
Place where he lives. Zavala. GWS

2189. WILLIAMS, ELIZABETH [E]
District of Bevil Nov 10th 1834
Certify Elizabeth Williams a native of Louisiana hath a family of three persons   John Bevil Alcalde

2190. WILLIAMS, HENRY [E]
San Augustine   22 Sept 1834
Certify Henry Williams a native of No Carolina a man of family of four-teen persons
        Benjamin Lindsey Alcalde

2191. WILLIAMS HEZEKIAH [E]
District of Bevil   Octr 10th 1834
Certify Hesakiah Williams a native
of Louisiana hath a family of nine
persons... John Bevil Alcalde
[Note] Wife and 7 children. Zavala
The place where he lives. G.W.S.

2192. WILLIAMS, HEZEKIAH   [E]
San Augustine   October 27th 1834
Certify Hezekian Williams a native
of Louisiana a single man...
            Benjamin Lindsey Al
[Note] The place he has improved.
    Zavala
2193. WILLIAMS HEZEKIAH REAMS   [E]
San Augustine   Octr 27, 1834
Certify Hezekiah Reims Williams a
native of Louisiana...
        Benjamin Lindsey Alcalde
[Note] Single. Zavala

2194. WILLIAMS, JAMES   [E]
San Augustine   Oct 10th 1835
Certify James Williams a native of
Tennessee a man of family of six
persons...emigrated in 1829 and has
taken the oath of allegiance...
        Saml Thompson Alcalde
2194a.
San Augustine   Oct 10, 1835
I authorize Samuel Stivers to peti-
tion for one league...James Williams
Witnesses E.O. Legrand
        Saml Thompson Alc

2195. WILLIAMS, JAMES W.   [E]
San Augustine   October 28th 1834
Certify James W. Williams a native
of North Carolina man of family of
twelve persons... James W. Bullock
        Cindico and Alcalde pro tem
[Note] Wife and ten children.
Housen Bayou. Zavala. G. McFarland

2196. WILLIAMS, JOHN   [E]
Tenoxtitlan   6 June 1834
To the Empresarios Austin & Williams
I have emigrated to Texas...
I am a widower & have 7 children.
My [age] 47 years. For John Williams
        S.H. Jack
2197. WILLIAMS, LEONARDO   [S]
Nacogdoches   24 November 1834
Certify foreigner Lionardo Williams
a man of good...married with family
        Vital Flores

2198. WILLIAMS, PARKER   [E]
Austin   Feby 15, 1832
To Mr. S.F. Austin Empresario
I have enmigrated to this Colony...
My name is Parker Williams unmar-
ried. 43 years old. Moved from Vir-
ginia and arrived in this Colony
August 1830. [Sig] Parker Williams

2199. WILLIAMS, RICHARD   [E]
District of Bevil   April 5th 1835
Certify Richard Williams of Louisi-
ana hath a family of two persons...
        John Bevil Alcalde pro tem
2199a.
District of Bevil   Aug 27th 1835
Certify Richard Williams native of
Louisiana, emigrated in 1829, hath a
family of two persons...
        Wm Williams Alcalde

2200. WILLIAMS, RICHARD   [E]
San Augustine   August 18, 1835
Certify Richard Williams a native of
Georgia a single man, emigrated 1831
        Nathan Davis Commissioner

2201. WILLIAMS, STEPHEN   [E]
San Augustine   April 16, 1835
Certify Stephen Williams a native of
North Carolina man of family of five
children...
        A. Hotchkiss Primary Judge

2202. WILLIAMS, STEPHEN   [E]
District of Bevil   Octr 28th 1834
Certify Stephen Williams junr a
native of Louisiana, single...
        John Bevil Alcalde
[Note] Single. The place he has
improved in Zavala's. G.W. Smyth

2203. WILLIAMS, WILLIAM   [E]
District of Sabine Sept 17th 1835
Certify William Williams a native of
Lousana family of three persons...
emigrated to Texas 1830...
        B. Holt Commissioner
2203a.
District of Sabine   17 Sep 1835
I, William Williams of the Sabine
District empower W.H. Landrum...
procuring order of survey according
to my headright as an old settler
and citizen having a family...
        William Williams
Witness   Thomas Lindsey Wm Earl

William Williams took the oath before me.   B. Holt Commissioner

2204. WILLIAMS, WILLIAM   [E]
San Augustine   22 Sept 1834
Certify William Williams native of
Georgia a man of family of seven
persons...Benjamin Lindsey Alcalde
2204a.
Nacogdoches   [S]   14 October 1834
Certify resident of this Villa and
Municipality William Williams a man
of good...   married with family...
      Luis Procela
[Note] Wm Williams on the head of
Angelina. Burnet. Wife and four
children.

2205. WILLIAMS, WILLIAM   [E]
District of Bevil   Octr 13th 1834
Certify William Williams a native of
N. Carolina hath a family of eleven
persons.   John Bevil Alcalde
[Note] Wife and 9 children. Place
he has improved. Zavala. GWS

2206. WILLIAMS, WILLIAM   [E]
                    March 24, 1835
This may serteyfy that Mr. William
Williams is a man of good moral
habits...
      John Bodine Alcalde pro tem
2206a.
Nacogdoches   20 March 1835
Major G.A. Nixon Dear Sir:
You will please to deliver to Mr.
H.H. Edwards my Title for one
League...   Wm Williams

2207. WILLIAMS, WILLIAM A.   [E]
San Augustine   Oct 5, 1835
Certify William A. Williams a native
of No Carolina, a man of family of
three persons...emigrated 1829 has
taken the oath   Saml Thompson Alcd
2207a.
San Augustine   5 October 1835
I, William A. Williams appoint James
C. Cain my attorney to petition for
one league and labor...
                William A. Williams
Witnesses   E.O. Legrand
      E.W. Cullene   Morris May

2208. WILLIAMSON, RUSSEL   [E]
San Augustine   Oct 7, 1835
Certify Russel Williamson a native
of Tennessee a man of family of
three persons emigrated in 1831 and
has taken the oath...
      Nathan Davis Commissioner
2208a.
San Augustine   7th Oct 1835
I authorize Franklin Fuller to petition for one league and labor...
      [Sig] Russel Williamson
Witnsses A.B. Davis   W.L. Scott
         E.M. Fuller E.O. Legrand
         James Morrison

2209. WILLIS, ARTHUR   [E]
San Augustine   Sept 1st 1835
Certify Arthur Willis a native of
Tennessee a man of family of five
persons...emigrated in 1823...
      Saml Thompson Alcalde

2210. WILLIS, WILLIAM J.   [S]
Nacogdoches   3 August 1835
Certify foreigner Wm J. Willis a man
of good...married with family...
resident of this Municipality since
1832...   Jn Egne
Michamps Alcalde Interim

2211. WILLS, WILLIAM   [S]
Nacogdoches   20 April 1835
Certify foreigner William Wills a
man of good...married with family...
Radford Berry
2211a.
Nacogdoches   16 September 1835
Certify foreigner William Wills a
man of good...married with family...
      Radford Berry
[Rev] Accepted in Vehlein. A.Henrie

2212. WILSON, ALVAH   [E]
Austin   24 Decr 1831
To Mr. S.F. Austin Empresario
I have emigrated to this Country...
Alvah Wilson 35 years of [age].
Married. Sophronia my wife 28 years
of age 2 Male 1 female children.
Occupation farmer. Moved from Geor-
gia and arrived in Texas in Novemr
1831.   Alvah Wilson

2213. WILSON, DAVID   [S]
Nacogdoches   9 August 1835
Certify foreigner David Wilson a man
of good...married with family...
                      Radford Berry
[Rev] Accepted in Vehlein A.Henrie

2214. WILSON, GEORGE W.   [E]
St. Francisville, La.   21 Sep 1834
George W. Wilson and his two brothers intending to leave this place
tomorrow, for Texas in consequence
of the great excitement that has
prevailed in some time past in regard to suspicious persons, have applied to me to relate what I know of
them. I have known George W. Wilson
and one of his brothers for several
years...George W. Wilson on the
first Monday in March last was
elected the Town Collector of Taxes.
James M. Bradford   Town Magistrate
[Additional tesimonials included]
[Reverse side notes]
[1] George W.Wilson has family wife
in   Texas. Accepted Vehlein
[2] James B. Wilson single
Accepted also Vehlein
[3] John Wilson single also accepted
2214a.
Nacogdoches   13 January 1835
Certify foreigner George W. Wilson
is a man of good...married with
family...   Radford Berry
[Note] Wife & 4 children. Adjoining
McCleans on the Sn Pedro. Burnet.
Strode
2214b.
Nacogdoches   Octr 23d 1835
Recd of J.A. Nixon Comr Titles for
George W. Wilson Daniel Parker Jun
James Maddens   [by] Arthur Henrie

2215. WILSON, JANE   [E]
San Augustine   September 1st 1835
Certify Jane Wilson native of Kentucky a widow woman of family of
eleven persons...emigrated in 1833
         Saml Thompson Alcd

2216. WILSON, JEFFERSON   [S]
Nacogdoches   28 May 1835
Certify foreigner Jefferson Wilson a
man of good...married with family...
   Jn Egne Michamps Alcalde Interim

2217. WILSON, DR. STEPHEN P.   [E]
San Augustine   26 Sept 1834
Certify Doct Stephen P. Wilson native of New York man of family of
six persons...
         Benjamin Lindsey Alcalde

2218. WILSON, THOMAS   [E]
San Augustine   May 9th 1835
Certify Thomas Wilson a native of
England a man of family of five
persons...
         John Rankin Alcalde pro tem

2219. WILSON, WILLIAM R.   [S]
Nacogdoches   23 March 1835
Certify foreigner William R. Wilson
a man of good...married to a woman
of the Country, with family...
                      Radford Berry

2220. WIN, JOHN   [E]
San Augustine   August 29th 1835
Certify John Win a native of Georgia
a man of family of two persons...
emigrated 1830   Saml Thompson Alcd
2220a. 2nd Sept 1835 I authorize
J.K. Allen and G. Logan to apply for
a Certificate of Citizenship and for
an Order of Survey [Sig] John Win
Witnesses James Rowe A.G. Kellogg
[Reverse] John Winn

2221. WIN, JOHN B.   [S]
Nacogdoches   21 October 1834
Certify foreigner John B. Win a man
of good...married with family...
                      Vital Flores
[Note] One child. Vehlein's Grant
Long Cane Bayou. About 30 miles from
the mouth. Hiroms Surveyor

2222. WINCHESTER, DAVID R.   [E]
Nacogdoches   Octr 4, 1835
Mr. Surveyor: You are to survey in
David G. Burnet's Grant the sitio
that Mr. David R. Winchester will
designate... Jorge Anto Nixon Comr

2223. WINTERS, JAMES   [S]
Nacogdoches   20 Novr 1834
Certify James Waters is a man of
good...married with family...
                      Vital Flores
[Note] Wife & 10 children on Camer-
on's Claim on the Sn Jacinto.
Vehlein. Rankin

2224. WINTERS, WILLIAM [E]
Precinctof Viesca   14th Feb 1835
Certify William Winters a native of
Tennessee a man of family of five
persons...   B.B. Goodrich Comr
[Reverse] Accepted in Vehlein

2225. WITT, HUGHES [E]
Tenoxtitlan   18th Feby 1834
To Empresarios Austin & Williams
I have emigrated to Texas...
I am single, my age is 34 years.
                [Sig] Hughs Witt
2225.
To Mr. S.F. Austin
I have emigrated to this Colony...
Hughs Witt 30 years of age.
Unmarried. Moved from Florida and
arrived in this Colony May 1830.
        [Sig] Hughs Witt

2226. WOLFENBARGER, SAMUEL [E]
Austin   November 13, 1832
To Mr. S.F. Austin Empresario
I have emigrated to this Country...
Samuel Wolfenbarger 27 years of age
Caroline my wife   25   do
1 Male 2 female children. From
Missouri. [Sig] Samuel Wolfenbarger

2227. WOMACK, MARK S. [S]
Nacogdoches   2 May 1835
Certify foreigner Mark S. Womack is
a man of good...married with family
                Radford Berry

2228. WOOD, MITCHEL [S]
Nacogdoches   20 November 1834
Certify Mitchel Wood a man of good
single...   Vital Flores
[Note] 1/4 sitio. 5 Surveys from
Baptist Village adjoining Cole
Gardner.   Vehlein

2229. WOOD, REUBEN [E]
San Augustine   Sept 22, 1834
Certify Reuben Wood a native of
Tennessee a man of family of three
persons...Benjamin Lindsey Alcalde

2230. WOODLASS, DR. JEROME [E]
San Augustine   May 27, 1835
Certify Dr. Jerome Woodlass a native
of Virginia...single man...
                Nathan Davis Comr

198

2231. WOODS, JAMES B. [E]
Jurisdiction of Liberty Dec 20, 1834
Certify James B. Woods a native of
Kentucky a man of family of his wife
and one child...   Wm Hardin Judge
[Note] On the waters of Big Sandy on
a nameless creek. F.Hardin. Vehlein

2232. WOODS, NORMAN [E]
Town of Austin   20 May 1830
To Mr. S.F. Austin Empresario
I have emigrated to this Colony...
Norman Woods 25 years old.
Unmarried. Moved from Misouri and
arrived in this   Colony Jany 1826.
Occupation farmer.
        [Sig] Norman Woods

2233. WOODWORTH, JONATHAN [S]
Villa de Austin   15 December 1830
To Stephen F. Austin Empresario
Certify that Johnathan Woodworth is
one of the Colonists...came to this
Colony December 1830. Married, fami-
ly of fourteen persons. Give this
Certificate ...
[Note] His family is in Connecticut
and has two years to bring them.
            Stephen F. Austin

2234. WOOTON, MOSES [E]
San Augustine   August 18, 1835
Certify Moses Wooton a native of
North Carolina a man of family of a
wife and six children...emigrated
1822... A. Hotchkiss Prmy Judge

2235. WORK, RICHARD [E]
San Augustine   22 March 1835
Certify Mr. Richard Work a native of
Kentucky a man of family of three
persons... emigrated in 1834...
            R.C. McDaniel C.P.O.
[Reverse] Accepted. A. Henrie
2235a.
Nacogdoches   Augt 13th 1835
Mr. Surveyor   You are to survey in
Zavala's Grant the sitio which Mr.
Richard Work will designate...
            Jorge A. Nixon Comr

2236. WRIGHT, ALEXANDER , [E]
San Augustine   Sept 22d 1834
Certify Alexander Wright a native of
Georgia...a man of family of five
persons... Benjamin Lindsey Alcalde

2237. WRIGHT, HARDIN [E]
San Augustine   August 17, 1835
Certify Hardin Wright a native of
Tennessee a man of family of a wife
and four children, emigrated 1832...
          A. Hotchkiss Prmy Judge

2238. WRIGHT, HENRY Q.   [E]
Mr. S.F. Austin Empresario
I have emigrated to this Colony...
Henry Q. Wright age 40 years married
Anne my wife 39 years old
One male 4 female children. Moved
from Ohio and arrived in this Colony
May 1830.   [Sig]   Henry Q. Wright

2239. WRIGHT, J.   [E]
Tenoxtitlan   29 April 1834
To Empresarios Austin & Williams
I have emigratd to Texas...
I am married my wife Permelia W. and
have 3 children.
My age 36 my wifes 29.   J. Wright
2239a.
San Felipe de Austin 1st Jan 1836
Gale Bordon Esqr.   Dear Sir:
I wish to enter a labor of land that
was originally granted to Jesse
Burnham adjoining a league granted
to Elizabeth Tumlinson on the
Colorado...   J. Wright

2240. WRIGHT, SHAROD   [E]
San Augustine   Sept 22d 1834
Certify Sharod Wright a native of
Georgia a man of family of ten
persons... Benjamin Lindsey Alcalde

2241. WROE, WILLIAM   [S]
Villa de Austin   12 April 1830
Certify William Wroe is one of the
Colonists...Came in the year 1825,
married, family of four persons...
          Estevan F. Austin
          by Samuel M. Williams

2242. WYLLIE, ANDREW   [S]
Nacogdoches   2 May 1835
Certify foreigner Andrew Wyllie ia a
man of good...single without family
          Radford Berry

2243. WYRES, ROBERT   [E]
San Augustine   August 22d 1835
Certify Robert Wyres a native of
Virginia a man of family of two
persons...emigrated in 1830...
          Saml Williams Alcalde

Nacogdoches   27 Aug 1835
Personally appeared Robert Wires and
took the oath of allegiance...
          Radford Berry

2244. XIMENES, JUAN   [S]
Nacogdoches   15 June 1835
Certify citizen Juan Ximenes Morales
is a man of good...widower with
family, has not received land...
          Jn Egne Michamps Alc Int
2244a.
Nacogdoches   August 12th 1835
Sir: You are to survey the sitio &
labor which Mr. Juan Ximenes will
designate... Geo W. Smyth Comr

2245. YANCY, JOHN   [E]
Nacogdoches   August 3d 1835
Sir: You are to survey the 1/3
sitio which Mr. John Yancy will
designate... Geo W. Smyth Comr
[Note] 9 miles from Nacogdoches
          near Colony line

2246. YARBROUGH, RANDOLPH   [E]
San Augustine   August 18, 1835
Certify Randolph Yarbrough a native
of Arkansas Territory, single man,
emigrated to Texas 1832...
          Nathan David Comr

2247.   YARBROUGH, SWANSON JR   [E]
San Augustine   August 18, 1835
Certify Swanson Yarbrough Jr a native of Louisiana, single man
emigrated 1832... Nathan Davis Comr

2248 YARBROUGH, SWANSON   [E]
San Augustine   August 18th 1835
Certify Swanson Yarbrough a native
of No Carolina a man of family of
ten persons...emigrated in Febr 1832
          Saml Thompson Alcd

2249. YARNAC, MARIA DOROTEA [S]
Nacogdoches   28 April 1835
Certify citizen Maria Dorotea Yarnac
is a resident of this Municipality
and born here, widow with family,
has not received land...
                 Radford Berry

2250. YATES, ANDREW J.   [S]
Nacogdoches   7 April 1835
Certify foreigner Andrew J. Yates a
man of good...married with family...
                 Radford Berry

2251. YATES, THOMAS   [E]
San Augustine   January 18th 1835
Certify that a citizen calling himself Thomas Yates fifty one years of
age a married man a native of Virgiania appeared this day before me
and took the oath...
           James S. Hanks Alcalde

2252. YBARBO, ANASTACIO   [S]
Nacogdoches   29 June 1835
Certify citizen Anastacio Ybarbo a
resident of the Municipality and
born here, man of good...married
with family...has not received
land...
Jn Egne Michamps Alcalde Interim

2254. YBARBO, DOMINGO   [S]
Nacogdoches   29 June 1835
Certify citizen Domingo Ybarbo a
resident of this Municipality and
born here, man of good...married
with family, has not received
land... Jn Egne Michamps Alc Int

2255. YBARBO, JOSE   [S]
Nacogdoches   1 June 1835
Certify citizen Jose Ybarbo a resident of this Municipality and born
here, man of good...widower with
family and has not received land...
      Jn Egne Michamps Alc Int
[Rev] Accepted in Burnet. A.Henrie

2256. YBARBO, JOSE   [E]
San Augustine   Sept 1, 1835
Certify Hosa Labarb a native citizen
a man of family of twelve persons a
man of good... Saml Thompson Alcd
[Reverse] Jose Ybarbo

2257. YBARBO, JUAN ANTONIO   [S]
Nacogdoches   7 May 1835
Certify Juan Antonio Ybarbo a resident of this Municipality and born
here is married with family, has not
received land...   Radford Berry
[Note] Wife 3 children

2258. YBARBO, MARIA TELESFORA   [S]
Nacogdoches   20 June 1835
Certify citizen Maria Telesfora
Ybarbo is a resident of this Munici-
pality and born here, woman of very
good...widow with family and has not
received land...
         G. Pollitt Alcalde Interim
2258a.
Nacogdoches   Sept 10hth 1835
Sir: You are to survey the sitio &
labor which Mrs. Maria Telesfora
Ybarbo will designate...
                 Geo W. Smyth Comr

2259. YBARBO, MIGUEL   [S]
Nacogdoches   April 27, 1835
Mr. Surveyor: You are to survey in
Zavala's Grant the sitio which Mr.
Miguel Ybarbo will designate...
                 Jorge Anto Nixon

2260. YBARBO, MIGUEL   [S]
Nacogdoches   27 April 1835
Certify citizen Miguel Ybarbo is
resident of the Municipality, born
here, man of good...married with
family, has not received land...
                 Radford Berry
2260a.
Nacogdoches   Sept 4th 1835
Sir: You are to survey the sitio &
labor which Mr. Miguel Ybarbo will
designate...   Geo W. Smyth

2261. YEAMANS, ASA   [E]
Town of Austin   15 May 1830
To S.F. Austin Empresario
I have emigrated to this Colony...
Asa Yeamans 57 years married
Jerusha my wife 52
Three male and one female children
Moved from New York and arrived in
this Colony in 1829 Jany.
              [Sig] Asa Yeamans

2262. YOCOM, THOMAS D.   [E]
Liberty   August 4th 1835
Majr G.A. Nixon Comr   Dear Sir:
You will please deliver my land
title to Mr. Joseph Bryan
    [Sig] Thos D. Yocom

2263. YOUNG, WILLIAM W.   [E]
San Augustine   7th May 1835
Certify William W. Young a native of
Georgia a man of family of three
persons...emigrated in 1834...
        R.C. McDaniel C.P.O.
[Reverse]   Accepted A.Henrie
2263a.
Nacogdoches   Augt 9, 1835
Mr. Surveyor   You are to survey in
Zavala's Grant the sitio which Mr.
Wm W. Young will designate...
        Jorge Anto Nixon Comr

2264. YOUNGBLOOD, POLLY   [E]
District of Bevil   April 14, 1835
Certify Polly Youngblood a native of
N. Carolina has a family of nine
persons...   Wm Williams Alcd

2265. ZAVALA, LORENZO DE JR   [S]
Nacogdoches   23 June 1835
Certify citizen Lorenzo de Zavala Jr
is a man of good...single without
family, has not obtained land...
    Jn Egne Michamps Alcalde Interim

[The following document is from a
copy made about 1980. The original
is not now in the Character Certificate file. A number has been
assigned for indexing.]

2266. HANCOCK, EDWIN
San Augustine   August 18, 1835
Edwin Hancock a native of Kentucky,
wife and two children...came to
Texas in 1824

UNFINISHED TITLES

The various land offices operating under the
Colonization Laws of the Republic of Mexico were
closed by the provisional government in late November 1835. Titles issued after 13 November 1835 were
later declared not legal. Papers relating to inva-
lid Titles were gathered together under the name of
each Commissioner as Unfinished Business or Unfinished Titles and bound into permanent volumes.

It was inevitable that many Titles would have
been in process when the surprise closing of the
land offices was decreed. The Mexican government
had delayed in appointing Commissioners for the
eastern part of Texas until 1834 and the one year
that land offices were open was not time enough for
many settlers to find money for the fees and pro-
ceed with their applications.

Some also abandoned applications under one
contractor in favor of another, and some may have
returned to the U.S.A. Those left without a Title
would wait until a land law was passed and a system
put into operation in January 1838 by the Republic
of Texas. They may have already been on the land of
their choice for ten or fifteen years.

The Petitions have been abstracted and trans-
lated to give all of the information considered to
be genealogically important. These records vary
from one to several pages and some are transcribed
complete.

An additional volume of Unfinished Business
was left from Padilla who was Commissioner for
Texas in 1829. It is variable in content and has
not been abstracted for this report.

Copies can be provided by the General Land
Office. They are in Spanish, and English transla-
tions may not have been made. One should give the
name of the settler, and if applicable, the Volume
and page number cited here. The 4-digit number
assigned to each record is for an index only and
does not appear in the original Unfinished Titles.

Titles Issued by C.S. Taylor Dated after the Closing of the Land Offices
[In Spanish. Petitions only abstracted]

2501. Nacogdoches   Sept 7, 1835
No. 2. David Anderson native of the
U.S. emigrated in 1828, single with-
out family   David Andeson

2502. Nacogdoches Sep 15, 1835
No. 6. Wade Horton native of the
U.S. single, emigrated about
1826...   Waid Horton

2503. Nacogdoches Noyr 16, 1835
No. 7. Thomas Bassett native of the
U.S. emigrated 1826 married with
family...
By attorney   Thomas Bassett

2504. Nacogdoches   July 28, 1835
No. 9. Augustin Basquez native of
Mexico, came to the State about
1826. Married with   family...
        Don Augustin X Basques

2505. Nacogdoches Sep 5, 1835
No. 10. George B. Brownrigg native
of the U.S. married with a family of
seven persons, emigrated in 1830...
G.B. Brownrigg   By attorney

2506. Nacogdoches   Aug 14, 1835
No. 11. James Adams native of the
U.S. married with family...
        James X Adams

2507. Nacogdoches   Nov 22, 1835
No. 18. John Bridges native of the
U.S. emigrated 1825, married with
family...
By attorney   John Bridges

2508. Nacogdoches   Nov 23, 1835
No. 19. Jabes Bradbury native of
the U.S. emigrated 1822, married
with family...
By attorney   Jabes Bradbury

2509. Nacogdoches   Nov 14, 1835
No. 20. Daniel Brake native of the
U.S. emigrated 1832, married with
family...   Daniel Brake

2510. Nacogdoches Nov 21, 1835
No. 24. Frederick Cooper native of
U.S. married with family...
By attorney   Frederick Cooper

2511. Nacogdoches Nov 24, 1835
No. 25. Roger Barfield native of
the U.S. emigrated in 1831, married
with family...
By attorney   Roger Barfield

2512. Nacogdoches   Nov 24, 1835
No. 26. James Calcote native of the
U.S. emigrated in 1830, married with
family
By attorney   James Calcote

2513. Nacogdoches   Nov 24, 1835
No. 27. Joseph L. Chambers native
of U.S. emigrated 1829, married with
family...
By attorney   Joseph L. Chambers

2514. Nacogdoches   Sept 5, 1835
No. 28. Rafael de la Cruz native of
Mexico married with family...
        Rafael X de la Cruz

2515. Nacogdohces   Nov 23, 1835
No. 32. Reuben Cole native of the
U.S. emigrated in 1825, married...
By attorney   Reuben Cole

2516. Nacogdoches   Nov 22, 1835
No. 35. John Crowder native of the
U.S. emigrated 1831, married with
family...
By attorney   John Crowder

2517. Nacogdoches Nov 4, 1835
No. 39. Adam Caraway native of the
U.S. emigrated 1829, married with
family...
By attorney   Adam Caraway

2518. Nacogdoches   Sep 17, 1835
No. 42. James C. Dewitt native of
the U.S. married with family...
        James C. Dewitt

2519. Nacogdoches   Nov 24, 1835
No. 47. G.W. Fergusson native of the
U.S. emigrated 1825, married with
family...
By attorney   G.W.Fergusson

2520. Nacogdoches   Nov 22, 1835
No. 48. Jacob Fulcher native of the

U.S. emigrated 1828, married with
family...By atty   Jacob Fulcher

2521. Nacogdoches   Oct 24, 1835
No. 49. Abraham Forman native of
U.S. married with a family of 6
persons...
By attorney   Abraham Forman

2522. Nacogdoches   Nov 16, 1835
No. 52. William Glass native of the
U.S. emigrated in 1824, married
with family...   William Glass

2523. Nacogdoches   Nov 3, 1835
No. 56. John Grissett native of U.S.
emigrated in 1832, married with
family of three persons...
John X Grissett

2524. Nacogdoches   Nov 23, 1835
No. 61. David Gristman native of
U.S. emigrated in 1822, married with
family...By atty   David Gristman

2525. Nacogdoches   Nov 16, 1835
No. 62. George M. Glass native of
U.S. emigrated in 1831, married with
family...By attorney George M. Glass
[The Plat has written W above M]

2526. Nacogdoches   Nov 21, 1835
No. 63. Joseph Hunter native of
U.S.A. emigrated in 1829, married
with family...
By attorney   Joseph Hunter

2527. Nacogdoches   21 Nov 1835
No. 65. Nathaniel Hodges native of
USA emigrated in 1829, married
with family
By attorney   Nathaniel Hodges

2528. Nacogdoches   Nov 23, 1835
No. 67. Daniel Hopkins native of USA
emigrated in 1826, married...
Daniel Hopkins

2529. Nacogdoches   Nov 23, 1835
No. 68. John Higgins native of USA
emigrated 1828, married with family
By attorney   John Higgins

2530. Nacogdoches   Nov 22, 1835
No. 69. William Howard native of
USA, emigrated 1830, married with
family...By atty   William Howard
204

2531. Nacogdoches Nov 22, 1835
No. 71. William Herring native of
the USA, emigrated 1831, married
with a family of 5 persons...
William Herring

2532. Nacogdoches   Nov 22, 1835
No. 72. John Hillis native of the
U.S. emigrated 1821, married with
family...By atty   John Hillis

2533. Nacogdoches   Novr 23, 1835
No. 73. Alexander Hughs native of
the U.S. emigrated 1823, married
with family...
By attorney   Alexander Hughs

2534. Nacogdoches   Nov 23, 1835
No. 75. Isaac Johnson native of the
U.S. emigrated 1829, married...
By attorney   Isaac Johnson

2535. Nacogdoches   Nov 21, 1835
No. 76. George Knox emigrated 1829,
married with family...
By atty,   George Knox

2536. Nacogdoches   Nov 11, 1835
No. 77. Levy Lusk native of the
U.S. married with family, emigrated
1827... By attorney   Levy Lusk

2537. Nacogdoches   October 9, 1835
No. 78. Guadalupe Lopez native of
Mexico, married with family...
Guadalupe X Lopez

2538. Nacogdoches   Nov 22, 1835
No. 80. Peter Lacy native of the
U.S. emigrated 1826, married with
family...By attorney   Peter Lacy

2539. Nacogdoches   Nov 21, 1835
No. 84. James Liddle native of U.S.
married with family...
By atty; James Liddle

2540. Nacogdoches   Nov 21, 1835
No. 85. John Lampkin native of U.S.
married with family...
By atty; John Lampkin

2541. Nacogdoches   Nov 16, 1835
No. 86. John Lacy native of U.S.
emigrated 1825, married with
family...By attorney John Lacy

2542. Nacogdoches Oct 8, 1835
No. 87. John Morehead native of U.S.
emigrated in 18--, married with
family...By atty   John Morehead

2543. Nacogdoches   Oct 8, 1835
No. 88. Peter Mendenhall native of
the U.S., emigrated 1830, married
with family
By attorney   Peter Mendenhall

2544. Nacogdoches   Nov 21, 1835
No. 90. Thomas Meredith native of
the U.S. emigrated 1819, married
with family...
By attorney   Thomas Meredith

2545. Nacogdoches Nov 22, 1835
No. 94. William Mays native of the
U.S. emigrated 1824, married with
family...By atty   William Mays

2546. Nacogdoches Nov 3, 1835
No. 95. H.T. Metcalf native of
U.S. emigrated 1831, married with
family of 4 persons...
              H.T. Metcalf

2547. Nacogdoches July 29, 1835
No. 96. Maria Dolores Menchaca native of Mexico, came to the State in
1820, widow with family of 6 persons
    Maria X Dolores Menchaca

2548. Nacogdoches Nov 16, 1835
No. 99. William Mott native U.S.
emigrated 1828, married with family
By attorney   William Mott

2549. Nacogdoches Nov 16, 1835
No. 102. Henry Middleton native of
U.S. emigrated 1830, married with
family...By atty Henry Middleton

2550. Nacogdoches Sep 5, 1835
No. 103. Crecencio Morales native of
Mexico, married with family...
       Crecencio Morales

2551. Nacogdoches Nov 16, 1835
No. 104. John Mayo native U.S.
emigrated 1831, married with family
By attorney   John Mayo

2552. Nacogdoches   Sept 28, 1835
No. 106. Patrick McDavid native of

Ireland emigrated 1827, single...
    Patrick X McDavid

2553. Nacogdoches   Nov 21, 1835
No. 108. Joseph Neilson native U.S.
married with family...
By attorney   Joseph Neilson

2554. Nacogdoches Nov 16, 1835
No. 110. Wm Nichols native U.S.
emigrated 1825, married with family
By attorney   William Nichols

2555. Nacogdoches Nov 21, 1835
No. 111. Jesse Norris native U.S.
emigrated 1835, married with family
By attorney   Jesse Norris

2556. Nacogdoches   20 Nov 1835
No. 112. Juan Prado native this
Villa, single...
By attorney   Juan Prado

2557. Nacogdoches   Sep 15, 1835
No. 114. Candelario Peres Mexican
citizen, married with wife and
children... Candelario X Perez

2558. Nacogdoches Nov 22, 1835
No. 115. John Parker native U.S.
emigrated 1831, married with family
By attorney   John Parker

2559. Nacogdoches   Nov 22, 1835
No. 118. Robert Pettit native U.S.
emigrated 1831, married...
By attorney   Robert Petit

2560. Nacogdoches Aug 5, 1835
No. 121. Jose Antonio Rodriguez
native Mexico, resident of this
Villa for 40 years, married with
family...Jose Anto X Rodriguez

2561. Nacogdoches   Oct 1, 1835
No. 123. Andres de Rojas native of
Mexico, single...Andres X de Rojas

2562. Nacogdoches Nov 2, 1835
No. 127. Piere Roblo native of
Mexico, married with family...
       Piere X Roblo

2563. Nacogdoches Nov 2, 1835
No. 128. John R. Rogers, native of
USA, emigrated in 1824, married with
family...By atty   John R. Rogers

2564. Nacogdoches   Nov 21, 1835
No. 129. Nicholas de la Rosa, native
of Mexico, married with family...
By attorney   Nicholas de la Roas

2565. Nacogdoches   28 Oct 1835
No. 130. Jose' del Rio born in this
Villa, married with family of three
persons...   Jose' del X Rio

2566. Nacogdoches   Nov 16, 1835
No. 131. Stephen Richardson native
of USA, emigrated in 1822, married
with family...
By attorney   Stephen Richardson

2567. Nacogdoches   Sep 23, 1835
No.138. Joseph S. Shackelford native
of USA, emigrated in 1829, without
family...   Joseph S. Shackelford

2568. Nacogdoches   Nov 19, 1835
No. 144. Jose' de los Santos born in
this Municipality, widower with
family of 2 persons...
  Jose' Santiago X de los Santos

2569. Nacogdoches   Sept 5, 1835
No. 147. Wiley S. Thomas native of
USA, emigrated in 1826, single...
              Wiley S. Thomas

2570. Nacogdoches   Oct 20, 1835
No. 150. Luis David native of Louisiana, emigrated in 1829, married
with family of 2 persons...
              Luis X David

2571. Nacogdoches   Nov 17, 1835
No. 151. John Deviny native of USA,
married with family of 3 persons...
              John Deviny

2572. Nacogdoches   Nov 25, 1835
No. 153. William Davis native of
USA, emigrated in 1830, married with
family...By atty   William Davis

2573. Nacogdoches   Nov 10, 1835
No.154. John Davidson native of USA
emigrated in 1823, married with
family...By atty   John Davidson

2574. Nacogdoches   Nov 21, 1835
No. 156. Zachariah Williams native

of USA, married with family...
By attorney   Zachariah Williams

2575. Nacogdoches Nov 21, 1835
No. 160. Isaiah Wroton native of
USA, emigratd in 1830, married with
family...By atty   Isaiah Wroton

2576. Nacogdoches   Nov 23, 1835
No. 161. Seth Ward native of USA.
emigrated in 1825, married...
By attorney   Seth Ward

2577. Nacogdoches   24 Nov 1835
No. 166. Juan Villareal, native of
Mexico, 26 years old, born and
raised in this Municipality, my wife
born here, have three children...
By attorney   John Villareal

2578. Nacogdoches   Aug 5, 1835
No. 169. Citizen Juan Francisco
Fermin Tobar, married with family of
three persons, born and raised in
this Villa...
   Juan Francisco X Fermin Tobar

2579. Nacogdoches   Nov 16, 1835
No. 170. John Todd native of USA,
emigrated in 1827, married with
family...By atty   John Todd

2580. Nacogdoches   Dec 14, 1835
No. 174. Jose Andres Torres over 25
years old, born in this Municipality, married with family of 3 persons
              Jose Ands Torres

2581. Nacogdoches   Oct 8, 1835
No. 31. William Clifton emigrated in
1830, married with family...
By attorney   William Clifton

2582. Nacogdoches   Nov 17, 1835
No. 44. John Faliepe native of
Mexico, married with family...
By attorney   John Faliepe

2583. Nacogdoches   Nov 17, 1835
No. 46. Joseph Feliepe native of
Mexico, married with family...
By attorney   Joseph Faliepe

2584. Nacogdoches October 8, 1835
No. 51. Joseph Fleming native of
USA, emigrated in 1825, married with
family...By atty   Joseph Fleming

2585. Nacogdoches   Oct 8, 1835
No. 79. Amsted J. Lilley native of
USA, emigrated in 1829, married with
family...By atty   Amsted J. Lilley

2586. Nacogdoches Nov 17, 1835
No. 92. William Murrell native of
Mexico, married with family...
By attorney   William Murrell

2587. Nacogdoches   Nov 17, 1835
No. 97. Samuel Maxlen native of
Mexico, married with family...
By attorney   Samuel Maxlen

2588. Nacogdoches   Nov 17, 1835
No. 98. Soto Montone native of Mexi-
co, married with family...
By attorney   Soto Montone

2589. Nacogdoches   Nov 21, 1835
No. 132. Amos Spring native of USA,
emigrated in 1830, single...
By attorney   Amos Spring

2590. Nacogdoches   Oct 8, 1835
No. 146. Peter Striker native of
Germany, emigrated in 1830, married
with family...
By attorney   Peter Striker

Volume 47
Unfinished Titles by Geo. W. Smyth. In two volumes.
[In Spanish. Petitions only are abstracted]

2601. San Augustine   Sept 1, 1835
No. 1. Joseph Howe, native of the
USA, emigrated in 1827, single...
             Joseph Howe

2602. San Augustine   Sept 1, 1835
No. 2. Nathaniel Hamilton, native of
the USA, emigrated 1831, single...
             Nathaniel X Hamilton

2603. San Augustine   Sept 1, 1835
No. 3. Cyreny McCrary native of the
USA, emigrated 1822, widow with
family of five persons...
             Cyreny McCrary

2604. San Augustine   Sept 1, 1835
No. 4. Samuel Porter native of the
USA, emigrated 1831, family of six
persons...   Samuel Porter

2605. San Augustine   Sept 1, 1835
No. 5. William Watson, native of
the USA, emigrated 1832, single...
             William Watson

2606. Nacogdoches   Sept 3d 1835
No. 6. Elizabeth White native of
Louisiana emigrated 1823, widow with
family of five persons...
             Elizabeth White

2607. Nacogdoches   Sept 3d 1835
No. 7. Mathew Earl native of Louisiana emigrated 1823, married with
family of seven persons...
             Matthew Earl

2608. Nacogdoches   Sept 3d, 1835
No. 8. William Earl native of Louisiana emigrated 1824, single...
             William Earl

2609. Nacogdoches   Sept 3d 1835
No. 9. Benjamin White native of
Louisiana emigrated 1823, single...
             Benjamin White

2610. Nacogdoches   Sept 3, 1835
No. 11. William Robert native of
Scotland emigrated 1825, single...
[not signed]

2611. Nacogdoches   Sept 3, 1835
No. 12. James Mason native of South
Carolina, emigrated 1830. married
with family of six persons...
             James Mason

2612. Nacogdoches   17 August 1835
No. 13. William Sherman native of
Carolina emigrated 1830, married
with family of three persons...
             Wm Sherman

2613. Nacogdoches   Sept 4. 1835
No. 14. Trinidad Gonzales native of
the Country, widow with family of 4
persons...   Trinidad X Gonzales

2614. Nacogdoches   Sept 4, 1835
No. 15. Isaac Renfro native of Missouri emigrated 1825, married with
family of 4 persons... Isaac Renfro

2615. Nacogdoches   August 27, 1835
No. 16. Robert Wire native of USA,
emigrated 1830, married with family
of 2 persons...   R. Wyre

2616. Nacogdoches   August 30, 1835
No. 17. Robert Earl native of Misouri, emigrated 1830, married with
family of 2 persons... Robert Earl

2617. Nacogdoches   August 30, 1835
No. 18. John Jacobs native of Pennsylvania emigrated 1830, single...
     John X Jacobs

2618. Nacogdoches   August 17, 1835
No. 19. Howard Bayley native of USA,
single...   Howard X Bailey

2619. Nacogdoches   30 August 1835
No. 20. Quintus Cincinatus Nujent
native of Mississippi, emigrated
1825, married with family of 2 persons...   Qunitus C. Nujent

2620. Nacogdoches   17 August 1835
No. 21. Wilson C. Brown native of
Virginia emigrated 1830, married
with family of 2 persons...
     Wilson C. Brown

2621. Nacogdoches   August 25, 1835
No. 22. Susana Latham widow with
family of 9 persons...
     Susana X Latham

2622. Nacogdoches   August 22, 1835
No. 23. William U. Sanderson native
of Ireland, emigrated Aug 1832,
single...   Wm U. X Sanderson

2623. Nacogdoches   Sept [1835?]
No. 24. Joseph Vannoy native of USA
emigrated 1831, married with family
of 5 persons...   Joseph Vannoy

2624. Nacogdoches   Sept 4, 1835
No. 25. Robert H. Lowther native of
USA emigrated 1832, married with
family...   R.H. Lowther

2625. Nacogdoches   Sept 30, 1835
No. 27. Thos Newlon native of USA,
emigrated 1832, married with family
of 2 persons... [Signed] Wm Newlon

2626. Nacogdoches   Sept 30, 1835
No. 28. John Win native of USA emigrated 1830, married with family...
     John Win

2627. Nacogdoches   Sept 7, 1835
No. 29. Isaac Burton native of USA
emigrated 1831, married with family
     I.W. Burton

2628. Nacogdoches   Sept 7, 1835
No. 30. John Bradley native of USA,
emigrated 1831, single without
family...   John Bradley

2629. Nacogdoches   Sept 7, 1835
No. 31. Redding A. Jorden native of
USA, emigrated 1831, single without
family... Redding A. Jorden

2630. Nacogdoches   Sept 7, 1835
No. 32. John D. Henry native of USA,
emigrated 1832 single without
family...   J.D. Henry

2631. Nacogdoches   Sept 7, 1835
     Mary X Earles
[This is a blank, signed and dated]

2632. Nacogdoches   Sept 8, 1835
No. 33. Feliciano Lopez native of
the Country, married with family...
     Feliciano X Lopez

2633. Nacogdoches   Sept 8, 1835
No. 34. Damien Rodriguez native of
the Country, married with family...
     Damien X Rodriguez

2634. Nacogdoches   Sept 8, 1835
No. 35. Merajeldo Ramires native of
the Country, married with family...
     Merajeldo X Ramires

2635. Nacogcoches   Sept 8, 1835
No. 36. Jose Andres Arrocha native
of Mexico, single...
       Jose Andres X Arrocha

2636. Nacogdoches   Sept 8, 1835
No. 37. Patricio de Torres native
of Mexico, married with family...
       Patricio de Torres

2637. Nacogdoches   Sept 9, 1835
No.38. Dolores Hernandez native of
Mexico, married with famiy...
       Dolores X Hernandez

2638. Nacogdoches   Sept 9, 1835
No. 39. Manl de Carmona, native of
Mexico married with family of 5
persons...   Manuel X Carmona

2639. Nacogdoches   Sept 9, 1835
No. 40. Guadalupe Calderon, native
of Mexico, widow with family of 5
persons...   Guadalupe X Calderon

2640. Nacogdoches   Sept 9, 1835
No. 41. Maria Getrudes Carmona native of Mexico, widow with family of
3 persons...
       Maria Gertrudes X Carmona

2641. Nacogdoches   Sept 9, 1835
No. 42. William Pace native of USA,
emigrated 1826, married with family
of seven persons... William Pace

2642. Nacogdoches   Septr 11, 1835
No. 43. William Defee native of USA
emigrated 1831, married with family
of nine persons...   William Defee

2643. Nacogdoches   Sept 11, 1835
No. 44. Silvera Pasquasin native of
Mexico widow with family...
       Silvera X Pasquasin

2644. Nacogdoches   Sept 12, 1835
No. 45. John Johnson native of USA
emigrated 1831, married with family
       John X Johnson

2645. Nacogdoches   Sept 14, 1835
No. 46. Amos King native of USA
emigrated 1830, single...
       Amos King

2646. Nacogdoches   Sept 14, 1835
No. 47. Hall Roddye native the of
USA emigrated 1832, single without
family...   Hall Roddye

2647. Nacogdoches   Sept 14, 1835
No. 48. Luther Smith native of USA
emigrated 1828, widower with family
       Luther Smith

2648. Nacogdoches   Sept 15, 1835
No. 50. Obediah Hendrick native of
USA emigrated 1826, single without
family...   O. Hendrick

2649. Nacogdoches   Sept 15, 1835
No. 51. Isaac Blover native of USA
emigrated 1823, married with family
of 3 persons...   Isaac Clover [?]

2650. Nacogdoches   Sept 17, 1835
No. 52. Charles Lindsey native of
USA emigrated 1826, married with
family of two persons...
       Charles Lindsey

2651. Nacogdoches   Sept 17, 1835
No. 53. Penangton Lindsey native USA
emigrated 1824, married with family
of 2 persons... Penangton Lindsey

2652. Nacogdoches   Sept 17, 1835
No. 54. Micajah Lindsey native of
USA emigrated 1824, married with
family of 2 persons...
       Micajah Lindsey

2653. Nacogdoches   Sept 17, 1835
No. 55. Elizabeth Carroll native of
USA widow with family of two
persons...   Elizabeth Carroll

2654. Nacogdoches   Sept 17, 1835
No. 56. Geo W. Ritter nativc of USA
emigrated in 1821, married with
family of three persons...
       George W. Ritter

2655. Nacogdoches   Sept 18, 1835
No. 57. Joseph Reynolds native of
USA emigrated 1833, single without
family...   Jos X Reynolds

2656. Nacogdoches   Sept 18, 1835
No. 58. Juan Franco Basques native

of Mexico, married with family of
four persons...
        Juan Francisco Basques

2657. Nacogdoches   Sep 19, 1835
No. 59. Pedro Murphy native of USA
emigrated 1812, single without
family...   Pedro X Murphy

2658. Nacogdoches   Sep 19, 1835
No. 60. William Burnett native of
USA emigrated 1830, married with
family of three persons...
        Wm Burnett

2659. Nacogdoches   Sep 19, 1835
No. 61. James Burnett native of USA
emigrated 1830, married with family
of four persons... Jas Burnett

2660. Nacogdoches   Sep 19, 1835
No. 62. Ramon Daley native of USA
emigrated 1829, married with family
of six persons...   Ramon Daley

2661. Nacogdoches   Sep 19, 1835
No. 63. William Williams native of
USA emigrated 1830, married with
family of three persons...
        William Williams

2662. Nacogdoches   Sep 19, 1835
No. 64. Narcece Monett native USA
emigrated 1829, married with family
of three persons... Narcece Monatt

2663. Nacogdoches   Sep 19, 1835
No. 65. James Hughes native USA
emigrated 1833, single without
family...   James Hughes

2664. Nacogdoches   Sep 19, 1835
No. 66. Burgess G. Hall native USA
emigrated 1828, single without
family...   Burgess G. Hall

2665. Nacogdoches   Sep 19, 1835
No. 67. Thomas Lindsey native USA
emigrated 1824, married with family
of two persons...   Thomas Lindsey

2666. Nacogdoches   Sep 19, 1835
No. 68. Wiley Waldrope native USA
emigrated 1827, married with family
of two persons...Wiley X Waldrope

2667. Nacogdoches   Sep 19, 1835
No. 69. Henry H. Hobson native of
USA emigrated 1822, married with
family of two persons...
        Henry H. X Hobson

2668. Nacogdoches   Sept 21, 1835
No. 70. Nathan B. Johnson native of
USA emigrated 1834, widower with
family of four persons...
        Nathan B. Johnson

2669. Nacogdoches   Sep 21, 1835
No. 71. Mathew Rolson native of
England emigrated 1831, married with
family of five persons...
Mathew Rolson   by Atty John Inman

2670. Nacogdoches   Sep 21, 1835
No. 72. Johnson Rawlins native of
USA emigrated 1812, married with
family of four persons...
John Rawlins   by Atty Wm Inglish

2671. Nacogdoches   Sep 21, 1835
No. 73. Isaac Freeland native of USA
emigrated 1830, married with family
of two persons...   Isaack Freeland
by Atty Wm Inglish

2672. Nacogdoches   Sep 23, 1835
No. 74. Alfred B. Davis native of
USA emigrated 1828, married with
family...   A.B. Davis

2673. Nacogdoches   Sep 24, 1835
No. 75. James Ford native of England
emigrated 1829, married with family
of four persons...   James X Ford

2674. Nacogdoches   Sep 28, 1835
No. 76. Charles H. Delaney native of
USA emigrated 1833, married with
family of four persons...
        C.H. Delaney

2675. Nacogdoches   Sept 28, 1835
No. 77. Samuel Faris native of USA
emigrated 1834, married with family
of four persons...   Samuel X Faris

2676. Nacogdoches   Sep 29, 1835
No. 78. Willis Donoho native of USA
emigrated 1831, married with family
of two   persons...Willis X Donoho

2677. Nacogdoches   Oct 2, 1835
No. 79. Franklin Mott native of USA
emigrated 1833, single.,..
                    Frankin Mott

2678. Nacogdoches   Oct 2, 1835
No. 80. Parthenia Courcy native of
USA emigrated 1833, widow with
family... Parthenia X Courcy

2679. Nacogdoches   Oct 2, 1835
No. 81. Lewis Donoho native of USA
emigrated 1831, married with family
of 4 persons...   Lewis Donoho

2680. Nacogdoches   Oct 2, 1835
No. 82. Fielding Walker native of
USA emigrated 1833, single...
                    Fielding X Walker

2681. Nacogdoches   Oct 3, 1835
No. 83. Samuel G. Hanks native of
USA emigrated 1827, single...
                    Samuel G. Hanks

2682. Nacogdoches   Oct 3, 1835
No. 84. William Jourdon native of
USA married with family of six
persons...   William Jourdan

2683. Nacogdoches   Oct 3, 1835
No. 85. John Faris native of USA
married with family of six persons
                    John Faris

2684. Nacogdoches   Oct 3, 1835
No. 86. Owen Taylor native of USA
married with family of 8 persons...
                    Owen Taylor

2685. Nacogdoches   Oct 3, 1835
No. 87. Gadie West native of USA
emigrated 1829, married with family
of 8 persons...   Gadi X West

2686. Nacogdoches   Oct 3, 1835
No. 88. William Nichols native of
USA emigrated 1826, married with
family of 6 persons...
                    William X Nichols

2687. Nacogdoches   Oct 3, 1835
No. 89. Richard Simmons native of
USA emigrated 1830, married with
family of 4 persons...
                    Richard Simmons

2688. Nacogdoches   Oct 3, 1835
No.90. Thomas Tanner native of USA
emigrated 1831, married with family
of 7 persons...   Thomas Tanner

2689. Nacogdoches   Oct 3, 1835
No.91. William Guthrie native of USA
emigrated 1830, married with family
of 5 persons...   William Guthrie

2690. Nacogdoches   Sept 23, 1835
No.92. Samuel Holmes native of USA
emigrated 1829, married with family
                    Samuel Homes

2691. Nacogdoches   Oct 3, 1835
No.93. Isaac Winfree native of USA
emigrated 1826, married with family
of 3 persons...   Isaac Winfree

2692. Nacogdoches   Oct 3, 1835
No.94. Alfred M. Bevil native of USA
emigrated 1823, single...
                    Alfred M. Bevil

2693. Nacogdoches   Oct 3, 1835
No.95. James D. Good native of USA
emigrated 1833, single...
                    James D. Good

2694. Nacogdoches   Oct 8, 1835
No.96.   Wm G. X Gates

2695. Nacogdoches   Oct 9, 1835
No.97.   John Gates

2696. Nacogdoches   Oct 9, 1835
No.98.   Jesse Walling

2697. Nacogdoches   Oct 9, 1835
No.99.   John Rannlet[?]

2698. Nacogdoches   Oct 9, 1835
No.100.   John C. Walling

2699. Nacogdoches   Oct 10, 1835
No.101.   Alfred Mayfield
        by James C. Cain Attorney

2700. Nacogdoches   Oct 10, 1835
No.102.   William A. Williams
    by James C. Cain Attorney

2701. Nacogdoches   Oct 10, 1835
No.103.   Nathan Hardwick
    by Attorney James C. Cain

2702. Nacogdoches   Oct 10, 1835
No.104.   Joseph Fish
    by Attorney James C. Cain

2703. Nacogdoches   Oct 9, 1835
No.105.   Henry Hoover
    by Attorney Henry Teal

2704. Nacogdoches   Oct 9, 1835
No.106.   James Faddes
    by Attorney Henry Teal

2705. Nacogdoches   Oct 9, 1835
No.107.   Peter Mason
    by Attorney James C. Cain

2706. Nacogdoches   Oct 12, 1835
No.108.   Thos H. Henly[?]

2707. Nacogdoches   Oct 12, 1835
No.109.   William M. Lumpkin

2708. Nacogdoches   Oct 13, 1835
No.110.   John M. Brown
    by Attorney Saml Stivers

2709. Nacogdoches   Oct 13, 1835
No.111.   Samuel Dickerson
    by Attorney Saml Stivers

2710. Nacogdoches   Oct 13, 1835
No.112.   Houdt[?] Farmer
    by Attorney Saml Stivers

2711. Nacogdoches   Oct 13, 1835
No.113.   James Williams
    by Attorney Samuel Stivers

2712. Nacogdoches   Oct 13, 1835
No.115.   John Locke
    by Attorney Saml Stivers

2713. Nacogdoches   Octr 13, 1835
No.116.   Walter Dickerson

2714. Nacogdoches   Oct 13, 1835
No.117.   William X Melton

[Nos.2694 through 2714 are blank
forms with only the above]

2715. Nacogdoches   Oct 13, 1835
No.118. Ross Law native of USA married with family...   Ross Law

2716. Nacogdoches   Oct 13, 1835
No.119. John B. Hixon native of USA
married with family...John B. Hixon

2717. Nacogdoches   Oct 13, 1835
No.120. Samuel Slaughter native of
USA emigrated 1826, single...
            Samuel Slaughter

2718. Nacogdoches   Oct 14, 1835
No.121. Samuel Eldridge native of
USA emigrated 1833, married with
family of 2 persons...
            Samuel Eldridge
    by Attorney Richard Haley

2719. Nacogdoches   Oct 14, 1835
No.122. James Howard native of USA
emigrated 1833, single...
            James Howard
    by Attorney Richard Haley

2720. Nacogdoches   Oct 14, 1835
No.123. John Lowry native of USA
emigrated 1821, single...
            John Lowery
    by Attorney Richard Haley

2721. Nacogdoches   Oct 14, 1835
No,124. George Slaughter native USA
emigrated 1826, single...
            George Slaughter
    by Attorney Richard Haley

2722. Nacogdoches   Oct 14, 1835
No.125. Edward Robertson native USA
emigrated 1831, married with family
of 9 persons...   Edward Roberson
    by Attorney Richard Haley

2723. Nacogdoches   Oct 14, 1835
No.126. William Clark native USA
widower with family of two persons
            William Clark
    by Attorney Richard Haley

2724. Nacogdoches   Oct 14, 1835
No.127. Sarah Rugg native USA emigrated 1833, widow with family...
          Sarah Rugg
     by Attorney Richard Haley

2725. Nacogdoches   Oct 14, 1835
No.128. Lewis H. Adams native USA
emigrated 1833, widower with family
          Lewis H. Adams
     by Attorney Richard Haley

2726. Nacogdoches   Oct 14, 1835
No.129. Charles Haley native USA
emigrated 1821 without family...
          Charles Haley
     by Attorney Richard Haley

2727. Nacogdoches   Oct 3, 1835
No.130. Oliver Lund native USA emigrated 1833, single without family
          Oliver Lund
     by Attorney Richard Haley

2728. Nacogdoches   Oct 3d 1835
No.131. Hardy Ware native USA emigrated 1824, widower with family...
          Hardy Ware
     by Attorney Richard Haley

2729. Nacogdoches   Oct 5, 1835
No.132. Isaac Barr native USA emigrated 1832, single without family
          Isaac Bear

2730. Nacogdoches   Oct 7, 1835
No.133. E. Grigsby native USA emigrated 1831 single without family...
          E. Grigsby

2731. Nacogdoches   Oct 3d 1835
No.134. William A. Irwine native USA
emigrated 1822, married with family
of two persons... Wm A. Irwine

2732. Nacogdoches   1st Oct 1835
No.135. William J. Harding native
USA emigrated 1831, single without
family... Wm J. Harding

2733. No.136. Margett Russell
     by Attorney Samuel Stivers
[This document and through 2736 are
forms, otherwise blank]

2734. No.137. John Mason
     by Attorney Saml Stivers

2735. No.138. Jessey Russell
     by Attorney Saml Stivers

2736. No.139. David Fuller
     by his Atty Saml Stivers

2737. Nacogdoches   Oct 24, 1835
No.140. John McCormick native of USA
emigrated January 1832 without
family... John X McCormick

2738. Nacogdoches   Oct 21, 1835
No.141. Mary Vanwinkle native USA
emigrated February 1832, widow with
family... Mary X Vanwinkle
[Pencil note across top: "U.S.,
widow, 2 Feb 1832"]

2739. Nacogdoches   Ocr 27, 1835
No.142. Ynes Moreno native Mexico
without family... Ynes Moreno

2740. Nacogdoches   Oct 28, 1835
No.143. Michael Castley native USA
emigrated 1832 married with family
          Michael Castley

2741. Nacogdoches   Oct 28, 1835
No.144. Joseph Smith native USA
emigrated 1830, married with family
          Joseph Smith

2742. Nacogdoches   Oct 19, 1835
No.145. John H. Irby native USA
emigrated 1832, single without
family... John H.Irby

2743. Nacogcohes   Oct 29, 1835
No.146. Jose' Lionicio Trevino native Mexico, married with family...
          Jose' Lionicio X Trevino

2744. Nacogdoches   Oct 30, 1835
No.147. Joseph Houndshell native USA
emigrated 1832, married with family
          Joseph Houndshell

2745. Nacogdoches   Oct 30, 1835
No.148. Wm Clark native USA emigrated 1834 married with family...
          Wm Clark

2746. Nacogdoches   Oct 30, 1835
No.149. Jose' Ramise native Mexico,
married with family...
          Jose' X Ramires

2747. Nacogdoches   Nov 2, 1835
No.150. W.H. Payne native USA emigrated 1833 married with family...
            W.H. Payne

2748. Nacogdoches   Aug 5, 1835
No.151. Citizen Adolfo Sterne as
Attorney for Citizen Juan Jose'
Alvarado...since the year 1826 has
occupied his ranch on the Attoyaque

2749. Nacogdoches   Sep 2, 1835
No.152. Before me Vicente Cordoba,
Judge of the First Instance, appeared Citizen Juan Jose' Albarado
and says: [Power Atty]

2750. Nacogdoches   15 Aug 1835
No.153. Julie Lazarin native of
Mexico (Bexar) single...
            Julie Lazarin

2751. Nacogdoches   5 Aug 1835
No. 154. John Coughran native Terr.
of Arkansas, emigrated 1830, single
            John Coughran

2752. Nacogdoches 29 Aug 1835
No. 157. Jose Gambo native Chihua-
hua emigrated this State 1812 married with family four persons...
            Jose' X Gamboa'

2753. Nacogdoches   Aug 29, 1835
No. 158. Theresa Thombleston native
Louisiana emigrated 1824, widow with
family of 6 persons...on Rio Neches
            Theresa X Thombleston

Vol. 48. [Volume 2 of the Geo W. Smyth Unfinished Titles, continued]

2754. Nacogdoches   3 Aug 1835
No.1. Hugh Henderson native Virginia
emigrated 1832, single...
            Hugh Henderson

2755. Nacogdoches   Aug 3, 1835
No.2. Wm J. Willis native South
Carolina emigrated 1832, married
with family of six persons...
            W.J. Willis

2756. Nacogdoches   Aug 3, 1835
No.3. Adam Johnson native Missouri
emigrated 1832, single...
            Adam Johnson

2757. Nacogdoches   Aug 3, 1835
No.4. William Marshall native Ohio
emigrated 1827, single...
            William X Marshall

2758. Nacogdoches   Aug 3, 1835
No.5. Maria Josefa Cadena native
City of Bejar, widow with family of
three persons Ma Josefa X Cadena

2759. Nacogdoches   Aug 3, 1835
No.6. Juan Lopez native Mexico,
married with family of two persons
            Juan X Lopez

2760. Nacogdoches   3 Aug 1835
No.7. Manuel Acosta native this
Villa, single... Manuel Acosta

2761. Nacogdoches   4 Aug 1835
No.8. Agapito Servantes native City
of Bejar, married with family of 4
persons... Agapito X Servantes

2762. Nacogdoches   4 Aug 1835
No.9. Santiago Bebe native this
Municipality, widower with family of
eight persons... Santiago X Bebe

2763.Nacogdoches   5 Aug 1835
No.10. Ma de la Cruz Rodriguez de
Cortes native this Villa, widow with
family of 5 persons...
Ma de la Cruz X Rodriguez de Cortes

2764. Nacogdoches   5 August 1835
No.11. James Taylor native Kentucky,
single, emigrated 1820...
            James X Taylor

2765. Nacogdoches   5 Aug 1835
No.12. Elenor Bradley native Pennsylvania emigrated 1831, widow with
family of five persons...
            Eleanor X Bradley

2766. Nacogdoches   5 Aug 1835
No.13. John Daugherty native Ireland, emigrated 1831, married with
family of five persons...
            John Daugherty

214

2767. Nacogdoches   5 August 1835
No.14. Juan Rodriguez native State
of Nuevo Leon, single...
                Juan Rodriguez
2768. Nacogdoches   August 8, 1835
No.15. Samuel Brimberry native North
Carolina, emigrated 1833, married
with family of 8 persons...
                Samuel Brimberry

2769. Nacogdoches   8 August 1835
No.16. Hesekiah George native State
of Main, emigrated 1828 single...
                Hezekiah George

2770. Nacogdoches   [no date]
No.17. Charles C. Hieskell native of
Virginia, emigrated 1822 single...
                Chs C. Hieskell

2771. Nacogdoches   10 August 1835
No.18. Charles H. Sims native of
Virginia emigrated 1829, married
with family of two persons...
                C.H. Sims
2772. Nacogdoches   10 August 1835
No.19. F.U.K. Day native Connecticut
emigrated 1834, single... F.U.K. Day

2773. Nacogdoches   10 August 1835
No.20. David Towns native of North
Carolina emigrated 1826, married
with family of eight persons...
                David Towns

2774. Nacogdoches   11 August 1835
No.21. David Bullock native South
Carolina emigrated 1833 single...
                David Bullock

2775. Nacogdoches   11 August 1835
No.22. David A. Huffman native Virginia married with family of three
persons...   D.A. Huffman

2776. Nacogdoches   11 August 1835
No.23. Thomas J. Hughes native Louisiana emigrated 1832, single...
                Thomas Hughs

2777. Nacogdoches   13 August 1835
No.24. Benjamin F. Cage native Tennessee emigrated 1832, single...
                B.F. Cage

2778. Nacogdoches   13 August 1835
No.25. Luis Holloway native South

Carolina emigrated 1821, married
with family of five persons...
                Lewis X Holloway

2779. Nacogdoches   13 August 1835
No.26. Mathew Doyal native Louisiana
emigrated 1831, married with family
of three persons... Matthew Doyal

2780. Nacogdoches   August 14, 1835
No.27. Henry Whiteside native Kentucky emigrated 1824, married with
family of four persons...
                Henry Whiteside

2781. Nacogdoches   August 14, 1835
No.28. William P. Chisum native
Tennessee emigrated 1833, single...
                William P.Chisum

2782. Nacogdoches   14 August 1835
No.29. William Harness native Virginia emigrated 1833, single...
                William Harness

2783. Nacogdoches   15 August 1835
No.30. Jose' Ma Arocha native this
Villa, married with family of three
persons... Jose' Ma Arocha

2784. San Augustine 17 August 1835
No.31. John English native Carolina
emigrated 1825, married with family
of seven persons... John English

2785. San Augustine 17 August 1835
No.32. Stephen English native Tennessee emigrated 1825, married with
family of four persons...
                Stephen English

2786. San Augustine 17 August 1835
No.33. James B.Tucker native Virginia emigrated 1834, married with
family of ten persons...
                James B. Tucker

2787. San Augustine Aug 17, 1835
No.34. Richard B.Haley native Tennessee emigrated 1824, married with
family five persons...Richard Haley

2788. San Augustine Aug 17, 1835
No.35. Richard Haley native North
Carolina emigrated 1822, married
with family ten persons...
                Richard Haley

2789. San Augustine Aug 17, 1835
No.36. Harbard L. Wiggins native
Carolina emigrated 1830, married
with family three persons...
      Harbard L. Wiggins

2790. San Augustine Aug 17, 1835
No.37. David Strickland native Kentucky emigrated 1821, married with
family of seven persons..
      David X Strickland

2791. San Augustine Aug 17, 1835
No.38. Archibald English native Tennessee emigrated 1831, single...
      Archibald English

2792. San Augustine Aug 17, 1835
No.39. Hardin Wright native Tennessee emigrated 1832, married with
family six persons...
      Hardin X Wright
2793. San Augustine Aug 17, 1835
No.40. Jonathan Anderson native Kentucky emigrated 1819, married with
family of eight persons...
      Jonathan Anderson

2794. San Augustine Aug 17, 1835
No.41. Alanson Barr native Vermont
emigrated 1821, married with family
of seven   persons... Alanson Barr

2795. San Augustine Aug 17, 1835
No.42. Chester Rockwell native New
York emigrated 1833, single...
      Chester X Rockwell

2796. San Augustine Aug 17, 1835
No.43. John C. Payne native Tennessee emigrated 1825, single...
      John C. X Payne

2797. San Augustine Aug 17, 1835
No.44. Henry Ashabraner native North
Carolina emigrated 1830, married
with family of three persons...
      Henry X Ashabraner

2798. San Augustine Aug 17, 1835
No.45. James English native Tennessee emigrated 1829, single...
      James English
2799. San Augustine Aug 17, 1835
No.46. Menan Smith native Louisiana
emigrated 1822, married with family
of four persons...   Menan X Smith
216

2800. San Augustine Aug 17, 1835
No.47. Jonas English native Tennessee emigrated 1824, married with
family of two persons...
      Jonas English
2801. San Augustine Aug 17, 1835
No.48. William Todd native Georgia
emigrated 1834[?] married with family of thirteen persons...Wm Todd[?]

2802. San Augustine Aug 17, 1835
No.49. Simpson Holloway native South
Carolina, emigrated 1821, married
with family of three persons...
      Simpson Holloway

2803. San Augustine Aug 17, 1835
No.50. Caleb Holloway native Mississippi emigrated 1821, single...
      [not signed]

2804. San Augustine Aug 17, 1835
No.51. John Weeks native Tennessee
emigrated Oct 1832, married with
family of seven persons...
      John X Weeks

2805. San Augustine Aug 17, 1835
No.52. Claiborn Walker native Tennessee emigrated 1832 Feb, single...
      Claiborn X Walker

2806. San Augustine Aug 17, 1835
No.53. Joseph Burleson native Tennessee emigrated 1833, married with
family eight persons...
      Joseph Burleson

2807. San Augustine Aug 17, 1835
No.54. Jesse McCelvey native Tennessee emigrated 1825, single...
      Jesse McCelvey

2808. San Augustine Aug 17, 1835
No.55. Thomas Roads native Georgia
emigrated 1832, married with family
four persons...   Thomas X Roads

2809. San Augustine Aug 17, 1835
No.56. Henry Scritchfield native
Louisiana emigrated 1822, single...
      Henry X Scritchfield

2810. San Augustine Aug 17, 1835
No.57. [blank] emigrated 1825,
widow with family of two persons...
      Elizabeth English

2811. San Augustine Aug 17, 1835
No.58. Jonas Haile native North
Carolina emigrated 1833, married
with family six persons...
              Jonas Haile

2812. San Augustine Aug 18, 1835
No.59. Ealey Ewing native Tennessee
emigrated 1833, married with family
six persons...   Ealey Ewing

2813. San Augustine Aug 18, 1835
No.60. Charles Gates native Kentucky
emigrated 1831, married with family
six persons...   Charles Gates

2814. San Augustine Aug 18, 1835
No. 61. Robert Ervin native South
Carolina emigrated 1832 March, mar-
ried with family seven persons...
              Robert Erwen

2815. San Augustine Aug 18, 1835
No.62. F. Swetenburg native South
Carolina emigrated 1832 May, single
              F. Sweetenburg

2816. San Augustine Aug 18, 1835
No.63. William J. Crain native Tennessee emigrated 1831, married with
family five persons...
              William J. X Crain

2817. San Augustine   18 Aug 1835
No.64. Abraham Smith native Tennessee emigrated 1831, married with
family four persons...
              Abraham X Smith

2818. San Augustine Aug 18, 1835
No.65. James Bowlin native Tennessee
emigrated 1826, married with family
three persons...   James X Bowlin

2819. San Augustine Aug 18, 1935
No.66. Jeremiah Bowlin native Virginia emigrated 1826, married with
family four persons...
              Jeremiah X Bowlin

2820. San Augustine 18 Aug 1835
No.67. Holland Anderson native Kentucky emigrated 1830, married with
family four persons...
              Holland X Anderson
2821. San Augustine Aug 18, 1835
No.68. James English native Carolina

emigrated 1827, married with family
nine persons...   James English

2822. San Augustine Aug 18, 1835
No.69. William M. Lloyd native Tennessee emigrated 1828, single...
              William M. Lloyd
2823. San Augustine Aug 18, 1835
No.70. Moses Wootan native North
Carolina emigrated 1822, married
with family eight persons...
              Moses X Wootan

2824. San Augustine Aug 18, 1835
No.71. Nathan Davis senior native
South Carolina, emigrated 1822, mar-
ried with family eight persons...
              Nathan Davis Senior

2825. San Augustine Aug 18, 1835
No.72. Harrison Davis native Illinois emigrated 1822, married with
family two persons...Harrison Davis

2826. San Augustine Aug 18, 1835
No.73. Bailey Anderson senior native
Virginia emigrated 1822, married
with family seven persons...
              Bayley X Anderson

2827. San Augustine Aug 18, 1835
No.74. Oliver H. Anderson native
Indiana emigrated 1821, married with
family three persons...
              Oliver X Hazard Anderson

2828. San Augustine Aug 18, 1835
No.75. Bailey Anderson junior native
South Carolina emigrated 1821, mar-
ried with family ten persons...
              Bailey Anderson jr

2829. San Augustine Aug 18, 1835
No.76. Samuel M. Rainer native Louisiana emigrated 1831, married with
family three persons... S.M. Rainer

2830. San Augustine Aug 18, 1835
No.77. John Beauchamp native Delaware emigrated 1830, married with
family six persons...John Beauchamp

2831. San Augustine Aug 18, 1835
No.78. Hezekiah Thomas native North
Carolina, emigrated 1831, married
with family six persons...
              Hezekiah Thomas

2832. San Augustine   Aug 18, 1835
No.79. James Smith native North
Carolina emigrated 1831, married
with family seven persons...
James Smith

2833. San Augustine   Aug 18, 1835
No.80. James Thomas native North
Carolina emigrated 1831 single...
James X Thomas

2834. San Augustine   Aug 18, 1835
No.81. Clinton Rice native Tennessee
emigrated 1826, single...
Clinton Rice

2835. San Augustine   Aug 18, 1835
No.82. Daniel Holloway native Vir-
ginia emigrated 1821, single...
Daniel Holloway

2836. San Augustine   Aug 18, 1835
No.84. Benjamin Bustin native Virginia emigrated 1821, married with
family four persons... Benj Bustin

2837. San Augustine   Aug 18, 1835
No.85. Jonas Harrison native New
Jersey emigrated 1821, married with
family nine persons... J. Harrison

2838. San Augustine   Aug 18, 1835
No.86. James McElvey native Tennessee emigrated 1824, married with
family two persons...James McElvey

2839. San Augustine   Aug 18, 1835
No.87. David Wilkerson native South
Carolina emigrated 1822, married
with family eight persons...
David X Wilkerson

2840. San Augustine   Aug 18, 1835
No.88. John McAdams native Alabama
emigrated Oct 1832, married with
family eight persons...John McAdams

2841. San Augustine   Aug 18, 1835
No.89. Jesse Sullins native Tennessee emigrated 1832, married with
family three persons...Jesse Sullins

2842. San Augustine   Aug 18, 1835
No.90. Jams McAdams native North
Carolina emigrated Jany 1832, mar-
ried with family five personss...
James McAdams

2843. San Augustine   Aug 18, 1835
No.91. Swanson Yarbrough native
North Carolina emigratd Feb 1832,
married with family ten persons...
Swanson Yarbrough

2844. San Augustine   Aug 18, 1835
No.92. Tire Buckley native Missis-
sippi emigrated 1822, single..
Tyre Buckley

2845. San Augustine   Aug 18, 1835
No.93. Richard Williams native Geor-
gia emigrated 1821, single...
Richard Williams

2846. San Augustine   Aug 18, 1835
No.94. Joshua English native Tennessee emigrated 1826, married with
family two persons...Joshua English

2847. San Augustine   Aug 18, 1835
No.95. Jeroboam Beauchamp native
Kentucky emigrated 1831, single...
Jeroboam B. Beauchamp

2848. San Augustine   Aug 18, 1835
No.96. Joseph English native Tennessee emigrated 1823, married with
family four persons...
Joseph X English

2849. San Augustine   Aug 18, 1835
No.97. Bart. Gates native Georgia
emigrated 1831, married with family
five persons...Bartholomew Gates

2850. San Augustine   Aug 18, 1835
No.98. Edwin Hendrick native Kentucky emigrated 1824, married with
family five persons...Edwin Hendrick

2851. San Augustine   Aug 18, 1835
No.99. Benjamin Holt native
Mississippi emigrated 1825, married
with family seven persons...B. Holt

2852. San Augustine   Aug 18, 1835
No.100. Everett Ritter native Tennessee emigrated 1831, married with
family five persons...
Everett X Ritter

2853. San Augustine   18 Aug 1835
No.101. B.H. Simpson native Tennessee emigrated 1831, married with
family 7 persons   B.H. Simpson

2854. San Augustine Aug 18, 1835 No.102. Archibald Smith native Louisiana emigrated 1822, married with family five persons...
Archibald X Smith

2855. San Augustine Aug 18, 1835 No.103. John Applegate native Kentucky emigrated 1829, married with family four persons...
John Applegate

2856. San Augustine Aug 18, 1835 No.104. Allen Haley native Tennessee emigrated 1822 single...
Allen X Haley

2857. San Augustine Aug 18, 1835 No.105. Samuel Davis native North Carolina emigrated 1832, married with family three persons...
Samuel Davis

2858. San Augustine Aug 18, 1835 No.106. Thomas Haley native Alabama emigrated 1822 single...Thos Haley

2859. San Augustine Aug 18, 1835 No.107. John Harma native Tennessee emigrated 1826, married with family two persons...   John Harmon

2860. San Augustine Aug 18, 1835 No.108. Jacob Walker native Tennessee emigrated 1820, married with family six persons... Jacob Walker

2861. San Augustine Aug 18, 1835 No.109. Andrew W. Gordon native Tennessee emigrated 1830, married with family three persons...
Andres X W. Goodwin

2862. San Augustine Aug --, 1835 No.110. William King native Georgia emigrated 1830 married with family six persons...   William X King

2863. San Augustine Aug 19, 1835 No.111. Edward Teal native Maryland emigrated 1824 widower with family 4 persons   E. Teal

2864. San Augustine Aug 19, 1835 No.112. Mason Van native South Carolina emigrated 1822 married with family eight persons... Mason X Van

2865. San Augustine Aug 19, 1835 No.113. John Hubbell native Missouri emigrated 1815 married with family two persons...   John X Hubbell

2866. San Augustine Aug 19, 1835 No.114. John Holly native North Carolina emigrated 1822, married with family twelve persons...
John Haley

2867. San Augustine Aug 19, 1835 No.115. John Inman native North Carolina emigrated 1831, married with family eight persons...
John Inman

2868. San Augustine Aug 19, 1835 No.116. James Forsyth native Kentucky emigrated 1821, married with family five persons... James X Forsyth

2869. San Augustine Aug 19, 1835 No.117. Edward A. Merchant native North Carolina emigrated 1829 married with family six persons...
Edward A. Merchant

2870. San Augustine Aug 19, 1835 No.118. Berry Merchant native Tennessee emigrated March 1832 single
Berry Merchant

2871. San Augustine Aug 19, 1835 No.119. John D. Merchant native South Carolina emigrated Feb 1832 married with family eight persons...
John D. Merchant

2872. San Augustine Aug 19, 1835 No.120. William Stout native Tennessee emigrated 1827, single...
William X Stout

2873. San Augustine Aug 19, 1835 No.121. Samuel Thompson native North Carolina emigrated 1826 married with family two persons... Saml Thompson

2874. San Augustine Aug -- 1835 No.122. John Usserry native Virginia emigrated 1832 married with family four persons...   John A. Usery

2875. San Augustine Aug 19, 1835 No.123. John Latham native North Carolina emigrated 1804 married with family nine persons...John X Latham

2876. San Augustine   Aug 19, 1835
No.124. Garret M. Lankford native
Tennessee emigrated 1829 married
with family eight persons...
          Garrett M. X Lankfort

2877. San Augustine   Aug 19, 1835
No.125. King Latham native this
State married with family five
persons...   King X Latham

2878. San Augustine   Aug 19, 1835
No.126. Samuel McFaden native Kentucky emigrated 1822 married with
family seven persons...
          Samuel X McFaden

2879. San Augustine   Aug 19, 1835
No.127. Jonathan McFaden native
Louisiana emigrated 1822 single...
          Jonathan X McFaden

2880. San Augustine   Aug 19, 1835
No.128. William T. Mallone native
Mississippi emigrated 1812 married
with family four persons...
          Wm T. Malone
2881. San Augustine   Aug 19, 1835
No.129. Maria Ann Haley native Georgia emigrated 1828 widow with family
four persons... Maria Anna X Haley

2882. San Augustine   Aug 19, 1835
No.130. Jehu H. Greenway native
Tennessee emigrated 1831 single...
          Jehu H. X Greenway

2883. San Augustine   Aug 19, 1835
No.131. Jose Santos native of the
Country married with family six
persons... Jose X Santos Senior

2884. San Augustine   Aug 19, 1835
No.132. Jose Santos native of the
Country single... Jose X Santos

2885. San Augustine   Aug 19, 1835
No.133. John Forsythe native Kentucky emigrated 1822 married with family 5 persons   John X Forsythe

2886. San Augustine   Aug 19, 1835
No.134. Feleppe Madregal native of
the Country married with family 4
persons   Feleppi X Madregal
220

2887. San Augustine   Aug 19, 1835
No.135. James Connally native New
York single... James Connally

2888. San Augustine   Aug 19, 1835
No.136. Domingo Gonzales native Mexico married with family four persons
          Domingo X Gonzales

2889. San Augustine   Aug 19, 1835
No.137. Mark Haley native USA emigrated 1825 married with family
three persons... Mark Haley

2890. San Augustine   Aug 19, 1835
No.138. Philip Graves native USA
emigrated 1824 single...
          Philip X Graves

2891. San Augustine   Aug 19, 1835
No.139. Martin Law native USA emigrated 1832 sigle... Martin Law

2892. San Augustine   Aug 19, 1835
No.140. Davis Renfro native USA
emigrated 1827 married with family 5
persons...   David Renfro

2893. San Augustine   Aug 20, 1835
No.141. H.T.Chappell native USA emigrated 1833 married with family two
persons... H.T. Chappell

2894. San Augustine   Aug 20, 1835
No.142. Clement Tutt native USA
married with family 9 persons...
          C. Tutt

2895. San Augustine   Aug 20, 1835
No.143. Sarah Chappell native USA
widow with family 2 persons...
          Sarah X Chappell

2896. San Augustine   Aug 20, 1835
No.144. Hartwell Howard native USA
emigrated 1823 married with family 5
persons   Hartwell X Howard

2897. San Augustine   Aug 20, 1835
No.145. Joseph Rice native USA emigrated 1826 married with family 5
persons... Joseph Rice

2898. San Augustine   Aug 20, 1835
No.146. Christian Gross native USA

emigrated 1828 married with family 3 persons   [Sig not legible]

2899. San Augustine   Aug 20, 1835 No.147. George Grounds native USA emigrated 1828 married with family 5 persons   George X Grounds

2900. San Augustine   Aug 20, 1835 No.148. Ahira Butler native USA emigrated 1828 single...Ahira Butler

2901. San Augustine   Aug 20, 1835 No.149. William Taylor native USA emigrated 1833 married with family eleven persons...   William Taylor

2902. San Augustine   Aug 20, 1835 No.150. Alfred Morris native USA emigrated 1833 married with family 3 persons...   Alfred Morris

2903. San Augustine   Aug 20, 1835 No.151. J.E. Cotton native USA emigrated 1833 married with family 6 persons...   John J.E. Cotton

2904. San Augustine   Aug 20, 1835 No.152. Randolph Yarbrough native USA emigrated 1832 single...   Randolph Yarbrough

2905. San Augustine Aug 20, 1835 No.153. James Alford native USA emigrated 1832 married with family 3 persons...   James Alford

2906. San Augustine   Aug 20, 1835 No.154. Grenberry Gates native USA emigrated 1831 single...   Greenberry Gates

2907. San Augustine   Aug 20, 1835 No.155. William Scurlock native USA emigrated 1834 single...   William Scurlock

2908. San Augustine   Aug 20, 1835 No.156. Jacob Anthony native USA emigrated 1831 married with family 3 persons...   Jacob X Anthony

2909. San Augustine   Aug 20, 1835 No.157. Rhoddy Anthony native USA emigrated 1831 arrived with family 8 persons...   Rhoddy Anthony

2910. San Augustine   Aug 20, 1835 No.158. Peter Stockman native USA emigrated 1810 married with family 3 persons   Peter X Stockman

2911. District of Bevil Aug 21, 1835 No.159. Martin Byarly native USA emigrated 1833 married with family 3 persons...   Martin Byerley

2912. District of Bevil Aug 21, 1835 No.160. William Byarly native USA emigrated 1833 single...   William Byerley

2913. Dictrict of Bevil Aug 26, 1835 No.161. James Denman native USA emigrated 1831 single...   James X Denman

2914. District of Bevil Aug 30, 1835 No.162. Martin B. Lewis native USA emigrated 1830 married with family 4 persons   M.B. Lewis

2915. District of Bevil Aug 26, 1835 No.163. J. Becker native USA emigrated 1830 single...   J. Becker

2916. District of Bevil Aug 29, 1835 No.164. Harman Lewis native USA emigrated 1825 single...   Harman X Lewis

2917. District of Bevil Aug 29, 1835 No.165. Samuel S. Lewis native USA emigrated 1830 married with family 4 persons   Samuel S. Lewis

2918. District of Bevil Aug 29, 1835 No.166. Henry Cochron native USA emigrated 1833 single...   Henry Cochron

2919. District of Bevil Aug 29, 1835 No.167. John T. Lewis native USA emigrated 1830 married with family 4 persons...   John T. Lewis

2920. District of Bevil Aug 29, 1835 No.168. James Chessher native USA emigrated 1824 married with family 8 persons   James Chessher

2921. District of Bevil Aug 29, 1835 No.169. Daniel Chessher native USA emigrated 1829 married with family 2 persons   Daniel Chessher

2922. San Augustine Aug 31, 1835 No.170. Isaac Caradine native USA emigrated 1827 married with family 3 persons...   Isaac Caradine

2923. San Augustine Sep 1, 1835 No.171. Charles Roberts native USA married   Charles Roberts

2924. San Augustine Sep 1, 1835 No.172. James Elder native USA emigrated 1831 single... James Elder

2925. San Augustine Sep 1, 1835 No.173. Samuel Robinson native USA emigrated 1831 single...
Samuel Robinson

2926. San Augustine Sep 1, 1835 No.174. Mary Ann Bowlin native USA emigrated 1826 with family 3 persons...   Mary Ann Bowlin

2927. San Augustine Sep 1, 1835 No.175. James Lesley native USA emigrated 1833 married with family 2 persons...   James Lesley

2928. San Augustine Sep 1, 1835 No.176. George Carter native USA emigrated 1824 married with family 3 persons...   George Carter

2929. San Augustine Sep 1, 1835 No.177. Elizabeth Grayham native USA widow with family 7 persons...
Elizabeth Grayham

2930. San Augustine Sep 1, 1835 No.178. R.B. Haley native USA emigrated 1822 married with family 2 persons...   R.B. Haley

2931. San Augustine Sep 1, 1835 No.179. Winney Jewel native USA emigrated 1830 married with 5 persons...   Winney Jowel

2932. San Augustine Sep 1, 1835 No.180. Cornelius Santos native Mexico single...   Cornelius Santos

2933. San Augustine Sep 1, 1835 No.181. Sidney O. Pennington native USA emigrated 1831 single...
Sydney O. Pennington

2934. San Augustine Sep 1, 1835 No.182. Samuel Strickland native USA emigrated 1821 married with family 5 persons   Samuel X Strickland

2935. San Augustine Sep 1, 1835 No.183. Robert Carodine native USA emigrated 1827 single...
Robert Carodine

2936. San Augustine Sep 1, 1835 No.184. Martin Lacey native USA emigrated 1831 single...
Martin X Lacey

2937. San Augustine Sepr 1, 1835 No.185. John C. Burk native USA emigrated 1820 married with family 7 persons...   John C. Burke

2938. San Augustine Sep 1, 1835 No.186. Presious Seets native USA emigrated 1834 widow with family 2 persons   Precious X Seets

2939. San Augustine Sepr 1, 1835 No.187. Robert O. Lusk native USA emigrated 1833 married with family two persons...   Robert O. Lusk

2940. San Augustine Sep 1, 1835 No.188. William Smith native USA emigrated 1831 married with family 3 persons...   William Smith

2941. San Augustine Sep 1, 1835 No.189. Shelby Turnage native USA emigrated 1831 single...
Shelby Turnage

2942. San Augustine Sept 1, 1835 No.190. Frederick Anthony native USA emigrated 1830 single...
Frederick Anthony

2943. San Augustine Sep 1, 1835
No.191. James C. Sanders native USA
emigrated 1832 single...
        James C. Sanders

2944. San Augustine Sepr 1, 1835
No.192. Edwin Smith native USA emigrated 1833 married with family five
persons...   Edwin Smith

2945. San Augustine Sep 1, 1835
No.193. Daniel Anding native USA
emigrated 1834 single...
        Daniel X Anding

2946. San Augustine Sep 1, 1835
No.194. Jane Wilson native USA emigrated 1833 widow with family eleven
persons...   Jane X Wilson

2947. San Augustine Sep 1, 1835
No. 195. Levi Sanders native USA
emigrated 1831 single...
        Levi Sanders
2948. San Augustine Sep 1, 1835
No.196. Alexander C. Thornburgh native USA emigrated 1829, married
with family five   persons...
        Alex C. Thornburgh

2949. San Augustine Sep 1, 1835
No.197. Thomas Yates native USA
emigrated 1832, married with family
seven persons...   Thos Yates

2950. San Augustine Sep 1, 1835
No.198. Swanson Yarbrough native USA
emigrated 1832 single...
        Swanson X Yarbrough
2951. San Augustine Sep 1, 1835
No.199. William H. Sewall native USA
emigrated 1826, married with family
two persons...   Wm H. Sewall

2952. San Augustine Sep 1, 1835
No.200. William Sinclair native USA
emigrated 1830 married with family
ten persons...   Wm Sinclair

2953. San Augustine Sep 1, 1835
No.201. E.D. Chinneth native USA
single   E.D. Chineth

2954. San Augustine Sep 1, 1835
No.202. Arthur Willis native USA
emigrated 1823 married with family 5
persons...   Arthur X Willis

2955. San Augustine Sep 1, 1835
No.203. Cornelius Crenshaw native
USA emigrated 1831 married with
family seven persons...
        Cornelius X Crenshaw

2956. San Augustine Sep 1, 1835
No.204. Daniel Crenshaw native USA
emigrated 1831 married with family
three persons... Daniel Crenshaw

2957. San Augustine Sep 1, 1835
No.205. Green Reaves [Reanes] native
USA emigrated 1830, married with
family five persons...Green X Reaves

2958. San Augustine   Sep 1, 1835
No.206. Thomas Loban [Lobar] native
USA emigrated 1831 married with
family two persons...Thomas X Loban

2959. San Augustine Sep 1, 1835
No.207. John V. Cherry native USA
emigrated 1833 married with family
three persons...   John V. Cherry

2960. San Augustine   Sep 1, 1835
No.208. Smith R. Cherry native USA
emigrated 1830 single...
        Smith R. X Cherry

2961. San Augustine   Sep 1, 1835
No.209. David Cherry emigrated 1830
married with family six persons...
        David Cherry

2962. San Augustine Sep 1, 1835
No.210. Elizabeth Michell native USA
emigrated 1830 widow with family two
persons   Elizabeth X Mitchell

2963. San Augustine   Sep 1, 1835
No.211. Jonathan Russell native USA
emigrated 1833 married with family
four persons...   Jonathan Russell

2964. San Augustine Sep 1, 1835
No.212. James T.P. Irvin native USA
emigrated 1830 married with family
three persons... James T.P. Irvine

2965. San Augustine   1 Sep 1835
No.213. Alexander F. Albright native
USA emigrated 1831 married with
family three persons...
        Alexander F. Allbright

2966. San Augustine   1 Sep 1835
No.214. Agaton Carro native Mexico
single   X Carro

2967. San Augustine   Sep 1, 1835
No.215. Anistacyo Carro native Mexico single...   Anistacio X Carro

2968. San Augustine   Sep 1, 1835
No.216. Jose Ybarbo native Mexico
married with family seven persons...
         Jose X Ybarbo

2969. San Augustine   Sept 1, 1835
No.217. Jose Francisco Sanches native Mexico single...
         Jose Francisco X Sanches

2970. San Augustine   Sep 1, 1835
No.218. John Norris native USA married with family six persons...
         John Norris

2971. San Augustine   Sep 1, 1835
No.219. Sarah H. Norris native USA
widow with family four persons...
         Sarah H. Norris

2972. San Augustine   Sep 1, 1835
No.220. Maria Jesusa de los Santos
Coy native Mexico widow with family
6 persons
  Maria Jesusa de los X Santos Coy

2973. San Augustine   Sep 1, 1835
No.221. Gertrudes Proselo native
Mexico widow with family six persons
  Gertrudes X Prosela

2974. San Augustine   Sep 1, 1835
No.22. Nimrod Smith native USA emigrated 1826 married with family
three persons...   Nimrod X Smith

2975. San Augustine   Sep 1, 1835
No.223. Juan Polvadore emigrated
1785 married with family seven
persons...   Juan X Polvadore

2976. San Augustine   Sep 1, 1835
No.224. Thomas Morris native USA
emigrated 1803 married with family
six persons...   Thomas Norris

2977. San Augustine Sep 1, 1835
No.225. Henry N. Quirk native Mexico
married with family two persons...
         Henry N. Quirk

2978. San Augustine   Sep 1, 1835
No.226. Richard B. English native
USA emigrated 1827 single...
         Richard B.English

2979. San Augustine   Sep 1, 1835
No.227. Benjamin Odle native USA
emigrated 1825 single...
         Benjamin Odell

2980. San Augustine   Sep 1, 1835
No.228. Susannah McKelvey native USA
emigrated 1824 widow with family
three persons...Susannah X McKelvy

2981. San Augustine   Sep 1, 1835
No.229. William McFaden native USA
emigrated 1833 married with family
three persons...William X McFadden

2982. San Augustine   Sep 1, 1835
No.230. Elithabeth McIntyre native
USA emigrated 1829 widow with family
nine persons...Elithabeth X McIntyre

2983. San Augustine   Sep 1, 1835
No.231. Polly McVay native USA emigrated 1829 widow with family two
persons...   Polly X McVay

2984. San Augustine   Sep 1, 1835
No.232. Marryweather Ussery native
USA emigrated 1832 single...
         Marryweather X Ussery

2985. San Augustine   Sep 1, 1835
No.233. Hesekiah McKelvy native USA
emigrated 1824 married with family
six persons... Hesekiah X McKelvy

2986. San Augustine   Sep 1, 111835
No.234. Elithabeth Melton native USA
emigrated 1824 widow with family
three persons...Elithabeth X Melton

2987. San Augustine Sep 1, 1835
No.235. Choyl Freeland native USA
emigrated 1827 married with family
three persons... Choyl Freeland

2988. San Augustine Sepr 1, 1835
No.236. William Hines native USA
emigrated 1823 married with family
7 persons... William Hines

2989. San Augustine Sep 1, 1835
No.237. Thomas McIntyre native USA
emigrated 1829 single...
Thomas McIntyre

2990. San Augustine Sep 1, 1835
No.238. Washington Orsment native
USA emigrated 1831 single...
Washington Orsment

2991. San Augustine Sepr 1, 1835
No.239. Elbert Hines native USA
emigrated 1823 married with family
six persons... Elbert Hines

2992. San Augustine Sep 1, 1835
No.240. Almone Harrison native USA
single Almond Harrison

2993. San Augustine Sepr 1, 1835
No.241. Minor Blossom native USA
emigrated 1831 single...
Minor Blossom

2994. San Augustine Sep 1, 1835
No.242. John Bryan native USA emigrated 1830 single... John Bryan

2995. San Augustine Sep 1, 1835
No.243. Henry Morgan native USA
emigrated 1829 single...
Henry Morgan

2996. San Augustine Sep 1, 1835
No.243. Harvey Hall native USA em-
grated 1829 single...Harvey X Hall

Volume 61. Milams's Colony at Mina, Unfinished Business
Talbot Chambers, Commissioner. 1835

3001. Mina 16 June 1835
No.1 Samuel W.Hamilton married with
a family... Samuel W. Hamilton

3002. Mina 16 June 1835
No.2. Stephen Townsend married with
family [not signed]

3003. Mina -- September 1835
No.3. Abner Spears married with
family... [not signed]

3004. Mina [no date]
No.5. Moses T. Martin single...
Moses T. Martin

3005. Mina [no date]
No.6. William Oldham single...
William Oldham

3006. Mina 16 July 1835
No.7. Logan Vandever single...
Logan Vandever

3007. Mina 16 July 1835
No.8. Nathan Mitchell single...
Nathan Mitchell

3008. Mina 1835
No.9. D.C. Barrett married with
family... [Not signed]

3009. Mina September 1835
No.21. Burleson Gage [signed blank]

[This volume also contains 65 completed Titles which appear in The Index
of Spanish Titles. They were all done at Mina (Bastrop) by Commissioner
Talbot Chambers]

Volume 62. Burnet's Colony. Unfinished Business
George Antonio Nixon, Commissioner, 1835

3011. Nacogdoches   May 8, 1835
No.1. Maria Gertru Herrero native
Mexico, widow with 3 children...
          Maria Ger X Herrera

3012. Nacogdoches   Feb 9, 1835
No.2. John F. Ryan native USA
single...   John F. Ryan

3013. Nacogdoches   March 21, 1835
No.3. Nicholas Adolfo Sterne native
Germany, married with family 4 per-
sons...   Nicolas Adolfo Sterne

3014. Nacogdoches   Oct 7, 1835
No.4. Eleanor Bradley native Ireland
with family 5 childlren...
          Eleanor X Bradley

3015. Nacogdoches   April 29, 1835
No.5. William Hampton native USA
with wife and 7 children...
          Wm Hampton

3016. Nacogdoches   June 11, 1835
No.6. Hance[?] C. Hamilton native
USA with wife...   H.C. Hamilton

3017. Nacogdoches   May 6, 1835
No.7. Haywood Hudson Hall native
USA...   Haywood Hudson Hall

3018. Nacogdoches   May 25, 1835
No.8. William Cheairs native USA
single...   William X Cheairs

3019. Nacogdoches   May 25, 1835
No.9. Jeremiah Courtnay native USA
married with family four persons...
          J.G. Courtnay

3020. Nacogdoches   May 21, 1835
No.10. Irdell D. Thomas native USA
married with wife and two children
          I.D. Thomas

3021. Nacogdoches   May 23, 1835
No.11. Durham Avent native USA has
come with children...
          Durham A[vent]

3022. Nacogdoches   April 13, 1835
No.12. John R. Taylor native USA
single...   John R. Taylor
226

3023. Nacogdoches   Dec 6, 1834
No.13. Ignacio Sanchez native Mexico
with wife...   Ignacio X Sanchez

3024. Nacogdoches   July 8, 1835
No.14. Robert Potter native USA with
family...   Robt Potter

3025. Nacogdoches   June 2, 1835
No.15. Thomas Y. Buford native USA
single   Thos Y. Buford

3026. Nacogdoches   April 13, 1835
No.16. Maxime Salazar native Mexico
with wife & 4 children...
          Maxime Salazar

3027. Nacogdoches   May 21, 1835
No.17. William C. Bullock native USA
wife and 4 children...
          Wm C. Bullock

3028. Nacogdoches   May 25, 1835
No.18. John Cheairs native USA family of three persons... John Cheairs

3029. Nacogdoches   May 25, 1835
No.19. Samuel Cheairs native USA
single...   Samuel Chaiirs

3030. Nacogdoches   Sep 26, 1835
No.20. William Miller native USA
wife and 8 children... Wm Miller

3031. Nacogdoches   Sep 12, 1835
No.21. John F. Downs native USA with
family...   John F. Downs

3032. Nacogdoches   June 10, 1835
No.22. George Neill native USA with
family of six persons...George Neill

3033. Nacogdoches   Aug 15, 1835
No.23. Jeremiah Enochs native USA
with family, widower... J. Enochs

3034. Nacogdoches   30 March 1835
No.24. Thomas Maxwell native USA
with family six persons...
          Thos Maxwell

3035. Nacogdoches   Sep 9, 1835
No.25. Richard Mooney native USA
with family... Richard Mooney

3036. Nacogdoches   May 19, 1835
No.26. Henry C. Clark native USA
with wife...   Henry C. Clark

3037. Nacogdoches   Nov 7, 1834
No.27. Henry Martin native USA with
wife and five persons...
                    Henry Martin

3038. Nacogdoches   Aug 18, 1835
No.28. John Mariwather native USA
came with family...John Mariwather

3039. Nacogdoches   Aug 29, 1835
No.29. Samuel Raimondo native USA
with family...   Samuel Raimond

3040. Nacogdoches   May 4, 1835
No.30. Augustin Padillo native this
Dept. single...Augustin X Padillo

3041. Nacogdoches   Aug 16, 1835
No.31. Rufus Holman native USA with
family   Rufus Holman

3042. Nacogdoches   June 4, 1835
No.32. Joseph Nations native USA
single...   Joseph Nations

3043. Nacogdoches   Aug 16, 1835
No.33. James F. Fowler native USA
with family...   Jame F. Fowler

3044. Nacogdoches   June 17, 1835
No.34. Jose' San Miguel native this
place single... Jose X San Miguel

3045. Nacogdoches   Dec 8, 1834
No.35. James Cooke native USA with
wife...   James Cook

3046. Nacogdoches   May 25, 1835
No.36. Joab Kirby native USA with
family three persons...Joab X Kirby

3047. Nacogdoches   Aug 22, 1835
No.37. Patrick Obriant native USA
with family...   Patrick O'Briant

3048. Nacogdoches   Aug 19, 1835
No.38. John T. Greenwood native USA
family of wife & children...
                John T. Greenwood

3049. Nacogdoches   June 3d 1835
No.39. William Jones native USA
single...   William Jones

3050. Nacogdoches   Sep 2, 1835
No.40. Bn L. Reed native USA with
family...   B.L. Reed

3051. Nacogdoches   May 26, 1835
No.41. James Grant native USA
single...   James Grant

3052. Nacogdoches   May 23, 1835
No.42. Stephen George native USA
single...   Stephen George

3053. Nacogdoches   Aug 22, 1835
No.43. Josiah M. King native USA
family of wife & children...
                J.M. King

3054. [Nacogdoches]
No.44. James T. Jones native USA
with family [nothing more]

3055. Nacogdoches   May 26, 1835
No.45. George V. Lusk native USA
with family of 5 persons...
                G.V. Lusk

3056. Nacogdoches   Sep 7, 1835
No.46. Robert Craig native USA came
with family...   Robert Craig

3057. Nacogdoches   May 22, 1835
No.47. John P. Lawson native USA
with wife & one child...
                John P. Lawson

3058. Nacogdoches   14 Aug 1835
No.48. James N. Garnett native USA
with family... James N. Garnett

3059. Nacogdoches   May 26, 1835
No.49. Amos Ladd native USA
single...   Amos Ladd

3060. Nacogdoches   Aug 15, 1835
No.50. Patrick R. McMullin with
family... Patrick R. McMullin

3061. Nacogdoches   May 15, 1835
No.51. Bartholomew Gates native USA
wife and 8 chidren...
          Bartholomew Gates

3062. Nacogdoches   May 15, 1835
No.52. Juan Antonio Ybarbo native
this territory, family of 3 persons
     Juan Antonio X Ybarbo

3063. Nacogdoches   May 11, 1835
No.53. William Ragland native USA
single   Wm Ragland

3064. Nacogdoches   June 11, 1835
No.54. Joel B. Crain native USA
single...   Joel B. Crain

3065. Nacogdoches   May 23. 1835
No.55. Michael Costley native USA
family two persons...
          Michael Costley

3066. Nacogdoches   April 3, 1835
No.56. John T. Copeland native USA
with wife and 2 children...
          John T. Copeland

3067. Nacogdoches   April 13, 1835
No.57. Solomon R. Peck native USA
single   S.R. Peck

3068. Nacogdoches   May 15, 1835
No.58. George Rawson native USA
single...   George Rawson

3069. Nacogdoches   April 20, 1835
No.59. William J. Wills native USA
with wife & 4 children...W.J. Wills

3070. Nacogdoches   May 26, 1835
No.60. Armstead White native USA
single...   Armstead White

3071. Nacogdoches   May 20, 1835
No.61. Chrisley Shultz native USA
wife and 6 children...
          Chrisley Shults

3072. Nacogdoches   May 25, 1835
No.62. Randolph DSpain native USA
single   Randolph D'Spain

3073. Nacogdoches   May 8, 1835
No.63. Elias K. Davis native USA
wife and 4 children...
          Elias K. Davis

3074. Nacogdoches   Nov 18, 1834
No.64. Andrew P. Cunningham native
USA wife and 2 children...
          A.P. Cunningham

3075. Nacogdoches   May 23, 1835
No.65. John Cheairs native USA
single...   John X Cheairs

3076. Nacogdoches   June 2, 1835
No.66. Sydney O. Pennington native
USA single...Sydney O. Pennington

3077. Nacogdoches   May 5, 1835
No.67. Jacob Mast native USA with
wife and seven children...
          Jacob Mast

3078. Nacogdoches   Aug 16, 1835
No.68. John S. Hoover native USA
with family...   John S. Hoover

3079. Nacogdoches   June 17, 1835
No.69. John W. Pait native USA married with family seven persons...
          John W. Pait

3080. Nacogdoches   May 18, 1835
No.70. John Pankins native USA
single...   John Pankins

3081. Nacogdoches   June 13, 1835
No.71. Josiah Pruit native USA with
family of 2 children...Josiah Pruit

3082. Nacogdoches   June 1, 1835
No.72. Jose' Ybarbo native USMex
widower family of 6 persons...
          Jose' X Ybarbo

3083. Nacogdoches   May 29, 1835
No.73. William J. Shields native USA
single...   William J. Shields

3084. Nacogdoches   Oct 18, 1834
No.74. Green B. Brewer native USA
family of wife & 5 children...
          Green B. Brewer

3085. Nacogdoches   Nov 7, 1834
No.75. Dennis B. Burts native USA
family of wife...Dennis B. X Burts

3086. Nacogdoches   May 21, 1835
No.76. Benjamin Anderson native USA
with family...   Ben Anderson

228

3087. Nacogdoches   May 20, 1835
No.77. Robert G. Cartwright native
USA single...   R.G. Cartwright

3088. Nacogdoches   Jan 26, 1835
No.78. Eliphalet Rollins native USA
family of 6 children...
      Eliphalet Rollins

3089. Nacogdoches   Oct 8, 1834
No.79. William Barnhill native USA
wife and 2 children... Wm Barnhill

3090. Nacogdoches   Oct 11, 1834
No.80. Juan J. Hammonds native USA
wife and 3 children...
      Juan J. Hammonds

3091. Nacogdoches   April 27, 1835
No.81. Wm F. Sparks native USA wife
and 6 children... Richard Sparks

3092. Nacogdoches   Oct 18, 1834
No.82. Jesse W. Stoddard native USA
wife and 2 children...
      J.W. Stoddard

3093. Nacogdoches   May 26, 1835
No.83. James Bradshaw native USA
with wife and 2 children...
      James Bradshaw

3094. Nacogdoches   Oct 19, 1835
No.84. William F.C. Butler native
USA with family...
      William F.C. X Butler

3095. Nacogdoches   May 11, 1835
No.85. Joseph Polvador native USA
with wife and 4 children...
      Jos X Polvador

3096. Nacogdoches   May 25, 1835
No.86. Robert Rogers Senr native USA
family 6 persons...
      Robert Rogers Sen

3097. Nacogdoches   June 1, 1835
No.87. William Ratliff native USA
with wife...   W. Ratliff

3098. Nacogdoches   May 26, 1835
No.88. Elbert Hines native USA wife
and 7 children...   Elbert Hines

3099. Nacogdoches   June 3, 1835
No.89. James L. Cheatham native USA
single   James L. Cheatham

3100. Nacogdoches   Aug 28, 1835
No.90. William R. Wilson native USA
wife and one child...   Wm R. X
Wilson

3101. Nacogdoches   Feb 20, 1835
No.91. Eusebio Davis native Louisiana with wife...   Eusebio X Davis

3102. Nacogdoches   Jan 19, 1835
No.92. Benjamin Van Sickle native
USA single...Benjamin Van Sickle

3103. Nacogdoches   March 31, 1835
No.93. Francisco Procela native US
of Mexico with wife and 5
children...   Francisco X Procela

3104. Nacogdoches   May 26, 1835
No.94. Bethany Rogers native USA
widow with family 6 persons...
      Bethany X Rogers

3105. Nacogdoches   June 10, 1835
No.95. Thomas Fields native USA
single...   Thomas Field

[Nos. 96 through 97 have no
petitions]

3106. Nacogdoches   Feb 7, 1835
No.98. Luther Smith native USA
widower without children...
      Luther Smith

3107. Nacogdoches   30 March 1835
No.99. Jose' Antonio Sepulveda, son
of the Villa of San Carlos, Tamaulipas, married to a daughter of this
Villa of Nacogdoches with 8 children
3 sons and 5 daughters...
        Jose' Antonio Sepulveda

3108. Nacogdoches   May 4, 1835
No.100. Buckley Kimbrough native USA
[nothing further] Buckley Kimbrough

3109. Nacogdoches   Nov 10, 1835
No.101. Reuben McKenzie native USA
wife and 5 children...
        Reuben McKenzie

3110. Nacogdoches   April 28, 1835
No.102. Maria Dorotea Juanca[?] native Mexico, family of 3 children...
        Maria Dorotea X Junca[?]

3111. Nacogdoches   Sep 18, 1835
No.103. Jesse R. Jones [faded] wife
and children...   Jesse R. X Jones

3112. Nacogdoches   Sep 2, 1835
No.104. Henderson Simmons native USA
with family...   Henderson Simmons

3113. Nacogdoches   Oct 7, 1835
No.105. Gray B. King native USA wife
and 3 children...   G. King

3114. Nacogdoches   [no date]
No.106. Solomon Rozell
        [signed blank]

3115. Nacogdoches   April 29, 1835
No.107. Felix A. Richardson native
USA wife and 3 children...
        Felix A. Richardson

3116. Nacogdoches   April 28, 1835
No.108. Benson Risenhoover native
USA wife and 4 children...
        Benson Risenhoover

3117. Nacogdoches   April 24, 1835
No.109. Samuel Rodgers native USA
with wife...   Samuel Rogers

3118. Nacogdoches   April 3, 1835
No.110. Jose Antonio Rodriguez na-
230

tive Mexico wife and 2 children...
        Jose' Antonio Rodriguez

3119. Nacogdoches   Oct 8, 1834
No.112 Isaac Roberts native USA wife
and 8 children... Isaac X Roberts

3120. Nacogdoches   May 2, 1835
No.113. Juliano Basilio Sanches native Mexico single...
        Juliano Basilio X Sanches

3121. Nacogdoches   Oct 28, 1834
No.114. Jaime Richards native USA
single   James Richards

3122. Nacogdoches   April 25, 1835
No.115. John D. Bell native USA with
wife   John D. Bell

3123. Nacogdoches   April 13, 1835
No.116. Geo B. Brownrigg native USA
with wife and 5 children...
        G.B. Brownrigg

3124. Nacogdoches   Sep 10, 1835
No.117. Hiram Little native USA with
wife and 3 children...Hiram X Little

3125. Nacogdoches   Nov 13, 1834
No.118. Jorge L. Bledsoe native USA
wife and one child...
        George L. Bledsoe

3126. Nacogdoches   May 8, 1835
No.119. Elisha H.R. Willis native
USA with wife and 8 children...
        Elisha H.R. Wallis

3127. Nacogdoches   May 30, 1835
No.120. Andres Vasces native Mexico
single   Andres Vasques

3128. Nacogdoches May 21, 1834[sic]
No.121. Mary Thomas native USA widow
with family of thirteen individuals
        Mary Thomas

3129. Nacogdoches   May 1, 1835
No.122. Shadrack D. Thomas native
USA with wife and 4 children...
        Shadrack D. Thomas

3130. Nacogdoches   June 10, 1835
No.123. Cyrus W. Thompson native USA
single...   Cyrus W. Thompson

3131. Nacogdoches   April 13, 1835
No.124. Wiley S. Thomas native USA
single   W.S. Thomas

3132. Nacogdoches   April 4, 1835
No.125. Maria Concepcion Alanis native Mexico with one child...
     Maria Concepcion X Alanis

3133. Nacogdoches   Sep 16, 1835
No.126. Thos Hinds Duggan native USA
with wife and one child...
         Thomas Hinds Duggan

3134. Nacogdoches   May 25, 1835
No.127. Thomas Choate native USA
with family 5 persons...
         Thos Choate

3135. Nacogdoches   May 15, 1835
No.128. Francis Ramsdall native USA
with family 4 persons...
         Francis Ramsdall

3136. Nacogdoches   June 6, 1835
No.129. Besheba Blunt native USA
widow with family 2 persons...
         Basheba X Blunt

3137. Nacogdoches   Nov 18, 1834
No.130. John Grigsby native USA with
wife and 8 children... John Grigsby

3138. Nacogdoches   Nov 18, 1834
No.131. Elias Gilliland native USA
with wife and 7 children...
         Elias X Gilliland

3139. Nacogdoches   Oct 7, 1834
No.132. Andres Gonzales native
Comargo with wife and 7 children...
         Andres X Gonzales

3140. Nacogdoches   Sep 30, 1835
No.133. Thomas Grubbs native USA
single...   Thomnas Grubbs

3141. Nacogdoches   Feb 28, 1835
No.134. Uriah Gibson native USA with
wife   Uriah Gipson

3142. Nacogdoches   April 9, 1835
No.135. Aaron Cherry Senr native USA

wife and 6 children...
         Aaron X Cherry Senr

3143. San Augustine Sep 26, 1834
No.136. Thomas Cartwright native USA
with family 7 persons...
         Thomas Cartwright

3144. Nacogdoches   Nov 22, 1834
No.137. Jeremias Christ native USA
with wife...   Jeremiah Crist

3145. Nacogdoches   Nov 22, 1834
No.138. Isaac Christ native USA with
wife   Isaac X Crist

3146. Nacogdoches   Sep 25, 1835
No.139. Wiley Colwill native USA
with wife and 4 children...
         Wiley Colwill

3147. Nacogdoches   May 3, 1835
No.140. A.B. Carr native USA with
wife and 4 children... A.B. Carr

3148. Nacogdoches   June 21, 1835
No.141. Daniel Cleavland native USA
single   Daniel Cleveland

3149. Nacogdoches   June 20, 1835
No.142. Martin Cannon native USA
[blank]   Martin X Cannon

3150. Nacogdoches   April 4, 1835
No.143. Maria Salomi Cortes native
Mexico widow with one child...
         Maria Salomi X Cortes

3151. Nacogdoches   Oct 1, 1834
No.145. Claiborn Garrett single native USA   Claibaun Garrett

3152. Nacogdoches   March 30, 1835
No.146. Marcos Garcia native Mexico
wife and 7 children...
         Marcos X Garcia

3153. Nacogdoches   Sep 18, 1835
No.147. Champion Blythe native USA
came alone, married... C. Blythe

3154. Nacogdoches   Oct 28, 1834
No.148. Charles Richards native USA
with wife and 8 children...
         Charles Richards

3155. Nacogdoches   Sep 28, 1835
No.149. Philip Walker native USA
single...   Philip Walker

3156. Nacogdoches   Aug 1, 1835
No.150. Charity Eaton native USA
widow with family of nine children
        Charity X Eaton

3157. Nacogdoches   Aug 5, 1835
No.151. John B. Trenary native USA
with wife and 7 children...
        John B. X Trenary

3158. Nacogdoches   Sep 8, 1835
No.152. Thomas C. Denson native USA
with wife and 8 children...
        Thomas C. Denson

3159. Nacogdoches   Sep 14, 1835
No.153. Abraham Vanordstran native
USA with family 4 persons...
        Abraham X Vanordstran

3160. Nacogdoches   April 28, 1835
No.154. Henry B. Lary native USA
single...   Henry B. Lary

3161. Nacogdoches   Sep 10, 1835
No.155. William Little native USA
with wife and 4 children...
        William Little
3162. Nacogdoches   Sep 28, 1835
No.156. George A. Lamb native USA
with wife and 5 children...
        George A. X Lamb
3163. Nacogdoches   May 25, 1835
No.157. William Love native USA
single   William X Love

3164. Nacogdoches   Sep 18, 1835
No.158. George W. Lemoyne native USA
single...   G.W. Lemoyne

3165. Nacogdoches   July 28, 1835
No.159. Greenville Mills native USA
with wife and 2 children...
        Greenville Mills
3166. Nacogdoches   April 6, 1835
No.160. Esteban Mora native Mexico
with wife and 4 children...
        Esteban X Mora

3167. Nacogdoches   June 6, 1835
No.161. James Mullen native USA
single...   James X Mullen
232

3168. Nacogdoches   May 4, 1835
No.162. Maria Soledad Menchaca native of this Department widow with
one daughter...
By Atty L. Mortimer Thorn
        Maria Soledad Menchaca

3169. Nacogdoches   May 14, 1835
No.163. Stephan Boynton native USA
        Stephen Boynton

3170. Nacogdoches   October 3, 1835
No.164. Nevel Washburn native USA
with wife...   Nevel Washburn

3171. Nacogdoches   Sep 22, 1835
No.165. John Thomas native USA with
wife   John Thomas

3172. Nacogdoches   Sep 18, 1835
No.166. Stephen W. Blount native USA
married, came alone...
        Stephen W. Blount

3173. Nacogdoches   Decr 8, 1834
167. The widow Sarah Odell native
USA with family 4 children...
        Sarah X Odell

3174. Nacogdoches   Jan 13, 1835
No.168. William M. White native USA
single   William M. White

3175. Nacogdoches   May 11, 1835
No.169. William Nelson native USA
widower with 6 children...
        William X Nelson

3176. Nacogdoches   April 8, 1835
No.170. Richard Williams native USA
with wife...   Richard X Williams

3177. Nacogdoches   April 20, 1835
No.171. William R. Dalton native USA
with wife and 4 children...
        William Dalton
3178. Nacogdoches   May 15, 1835
No.172. Romaldo Trevino native Mexico single...   Romaldo X Trevino

3179. Nacogdoches   April 21, 1835
No.173. Theophilus Thomas native USA
single...   Theophilus Thomas

3180. Nacogdoches   April 4, 1835
No.175. James Thompson native USA

with wife and seven children [faded record]   James Thompson

3181. Nacogdoches   May 1, 1835
No.176. Oliver Peterson native USA
wife and one child...
    Olof Peterson

3182. Nacogdoches   April 13, 1835
No.177. Gavin Rigby native USA
single...   Gavin Rigby

3183. Nacogdoches   May 11, 1835
No.178. Felix F. Cordova native
Mexico single...
    Felix fro X Cordova

3184. Nacogdoches   April 23, 1835
No.179. John Faulk native USA with
wife and 6 children...   John Faulk

3185. Nacogdoches   June 1, 1835
No.180. Benjamin Freeman native USA
single   Benjamin Freeman

3186. Nacogdoches   Sep 15, 1834
No.181. Josue' Fulcher native USA
with wife and 1 child...
    Josue Fulcher

3187. Nacogdoches   April -- 1835
No.182. Dyer Blithe native USA
single...   Dyer Blythe

3188. Nacogdoches   Sep 11, 1835
No.183. M.B. Clark native USA
single...   M.B. Clark

3189. Nacogdoches   Sep 21, 1835
No.184. Jas H. Duncan native USA
married   James H. Duncan

3190. Nacogdoches   Jan 24, 1835
No.185. Hervey Whiting native USA
with wife and 6 children...
    Hervey Whiting

3191. Nacogdoches   Sep 15, 1835
No.186. William Mills native USA
with wife and 3[?] children...
    William Mills

3192. Nacogdoches   May 28, 1835
No.187. William Nash native USA wife
and 3 children...   William Nash

3193. Nacogdoches   Oct 20, 1834
No.188. Nathaniel Norris native Ireland with wife and 6 children...
    Nathaniel Norris

3194. Nacogdoches   Oct 1, 1834
No.189. Francisco Jacinto Villanova
of this Pueblo with wife and 3
children...
    Francisco Jacinto X Villanova

3195. Nacogdoches   April 27, 1835
No.190. Walter Ozbourne native USA
with wife...   Walter Ozbourn

3196. Nacogdoches   June 1, 1835
No.191. Oliver W. Ogden native USA
with family 4 persons...
    Oliver W. Ogden

3197. Nacogdoches   May 29, 1835
No.192. Sebastian Hogan native USA
single   Sebastian Hogan

3198. Nacogdoches   Nov 14, 1835
No.193. Isaiah Harlan native USA
with wife and nine children...
    Isaiah Harlan

3199. Nacogdoches   May 16, 1835
No.194. Charles C. Hieskell native
USA single...   Chs Hieskell

3200. Nacogdoches   Feb 7, 1835
No.195. William B. Hardin native USA
with wife and 3 children...
    W.B. Hardin

3201. Nacogdoches   Jan 26, 1835
No.196. Claibourne C. Houlhousen
native USA single...
    Claiborne C. Holshausen

3202. Nacogdoches   Jan 3, 1835
No.197. Agustin B. Hardin native USA
with wife and 2 children...
    A.B. Hardin

3203. Nacogdoches   Sepr 24, 1835
No.198. Jno Heffran native USA
single...   [not signed]

3204. Nacogdoches   Aug 15, 1835
No.199. Nath Halbert native USA
with wife and one child...
    Nathan Halbert

3205. Nacogdoches   Oct 5, 1834
No.200. Guillermo H. Smith native
Louisiana with wife and two
children...   Wm H. Smith

3206. Nacogdoches   Sep 11, 1835
No.201. Wm C. Stanley native USA
single...   Wm C. X Stanley

3207. Nacogdoches   Nov 10, 1835
No.202. William Sherman native USA
with wife and one child...
            William Sherman

3208. Nacogdoches   Sep 24, 1835
No.203. Nathan Wade native USA
single...   Nathan Wade

3209. [Nacogdoches]
No.204. Minister L. Milton native
USA single...   M.L. Milton

3210. Nacogdoches   Oct 3, 1835
No.205. Mary Drake native USA widow
with six children... Mary X Drake

3211. Nacogdoches   Sep 23, 1835
No.206. Henry Geough native USA with
wife and one child... Henry Geough

3212. Nacogdoches   Sept 28, 1835
No.207. Joseph Burns native USA
single...   Joseph Burns

3213. Nacogdoches   Oct 8, 1835
No.208. Whitney Britton native USA
with wife...   Whitney Britton

3214. Nacogdoches   Oct 9, 1835
No.209. Francis Bradley native USA
with family 3 persons...
            Francis X Bradley

3215. Nacogdoches   Sep 25, 1835
No.210. William Colwill native USA
single   William Colwill

3216. Nacogdoches   Sep 4, 1835
No.211. Edwd B. Davis native USA
with wife   Edward B. Davis

3217. Nacogdoches   Sep 18, 1835
No.212. Kincheon A. Wilborn native
USA married without family...
            K.A. Wilborn

3218. Nacogdoches   Sep 24, 1835
No.213. George W. Welsh native USA
single   Geo W. Welsh

3219. Nacogdoches   April 10, 1835
No.214. Joseph Squires native USA
with wife and 9 children...
            Joseph Squyres

3220. Nacogdoches   April 20, 1835
No.215. Jose' Andres Torres native
Peru with wife, a Mexican, and 5
children... Jose' Andres X Torres

3221. Nacogdoches   Dec 6, 1834
No.216. Francisco Xavier Mora native
Sn Nicholas with family of wife...
            Franco Xabier X Mora

3222. Nacogdoches   March 30, 1835
No.217. Jose' Vicente Micheli native
Arkansas with wife...
            J. Vicente Micheli

3223. Nacogdoches   April 23, 1835
No.218. Jackson H. Griffin native
USA with wife...   J.H. Griffin

3224. Nacogdoches   April 23, 1835
No.219. Benjamin M. Green native USA
with wife and one child...
            Benjamin M. Green

3225. Nacogdoches   Jan 13, 1835
No.220. Nathaniel Moss native USA
with wife and 2 children...
            Nathaniel Moss

3226. Nacogdoches   Sep 30, 1835
No.221. S.P. Johnson native USA with
family...   S.P. Johnson

3227. Nacogdoches   May 1, 1835
No.222. William Frisby native USA
with wife and 6 children...
            Wm X Frisby

3228. Nacogdoches   May 25, 1835
No.223. James Clarkson native USA
with family of 6 persons...
            James Clarkson

3229. Nacogdoches   April 8, 1835
No.224. John Cherry native USA with
wife and 3 children...John X Cherry

3230. Nacogdoches   Dec 4, 1835
No.224A. David Milhomme native USA
[otherwise blank]   David X Milhomme

3231. Nacogdoches   Oct 12, 1835
No.224B.   Wm A. X Corder
[otherwise blank]

3232. Nacogdoches   Oct 10, 1835
No.224C.   James B. Wilson
[otherwise blank]

3233. Nacogdoches   Oct 10, 1835
Mo.224D.   George W. Wilson
[otherwise blank]

3234. Nacogdoches   Feb 5, 1835
No.225. Juliana Maly native Germany
with family of 2 children...
    Juliana X Maly

3235. Nacogdoches   Jan 31, 1835
No.226. James Coale native USA with
wife and 10 children...Jaime X Coale

3236. Nacogdoches   Sep 14, 1835
No.227. Isaac Ruddell native USA
single...   Isaac Ruddell

3237. Nacogdoches   Oct 5, 1835
No.228. Robert Randolph native USA
single   Robert Randolph

3238. [No place or date]
No.229. William Harkins native USA
with family...   Wm Harkins

3239. San Augustine Sep 21, 1834
No.230. William English native USA
with family nine persons...
    Wm Inglish

3240. Nacogdoches   Aug 18, 1835
No.231. Eli W. Hall native USA with
family   Eli W. Hall

3241. Nacogdoches   Sep 23, 1835
No.232. Peter S. Thompkins native
USA with family...
    Peter S. Thompkins

3242. Nacogdoches   Oct 3, 1834
No.233. Santiago Dewitt native USA
with wife and one child...
    James Dewitt

3243. Nacogdoches   Dec 2, 1834
No.234. John Dickerson native USA
with wife and 6 children...
    John Dickerson

3244. Nacogdoches   Aug 26, 1835
No.235. John Roydon native USA with
family   John Roydon

3245. Nacogdoches   Nov 1, 1834
No.236. Jonathan C. Pool native USA
with wife and 5 children...
    Jonathan C. X Pool

3246. Nacogdoches   Sep 20, 1835
No.237. Jonathan Ping native USA
with wife and 2 children...
    Jonathan Ping

3247. Nacogdoches   Feb 2, 1835
No.238. George R. Peters native USA
single   George R. Peters

3248. Nacogdoches   Sep 10, 1835
No.239. James Patton native USA with
wife   James Patton

3249. Nacogdoches   Mar 30, 1835
No.240. Concesion Ybarbo native Mexico with wife and 4 children...
    Concesion X Ybarbo

3250. Nacogdoches   June 13, 1835
No.241. Hearrison Johnston native
USA single...Harrison X Johnston

3251. Nacogdoches   Oct 14, 1834
No.242. Ventura Tejeda native of the
State, single...   Ventura X Tejada

3252. Nacogdoches   Sep 14, 1835
No.243. Jas E. Watkins native USA
single   James E. Watkins

3253. Nacogdoches   April 27, 1835
No.244. Alexander A. Scott native
USA single...   A.A. Scott

3254. Nacogdoches   Oct 9, 1835
No.245. Woodrough Stublefield native
USA with wife and 8 children...
    Woodruff Stubblefield

3255. Nacogdoches   Dec 1, 1834
No.246. Charles H. Sims native USA
single   C.H. Sims

3256. Nacogdoches   Dec 29, 1834
No.247. John J. Stubblefield native
USA with wife and 2 children...
      John J. Stubblefield

3257. Nacogdoches   Nov 22, 1834
No.248. William Smith native USA
with wife...   William X Smith

3258. Nacogdoches   April 6, 1835
No.349. James Smith native USA with
wife and eleven children...
      James Smith

3259. Nacogdoches   Sepr 2, 1835
No.250. Saml Glenn native USA with
family   Samuel Glenn

3260. Nacogdoches   Jan 3, 1835
No.251. Thomas Cope native USA
single   Thos Cope

3261. Nacogdoches   Aug 20, 1835
No.252. James L. Glenn native USA
with family...   James L. Glenn

3262. Nacogdoches   Nov 10, 1834
No.253. George H. Duncan native USA
with family...   Jorge H. X Duncan

Volume 63. Zavala's Colony Unfinished Business
George Antonio Nixon, Commissioner. 1835.

3263. San Augustine   Sep 25, 1834
No.1. Clement Tutt native USA with
family nine persons...
      Clement X Tutt

3264. Nacogdoches   Oct 6, 1834
No.2. Samuel Whiting native USA with
wife and 3 children...
      Samuel Whiting

3265. Nacogdoches   May 28, 1835
No.3. Aaron Castleberry native USA
married with family eleven persons
      Aaron Castleberry

3266. Nacogdoches   May 28, 1835
No.4. William H. Castleberry native
USA married with family 6 persons...
      William H. Castleberry

3267. Nacogdoches   May 26, 1835
No.5. Pedro Castenada native this
Territory, married with family four
and wife...   Pedro X Castenada

3268. [No place or date]
No.6. Benjn McGahey native USA
married with family of wife and one
child...   Benjamin X McGahey

3269. Nacogdoches   May 1, 1835
No.7. William McDonald native USA
married with wife and 2 children...
      Wm McDonald

3270. Nacogdoches   June 5, 1835
No.8. Alexander McRae native USA
married with family eight persons...
      Alex McRae

3271. Nacogdoches   May 11, 1835
No.9. John Pool native USA single...
      John Pool

3272. Nacogdoches   May 27, 1835
No.10. Maria Estefania Padilla native this Province widow with family
of 5 persons...
      Mara Estefa X Padilla

3273. Nacogdoches   Dec 19, 1834
No.11. Hardy Pace native USA married
with family wife and 5 children...
      Hardy X Pace

3274. Nacogdoches   May 28, 1835
No.12. Samuel McParsons native USA
with wife...   Saml M.Parsons

3275. Naccogdoches   Dec 27, 1834
No.13. Thomas Parmer native USA with
wife   Thos Parmer

3276. Nacogdoches   May 22, 1835
No.14. Ira Parker native USA with
wife and 4 children...   Ira Parker

3277. Nacogdoches   Dec 2, 1834
No.15. Isaac Lindsey native USA with
wife and child...   Isaac Lindsey

3278. Nacogdoches   May 30, 1835
No.16. George Forbes native USA with
wife and child...   George Forbes

3279. Nacogdoches   June 2, 1835
No.17. Edward Fitzgerald native USA
single   Edward Fitzgerald

3280. Nacogdoches   May 28, 1835
No.18. Daniel Fuller native USA
married with family 5 persons...
Daniel Fuller
3281. Nacogdoches   Feb 28, 1835
No.19. Elizabeth Fulcher native USA
with family of 2 persons...
Elizabeth Fulcher

3282. Nacogdoches   Oct 3, 1835
No.20. Nathaniel Mix native USA
single...   Nathaniel Mix

3283. Nacogdoches   July 10, 1835
No.21. Archibald McLaughlin native
USA with family... A. McLaughlin

3284. Nacogdoches   June 18, 1835
No.22. William Lewis native USA
married with wife and 2 children...
William X Lewis
3285. Nacogdoches   Sepr 29, 1835
No.23. Alfred McLaughlin native USA
single   Alfred McLaughlin

3286. Nacogdoches   March 3, 1835
No.24. Alexander McLeod native USA
with wife and 2 children...
Alex McLeod
3287. Nacogdoches   Jan 31, 1835
No.25. Frederic Miller native USA
married with wife and 7 children...
Fredric X Miller
3288. Nacogdoches   June 24, 1835
No.26. Lorenzo de Zavala Junr native
Mexico single...
Lorenzo de Zavala Junr

3288A.San Augustine Sept 26, 1834
No.27. Stephen P. Wilson native USA
with my family six persons...
S.P. Willson

3289. Nacogdoches   April 13, 1835
No.28. Polly Youngblood native USA

widow with family of eight children
Polly X Youngblood

3290. Nacogdoches   April 13, 1835
No.29 Elizabeth Williams native USA
widow with 2 children...
Elizabeth X Williams

3291. Nacogdoches   April 13, 1835
No.30. Stephen Williams native
USA widower with 5 children...
Stephen Williams

3292. San Augustine Sepr 24, 1834
No.31. John S. Rummel single native
USA   John Rumel

3293. San Augustine Sep 25, 1834 No
James Davis native USA single...
J. Davis

3294. Nacogdoches   March 30, 1835
No.33. Miguel Ybarvo native this
Villa of Nacogdoches family of wife
and four children...
Miguel X Ybarvo

3295. Nacogdoches   April 13, 1835
No.34. Martin B. Lewis native USA
wife and 5 children...
Martin B. Lewis

3296. Nacogdoches   May 30, 1835
No.35. James McMahon native USA with
wife   James R[?] McMahon

3297. Nacogdoches   Feb 9, 1835
No.36. John G. Pemberton native USA
with family of wife and five
children... [Nothing further]

3298. Nacogdoches   March 31, 1835
No.37. Alexander Porter native USA
married with wife...
Alexander Porter
3299. Nacogdoches   April 13, 1835
No.38. Samuel S.Lewis native USA
came with wife and seven children...
Samuel S. Lewis
3300. Nacogdoches   April 24, 1835
No.39. Loreno Taylor Lewis native
USA widow with 2 children...
Loreno Taylor X Lewis

3301. Nacogdoches   April 21, 1835
No.40. Robert H. Smith native USA
single   Robt H. X Smith

3302. Nacogdoches   June 4, 1835
No.41. James Hughes native USA
single...   James Hughes

3303. [Incomplete]
No.42. Thos C. Holt native USA

3304. Nacogdoches   June 10, 1835
No.43. John McCleod native USA
single...   John McCleod

3305. Nacogdoches   June 6, 1835
No.44. William S. Mussett native USA
single...   William S. Mussett

3306. Nacogdoches   Feb 16, 1835
No.45. Edmundo Morrison native USA
with wife and 4 children...
     Edmund X Morrison

3307. Nacogdoches   Dec 29, 1834
No.46. John McGaffy native USA with
wife and 3 children...
     John McGaffey

3308. Nacogdoches   June 9, 1835
No.47. James Michell native USA
single...   James Michell

3309. Nacogdoches   May 27, 1835
No.48. Mastain S. Ussery native USA
with wife...   Matain S. Ussery

3310. Nacogdoches   May 27, 1835
No.49. Nancy Ussery native USA widow
with family of 4 persons...
     Nancy X Ussery

3311. Nacogdoches   June 5, 1835
No.50. Daniel Joyner native USA
married with family six persons...
     D. Joyner

3312. Nacogdoches   Sep 27, 1834
No.51. Isabella Hanks native USA
with family two persons...
     Isabella X Hanks

3313. Nacogdoches   Apr 5, 1835
No.52. William K. Hill native USA
with wife and 5 children...
     Wm K. Hill

3314. Nacogdoches   July 10, 1835
ETUP3. Stephen McLaughlin native USA
came with family...
     Stephen McLaughlin

238

3315. Nacogdoches   May 4, 1835
No.54. Benjamin Holt native USA with
family 9 persons...   B. Holt

3316. Nacogdoches   May 2, 1835
No.55. John Johnson native USA with
wife and 2 children...
     John X Johnson

3317. Nacogdoches   Oct 5, 1835
No.56. Wm B. Taylor [blank, nothing
more]

3318. Nacogdoches   May 15, 1835
No.57. John Droddy native USA with
wife and 4 children...John Droddy

3319. Nacogdoches   May 16, 1835
No.58. John Dooling native Ireland
widower with one daughter...
     John Dooling

3320. Nacogdoches   May 1, 1835
No.59. Aaron Ashworth native USA
with wife and 6 children...
     Aaron Ashworth

3321. Nacogdoches   May 2, 1835
No.60. Hiram Richley native USA with
wife and one child... Hiram Richley

3322. Nacogdoches   Feb 7, 1835
No.61. Thomas C. Holmes native USA
with wife and 3 children...
     Thos C. Holmes

3323. Nacogdoches   Dec 13, 1834
No.62. George W. Tevis native USA
single   George W. Tevis

3324. Nacogdoches   May 15, 1835
No.63. Barry West native USA with
wife and 4 children...Barry X West

3325. Nacogdoches   Oct 31, 1834
No.64. Richard Simmons native USA
with wife and 2 children...
     Richard Simmons

3326. Nacogdoches   Jan 28, 1835
No.65. John Stevenson native USA
with wife... John Stephenson

3327. Nacogdoches   July 29, 1835
No.66. John Noblit native USA
single...   John Noblit

3328. Nacogdoches   July 28, 1835
No.67. Stewart Newell native USA
with wife and one child...
              Stewart Newell

3329. Nacogdoches   May 26, 1835
No.68. Jose' Moran native USA with
wife and one child... Jose' X Moran

3330. Nacogdoches   March 7, 1835
No.69. Morris May native USA with
family of two persons...
              Morris May

3331. Nacogdoches   Dec 8, 1834
No.70. Wm Milspaugh native USA
single...   William Milspaugh

3332. Nacogdoches   Jan 31, 1835
No.71. Abner Ashworth native USA
with wife and 5 children...
              Abner X Ashworth

3333. Nacogdoches   June 18, 1835
No.72. Edmond Altig native USA with
wife and 2 children... Edmond Altig

3334. Nacogdoches   June 2, 1835
No.73. John Bowie native USA without
family, single...   John X Bowie
[Note added] Null because according
to Dr. Veatch land not vacant.

3335. Nacogdoches   Jan 24, 1835
No.74. Isabel Bridges native USA
widow with family 3 children...
              Isabel X Bridges

3336. Nacogdoches   Feb 28, 1835
No.75. David Burrell native USA with
wife   David Borell

3337. Nacogdoches   Dec 9, 1834
No.76. Isaac Bunker native USA with
wife and 9 children...Isaac Bunker

3338. Nacogdoches   May 30, 1835
No.77. William Smith native USA
single...   William Smith

3339. Nacogdoches   Dec 9, 1834
No.78. David Bullock native USA with
wife and 3 children...David Bullock

3340. Nacogdoches   [No date]
No.79. William S. Blount native USA

with wife and one child...
              Wm S. Blount

3341. Nacogdoches   May 30, 1835
No.80. James Allison native USA with
family 4 persons...   James Allison

3342. Nacogdoches   Jan 19, 1835
No.81. Hannah Allen native USA widow
with 3 children...   Hannah Allen
   By Attorney G.A. Pattillo

3343. Nacogdoches   Jan 19, 1835
No.82. Elisha Allen native USA
single...   Elisha Allen

3344. Nacogdoches   Oct 10, 1834
No.83. A.C. Allen native USA with
family of wife...   A.C. Allen

3345. Nacogdoches   Jan 31, 1835
No.84. William Ashworth native USA
with family of six persons...
              Guillermo X Ashworth

3346. Nacogdoches   May 27, 1835
No.85. Calvin Barco native USA with
spouse   Calvin Barco

3347. Nacogdoches   May 1, 1835
No.86. Bradley Garner native USA
with family of wife and seven
children... Bradley Garner

3348. Nacogdoches   May 31, 1835
No.87. Amos Smith native USA with
family wife and 2 children...
              Amos Smith

3349. Nacogdoches   June 9, 1835
No.88. George Fassett native USA
single... George A. Fassett

3350. Nacogdoches   Sep 26, 1834
No.89. James Bridges native USA with
family eight persons...James Bridges

3351. San Augustine Sep 27, 1834
No.90. John Bodine native USA with
family six persons... John Bodine

3352. Nacogdoches   May 29, 1835
No.91. John Barlington native USA
single ·   John Burlington

3353. San Augustine Sep 24, 1834
No.92. Squire Brown single native
USA...   Squire Brown

3354. Nacogdoches Dec 22, 1834
No.93. Alfred M. Bevil native USA
single   Alfred M. Bevil

3355. Nacogdoches Dec 22, 1834
No.94. Adan Byerley native USA
single...   Adan Byerley

3356. Nacogdoches May 6, 1835
No.95. Henry Cochran native USA
single...   Henry Cochran

3357. Nacogdoches Feb 4, 1835
No.96. John W. Cleghorn native USA
with family of wife and 2 children
          John W. Cleghorn

3358. Nacogdoches May 2, 1835
No.97. John Cole native USA with
wife and 5 children...John Cole

3359. Nacogdoches Feb 28, 1835
No.98. William Carr native USA with
family of wife and 8 children...
          William Carr

3360. Nacogdoches Jan 31, 1835
No.99. David Choat native USA
single...   David Choat

3361. Nacogdoches May 23, 1835
No.100. John Carson native USA widower with 8 children... John Carson

3362. Nacogdoches April 13, 1835
No.101. Greenberry Cook native USA
married with wife...
          Green Berry Cook

3363. Nacogdoches Oct 18, 1834
No.102. Robert Conn native USA with
wife and one child... Robert Conn

3364. Nacogdoches Oct 13, 1834
No.103. John M. Taylor native USA
single   John McTaylor

3365. Nacogdoches Dec 8, 1834
No.104. George W. Watson native USA
with wife and one child...
          Geo W. Watson

3366. Nacogdoches Jan 31, 1835
No.105. Jesse Dyson native USA with
wife and one child... Jesse X Dyson

3367. Nacogdoches June 18, 1835
No.106. Josiah Dyckes native USA
with wife and one child...
          Josiah Dyckes

3368. Nacogdoches June 17, 1835
No.107. Calaway Dean native USA
single...   Calaway Dean

3369. San Augustine Sep 22, 1834
No.108. Timothy Devore native USA
with family 4 persons...
          Timothy X Devore

3370. Nacogdoches July 6, 1835
No.109. Lewis Donaho native USA with
family 3 persons... Lewis Donaho

3371. Nacogdoches May 28, 1835
No.110. Juan M. Dorr native France
single   Juan M. Dor

3372. Nacogdoches May 28, 1835
No.111. Elias M. Eubanks native USA
with family six persons...
          Elias M. Eubanks

3373. Nacogdoches June 13, 1835
No.112. Manuela del Rios native this
Department, widow with 2 children...
          Manuela X del Rio

3374. Nacogdoches Dec 2, 1834
No.113. Samuel Ralph native Ireland
with wife and one child...
          Samuel Ralph

3375. Nacogdoches Oct 20, 1834
No.114. Widow Elizabeth Roebuck native USA with 4 children...
          Elizabeth X Roebuck

3376. Nacogdoches Jan 17, 1835
No.115. Henry Teal native USA single
          Henry Teal
3377. Nacogdoches June 2, 1835
No.116. Williston J. Talbot native
USA single... Williston J. Talbot

3378. Nacogdoches Jan 14, 1834
No.117. Josiah W. Turner native USA
with wife and one child...
          Jose' W. X Turner

3379. Nacogdoches   May 27, 1835
No.118. Joseph Roberts native USA
with wife and 2 children...
        Joseph Roberts

3380. Nacogdoches   Oct 29, 1834
No.119. Jaime W. Williams native USA
with wife and 10 children...
        James W. Williams
3381. San Augustine Sep 24, 1834
No.120. Owen Gaylor native USA with
family nine persons...
        Owen X Gaylor
3382. Nacogdoches   June 2, 1835
No.121. Jackson Todd native USA
single...   Jackson Todd

3383. Nacogdoches   March 24, 1835
No.122. William Willis native USA
with wife and 2 children...
        William X Willis
3384. San Augustine Sep 22, 1834
No.123. James Bridges native USA
with family 3 persons...
        James Bridges
3385. San Augustine Sep 26, 1834
No.124. Joseph Rowe native USA with
family 2 persons...   Joseph Rowe

3386. San Augustine Sep 27, 1835
No.125. Noel J. Roberts native USA
with family two persons...
        N.J. Roberts

3387. Nacogdoches   April 3, 1835
No.126. John Miller native USA with
wife and eleven children...
        John Miller

3388. Nacogdoches   Dec 29, 1834
No.127. James Mason native USA with
wife and 5 children...   James Mason

3389. Nacogdoches   May 28, 1835
No.128. Eugine Michamps native
France widower with family 4 child-
ren of both sexes
        Jn Egne Michamps

3390. Nacogdoches   Dec 29, 1834
No.129. James Jett native USA with
wife and 2 children... James Jett

3391. San Augustine Sep 24, 1834
No.130. William Jordan native USA
with family 6 persons...
        William Jordan

3392. Nacogdoches   June 2, 1835
No.131. Jno Jackson native USA
single... John Jackson

3393. Nacogdoches   Dec 12, 1834
No.132. William H. Irion native USA
with family of wife and 2 children
        William H. Irion

3394. San Augustine Sep 26, 1834
No.133. Jane Irvine native USA with
family three persons...
        Jane X Iravine

3395. Nacogdoches   June 8, 1835
No.134. John Sternes with family two
persons...   John Sternes

3396. Nacogdoches   May 30, 1835
No.135. Antonio Daniel Keller native
USA widower with 4 children...
        Antonio Dan. Keller

3397. Nacogdoches   June 5, 1835
No. 136. Joshua James native USA
with family 8 persons...
        Joshua James

3398. Nacogdoches   May 30, 1835
No.137. James T.P. Irvine native USA
married with family two persons...
        James T.P. Irvine

3399. Nacogdoches   May 28, 1835
No.138. Isaac Holman native USA
married with family 5 persons...
        Isaac Holman Jr

3400. Nacogdoches   June -- 1835
No.139. Murdoch A. McKensie native
USA with family 2 persons...
        M.A. MacKenzie

3401. Nacogdoches   Nov 1, 1834
No.140. Jese Terry native USA with
family of wife and 3 children...
        Jesse Terry

3402. Nacogdoches   Sep 27, 1834
No.141. Miguel Sacco native Genoa in
Italy with wife and 6 children...
        Michel Sacey

3403. San Augustine Sep 23, 1834
No.142. Antonio del Rio native USA
with family 7 persons...
        Antonio X del Rios

241

3404. Nacogdoches   Dec 2, 1835
No.143. Benjamin Richardson with
family of wife and eight children...
              Benjn Richardson

3405. Nacogdoches   Jan 25, 1835
No.144. William Shipp native USA
with famiily of wife...
              William Shipp

3406. Nacogdoches   Dec 11, 1834
No.145. John Stevenson native USA
with family of wife and 10 children
              John Stevenson

3407. Nacogdoches   Feb 4, 1835
No.146. Lewis Walker native USA with
family wife and 3 children...
              Lewis Walker

3408. Nacogdoches   July 28, 1835
No.147. Seth Swift native USA with
wife and 5 children... Seth Swift

3409. Nacogdoches   Jan 31, 1835
No.148. John C. Read native USA with
wife and·one child... John C. Read

3410. Nacogdoches   April l7, 1835
No.149. Henry Stagner native USA
married with wife and one child...
              Henry Stagner

3411. Nacogdoches   Dec 11, 1834
No.150. Gilbert Stevenson native USA
with wife and one child...
              Gilbert Stevenson

3412. Nacogdoches   Feb 3, 1835
No.151. Edwin Smith native USA with
wife and 3 children... Edwin Smith

3413. Nacogdoches   June 2, 1835
No.152. Thomas Hunt native USA without family...   Thomas Hunt

3414. Nacogdoches   Dec 10, 1834
Np.153. Obediah Hendrick native USA
single without family...
              Obah Hendrick

3415. Nacogdoches   May 28, 1835
No.154. Wesley W. Hanks native USA
single   Wesley W. Hanks

3416. Nacogdoches   May 28, 1835
No.155. Francis L. Green native USA
came with wife...   F.L. Green

3417. Nacogdoches   May 29, 1835
No.156. Christiana Garling native
USA widow without family...
              Christiana Garling

3418. Nacogdoches   May 28, 1835
No.157. James L. Gibson native USA
came with family...James L. Gibson

3419. Nacogdoches   May 28, 1835
No.158. John Gates native USA married with family...   John Gates

3420. Nacogdoches   May 2, 1835
No.159. David Garner native USA with
wife   David Garner

3421. Nacogdoches   Jan 14, 1835
No.160. John Gilchrist native USA
with wife and 7 children...
              Juan X Gilchrist

3422. San Augustine Sep 27, 1834
No.161. James S. Hanks native USA
with family 3 persons...
              James Hanks

3423. San Augustine Sep 24, 1834
No.162. George W.Jones native USA
with family 3 persons...
              George W. Jones

[No personal record in Nos. 163-165]

3424. Nacogdoches   Oct 31, 1834
No.166. William Guthrie native USA
with wife and 3 children...
              William Guthrie
3425. San Augustine Sep 23, 1834
No.167. Samuel Pharis native USA
with family 3 persons...
              Samuel Pharis
3426. Nacogdoches   May 28, 1835
No.168. John Moore native USA with
wife...   John M---

3427. Nacogdoches   May 6, 1835
No.169. John [J.] Lewis native USA
with family 3 persons...
              John T. Lewis

[The 4-digit numbers in the Unfinished Titles were assigned as indexing
numbers and are not found in the records in the Archives]

PERSONAL NAMES INDEX

Principal names in the Character Certificates are already in alphabetical order and have not been repeated. Officials and Attorneys are not completely indexed. The numbers used here are Document numbers.

Brake Daniel 2509
Breece see also Bruce
Brewer Green B 3084
Bridges Isabel 3335
Bridges James 3350,3384
Bridges John 2507
Bridges Robt 761
Brimberry Samuel 2768
Britton Whitney 3213
Brookfield Wm
529,1045,1625,1925,2019
Brooks Gilbert 1560
Brooks T.D. 1078
Brookes Thos D 1241
Brown David
1733,1821,2021
Brown Hiram 1934
Brown John M 2708
Brown Squire 3353
Brown Susan 215
Brown Wilson C 2620
Brownrigg George B
2505,3123
Bryan Jos 128,129
Bryan John 2994
Bryan Joseph
141,2005,2262
Buckes see Buckel
Buckley Tyre 2844
Buford Thomas Y 3025
Bullock David 2774,3339
Bullock James W
130,477,1185,2195
Bullock William C 3027
Bunker Isaac 3337
Burk see also Birk
Burk John C 2937
Burleson Edward 244
Burleson Elizabeth 239
Burleson James 243,244
Burleson Joseph 2806
Burleson Rebecca 242
Burleson Sarah 238
Burleson William 1960
Burlington John 3352
Burnapp 1877
Burnet Anne 246
Burnett James 2659
Burnett Nancy 249
Burnett William 2658
Burnham Jesse 2239
Burns Joseph 3212
Burny R.A. 512
Burrell David 364,3336
244

Burton Isaac 1828
Burtin Isaac W
1474,2627
Burts Dennis B 3085
Busby William 990
Bustin Benjamin 2836
Butler Ahira 2900
Butler William F.C.3094
Byerly Adan 3355
Byerley Martin 2911
Byerley William 2912
Cadena Ma Josefa 2758
Cage Benjamin F 2777
Cain James C 668,877
1001,1063,1273,1282
1768,2207,2699,2700
Calcote James 2512
Calderon Anto 915,1935
Calderon Guadalupe 2639
Caldwell William 1421
Canfield A.W. 318
Canfield Harriet 286
Canfield Henry 318
Cannon Martin 3149
Canoles John 1155
Cantun Maria de 2158
Caradine Isaac 2922
Carodine Robert 2935
Caraway Adam 2517
Carmon Juan 1205
Carmona Maria Getr 2640
Carmona Manl de 2638
Carr A.B. 3147
Carr William 698,3359
Carro Agaton 2966
Carro Anistacio 2967
Carroll Elizabeth 2653
Carroll John 1576,1596
Carson John 3361
Carter George 2928
Carter James 1684
Cartwright John 639
Cartwright M. 316,1869
Cartwright Mary 317
Cartwright Matthew 318
Cartwright RobertG 3087
Cartwright Thomas
213,3143
Casanoba Maria M.de S.
1843
Castenada Pedro 3267
Castleberry Aaron 3265
Castleberry Wm H 3266

Castley Michael 2740
Cazenave Jn Bt 116
Cazanova M.N.S. de 18
Chamar Cesario 1723A
Chamar Mara Jaca 2019
Chamber Jesse 915
Chambers Jesse H
1268,2095
Chambers Joseph L 2513
Chappell H.T. 2893
Chappell HumphreyT 1824
Chappell Sarah 2895
Cheairs John
3028,3075
Cheairs Samuel 3029
Cheairs William 3018
Cheatham James L 3099
Cherena Bautista 1935
Cherry Aaron Sr 3142
Cherry David 2961
Cherry John 3229
Cherry John V 2959
Cherry Smith R 2960
Chessher Daniel 2921
Chessher James 2920
Chevana Santiago 1935
Childers John 18
Chinneth E.D. 2953
Chisum Wm P
1389,2122,2781
Choate David
509,750,3360
Choat Edward 368
Choat John 237
Choate Thomas 3134
Christian Mary 378
Christy Ramsey 1335
Chumney John
327,705A,1290
Clark George 2003
Clark Henry B 169
Clark Henry C 3026
Clark James389,758,1314
Clark John 394
Clark M.B. 3188
Clark Susan S 387
Clark Wm 18,2723,2745
Clark Wm F 1580
Clarkson James 3228
Clay N. 1069
Cleghorn John W 3357
Cleveland Daniel 3148
Clifft Mary 402
Clifton William 2581

Good James D 2693
Goodman Rebecca 778
Goodrich B.B. 1125,2224
Goodwin Andrew W 2861
Gordon Andrew W 2861
Graham W.B. 210
Grant James 3051
Grason Isaac 810
Graves Philip 2890
Gray Ann 169
Grayham Elizabeth 2929
Green Benjamin M 3224
Green Francis L 3416
Greenway Jehu H 2882
Greenwood Garrison
  1080,145
Greenwood John T 3048
Greeson Isaac 318
Griffin Jackson H 3223
Grigsby E 2730
Grigsby John 3137
Grigsby Joseph 1934
Grigsby Nathaniel 1934
Grimes Jesse
  778,808,1319,1413
Grissett John 2523
Gristman David 2524
Groce Elizth 2003
Gross Christian 2898
Gross Larkin 1190
Grounds George 2899
Grubbs Thomas 3140
Guerra Ventura 1935
Guthtrie Wm
  2012,2689,3424
Gutierez Isabell 1705

Hagerty Thos J 18
Haile Jonas 2811
Halbert Nathan 3204
Haley Allen 2856
Haley Charles
  792,838,1401,2726
Haley John 210,237
838,1229,1401,1869,2866
Haley Maria Anna 2881
Haley Mark
  838,1041,1824,2889
Haley Michael 2076
Haley R.B. 2930
Haley Richard 5,393,601
833,838,984,1041,1218
1229,1732,1736,1832
1889,1890,2788

Haley Richard B 2787
Haley Susaannah 1869
Haley Thomas 2858
Hall Briton 478
Hall Burgess G 2664
Hall Eli W 3240
Hall Harvey 2996
Hall Haywood Hudson3017
Hall Wineford 848
Hamilton Hance C 3016
Hamilton Nathaniel 2602
Hamilton Samuel W 3001
Hammonds Juan J 3090
Hampton William 3015
Hancock Edwin 2266
Hanks Horatio 560
Hanks Isabella 3312
Hanks James S
  930,1958,2251,3422
Hanks Samuel G 2681
Hanks Sarah Anne 862
Hanks Wesley W 3415
Hanks Wyatt 236
Hardin Agustin B 3202
Harding F. 352
Harding John 237
Hardin William B 3200
Harding William J 2732
Hardwick Nathan 2701
Harelson A. 137
Harkins William 3238
Harlan Isaiah 3198
Harmon John 2859
Harness William 2782
Harper Benj J 1042
Harper Joseph 1383
Harrell Elisa 887
Harris Anthony 882
Harris John R 1862
Harris Martha 890
Harrison Almond 2992
Harrison Jonas 2837
Hart Wm 958
Harvey John 319
Haskell also Hieskell
Hatch Mary 900
Hatton Wm T 1722
Hawkins Thomas 1383
Heath Wm 1982
Heffron Jno 3203
Hegerty Dennis 318
Heley Michael 1840
Henderson Hugh 2754
Henderson Jesse 1401

Hendrick Edwin 2850
Hendrick Obediah
  2648,3414
Henly Thomas H 2706
Henry J.D. 683
Henry John D 2630
Hensley Mary 921
Hernandez Dolores 2637
Herrero Maria Gert 3011
Herring William 2531
Herron Nicholas 1877
Hertz Joseph 1960
Hiden Nathaniel 958
Hieskell Charles C
  899,2770,3199
Higgins John 2529
Hill William K 3313
Hillis John 2532
Hines Elbert 2991,3098
Hines William 2988
Hiroms S.C. 610,1360
Hiroms Samuel C
  728,870,1546
Hixon John B 2716
Hobson Henry H 2667
Hodges Nathaniel 2527
Hodges Newton C 1726
Hogan Sebastian 3197
Holland Francis
  1413,1851
Holloway Caleb
  1389,2122,2803
Holloway Daniel
  1389,2122,2835
Holloway Lewis
  1389,1725,2122,2778
Holloway Simpson
  1389,2122,2802
Holly John 2866
Holman Isaac 3399
Holman John H 958
Holman Rufus 3041
Holmes Isaac 958
Holmes Samuel 2690
Holmes Thomas C 3322
Holt B.417,588,843,1335
Holt Benjamin 2851,3315
Holt Thomas C 2165,3303
Hoover Henry 2703
Hoover John S 3078
Hopkins Daniel 2528
Horet see Horst
Hornsby Sarah 973
Horton A. 592,975

Mason J.W. 1212
Mason James
852,885,891,2611,3488
Mason John 2734
Mason Peter 2705
Mast see Most
Maxlen Samuel 2587
Maxwell Thomas 3034
May Morris 668,1273
1768,1979,2207,3330
Mayfield Alfred 2699
Mayo John 2551
May[s] Geo 599,770
Mayes Mary Anne 1280
May[s] Morris 668,877
1063,1273,1282,1768
1979,2207
Mays William 2545
Means Hugh 18
Means William 18,1286
Meirs William 1740
Melton Elizabeth 2986
Melton William 2714
Menard M.B.
256,473,728,1667
Menard Peter 1016
Menchaca Anton 480,1304
Menchaca Maria Dolores
2547
Menchaca Maria Soledad
3168
Mendenhall Peter 2543
Mendes Cateleno 1705
Mensola Antonio 1705
Merchant Berry 2870
Marchand Edward A 2869
Merchant John 83
Merchant John D
1749,2871
Meredith Thomas 2544
Merrell G. 1877
Merry John 1560
Metcalf H.T. 2546
Michamps John Egne
1684,3389
Micheli Jose' Vicente
3222
Michell Elizabeth 2962
Michell James 3308
Middleton Henry 2549
Milhomme David 3230
Miller Frederic 3287
Miller John 3387
Miller Solomon1316,1317
250

Miller William 3030
Mills Greenville 3165
Mills William 3191
Milspaugh William 3331
Milton Minister L 3209
Mitchell Asa 784
Mitchell Eliza. 2962
Mitchell James 210
Mitchell Nathan 3007
Mix Nathaniel 3282
Molina Cannon 1691
Monett Narcese 2662
Manson Lewis C 1901
Montone Soto 2588
Mooney Richard 3035
Moore Ester 1347
Moore John 3426
Moore S.D. 1421
Mora Esteban 3166
Mora Francisco Xavier
Mora Juan 1540
Morales Crecencio 2550
Moran James 1722
Moran Jose' 3329
Morehead John 2542
Moreland J.W. 565
Moreno Ynes 2739
Morgan Henry 2995
Morgan Hugh 18
Morgan Jas 1560
Morgan Joseph 872
Morgan W. 1388
Morris Alfred 2902
Morriss John 774
Morris Minerva 1363
Morrison Edmund 3306
Morrison James 2208
Morrow Elizabeth 1372
Morse Elisa W 1367
Morton Mary 1368
Moseley Socrates S 1373
Moses D. 852
Moss Nathaniel 3225
Most Jacob 1378,3077
Mott Franklin 2677
Mott William 2548
Mudd B.H. 1005
Muldoon Michael 1736
Mullen James 3167
Mullin Patrick 210
Murchison M. 808
Murchison Martin 309
Murphy Anne 1386

Murphy Pedro 2657
Murrell William 2586
Mussat William 526
Mussett William S 3305
Myers Elias 1940
Nash Hannah 1560
Nash William 3192
Nations Joseph 3042
Navaro M.C. 1935
Neill George 3032
Neely John M 210
Neilson Joseph 2553
Nelson S. 481
Nelson William 3175
Neville James 2069
Newell Stewart 3328
Newlon Thos 2625
Newlon Wm 2625
Newman Hannah 1487
Nexsen Katharine Mary
1489
Nichols Wm 2554,2686
Nicholson Mary Anne1493
Nicholson Stephen 1560
Noblit John 3327
Norris Jesse 2555
Norris John 1499,2970
Norris Nathaniel 3193
Norris Sarah H 2971
Norris Thomas 2976
Nujent Quintus Cin.2619
O'Boyle Edward 912
O'Boyle Juan 1509
O'Boyle Roderick 1594
Obriant Patrick 3047
Odell Benjamin 2979
Odle James 1516
Odell Sarah 3173
O'Docherty George 1801
Odum Birtan 18
Ogden Oliver W 3196
Oldham William 3005
Orr 870
Orsment Washington 2990
Owen Christine 1527
Ozbourn Walter 3195
Pace Albert Gallatin
1529
Pace Dempsey Council
1529
Pace Gideon 1529

Name	No.	Name	No.	Name	No.
Roblow P	636	San Miguel Jose'	3044	Skinner William	1723A
Roblo Piere	2562	Santos Cornelius	2932	Slaughter George	2721
Rockwell Chester	2795	Santos Jose Sr	2883	Slaughter Samuel	2717
Roddye Hall	2646	Santos Jose	2884	Small Emeline	1892
Rodgers Samuel	3117	Santos Jose' S.de los	2568	Small Rhody	1892
Rodriguez Damien	2633			Smedlie Wm	526
Rodriguez Jose Ant. Santos Manuel	1805	Smith Abraham	2817
2560,3118	Savery A.	232	Smith Amos	3348
Rodriguez Juan	2767	Sazarin Juiio	86	Smith Arabel	1401
Rodriguez Ma dela Cruz		Scott Alexander A	3253	Smith Archibald	
2763	Scott James	210		1229,2854
Rodriguez Ma Josefa	326	Scott W.L.	137,852	Smith Christian Jr	1560
Roebuck Elizabeth	3375	885,1508,1997,2208	Smith Edwin	2944,3412
Rogers Bethany	3104	Scritchfield Henry	2809	Smith Henry	1336
Rogers James	244	Scurlock Wm	2907	Smith James	
Rogers John R	2563	Seets Precious	2938	1369,2832,3528
Rogers R.C.	1705	Self	1877	Smith John S	1624
Rogers Rebecca	1762	Selser Nimrod	210	Smith Joseph	2741
Rogers Robert Sr	3096	Sepulveda Jose Ant.		Smith Luther	2647,3106
Rojas Andres de	2561	344,3107	Smith Menan	2799
Roland John	1389,2122	Servantes Agapito	2761	Smith Nathan	963
Rollins Eliphalet	3088	Servantes J.M.	1935	Smith Nimrod	2974
Rolson Mathew	2669	Servantes P.	1935	Smith R.	773
Rosa Nicholas de la	2564	Sewall William H	2951	Smith R.W.	1268,1688
Roth Jacob	18	Shackleford Jos S	2567	Smith Robert	381,481
Rowe James		Shannon Wm P	958	496,774,915,2095
130,1089,2220	Shannon Wm T	958	Smith Robert H	3301
Rowe Joseph	3385	Shears John	1421	Smith RobertW	1078,1241
Roydon John	3244	Sheldon Eliza	1854	Smith Sarah	1907
Rozell Solomon	3114	Shepherd Hugh	2046	Smith William	
Ruddell Isaac	3236	Sherman Wm	2612,3207	1905,2940,3257,3338
Rueg Henry	1725	Shields William J	3083	Smith William D	1906
Rugg Sarah	2724	Shipman J.M.	1862	Smith Wm H	3205
Rummel John S	3292	Shipp William	3405	Smullen	944
Rusk Thos J	1725	Shreves Michael	210	Smullin Thomas	1272
Russell James	1795	Shultz Chrisley	3071	Smullin Thomas M	705B
Russell Jessey	2735	Siglar Wm N	1725,1731	1134,1274,1793,1795
Russell Jonathan	2963	Simmons Henderson	3112	Snively J.	716,1935
Russell Margett	2733	Simmons Richard		Spain Randolph D	3072
Russell Widow	318	2687,3325	Sparks Wm F	111,3091
Ryan John F	3012	Simpson B.H.	2853	Spears Abner	3003
		Simpson Isaac	1839	Splanne Margaret	1945
Sacco Miguel	3402	Simpson John J	753,2037	Spring Amos	2589
Sadler John	413	Sims B.	1877	Squires Joseph	3219
Salazar Maxime	3026	Sims Bartlett	880	Stagner Henry	3410
Sanchez Ignacio	3023	Sims C.H.	1466	Stanback Martha	1368
Sanches Jose Franc	2969	Sims CharlesH	2771,3255	Stanley Stephen J	483
Sanchez Jose Maria		Sims Mathew	404	Stanley Wm C	3206
1723A	Sinclair William	2952	Steel Wm H	1721
Sanches Juliano Basilio	Singleton Elizab	1882	Steenson John	913
3120	Singleton Jesse	1388	Stephens Miles G	990
Sanders James C	2943	Skeers John	1934	Stephenson John	3326
Sanders Levi	2947	Skelton	1805	Sterne A.	1269
Sanderson Wm U	2622	Skerrett Mary	1884	Sterne Adolfo

1253,1756,2065,2748

Walling John C			Williams James	2711	Yancey John	1037
1389,2122,2698			Williams James W	3380	Yarbrough Randolph	2904
Wallis Elisha H.R.	3126		Williams Jno A	577,1043	Yarbrough Swanson	
Ward Seth	2576		Williams Leonard			2843,2950
Ware Georgeanne	2128			507,1626	Yates Andrew J	18
Ware Hardy	2728		Williams Richard		Yates Thomas	2949
Ware John	1722			2845,3176	Ybarbo Concesion	3249
Ware William	416,1125		Williams Samuel M		Ybarbo Domingo	18
Warren David	244			1693,2101,2241	Ybarbo Jose	2968,3082
Washburn Nevel	3170		Williams Stephen	3291	Ybarbo Juan Anton	3062
Watkins James E	3252		Williams Thomas	1997	Ybarbo Miguel	3294
Watson George W	3365		Williams William	2661	Yeamans Jerusha	2261
Watson William	2605		Williams William A	2700	York John	1892
Wattson Willis B	18		Williams Zachariah	2574	Young John	1037
Waugh John	685		Willis Arthur	2954	Youngblood Polly	3289
Weeks John	2804		Willis William	3383		
Welsh Geo W	3218		Wills Wm J	2755,3069	Zavala Lorenzo	958
Welsh John	289		Wilson David	685	Zavala Lorenzo Junr	3288
West Barry	3324		Wilson George W	3233	Zigler William	483
West C.	1038		Wilson JamesB	2214,3232		
West Gadie	2685		Wilson Jane	2946		
Wetherby Alvan	2155		Wilson Jefferson	316,958		
Wharton Sarah Anne	2156		Wilson John	2214		
Whitaker Nancy	2159		Wilson Sophronia	2212		
Whitaker Wm	233		Wilson Stephen P	3288A		
White Armstead	3070		Wilson Thomas	210,750		
White Benjamin	2609		Wilson William R	3100		
White Elizabeth	2606		Win John	2626		
White Geo	1560		Winfree Isaac	2691		
White Henry	1560		Winters William	990		
White J.	1284		Wire Robert	2615		
White James T	2165		Wolfenbarger Caroline			
White Margaret	2163			2226		
White Martin	617		Womack M.S.	610		
White Walter C	1892		Woodlief D.J.	1043		
White William M	3174		Woodlief D. Jerome	1749		
Whitesides Henry			Woods J.B.	129,354		
2122,2780			Woods James B			
Whiteside James	1892			128,844,1042		
Whiting Hervey	3190		Woods Michael	990		
Whiting Samuel	3264		Wood R.D.	210		
Whitlock	870		Wootan Moses	2823		
Wiggins H.L.	237		Wright Anne	2238		
Wiggins Harbard L	2789		Wright Benjamin F	1001		
Wilborn Kincheon A	3217		Wright Hardin	2792		
Wilkerson David	2839		Wright Permelia W	2239		
Williams Charles			Right Philip	1117		
1828,1934			Wright Ralph	1558		
Williams Elizabeth	3290		Wright Thomas	1368		
Williams Henery	1089		Wright Wm	1368		
Williams Hezekiah			Wrightsell John	477		
1398,1934			Wroton Isaiah	2575		
Williams Hez. Reines						
1934						

www.ingramcontent.com/pod-product-compliance
Lightning Source LLC
Chambersburg PA
CBHW050414280326
41932CB00013BA/1852